Acts of Dissent

Acts of Dissent

New Developments in the Study of Protest

edited by
Dieter Rucht, Ruud Koopmans,
and Friedhelm Neidhardt

ROWMAN & LITTLEFIELD PUBLISHERS, INC.
Lanham • Boulder • New York • Oxford

ROWMAN & LITTLEFIELD PUBLISHERS, INC.

Published in the United States of America
by Rowman & Littlefield Publishers, Inc.
4720 Boston Way, Lanham, Maryland 20706
http://www.rowmanlittlefield.com

12 Hid's Copse Road
Cumnor Hill, Oxford OX2 9JJ, England

British Library Cataloguing in Publication Information Available

Library of Congress Cataloging-in-Publication Data

Acts of dissent : new developments in the study of protest / edited by Dieter Rucht,
Ruud Koopmans, and Friedhelm Neidhardt.
    p. cm.
    Includes bibliographical references and index.
    ISBN 0-8476-9856-4 (alk. paper)—ISBN 0-8476-9857-2 (pbk. : alk. paper)
    1. Protest movements—Research—Methodology—Congresses. 2. Protest
movements in mass media—Congresses. I. Rucht, Dieter. II. Koopmans,
Ruud. III. Neidhardt, Friedhelm.
HN3.A27   1999
303.48'4'072—dc21   99-045880

Printed in the United States of America

⊗ ™ The paper used in this publication meets the minimum requirements of American
National Standard for Information Sciences—Permanence of Paper for Printed Library
Materials, ANSI Z39.48—1992.

Contents

I. Methodological Issues

II. Protest and the Mass Media

III. Applications: Protest in Different Contexts

Introduction: Protest as a Subject of Empirical Research

Dieter Rucht, Ruud Koopmans and Friedhelm Neidhardt[1]

Few people would claim to be completely satisfied with the conditions of life. However, while feelings of deprivation are common, they do not necessarily generate acts of manifest dissent which can be labeled "protest." At least two conditions must be fulfilled in order to translate dissatisfaction into protest. First, people must attribute a deplorable situation not to fate but to the actions of another person or group of people who are thus seen as culpable. Second, people must perceive that protest may improve their situation. In the absence of one or both of these conditions, people would likely opt to wait for a better opportunity to protest, seek other avenues to improve their situation, or become apathetic.

Looking back in history, we have good reason to assume that protest is a ubiquitous phenomenon. Some would argue that, in the course of history, average living conditions have improved, thus diminishing the catalysts of protest. Instead, protest seems to have increased and become a normal phenomenon in modern societies. It remains to be proven empirically whether or not the average level of protest has risen in modern societies, particularly within the last two centuries. At least for the last few decades, we have strong evidence that protest (probably with the exception of strikes and violence) has increased rather than decreased. Some observers even perceive protest as a typical feature of contemporary Western society, which they consequently refer to as "demonstration democracy" (Etzioni 1970), "protest society" (Pross 1992) or social "movement society" (Neidhardt and Rucht 1993; Tarrow 1994: 187). Assuming that the increase in protest is a matter of fact, we still lack empirically grounded theories as to how and why this is the case.

One hypothesis is that, although problems such as poverty, hunger and violations of democratic rights may have been reduced in advanced Western societies, a variety of other problems have emerged and multiplied the reasons and leverages for protest - problems that, at least in part, are unintended side-effects of modernization. Among these problems are the risks stemming from new technologies and their impacts on the natural environment. As for East European countries that are still in the process of transition, it is obvious that there are still many reasons for dissatisfaction which make protest very likely.

---

1   The editors would like to thank Gabi Rosenstreich for her invaluable editorial assistance as well as for the formatting of this volume.

A second hypothesis which is particularly pertinent to Western societies is that levels of aspiration and sensitivity have risen among the populace. For example, democratic rights are demanded beyond the political sphere, and have therefore become an issue in areas which were traditionally organized strictly according to hierarchical principles (e.g. universities, firms and armies). This demand can be partially explained by the fact that people, corresponding with their increased educational attainment, are better informed about societal defects and their underlying causes and have improved capacities and numerous means to articulate their dissatisfaction.

Finally, one could argue that the modern interventionist state has gradually multiplied its competences and steering capacities for regulating societal conditions. However, despite the expansion of state control, societal conditions have not been significantly improved. Therefore, the state increasingly becomes a target of focused critique that otherwise would have resulted only in diffuse feelings of discontent. This and other hypotheses have been formulated using various theoretical frameworks, such as that of the "risk society," "cognitive liberation," "rising expectations," "political overload" and "participatory revolution."

Regardless of which conditions one identifies as generating and fostering protest activities, it is of central importance that theories concerning protest describe the impacts of protest on society. Of particular interest are the political functions of protest in modern democratic societies which have created intermediary institutions such as voting, political parties and pressure groups. The task of these institutions is to register the feelings and demands of citizens with regard to political decision-making. Under these conditions protest is a telling indicator for problems which are neither registered nor dealt with in an adequate manner.

Seen from this angle, protest can be interpreted as a non-institutionalized impulse for political acting of institutions with formal powers and responsibilities. Protest exerts pressure for social change. Through the use of protest, distinct actors try to set particular issues on the political agenda in order to change the status quo. The crucial question is: under which conditions do these actors succeed? One can assume that the first hurdle for successful protest is erected by the mass media. Mass media reporting transforms protest into a relevant societal event. It enables and sometimes induces subsequent political acts which take the form of protest. Whether or not these acts occur, and if so, whether they correspond to the protestors' demands is not only dependent on the features of the political system but also on the characteristics of the protest itself.

In order to analyze such causal relations more systematically, one first has to describe the dependent variable "protest" in greater detail. Unlike other forms of social and political activities, e.g. electoral behavior, protest is by its very nature a complex phenomenon. It is highly contingent in terms of content, target, size, form, intensity, duration, social recruitment, etc. Whereas political voting is a strictly channeled activity designed for easy calculation, protest tends to be multifaceted, flexible, often unnoticed by the wider public, and unclear in its consequences. Not only for this latter reason, but also because of the difficulties in grasping and measuring protest, protest has been, until most recently, a widely neglected field of social research in contrast to, for example, voting behavior.

These difficulties, however, should not prevent us from empirically studying protest behavior, particularly once we acknowledge that protest, contrary to the assumptions made by earlier theorists, is not a form of irrational and spontaneous behavior resulting from "contagion." Protest is, rather, a rationally chosen, organized and strategically applied form of articulating and pursuing political interests.

For the most part, protest is not a matter of individuals but rather of groups and organizations. Although protest may occasionally be sponsored by political parties and established interest organizations, it is typically a domain of particular groups that, once they coordinate themselves and stabilize over time, may become a social movement. From an analytical standpoint, however, we should not equate the study of protest with the study of social movements. Social movements tend to protest, but not all protests are conducted by social movements.

In order to obtain a comprehensive and detailed picture of protest behavior, we must answer a set of elementary questions similar to those posed by journalists or police investigators: What is at stake, who acts (i.e. who protests), where and when does the action take place, what kind of action is taken, and who is the subject or target of action? Of course, before trying to answer such questions, one has to identify what should be counted as protest. Although students of protest tend to provide different answers, there is broad agreement about a core definition. In a very general way, (collective) protest can be understood as a public expression of dissent or critique that is often combined with making claims which, if realized, would affect the interests of particular groups in society.

Protest Event Analysis: An Overview of Research

Apart from historical research, systematic quantitative research on collective action and, more particularly, collective protest only commenced in the 1960s. As far as we can see, there are three lines of research that began more or less parallel but probably also influenced each other.

The Initiators

The first line of research is part of a broader attempt to gather data in the context of the *World Handbook on Political and Social Indicators*. This strand is an outgrowth of the social indicator school that aimed to collect various kinds of data over as many countries and as long time periods as possible. So far, three editions of the handbook have been published (Russet et al. 1964; Taylor and Hudson 1972; Taylor and Jodice 1983). They cover 136 countries and, taken together, the time period from 1948 through 1977. The data on political protests documented in the handbook include basic forms such as demonstrations and political murder. Information on these activities is mainly derived from one source, the *New York Times*, based on an index-guided search. Various other sources have been used to supplement the information from the *New York Times*. However, these additional sources were not consistently used over time. Moreover, they were used only for some geographic areas. Based on the *World Handbook*, we have rough estimates of the numbers of certain types of events that took place in particular countries, but not more. Only a few variables were coded per event, and the events are largely decontextualized. Several authors have used these data for cross-national analysis, mostly without acknowledging the obvious limits of the sources and coded information, but investing a substantial amount of energy in sophisticated data analysis and interpretation (e.g. Zimmerman 1989).

A second line of protest research, similar to that of the *World Handbook*, is represented by authors who were less concerned about establishing an extensive data base but more interested in studying the causes, dynamics and effects of collective violence. Robert Gurr is one of the foremost representatives of this scholarly strand (e.g. Gurr 1968). Beyond scientific motives, this interest in collective violence was also strongly fostered by political concerns about the wave of riots that occurred in many U.S. cities during the 1960s (e.g. Lieberson and Silverman 1965; Spilerman 1970). Studying the causes of these violent eruptions was perceived as a precondition to preventing such violent outbursts in the future. Like the authors who used the *World Handbook* data, most representatives of the collective violence approach were interested in correlations of variables without going into too much detail regarding the meaning and the specific context of protest.

Finally, a group of historical sociologists around Charles Tilly began to study protest in particular countries over relatively long periods. Initially, the focus was on strikes (Snyder and Tilly 1972) and collective violence (Tilly 1969; Tilly et al. 1975). But later, in the context of a broader theoretical focus on repertoires of contention, the whole range of protest forms became a subject of investigation (Tilly 1978). Unlike the two approaches mentioned above, this historically oriented research was deliberately geared not only toward finding statistical correlations among a relatively small set of variables but also toward enriching quantitative findings through the use of historical accounts, secondary literature, and other pieces of information. Scrutiny of these sources was important so that these data could be interpreted in a context-sensitive manner. In his later work, Charles Tilly and his collaborators expanded and refined the collection and analysis of protest event data. Most recently, Tilly published "Popular Contention in Great Britain, 1758-1834" (1995) for which he collected information on thousands of contentious gatherings. Nevertheless, he used these data as just one component in order to carry out an analysis that is still predominantly directed towards tracing and interpreting qualitative changes. Other historians have followed Tilly's path-breaking work, though they generally cover much less ground (Bergmann and Volkmann 1984; Gailus 1990).

Expanding the Field

Strongly influenced by these forerunners, a second generation of researchers began to study protest events in different territorial contexts during the 1970s. They all used print media and, in particular, newspapers in order to cover protest activities in one or several countries. Moreover, nearly all researchers of this second generation were strongly anchored in the social movement paradigm.

In a project initiated by Charles Perrow, several young sociologists covered protest activities of various kinds of progressive movements in the United States. Although the project did not result in a comprehensive collective product and some of the data were never used, two members of the group pursued their course individually and eventually published their findings. One was Doug McAdam (University of Arizona) who focused on the civil rights movement (McAdam 1982), the other Craig Jenkins (Ohio State University) who studied the farm workers' movement (Jenkins 1985).

Inspired by Tilly's work, in the early 1980s Sidney Tarrow, a U.S. political scientist from Cornell University, began to collect data on protest events occurring in Italy. Based on all issues of one national newspaper (the *Corriere della sera*), he collected some 7,000 events in the period from 1967 to 1973, thus covering a major protest cycle in recent Italian history. The results of this research were published in his book *Democracy and Disorder* (Tarrow 1989).

Also influenced by Tilly, Hanspeter Kriesi, a Swiss social scientist, initiated a study on collective actions in Switzerland spanning the period from 1945 to 1981. This group of researchers used several national and regional newspapers, without, however, systematically controlling for selectivity of the papers.

Moreover, the information collected per event was relatively limited so that the quantitative data were only used in a limited way (Kriesi 1985).

In a further step, Kriesi, who was then at the University of Amsterdam, together with some collaborators conducted a comparative research project that focused on new social movements' protests in France, West Germany, The Netherlands and Switzerland in the period from 1975 through 1989. Unlike the earlier study on Switzerland, this new research was based on only one newspaper per country, a systematic sampling procedure (mainly Monday issues), a broader set of variables and a strictly comparative perspective that, in this strand of research, has yet to be matched. The outcome of the Swiss-Dutch group is represented in several collective comparative publications (Kriesi et al. 1992, 1995) as well as in studies covering each one of the four countries (Duyvendak et al. 1992; Duyvendak 1995; Koopmans 1995; Giugni 1994).

Inspired by the methodology used by Tarrow in his study on Italy, Grzegorz Ekiert (Harvard University) and Jan Kubik (Rutgers University), both Polish immigrants, decided to study protest in four East European countries (Poland, Slovakia, Hungary and the former GDR, i.e. East Germany) during a crucial period of transition, namely 1989 through 1994. Later they were joined by Máté Szabó (Budapest) and Christiane Lemke (Berlin) who took responsibility for the Hungarian and East German study respectively. Currently, most of the data collection has been completed, and first analyses have been presented (see Ekiert and Kubik in this volume; Lemke 1996; Szabó 1996).

Independently of this group, the U.S. political scientist Mark Beissinger had begun to collect data on protest in the former Soviet Union for the period between 1987 and 1992. Probably more than any other researcher in this field, he encountered difficulties in relying on particular sources over time. Therefore he chose a flexible strategy, drawing on multiple sources in order to by and large neutralize the specific shortcomings of each single source (see Beissinger in this volume).

Susan Olzak, a U.S. sociologist (Stanford University), went further back in history than most of her colleagues mentioned above. Again using essentially the same methodology of data collection as Tarrow and others, she documented ethnic conflicts in the U.S. from 1877 through 1914. The specificity of her research is not only the much longer time span she covered but, above all, the sophisticated use of time series and event history analysis (Olzak 1992). Johan Olivier, a former student of Olzak, adopted her research method and her focus on ethnic conflict in order to apply it to contemporary conflicts in his home country of South Africa (see also Olzak and Olivier in this volume).

Finally worth mentioning is the work of James W. White, a political scientist at the University of North Carolina. He is using a large data set "based on 7,664 incidents of social conflict and protest occurring in Japan during the period

1590-1877" (White 1995b: 145). These data were been collected by K. Aoki, from Japan, who used various sources such as official reports, diaries of observers, arrested persons' confessions, etc. White is particularly interested in studying major cycles of contention and how they relate to other developments, such as wages, food prices, natural disasters, and political and social reforms (White 1995a).

Broadening Sources and Controlling for their Selectivity

Whereas historians, because of their professional training, tend to be highly aware of potential biases in their sources, this concern was less common among sociologists and political scientists in the 1960s. Hence the authors of the *World Handbook* and various other researchers who have relied mainly or even exclusively on newspapers to collect event data did not pay particular attention to potential flaws in their sources. It was not until the mid-1970s that the selectivity of newspaper reports became a subject of study in its own right for those who used newspapers for event data collection (e.g. Danzger 1975; Snyder and Kelly 1977). Although the results of these selectivity controls were not fully conclusive (Mueller 1994), it became clear that several factors (e.g. size and location of the event) influence media coverage and may therefore lead to a misrepresentation of the events that actually occur. Another conclusion drawn from these investigations in media selection biases was not to rely only on national sources but also to look at local newspapers. Of course, considering such aspects makes research more complicated and costly. This probably led most researchers to shy away from the systematic control of bias in their sources for event analysis.

Only very recently have several researchers begun to take up the issue of media selectivity in reporting on protest events again. In terms of documenting protests using mass media, on the whole they followed the path paved by Tarrow and others. In contrast to these forerunners, however, this new generation of projects was geared to complement media-generated data with information drawn from independent extra-media sources - police archives were of particular importance. The rationale of this approach is not so much to increase the number of events but rather to control for the selectivity of data drawn from the mass media. Police archives may have their own biases, particularly when it comes to reporting on "soft" aspects of protest and the role of police authorities themselves. However, these archives have the advantage of providing more exhaustive coverage of at least certain kinds of events and variables when compared to mass media reports. Thus these archival data can be used as a baseline in order to study the over- and underreporting of various kinds and certain aspects of protests. They also allow researchers to test more general assumptions on theories of mass media, such as concepts of news-worthiness and news value factors (Rosengren 1979; Staab 1990). Moreover, based on these data from public authorities, one can also make grounded estimates of the total numbers of certain kinds of events that actually occur in a distinct territory within a specific time period.

Because several authors who set great store by the control of media selectivity are represented in this volume, it may suffice to provide only some elementary information on the issue in this introductory chapter.

Unlike most of her colleagues within this group sensitive to media biases, the sociologist Carol Mueller (Arizona State University) did not use an extra-media data base as a means of selectivity control, but rather coded reports from different kinds of media on the same class of events, namely protests occurring in East Germany in the crucial year of 1989. By comparing the reports of three pairs of newspapers - two each in Germany, Great Britain and the U.S. - she could demonstrate that reports on protest events in these media only partially overlap. Her research confirms earlier findings on the differential impact of the location of the media with respect to the location of the event. For instance, in terms of numbers of reported events, the German newspapers were more inclusive than the British and these more inclusive than the U.S. newspapers (Mueller 1995).

McCarthy et al.'s (1996) study focuses on protests in Washington, D.C. in selected years (presently 1982 and 1991). This research group not only covered reports from different kinds of media (Washington Post, New York Times and the news from three television stations) but also coded information gathered from the local police authorities (see also McCarthy et al. in this volume). As in many other places, protesters in Washington need an official permit for which various kinds of information are required. Based on these two types of data sources, McCarthy et al. are able to control for various biases that different media exhibit when reporting on protest events in the capital.

In France, Olivier Fillieule has coded a large number of protest events based on follow-up reports by the police. So far, he has investigated the patterns of protest in three major cities (Paris, Marseille and Nantes) for the period from 1979 through 1989 (see Fillieule 1996 and in this volume). Moreover, he has coded reports on protest events from one national newspaper *(Libération)* for a six month period, enabling him to assess the selectivity of these media reports. Because he can access police reports - stored in a central archive in Paris - from virtually every major city, he may also expand his data base in the future.

Finally, an ambitious project on protest in Germany, initiated by Dieter Rucht, is underway. Currently, it covers protest events from 1950 through 1992 based on a sample of reports from two national newspapers (see Rucht and Ohlemacher 1992; Rucht and Neidhardt in this volume). This project is also complemented by a coding of protests from police archives in one medium-sized city in southwestern Germany from 1983 through 1987 (see Hocke in this volume). In addition, data on the issue of nuclear power have been coded from various sources, including newspapers and documents from the protest groups. Finally, events from one left-libertarian newspaper *(die tageszeitung)* that is highly sensitive to protests will be coded. Together, these complementary data sets will enable Rucht to control for the selectivity of the core data from various angles.

Overall we can observe a move from what Carol Mueller (1996) has called "extensive approaches" to "intensive approaches." Whereas the former take the selectivity of newspapers for granted and argue that, in spite of their selectivity, they provide a sufficient basis to study the levels and trends of protests, intensive approaches are more concerned with the possibility of changing patterns of media attention as well as with the patterns of protests that are neglected by mass media.

A Brief Assessment

In reviewing past and present work on protest event analysis, it seems that most new research attempts are only partially done with an awareness and knowledge of previous research. Thus, the field fails to develop as cumulatively as it could. Moreover, some researchers are reluctant to adopt certain standards and categories that have been set by their forerunners. As a result, we are confronted with much heterogeneity, and even incompatibility, as far as the units of analysis, the coded variables, and sampling procedures are concerned. Nevertheless, it seems that work in this area is becoming more sophisticated in terms of data collection and data analysis - both considerably facilitated by modern information technology and computer programs. Researchers are also becoming more sensitive to the various problems and limits of protest event analysis. Finally, closer communication and sometimes even cooperation among people under-taking this kind of research are likely to create a scientific community which allows the sharing of technical and other expertise and, hopefully, the production of more comparable data across time and space.

The Berlin Conference on Protest Event Analysis

In response to the above described situation in this field of research, Friedhelm Neidhardt and Dieter Rucht of the Social Science Research Center Berlin (WZB) launched the idea of an international conference that would bring together a considerable number of scholars working in this area. The conference took place in Summer 1995 at the WZB, gathering some 26 scholars from seven countries. With only a few exceptions, the authors and co-authors represented in this volume were also participants in this conference.

This conference was the first major gathering devoted to protest event analysis. It had a particular emphasis on methodological aspects, with a focus on the selection of units of analysis, sources and sampling strategies. Furthermore, as can be seen from the contributions to this volume, successful empirical applications of protest event analysis were also presented.

This conference should not remain an isolated attempt. There are already plans to organize a follow-up meeting at the WZB in 1998 which, unlike the first conference, will focus mainly on data analysis and problems of interpreting event data. Through these attempts, we hope to contribute to the spread of knowledge and sharing of experiences in this field, to more communication and collaboration among the scholars working with protest data, and finally to some degree of standardization of research projects so that data can be compared across time, territories and issues.

Aims and Structure of this Volume

As has been stated, this volume is a fruit of the conference mentioned above, providing a wider audience with access to revised versions of the papers presented. Although the emphasis of the conference was on methodological questions, we have also tried to represent substantive empirical analyses of protest data.

The volume is divided into three parts. First, several chapters focus on research designs and methodological questions of data collection. The second part is devoted to the representation and misrepresentation of protest events by the media and other sources. This is a critical issue because media reports are likely to remain the primary source for covering large numbers of protests in large territories. Finally, we present empirical applications of protest event analysis from different projects and different national contexts.

Methodological Issues

In the first part of the volume, a number of conceptual and methodological issues central to protest event analysis are discussed. Sidney Tarrow takes up the fundamental issues of the conceptual status of the "event" and the different conceptualizations of the relationships both between protest events and between protest events and contextual events and what he calls "non-eventful" processes. Of the four different models Tarrow discusses, William Sewell's focus on "great events," such as great revolutions, which constitute qualitative watersheds in history, is the least compatible with the basically quantifying thrust of protest event analysis. On the contrary, event history analysis - in the field of protest research, most prominently advanced by Susan Olzak - pushes this quantitative approach to its limits. However, according to Tarrow, despite the methodological rigor and sophistication of this approach, a price is paid in the form of its inability to grasp qualitative shifts in the causal relations between protest and contextual variables. These relationships include structural processes and changes which are difficult to conceptualize in terms of events. Charles Tilly's focus on "repertoires of contention" and recent work on "protest cycles," by Tarrow himself among others, constitute different attempts to find a middle ground between the qualitative reification of "great events" and the ahistoric tendencies of event history analysis. Both use protest event data to analyze causal processes within historical periods (the "short rhythm" of collective action) delimited on basically qualitative grounds and to compare different periods with each other (so as to gauge contention's "long rhythm"). This approach acknowledges that causal patterns are often limited in time and space. Still, the time-space limits it sets are broad enough to allow for causal analyses, and by comparing different historic periods, the impacts of long-term social-structural processes as well as of episodic events that may change causal configurations enter the analysis. Thus, Tarrow argues, this "events-in-history" approach, focusing on and comparing "cycles of contention" is both more historical than event history analysis and more sociological than Sewell's theorized narrative.

Another fundamental question concerns the relationship between protest events and social movements. Tarrow, Rucht and Neidhardt agree that social movements are both more and less than a mere aggregation of protest events. They are more because a certain degree of organizational and strategic interconnection is necessary for a series of events to classify as a social movement. At the same time, social movements are less then a mere aggregation of protest events because not all protest events can be ascribed to social movements. A methodological solution to this problem, however, remains to be found.

Rucht and Neidhardt go on to discuss the problems which arise in defining the empirical limits of "protest" and "event," illustrated by examples from an ambitious project on more than forty years of collective action in Germany. Should conventional political events (i.e. press releases, litigation, lobbying) by social movement organizations be included? And what about demonstrations or strikes by established members of the political system such as political parties or labor unions? And how does one delimit the boundaries of events in time and space? The authors conclude that there is always bound to be a certain degree of arbitrariness in these decisions, which, however minor they may sometimes seem, may have important consequences for the data one collects. Therefore it is important to make such decisions consciously and to expose them to the criticism of the scientific community. Only in this way, the authors argue, can a certain degree of standardization across projects be achieved.

The next question that arises concerns the kind of sources one may draw protest events from. In the eyes of Neidhardt and Rucht as well as Koopmans, the mass media, and in particular daily newspapers, have a number of distinct advantages over other sources. The reasons for this choice are both theoretical and pragmatic. Theoretically, it is important to realize that not all protest events are created equal: They differ both in their intensity (size, level of disruption, etc.) and in their relevance for social and political change. The selective coverage of protest events by the mass media is to a large extent a function of their intensity. Because in modern societies mass media coverage is often a necessary precondition for protests to have a social and political impact, media-reported protests may actually be a more valid indicator than the whole range of actual protests, which include many events of an extremely low intensity with little relevance to the wider society.

Pragmatically, newspapers have important advantages over other sources such as official statistics and police archives. The most important advantages are that newspapers tend to be more continuous, more easily accessible and more detailed than any of the alternatives. Moreover, as Koopmans argues on the basis of material from a comparison of protest mobilization in four Western European countries, they are more useful for comparative purposes than alternatives, such as official statistics, because they leave the researcher more freedom regarding definition of the unit of analysis, the range of variables to be included and the categorizations to be used.

Insecurity about the representativeness of media sources has often led researchers to fall victim to what Tarrow once labeled the "fetish of thorough-ness," i.e. a tendency to include as many sources and as much of each source as possible in the analysis. Koopmans argues that there is no reason why the method of sampling that is widely accepted in survey research cannot also be applied to protest event analysis. Sampling among and within sources can significantly reduce the resource investments required for gathering protest event data, making the method available to a larger number of researchers and allowing it to be extended over longer time periods and into cross-national designs. This argument is supported by a comparison of data on protest events in Germany drawn from two different projects, which show that, despite considerable differences in the definition of the unit of analysis as well as the sources and samples used, highly similar results are found. Thus, media-based protest data seem to be much more robust than one might think and easily satisfy conventional standards of methodological reliability.

Protest and the Mass Media

The second part of the volume consists of three chapters that analyze to what extent and according to which selective criteria protest is represented in the mass media. A close look at the role of media in ignoring or covering protest is of relevance for both the protesters, who try to use the media as a sounding board, and for the researchers, who use media as sources of information.

Media are a vital reference point for protesters. Because they have hardly any direct access to the polity, they try to influence political decision-making indirectly by stimulating public attention and support. In modern societies, this means first of all attracting media coverage in order to reach the larger populace (Kielbowicz and Scherer 1986; Gamson and Wolfsfeld 1993; Rucht 1994). To the extent that the media not only attentively report on but also support the protesters' claims, it is likely that this has an impact on the wider public. If so, protest can no longer be ignored by political decision-makers who depend on public support and, in particular, voters' opinions and behaviors. Consequently, many protest groups and, more generally, political actors of various sorts, invest much energy into getting a positive response from the mass media. In this sense, what the German political scientist Joachim Raschke has stated in reference to large segments of the population holds true: "Protests that are not reported by media do not take place" (Raschke 1985: 343).

Media are crucial for many researchers studying large numbers of protests because, as argued in the contributions by Rucht and Neidhardt, Koopmans and other researchers, they represent an easily accessible, continuous and relatively reliable source of information on the whole range of "public affairs," including political protest. However, media adhere to their own protocols and do not necessarily meet researchers' requirements and criteria.

First of all, media are highly selective, as the chapters by McCarthy et al. and Hocke show. They cover only a very small percentage of all protests that actually occur - "the tip of the iceberg," as McCarthy et al. aptly put it. In order to determine the number of protests missed by the media, one must create an independent data base derived from other sources. Protest groups' own files and documents on their activities provide one source. However, many protest groups do not produce such documents, and even if they do so, they rarely create and archive such documents in a continuous and consistent way. An alternative that has proven far superior is police archives. At least as far as certain forms of protests are concerned, police archives tend to be relatively exhaustive, systematic and accurate. This is not to say that these files are unbiased. But at least as far as "hard" information such as the form, location, duration, size and major claims of protest are concerned, police data seem to be fairly accurate, as several researchers from different countries have argued.

Though getting access to such archives may be extremely difficult and usually requires a cumbersome process of negotiation and trust-building, it seems to be a rewarding effort. Based on police data, McCarthy et al. in Washington, D.C., Hocke in Freiburg in southwestern Germany, and Fillieule in France (for the latter, see Part III of this volume) were able to use police data and to compare these with data derived from mass media. Whereas McCarthy et al. could only access data based on the permits required in advance of the protest, Hocke was also able to tap, beyond these permits, follow-up reports on the events. Obviously, for some kinds of information, e.g. protester numbers, these follow-up reports are more reliable than the estimates provided by the protest organizers in filling out the permit forms.

Second, the comparison of data from media and other sources not only allows researchers to control for the share of protests ignored by media, but also to gauge which types of protest are likely or not so likely to be covered. As one might expect, the size of the protest is a strong predictor of media coverage. Aspects such as size, location, participation of prominent public figures and other features are considered to be news values that, taken together, can explain which kinds of protests have a good chance of being covered while others are ignored. In the larger study that underlies his contribution to this volume, Hocke employs a highly complex revision of this approach as he aims at a systematic operationalization and test of the so-called "new values theory."

Third, by comparing the information drawn from different sources, this kind of research makes possible the study of particular aspects that are neglected, highlighted or distorted in media reports. This is what McCarthy et al. have called "the description bias." For example, accounts of a protest might emphasize the protesters' claims and their underlying motives and arguments, but might also focus on other aspects such as the protesters' organization, their actual behavior and their apparel. In controlling for description bias, the approach employed by McPhail and Schweingruber is of particular relevance. Based on a sophisticated technique of participant observation, they invest much more energy than anybody else in this field to studying the actual pattern and course of protest. This technique is so multifaceted, that it requires a large number of observers to adequately capture even one single protest event. The advantage of this method is that it provides us with detailed and systematic information on a large variety of aspects, ranging from the physical constellation of the participants to their individual behaviors and slogans - aspects that are widely neglected in the summary accounts and broad descriptions of protests we are usually confronted with in media reports and police archives. The obvious disadvantage of this method of systematized participant observation is the high investment per event in terms of preparation, training observers, and analyzing the mass of data. This makes it likely that the method will be used mainly for in-depth studies of single events and their underlying structures rather than for documenting larger numbers of protests or for studying description biases of media and other sources beyond an individual case.

Fourth, by comparing different kinds of media, McCarthy et al. and Hocke provide us with some insights regarding the selective reporting of these media. The research design used by McCarthy et al. has the particular advantage of systematically comparing different kinds of media, namely newspapers and television. Hocke, instead, compares two categories of newspapers, namely a local newspaper and two national newspapers.

Overall, this strand of research focusing on the inherent biases of various sources helps us to move beyond a naive treatment of mass media (or other sources) as more or less "objective" sources of information. At first glance, it seems that this research undermines the use of such sources insofar as it reveals their selectivity and other deficiencies. Taking a closer look, however, this research also shows that the biases of particular sources are fairly consistent as far as certain kinds of media and features of protest are concerned. The more we learn about these selective patterns, the better we are able to correct and to interpret the data generated from these admittedly biased sources. Based on this knowledge, we may eventually be able to reduce the investment of resources required by using sampling techniques in data collection or by applying methods of statistical extrapolation when the sources tend to misrepresent certain aspects.

This task, however, is more demanding than most of us might assume. We would also have to take into account the existence of media attention cycles that may follow complex rules. Protests may be underreported at an early stage when journalists do not know much about the issue and its potential significance. Journalists' interest in reporting may decline even when, and precisely because protests go on and on. Attention to protest may be unusually high when an issue gains great relevance for reasons that have nothing to do with the protest itself. Protests around a particular issue may also be overshadowed by an extraordinary event that captures most of the attention of the media. These aspects which are well-known to media researchers should make us cautious about taking media-generated data to be a faithful mirror of protest reality. Nevertheless, it is the reality as represented in media, and not as experienced by the myriad of protest groups and their immediate bystanders, which can be watched by the wider public and which may eventually impress those who are in power. Thus, when one is interested in the impacts of protests and the social change they might initiate, the media, who in modern societies have become a crucial factor in influencing public opinion and the political process, appear to be the most appropriate source.

Applications: Protest in Different Contexts

Although the Berlin conference's primary focus was on questions of method, we had good reasons to also include a number of contributions demonstrating some possible applications of protest event analysis. After all, in the end it is above all by its fruits, and not by its technical and statistical sophistication, that one can judge the merits of a particular method. The five chapters comprising the third part of this volume demonstrate the wide range of questions and topics protest event analysis can deal with. They present data on six countries, describing different protest forms, issues and actors, and dealing with different societal contexts and historical phases.

Olivier Fillieule focuses on demonstrations in France during the 1980s, concentrating on the examples of the cities of Marseille and Nantes, and to a lesser extent Paris. He was able to utilize police archive materials collected on the basis of the detailed guidelines of the French Ministry of the Interior. These ensure, particularly in the case of demonstrations, a highly standardized registration of a multitude of protest events all over the country - a rare case, scarcely rivaled by comparable sources in other countries. This circumstance allowed the author to analyze a wide range of variables and some of their interrelationships. Interesting, for example, are his findings about the "rhythm of demonstrations," not only for longer periods of time, but also for "seasonal cycles" and day-by-day patterns within the week. Obviously, protest actors, like other citizens, go on summer vacation, and within the week demonstrators' availability for participation in protest activities depends on the availability of leisure time.

Above all, Fillieule's results confirm some particularities of the French protest "industry" known from earlier social movement research: The new social movements are less developed in France than in other Western European countries and the United States. The dominant protest actors are still "traditional organizations," above all the unions and, to a quite remarkable degree, also the "educational community," i.e. teachers, students and parents of students. This corresponds to another finding: "Materialist" causes, such as jobs, wages, the standard of living, and the financing of education, continue, in effect, to dominate to a large extent. Post-materialist causes, including actions linked to moral issues, to the environment, to the right to abortions, or opposition to the military, play a relatively marginal role. The author concludes:

> It is therefore necessary to qualify the ideas developed by Ronald Inglehart with regard to the radical novelty of protest movements in the 1980s. As far as protest action in France is concerned, our results clearly contradict these conclusions ... (Fillieule).

Using multiple source data about more than two thousand political events, Pierre Gentile reports on radical right protest in Switzerland for the period from 1984 until 1993. He describes the mobilization of radical right parties and extra-parliamentary groups as well as the counter-mobilization of organizations and groups, backed above all by the Protestant churches, against radical right racism and anti-Semitism. Striking is the overrepresentation of right-wing activism in the German-speaking cantons in comparison with those where French is spoken. Striking, too, is the predominance of violence within the action repertoire of the extra-parliamentary groups. In contrast to left-wing radicalism,

> ... it appears that the extra-parliamentary radical right devoted little effort to attracting public attention. Instead of attempting to persuade the public, it sought to affect directly those it considers its enemies ... Violence against people appeared from the beginning of the mobilization in the late eighties; it was neither a response to repression nor a radicalization of groups refusing to undergo institutionalization (Gentile).

In other words, the violence of the radical right cannot be explained by the kind of escalation processes that have often been observed in the case of left-wing movements.

When considering radical right violence, there is good reason to ask whether there is a link between the activity of extreme right parties and extra-parliamentary mobilization. For some Western countries findings from other research support the hypothesis that the existence of organized right-wing parties tends to reduce the violence level of less institutionalized extremist groups (e.g. Koopmans 1996).

This postulate is not confirmed by Gentile's analysis. He found a "positive relationship between the actions of the parties and those initiated by extra-parliamentary groups or activists in the 26 cantons," and concludes that this "proves that the existence of an established radical right party at the cantonal level did not prevent the development of violence by the late eighties in Switzerland" (Gentile). It might be a subject of further and more refined analyses to validate and, perhaps, to differentiate this finding in light of intervening variables. The explanation Gentile provides for his findings seems a plausible starting point for such an endeavor:

> It is probable that in a canton where one or more radical right party tried to put their priorities onto the political agenda (and they proved to be able to do so at the federal as well as at the cantonal level through referenda and initiatives), other radical right groups became aware of a diffuse public sympathies for some of their ideas and perceived a real opportunity to act (ibid.).

The main emphasis of the contribution by Susan Olzak and Johan Olivier is on methodological problems not related to the gathering, but to the analysis of protest events, illustrated with data on black civil rights protests in South Africa and the United States. Their primary aim is to compare the results of different statistical techniques applied to the analysis of two types of interaction effects: First, diffusion effects across time and space, assuming that protest events are path-dependent, and, second, repression effects concerning the interplay between protest events and state repression.

Two central hypotheses are examined for urban areas in South Africa (1970 to 1986) and the United States (1954 to 1993): (1) Regions that have recently experienced racial protest, violence, and race riots have higher rates than regions that have experienced fewer cases of racial unrest; (2) periods that have high levels of police violence during racial unrest have higher rates of subsequent racial unrest. The divergent results regarding these hypotheses in the two countries suggest that both diffusion and repression effects are highly context-dependent. In addition, the authors show that the results may also be affected by the type of analytical model used (count analysis versus transition rate analysis).

Mark Beissinger's chapter on protest mobilization in the former Soviet Union demonstrates the extraordinary difficulties faced when conducting empirical research dealing with revolutionary periods and anomic states of political systems. Beissinger responds to this challenge with a remarkable data collection effort: Employing a "blanketing" strategy, and utilizing over 150 news sources and multiple types of information, he identifies several thousands of mass demonstrations, violent events, and strikes for the years 1987 through 1992. The time distribution of these events allows him to identify a "'glasnost' mobilization cycle" with peaks in 1990 (number of demonstrations) and late 1988 (number of participants). Particularly striking is the finding that the number of violent events increased in correspondence with decreasing mass participation. This seems to be a result of the changes of mobilization issues and dominant actors.

> In general violent contestation in the former Soviet Union evolved ... away from forms of mob violence (pogroms, riots and communal violence) towards more organized and sustained forms of armed combat. By 1991 and 1992 nationalist mass violence shaded off into organized warfare; where the line stood between the state-sponsored and mass violence was impossible to tell, much as it was difficult to draw clear lines between social movements, the para-military organizations that frequently carried out these acts, and the state (Beissinger).

This tendency reflects "the broader breakdown of the USSR government and its inability to control processes over its territory, and the institutionalization of mass violence as a result of the growing role played by republican and local governments in its organization" (ibid.). In a disintegrating political system the mobilizing force of civil society was marginalized by the growing power of the organized entrepreneurs of collective violence.

These disintegrating tendencies in the former Soviet Union stand in sharp contrast to developments in Poland. This is made clear by Grzegorz Ekiert and Jan Kubik's study of democratic consolidation in Poland between 1989 and 1993. The authors analyze protest event data within a systematic reference scheme derived from theoretical assumptions about the processes of "democratic consolidation." With material about 1,476 protest events they find, for example, (1) that for the transformation period 1989 to 1993 Poland is characterized by a high and rather stable level of protest activities, (2) that the demands leading to mobilization concern primarily economic issues and are "decisively reformist," (3) that these demands are promoted by "'old' well-institutionalized organizations" of civil society (above all unions and peasant organizations), (4) that the prevailing means of protest activities are "decidedly non-violent" (strikes, demonstrations, rallies, etc.), and (5) that their targets are mainly state institutions.

The authors conclude that Poland exhibits a functioning civil society and a highly institutionalized protest sector that fulfill important complementary and supplementary political roles. The political salience of protest is further magnified in light of the "general weakness" of the institutionalized political system, a weakness which stems from the over-differentiated structure of the party system and the failure of the legislative bodies and the government to adequately represent the population. The fundamental problem of civil society is described as "its lack of systematic linkages with the party system." This implies that protest activity can hardly be translated into "interorganizational negotiation and mediation." The authors assert that

> ... Poland is an excellent example of the disjointed and chaotic development of the institutional realms of the polity during a period of consolidation. The state, political society and civil society had their own transformational dynamics and the formation of institutional structures *within* each of them was far more advanced than the formation of the institutional linkages *between* them (Ekiert and Kubik).

This constellation obviously led to the "institutionalized contentiousness" of civil society without - up to now - destabilizing the political regime.

Open Questions and Suggestions for Further Research

Together, the contributions in this volume demonstrate how protest event analysis can help shed new light on a wide variety of research questions in a range of social and political contexts. The recent development of this new methodological tool for quantifying protest creates new opportunities for systematic comparative analyses of protest across time, space and collective actors, which this volume has only begun to explore. At present, however, a number of - certainly not insurmountable - obstacles still hinder the full development of this potential.

Although, as we have seen, relatively complete extra-media sources for protest events are sometimes available, they tend to only be available at a high cost and to be limited in their scope. Therefore, protest event analysis has to rely primarily on the mass media. The use of this source, however, necessarily implies that the range of protest events be restricted to the relatively small number that meet the selection criteria of the media. This is, as several authors have argued, not necessarily a problem in itself, since in modern societies it is primarily through their representation in the media that protest events become socially and politically "real in their consequences." Nevertheless, it is important that we learn more about the processes and mechanisms that govern this media construction of protest reality and thus about the nature and extent of the biases in our sources. This not only involves further studies of the criteria governing protest coverage, but also of the ways in which protest actors react to and try to make use of the media's selection mechanisms. In contrast to the extensive literature on the relation of protest to economic and political contexts, the relation between protest and the mass media has thus far been a neglected subject of theorizing and empirical research - a fact which is surprising given the importance that is generally attributed to the mass media by protest organizers. Hopefully, the recent methodological focus on the mass media as a data source will also stimulate theoretical reflections on the role of the modern mass media in the development of protest.

A second problem is the relatively low level of standardization that has been reached in protest event analysis. This limits the possibilities for cross-project comparisons and generalizations. Of course, such standardization is only possible to some extent, since decisions made on sources, sampling methods, variables, categorizations and operationalization will always depend partially on the kind of protests and research questions one is primarily interested in. At the very least, however, a rough consensus on the definition and boundaries of the unit of analysis - i.e. what constitutes protest, and what are the boundaries of an event - seems to be a precondition for cumulative progress. For a convergence on such issues to occur, it is imperative that protest event researchers make such decisions consciously and not intuitively and provide others with a careful documentation of their coding decisions and rules.

The most important weakness of the majority of protest event research so far, however, may be its largely descriptive character. In view of the limited factual knowledge we had until recently about even the most basic quantitative characteristics of protest, this descriptive element should not be underestimated and in itself constitutes a major advance in the field. Nevertheless, this should only be the beginning and must be followed by relating measures of protest to measures of covariates, allowing us to systematically investigate the causes and consequences of protest.

To begin with, such covariates may be derived from available data on, for instance, economic conditions, demographic changes, and the scope of social problems. Second, from a resource mobilization perspective, data on the resources of social movement organizations (funding, membership, access to the polity, etc.) seem relevant. Third, given the importance of political opportunity structures to the development of protest, we may look for sources that allow us to measure the actions and reactions of conventional political actors such as legislative decisions, programmatic statements of political parties or court rulings on issues relevant to the movement or movements studied. Finally, the discursive context of protest, i.e. collective processes of problem definition, attribution, and framing, have been identified as important determinants and objectives of protest. All four types of covariates are increasingly difficult to come by, and it is therefore no coincidence that the first, and to some extent also the second type have thus far been the most frequently used.

One possibility for collecting data on protest covariates is the use of already available external data, either derived from official statistics or from other research projects. Though this is the least cost-intensive strategy, the obvious problem with such external data is that they are usually imperfectly geared to the questions asked in research on protest and often do not match the temporal and spatial dimensions of the protest event data gathered. A second possibility is for the protest researcher to gather data him- or herself on covariates from other sources. Thus, in addition to newspaper-based protest event data, one may for instance code parliamentary proceedings, party programs or governmental decisions on relevant issues to get an idea of conventional political acts as possible causes and consequences of protest. The disadvantage of this approach is of course that it is extremely resource-intensive, especially if one is interested in a broader range of issues, actors and events.

A possible intermediate solution that has thus far hardly been explored is to use the mass media as a source not only for protest acts, but also for the activities of other actors that influence and are affected by protest. This may range from direct reactions to protest, such as police repression or counter-mobilization, to a much broader range of activities including a wide variety of contextual actors and acts. After all, protest event analysis based on media sources is just a special form of content analysis, and can therefore be extended without much difficulty to include other forms of relevant actors, acts and events. This strategy may give the researcher direct measures of, for instance, aspects of political opportunity structures and framing processes, measured with the same sources and samples and along the same temporal and spatial dimensions as protest.

Given that the gathering of protest event data is already very time and resource-consuming, the additional inclusion of relevant covariates is certainly a formidable task. The increasing availability of media and other sources in on-line format and the possibilities for electronic searching may to some extent help to overcome the obstacles involved. Whatever the remaining difficulties, however, the challenge must be met. It is in the systematic inclusion of the context of protest and the related possibilities for multivariate cross-sectional and time series analyses that the real promise of protest event analysis lies.

References

Danzger, M. H. 1975. "Validating Conflict Data." *American Sociological Review* 40: 70-584.
Duyvendak, J. W. 1995. *The Power of Politics. New Social Movements in France.* Boulder, Colo.: Westview.
Duyvendak, J. W. et al. 1992. *Tussen verbeelding en macht. 25 jaar niewe sociale bewegingen in Nederland.* Amsterdam: SUA.
Etzioni, A. 1970. *Demonstration Democracy.* New York; London; Paris: Gordon and Breach.
Fillieule, O. 1996. *Quand la France manifeste. Engagements, modes de participations et manifestations dans la France des années quatre-vingts.* Paris: Presses de la Fondation des Sciences Politiques.
Gailus, M. 1984. "Soziale Protestbewegungen in Deutschland 1847-1849." Pp. 76-106 in *Sozialer Protest. Studien zur traditionellen Resistenz und kollektiven Gewalt in Deutschland vom Vormärz bis zur Reichsgründung,* ed. H. Volkmann and J. Bergmann. Opladen: Westdeutscher Verlag.
Gamson, W. A. and G. Wolfsfeld. 1993. "Movements and Media as Interacting Systems." *American Academy for the Advancement of the Social Sciences* 528: 114-125.
Giugni, M. 1994. *La mobilisation des nouveaux mouvements sociaux en Suisse 1975-1989.* Université de Genève. Département de Sciences politiques. Traveaux et communications No. 2.
Gurr, T. 1968. "A Causal Model of Civil Strife: A Comparative Analysis Using New Indices." *American Political Science Review* 62: 1104-1124.
Jenkins, C. 1985. *The Politics of Insurgency: The Farm Worker Movement in the 1960s.* New York: Columbia University Press.
Kielbowicz, R. B. and C. Scherer. 1986. "The Role of the Press in the Dynamics of Social Movements." Pp. 71-96 in *Research in Social Movements, Conflicts and Change 9,* ed. L. Kriesberg. Greenwich, Conn.: JAI.
Koopmans, R. 1995. *Democracy from Below. New Social Movements and the Political System in West Germany.* Boulder, Colo.: Westview.
Koopmans, R. 1996. "Explaining the Rise of Racist and Extreme Right Violence in Western Europe: Grievances or Opportunities?" *European Journal of Political Research* 30: 185-216.

Kriesi, H., ed. 1985. *Bewegung in der Schweizer Politik. Fallstudien zu politischen Mobilisierungsprozessen in der Schweiz.* Frankfurt/M.; New York: Campus.

Kriesi, H., R. Koopmans, J. W. Duyvendak and M. Giugni. 1992. "New Social Movements and Political Opportunities in Western Europe." *European Journal of Political Research* 22: 219-244.

Kriesi, H., R. Koopmans, J. W. Duyvendak and M. Giugni. 1995. *New Social Movements in Western Europe: A Comparative Perspective.* Minneapolis and St. Paul: University of Minnesota Press.

Lemke, C. 1996. "Protestverhalten in post-kommunistischen Transformationsgesellschaften: Ostdeutschland im Vier-Länder-Vergleich. Komparative Dimensionen der Demokratisierung und empirische Ergebnisse." Unpublished paper.

Lieberson, S. and A. R. Silverman. 1965. "The Precipitants and Underlying Conditions of Race Riots." *American Sociological Review* 30: 343-353.

McAdam, D. 1982. *Political Process and the Development of Black Insurgency.* Chicago: University of Chicago Press.

McCarthy, J. D., C. McPhail and J. Smith. 1996. "Images of Protest: Dimensions of Selection Bias in Media Coverage of Washington Demonstrations, 1982, 1991." *American Sociological Review* 61 (3): 478-499.

Mueller, C. 1994. "A Test of Snyder and Kelly's Validity Model on International Press Coverage of Protest Events in East Germany, 1989." Paper presented at the International Sociological Association Meetings. Bielefeld, Germany. July 18-24.

Mueller, C. 1996. *Intensive and Extensive Approaches to Protest Event Analysis.* International Institute. University of Michigan. Working Paper Series No. 24.

Neidhardt, F. and D. Rucht. 1993. "Auf dem Weg in die 'Bewegungsgesellschaft'? Über die Stabilisierbarkeit sozialer Bewegungen." *Soziale Welt* 44 (3): 305-326.

Olzak, S. 1992. *The Dynamics of Ethnic Competition and Conflict.* Stanford, Cal.: Stanford University Press.

Pross, H. 1992. *Protestgesellschaft. Von der Wirksamkeit des Widerspruchs.* München: Artemis and Winkler.

Raschke, J. 1985. *Soziale Bewegungen. Ein historisch-systematischer Grundriß.* Frankfurt/M.; New York: Campus.

Rosengren, K. E. 1979. "Bias in News: Methods and Concepts." *Studies in Broadcasting* 15: 31-45.

Rucht, D. 1994. "Öffentlichkeit als Mobilisierungsfaktor für soziale Bewegungen." Pp. 337-358 in *Öffentlichkeit, öffentliche Meinung, soziale Bewegungen,* ed. F. Neidhardt. Kölner Zeitschrift für Soziologie und Sozialpsychologie (Special Edition).

Rucht, D. and T. Ohlemacher. 1992. "Protest Event Data: Collection, Uses and Perspectives." Pp. 76-106 in *Issues in Contemporary Social Movement Research,* ed. R. Eyerman and M. Diani. Beverly Hills: Sage.

Russett, B. M. et al. 1964. *World Handbook of Political and Social Indicators* (1st Edition). New Haven: Yale University Press.

Snyder, D. and W. R. Kelly. 1977. "Conflict Intensity, Media Sensitivity and the Validity of Newspaper Data." *American Sociological Review* 42 (1): 105-123.

Snyder, D. and C. Tilly. 1972. "Hardship and Collective Violence in France, 1830-1960." *American Sociological Review* 37: 520-532.

Spilerman, S. 1970. "The Causes of Racial Disturbances: A Comparison of Alternative Explanations." *American Sociological Review* 35 (4): 627-649.

Staab, J. F. 1990: *Nachrichtenwerttheorie. Formale Struktur und empirischer Gehalt.* München; Freiburg: Alber.

Szabó, M. 1996. "Trends of Collective Protest in Hungary 1989-1994." Unpublished paper. Budapest, University ELTE. Department of Political Science.

Tarrow, S. 1989. *Democracy and Disorder. Protest and Politics in Italy 1965-1975.* Oxford: Clarendon Press.

Tarrow, S. 1994. *Power in Movement: Social Movements, Collective Action and Politics.* Cambridge: Cambridge University Press.

Taylor, C. L. and M. C. Hudson. 1972. *World Handbook of Political and Social Indicators* (2nd Edition). New Haven: Yale University Press.

Taylor, C. L. and D. A. Jodice. 1983. *World Handbook of Political and Social Indicators* (3rd Edition). New Haven: Yale University Press.

Tilly, C. 1969. "Methods for the Study of Collective Violence." Pp. 15-43 in *Problems of Research on Community Violence*, ed. R. Conant and M. A. Levin. New York: Praeger.

Tilly, C. 1978. *From Mobilization to Revolution.* Reading, Mass.: Addison Wesley.

Tilly, C. 1995. "Popular Contention in Great Britain, 1758-1834." Pp. 15-42 in *Repertoires and Cycles of Collective Action*, ed. M. Traugott. Durham; London: Duke University Press.

Tilly, C., L. Tilly and R. Tilly. 1975. *The Rebellious Century: 1830-1975.* Cambridge, Mass.: Harvard University Press.

Volkmann, H. and J. Bergmann, eds. 1984. *Sozialer Protest. Studien zur traditionellen Resistenz und kollektiven Gewalt in Deutschland vom Vormärz bis zur Reichsgründung.* Opladen: Westdeutscher Verlag.

White, J. W. 1995a. *Ikki: Social Conflict and Political Protest in Early Modern Japan.* Ithaca, N.Y.; London: Cornell University Press.

White, J. W. 1995b. "Cycles and Repertoires of Popular Contention in Early Modern Japan." Pp. 145-171 in *Repertoires and Cycles of Collective Action*, ed. M. Traugott. Durham; London: Duke University Press.

Zimmermann, E. 1989. "Political Unrest in Western Europe: Trends and Prospects." *West European Politics* 12 (3): 179-196.

I.

Methodological Issues

Studying Contentious Politics: From Event-ful History to Cycles of Collective Action

Sidney Tarrow[1]

Introduction

The *Oxford English Dictionary* (Compact Edition 1971: 338) gives us the following as its main definition of the term "event":

> The (actual or contemplated) fact of anything happening; the occurrence *of*. Now chiefly in phrase *In the event of*: in the case (something specified) should occur.

The *Oxford English Dictionary* doesn't stop there: a second meaning of the term is "anything that happens ... an incident or occurrence; a third is "that which follows upon a course of proceedings"; a fourth is "what becomes of or befalls (a person or thing)" (p. 339); and a fifth is a combination of meanings two and three. A lot of meanings - and not all of them easily transmutable into operational terms!

Historians have been no more univocal. Fernand Braudel looked down his Gallic nose at events as no more than "surface disturbances, crests of foam that the tides of history carry on their strong backs" (1949, quoted in Appelby, Hunt and Jacob 1994: 83). More recent French historians have softened; Olivier Dumoulin tried to retrieve the event from its Braudelian exile, calling it "the historical fact that leaves a unique and singular trace, one that marks history by its particular and inimitable consequences" (1986: 271). Across the Channel, where narrative history never suffered the eclipse that Braudel hoped for it, Philip Abrams gave the concept theoretical power when he wrote that an event

> ... is a transformation device between past and future ... It is not just a happening there to be narrated but a happening to which cultural significance has successfully been assigned ... Events, indeed, are our principal points of access to the structuring of social action in time (Abrams 1982: 191).

Further west, Lawrence Stone tried to recapture the value of narrative from what he considered its anti-historical flattening at the hand of the cliometricians (1979).

---

1   Extremely helpful comments were offered on earlier drafts of this paper by Lissa Bell, Jack Goldstone, Larry Griffin, Doug Imig, Hanspeter Kriesi, David Laitin, Susan Olzak, Doug McAdam, Liz Perry, Dieter Rucht, Sarah Soule and Charles Tilly.

But just as historians like Abrams, Dumoulin and Stone were rejecting the event-less macrohistory of the *longue durée*, a combination of postmodernist critics, anthropologized historians and Foucaultian social constructionists were casting doubt on the ultimate reality of historical narrative. A healthy dose of relativism about the meaning of historical events was all that some of them wanted; but for others, all of history was turning into text. Who made the French revolution? Not Lafayette, not the Abbé Sieyes, not Robespierre with his head rolling on the ground nor Marat in his bath while Charlotte Cordey stood over him with a knife! It was rather those who *interpreted* - nay, "imagined" - the French Revolution who have created its current meaning.[2]

The problem with historical constructionism was not that historical events do not give rise to social construction but that it shifts the focus of historical work from what happens to glosses on what happens, from context to text, from archives to authors: away from the connections among people's "material conditions ... the languages they spoke, the collective interaction they carried on, and the impact of that collective interaction on the subsequent structure of power" (Tilly 1995: 38) to historians' own imaginings. For the strong constructionism that began to flourish in the 1980s, historical happenings were no more than the essentialist chaff that had to be peeled away from the grain of an interpretive history whose content was becoming ever more opaque.

The "Event-ful Re-turn"

But in recent years, there has been an "event-ful turn" in several branches of history, away from both Braudelian macrohistory and postmodern deconstruction, and towards something approaching Abrams' apotheosis of the event. At the same time, using new and swifter computational technologies, more social scientists are using events as their main data points as they employ systematic empirical methods to analyze population ecologies, social conflicts and political struggles. Qualitatively-oriented social scientists are focussing on agency and actions too, promising a convergence - after years of growing distance - between cliometrics and interpretive history.

But there are contentious issues as well. How do we recognize and analyze the *key* event in a historical sequence? How far can we go in construing history as a series of events (what will be called in this essay "event histories") without losing the sense of which are the important and which the incremental ones? And how can we relate these events to other events and to institutions and

---

2   If my sociological readers find this a caricature of social constructionist historiography, let them read Keith Michael Baker's *Inventing the French Revolution* (1990), especially pp. 203-223.

political processes in sequences, cycles and revolutions? Finally, how can we relate events - whether the Great Events of narrative history or the sequential ones of event histories - to social movements, contentious politics, the struggle for power?

This essay will not answer these questions, but will serve as an attempt to begin such an effort. Rather than attack the subject deductively, or summarize vast bodies of empirical research, I will use examples of what I take to be four major ways in which scholars have recently been employing events in historically-based collective action research. I call these approaches, first, *event-ful histories*, adopting that term from William Sewell's recent apotheosis of the theorized narrative; second, *event histories*, as the term has been developed in the organizational ecology tradition of North American sociology; third, *events-in-history*, the approach developed by Charles Tilly, beginning with his 1964 study, *The Vendée* and culminating in his recent *Popular Contention in Great Britain, 1758-1834* (1995); and fourth, *cycles of collective action*, drawing on recent works in the field, and especially on my own work on collective action and social movements in Italy (1989) and elsewhere in the world (1994).

I will argue that each approach has advantages and defects, but each one - if pursued too single-mindedly, at the cost of ignoring complementary forms of data and interpretation - may drive event-based historical research into diverging channels, to the detriment of our historically-based knowledge of the processes of collective action. Moreover, each approach offers a different answer to a key question for social movement scholars: how can collective events be used to trace the presence, the dynamics and the outcomes of contentious politics?

The Return to Eventful History

The return to event-ful history (though for many British and North American historians there was never a departure) dates from Lawrence Stone's polemical charge against quantitative social history in the 1970s (1979). Stone's attack was forceful and penetrating, but it had its ironies. Since he himself had broken new ground in the systematic use of historical statistics to reinterpret the meaning of marriage and the family in early modern England (1982), his assault on the "new" social history might seem a step backward. His special target was quantitative history; "forced into a choice between *a priori* statistical models of human behavior, and understanding based on observation, experience, judgement and intuition," he wrote, some of the new historians "are now tending to drift back towards the latter mode of interpreting the past" (1979: 19).

Stone's polemical attack on the new history in the name of narrative gave pause to a whole generation of students, but it did not lead to a research program. More subtle, and thus more effective, was the influence of a *non*-historian, Clifford Geertz, whose pellucid prose and microscopic dramatic portrayal of ritual-laden events convinced many younger scholars that "thick" description could peel layers of meaning even from things that had happened centuries ago (1973). Thus, Robert Darnton interpreted the sporadic killing of cats in late eighteenth century France as a cultural ritual pregnant with implications for the revolution that was about to occur (1984); Carlo Ginzburg re-interpreted the changing meaning of witchcraft in Friuli in the light of the cultural pressures of the Inquisition on popular culture (1984); Lynn Hunt interpreted a dispute about statuary among French revolutionaries as a symbolic struggle over the meaning of the revolution (1984); and William Sewell took the declaration of the Abbé Sieyes in favor of the Third Estate as the liminal event in the Revolution (1994). For these historians, events were singular, pregnant with meaning, and occasions for enlisting their cultural sensitivities in interpretive efforts. But for the empirically-oriented social scientist, they could seem idiosyncratically selected, subjectively analyzed and marked by rhetorical flair instead of analytic rigor.

In the meantime, historical sociology was going a different route than the caricature of mindless cliometricians poring over stacks of figures that Stone had airily dismissed. One strand was using historical demography to understand the social dynamics of the past.[3] Another was turning away from statistics to macro-historical comparisons between whole states and societies.[4] A third took the Big Historical Event as its focus, but strove to embed it in theoretically-robust concepts of structural change and cultural interaction (Sewell 1994). Back to the Old Political History, or a new level of theorization of historical narrative?

Sewell and the Culturation of Narrative

One of the historical sociologists who has tried to re-install the event at the center of historiographic practice is William H. Sewell Jr. In three sharply polemical but historically-informed articles, Sewell proposes that historical

---

3   For example, see the path-breaking use of military recruitment data by Roderick Floud
      to understand class differences in nutrition in England (1990).

4   See the survey and interpretation of this approach by Skocpol and Somers (1980,
      republished in Skocpol 1994); also see the sweeping interpretation of this school by
      Charles Tilly (1984) and the debate on macrohistorical sociology among Emirbayer,
      Goodwin and Tilly (1995).

sociology be rebuilt around event analysis (1990, 1992, 1996a). He has taken his own advice with an in-depth analysis of an Event that was to mark the entire French Revolution and much else besides: the publication of Abbé Sieyes' *Qu'est que c'est le tiers état?* (1994). And he has engaged macrohistorical sociologists like Skocpol, Tilly and Wallerstein in the name of a more narrativized history than what he sees their general structuralism producing (1996b).

But as if the various dictionary meanings of the term "event" surveyed at the outset of this chapter were not enough, Sewell proposes another, more cultural and sociological meaning. Events, according to Sewell, constitute unpredictable *ruptures* of normal causality, moments of fluidity in which small and momentary causes may have gigantic and enduring consequences (1996a: 843-844).[5] Sewell has been moving towards an emphasis on the particularity of great historical events for some time.[6] In his 1996a article, he offers the taking of the Bastille on 14 July 1789 as an archetypal example of his definition. For Sewell, it was not the raw *facts* of milling crowds, reluctant defenders, the dramatic charge on the fortress, the forced entry, the freeing of the few miserable prisoners and the beheading of the unfortunate governor that rendered the invasion a noteworthy Event. These would have been lost under the unfolding series of *journées* that followed, had they not been given political impact by the "multiple insecurities" that the occurrence produced, which in turn gave rise to a process of "collective creativity" and thus to important structural transformations. These transformations forced the King to recognize the National Assembly and crystallized during the debates that followed into a new and transformed concept of revolution (Sewell 1996a: 852-860).

The sequence of occurrences that followed the taking of the Bastille was sensational,[7] but its ultimate importance was to link two modes of activity previously thought to be unconnected: political and philosophical claims about

---

5   Note the striking similarity (possibly unconscious) between Sewell's concept of events and that of Pierre Nora, who writes: "l'évenement est précisément la rupture qui mettrait en cause l'équilibre sur lequel [les sociétés en place] sont fondées" [the event is precisely the rupture which disturbs the equilibrium on which today's societies are based] (1974: 220).

6   See, for example, Sewell's polemic against Tilly's generalizing tendency (1990), and his "Three Temporalities: Towards an Eventful Sociology" (1996b), in which he takes to task Skocpol, Tilly and Wallerstein.

7   "The king's troops pulled back from Paris, and the king, recognizing that the troops could not be trusted to act against the Parisians, ordered them back to the frontiers, thereby giving up his effort to intimidate the National Assembly. The National Assembly, which had seemed utterly at the king's mercy, emerged triumphant, thanks to the actions of the Parisian people" (Sewell 1996a: 850).

popular sovereignty; and acts of crowd violence (p. 852). It was because it came to be *construed* as an act of the people's sovereign will - and here Sewell emerges as a full-blown social constructionist - that the taking of the Bastille became "the establishing act of a *revolution* in the modern sense" (p. 852).

From Structure to Events

The importance of Sewell's proposal goes well beyond French historiography. In his theoretical work over the past five years, he has developed a structurally-related, causally-heterogeneous, path-dependent and contingent concept of events that grows out of both his critique of other historical sociologists and his cultural reading of French history. In an earlier paper in the series, he argued that most historical sociologists mistakenly limit themselves to two conventional notions of time - what he calls "teleological" and "experimental" temporality (Sewell 1996b).[8] He argues that both of these are deficient - even fallacious - forms of temporality and that "historical sociology needs to adopt a much more subversive eventful notion of temporality - which sees the course of history as determined by a succession of largely contingent events" (1996b: ms 3-4). History, writes Sewell, is made up of happenings, most of which merely reproduce social and cultural structures without significant changes. These, for him, are not events. Events are that relatively rare subclass of happenings that significantly transform structures (1996a: 842-844). An eventful conception of temporality, hence, is one that takes into account the transformation of structures by events. But happenings only become events when structures are already massively dislocated and insecurities are rife (p. 861). It is then that

---

8   This is a citation of Sewell's manuscript prior to publication. Page references thus refer to the draft manuscript (ms) rather than the published work. The terms need some explication. "Teleological" temporality, Sewell argues, is the view that sees history as a consequence of long-term, anonymous causal forces (1996b: ms 4) and "abstract transhistorical processes leading to some future historical state" (ms pp. 4-5). Such a logic leads, among other things, to what Sewell calls Emanuel Wallerstein's "astronomical" world system (ms pp. 6-11) and to Tilly's transmutation of fixed socio-geographical differences in social organization "into putative stages in the linear development of the abstract master process of urbanization" (ms p. 14). As for "experimental" teleology, it sets up comparative "natural experiments" thought to be capable of sorting out the causal factors that explain the occurrence of such events as social revolutions (ms p. 17). This leads such authors as Theda Skocpol to the identification of a few universal variables that are seen as necessary wherever and whenever such phenomena occur; for Sewell, it "freezes history," both ignoring particularities in individual cases and their lack of real world independence from one another (ms pp. 23-26). For Skocpol's commentary, see her essay (1994: 326-334).

events rearticulate structures; and become the source of "cultural transformations" which create new terms and cause old ones to take on authoritative
new meanings (ibid.). Events, for Sewell, are "globally contingent." They can
undo or alter even the most durable trends in history (1996b: ms 34). Path
dependency, causal heterogeneity and global contingency are the hallmarks of
Sewell's concept of event-ful history (ibid.).

Sewell is right to seize the moment when the major modern metanarrative -
Marxism - has collapsed, to place the concept of events squarely on the agenda
of historiography. He is also right to observe that the event must be thought
about as a central theoretical category - although he is by no means the only
scholar to have had this idea.[9] He should also be praised for his growing
recognition of role of structure in history (1994: 60; cf. Sewell 1992). But is he
as wise to limit his concept of events to unpredictable ruptures of normal
causality (1996a: 843)? And to allocate to later social constructors the power to
decide whether a given happening becomes an Event or remains a mere
occurrence? This move leads him to exclude from his chains of events
surrounding the taking of the Bastille occurrences which were not *seen to*
produce ruptures, as well as those whose effects on history were incremental. If
followed mechanically, such a historiographic strategy is likely to end up
choosing those events that can be *visibly* linked to later changes, as the taking of
the Bastille could be linked to the later policies of the National Assembly but
as, for example, changes in demography could not. The danger is that, if
followed rigorously, Sewell's method may relegate to the musty attic of
"metanarrative" event-poor yet structurally-rich processes that have a profound
effect on history.

To write history is to choose, but if the choice of Great Events for an event-
ful history leaves out both occurrences that cannot be seen to bring about
rupture as well as non-eventful processes, doesn't Sewell's proposal return to a
more traditional form of narrative history than he wishes to foster? Might it not
produce, in the words of one of Sewell's favorite targets, "the temptation to let a
few spectacular and well-documented conflicts dominate interpretations of
change" (Tilly 1995: 65)? An alternative approach is developing in sociology,
which begins with *populations of events* and relates them both to one another
and to non-eventful phenomena through statistical elaborations. Let us turn to it
now.

---

9   See, for example, Sewell (1996a: 897, note 2), whereby it should be noted that he
     neglects the anthropologist Sally Falk Moore (1987), and the historians David William
     Cohen (1994) and Christopher Lloyd (1993) as authorities on event-ful history.

Events within History

As Stone, Sewell and others[10] have been re-thinking and theorizing narrativity at the qualitative end of social history, a loose archipelago of historical sociologists and political scientists at its quantitative end has been applying advances in computational technology to the systematic analysis of contentious events. The first in this line of event analysts were, of course, students of strikes. They had ready-made official series of comparable events available to them with detectable properties and outcomes (e.g. was a union present in the strike? How long did it last? What proportion of the workers participated? Did the strike succeed or fail?). They were able to find out much about the relation-ship between strikes and economic trends and to ferret out changes in the structure of the strike over long time periods.[11] They were not as sensitive to cultural changes in the strike, and their dependence on official statistics left them somewhat insensitive to their connections with political conflict or other forms of collective action.

Most strike analysts were economists or economic sociologists, but in the 1960s the methods they used were applied to other forms of collective action - protests, demonstrations, riots, and violence in general. As statistically-trained political scientists and political sociologists turned their attention to contentious politics, the dominant tradition of focussing on social movement organizations or on individual protestors began to give way to the systematic study of incidents of contention.[12] And as the older concept of the crowd as a wild and anarchic gathering gave way to more down-to-earth conceptions of groups contending over interests and ideals, British historians also turned to the systematic analysis of contention.[13]

---

10   Mention should be made of the stimulating re-thinking of narrativity by Margaret Somers(1992, 1993). She focuses on the formation of collective identities and their relationship to conceptions of citizenship. Her work shows an increasing tendency to relativize historical epistemologies, which risks taking it away from the incredibly rich narrative tapestry that she displays in her re-interpretation of English working class formation and that will presumably reappear in her forthcoming book.

11   For some major sources, see the tradition begun by Ashenfelter and Pencavel in the United States in 1969. For France, see Perrot (1987) and Shorter and Tilly (1974). For Italy, see Franzosi's apotheosis of the tradition and his summary of the literature (1995).

12   The major stimulus was, of course, "the riots" of the American ghettos, but scholars of collective violence went on to study civil violence cross-culturally was well. The major sources can be found in Gurr (1989), and in Gurr's transnational study in 1970.

13   The major sources in the British tradition are Rudé (1964), Hobsbawm and Rudé (1968), Bohstedt (1983), Harrison (1988), Charlesworth (1983). See the review in Tilly (1995: Ch. 2).

But because of their lack of institutional structuring - in contrast to the strike - the forms of contention studied by these scholars could less easily be related to outcomes than is the case in strike research. And because protests produced few reliable official sources of statistics, analysts turned instead to the aggregation of quantitative indicators from narrative sources (Favre 1990; Gamson 1975), to police sources (Fillieule 1994, 1995) and especially to newspaper records (Jenkins 1985; McAdam 1982; Tarrow 1989). And although some analysts attempted to encompass all forms of contentious politics (Tilly 1995) or all types of protest events (Tarrow 1989), many specialized on specific series of events, like violent ones (Gurr 1970, 1989), on civil rights protests (McAdam 1982) or on communal and ethnic conflicts (Gurr 1993; Olzak 1992).

Since it began in the 1960s, there has been an explosion of methodological sophistication in the tradition of event-based statistical work on contentious politics. Where early analysts had to employ armies of assistants to pore over dusty archives and yellowing newspaper files and were usually content to portray their findings graphically or in tabular form, more recently there have been two major methodological developments.

First, researchers are turning experimentally to the enumeration of events by machine coding them from on-line newspaper or press agency records (Bond and Bond 1995; Franzosi 1987; Imig and Tarrow 1996). This procedure risks losses in accuracy and detail while offering immense gains in time and expense over manual coding procedures. While still critically in need of validation and elaboration through more sensitive computer programs, machine coding holds special promise for scanning large data sets over long periods of time where general trends or broad comparisons are more important than subtle changes.[14] At the same time, John McCarthy, Clark McPhail and their associates have been examining the validity and reliability of newspaper and press agency data on protest events through their examination of demonstrations in Washington, D.C., for which they have independent indicators of the numbers and properties of protest events.[15]

---

14   For example, Imig and Tarrow examine the hypothesis that the integration of Europe is bringing a relative increase in collective action aimed at the European Union or triggered by its policy initiatives, and a consequent decline in the national state's role as mediator of contentious politics. Employing the PANDA data processing program (Bond and Bond 1995), they use Reuters' press releases available on-line through Lexis/Nexis to examine protest profiles of twelve European Union members over an eleven year period - an impossible task using manual coding techniques.

15   All the reference listings under "McCarthy, John" and "McPhail, Clark" come out of this research project, as does the citation to Schweingruber and McPhail (1995).

Concurrently, some sociologists have begun to employ a family of data analysis methods first developed in population ecology, called "event history" methods (Allison 1982; Tuma and Hannan 1979). These have been applied to collective violence and protest by a number of sociologists (see the review in Olzak 1989). Coming out of the organizational ecology tradition, they have been applied to the founding and death of movement organizations by Debra Minkoff (1995). These methods have in common their compatibility with time-series, cross-sectional analysis of large numbers of homogeneous events. Susan Olzak's study of North American ethnic conflict (1992) can serve as a micro-cosm of the strengths and the difficulties of newspaper-based, statistically-organized series of protest events.

Olzak and the Practice of Event History

Moving from William Sewell's sonorous prose to Susan Olzak's statistical syntheses in her *Dynamics of Ethnic Competition and Conflict* (1992) leaves the reader feeling like a time traveler. While Sewell investigates meaning, Olzak is often satisfied with describing her data - or even the procedures she used in manipulating them. Nor are the statistical manipulations that Olzak carries out always easy to understand.[16] The result is a much less exciting read, albeit a marvelously well-documented and well-organized one which focuses on one form of social conflict - ethnic conflict - as measured through the techniques of event history analysis.

But if Olzak's language is forbidding and if she often tells the reader how to read her tables rather than what the dramatic history of ethnic conflict she describes was like, her book is a superb example of the systematic enumeration of very contentious events and an analysis of their relations with broader social and economic processes - migration, business cycles, employment opportunities and ethnic competition - exactly the kinds of processes that Sewell's focus on Great Events makes it difficult for him to tap into. Especially given the growing urgency of issues of race, immigration and ethnic conflict in the world today, her book is likely to be a model for statistically-based sociologists for years to come.

---

16   A certain amount of methodological information in the body of a book cannot be avoided, but not all readers will warm to passages like: "Does the rate of occurrence [of events] vary as the time since the previous event varies? One way to explore this question is to consider plots of the integrated hazard by duration. If the rate does not vary with duration, then the plot of an integrated hazard (or the minus-log survivor function) against duration will be approximately linear" (Olzak 1992: 73).

Olzak's work is familiar in some ways and path-breaking in others. It is familiar in her strategy of studying a standardized set of collective and contentious activities for the same set of spatial units over the same time period. In this respect, her book reminds us of two parallel traditions of collective action research: strike research and research on the North American social movements of the 1960s. Olzak's book is reminiscent of the tradition of statistical research on strikes that was referred to above. However, her procedure differs from this tradition - which is usually based on official statistics - in her almost complete reliance on newspaper sources, rather than official statistics. Olzak believes - and I think she is right - that the sacrifice in numerical exhaustiveness that she incurs in avoiding official statistics is more than compensated for by the greater richness of detail and interpretation that she finds in newspaper sources.[17]

Using newspaper sources so plentifully lends Olzak's work a resemblance to some of the social movement research on the 1960s carried out in the United States (Burstein 1995; Jenkins 1985; McAdam 1982). But she departs from this tradition both in confronting a much longer time span (37 years) and in basing her enumeration and coding of the newspaper sources on entire articles, rather than on headlines or newspaper indexes (Olzak 1992: 234-235). A number of studies of European collective action have followed the same time-consuming procedure (Beissinger, all citations; Ekiert and Kubik, all citations; Kriesi et al. 1992, 1995; Rucht and his collaborators, all citations; Tarrow 1989). The availability of relatively cheap, fast computational facilities and computer programs capable of reading text and transforming it into calculable units has made the use of newspaper headlines or indexes obsolete.

But Olzak's book differs from these studies in a number of important ways. First, where the Europeanists have been catholic in the kinds of collective action they have chosen to study, Olzak restricts her attention to only one type - *ethnic* collective action - and, within that category, to two sub-types - ethnic conflict and ethnic protest.[18] Second, where these scholars all use one or

---

17 Moreover, it is not always clear that official statistics are as complete or as accurate as their compilers would have us think. For example, for understandable reasons, the police are invariably more interested in violence than in peaceful behavior; can we believe that their data on peaceful assemblies are as complete as those on riots? Or that their counts of protester numbers are any more accurate than those of the protest organizers? For all their unevenness of coverage and big-city biases, newspapers at least provide qualitative information on the protesters and their claims that official statistics usually lack.

18 Ethnic conflict involves a confrontation between members of two or more ethnic groups, and ethnic protest is defined as the presentation of a grievance to the general public or some office of government (Olzak 1992: 8-9).

another sampling technique,[19] Olzak enumerates her events from a *daily* set of records. Third, she does not draw on secondary sources systematically, but relies principally on the statistical record provided by her primary data.[20]

Analyzing Ethnic Events

We can also use Olzak's study to examine the more general properties of "event history" approaches. First, there is little attempt in this tradition to theorize the meaning of events. When we try to glean what Olzak means by them, we find that the concept lacks the theorized structural and cultural prominence given it by Sewell. She defines her conflict events as "nonroutine, collective and public acts that involve claims on behalf of a larger collective" (Olzak 1992: 53).

Second, Olzak's procedure in compiling "event histories" is nominal, where Sewell's is purpose-built. As she describes the technique, it begins with recording exact information on the timing of a series of events and on their locales. She then uses this information to estimate the rates of transition between discrete events (making the procedure extremely sensitive to the bunching of events that are typical of cycles of protest) and relates their density to structural covariates, like changes in the rate of immigration, that are also specified over time and between cities. In Olzak's words, "event-history analysis can use information on the timing of events in a series of localities to estimate models that take both unit-specific characteristics and the timing of events [into account]" (1992: 63, 232).[21]

Third, Olzak's analysis of her data is relentlessly statistical, using the entire period of the study as her evidentiary basis and paying little attention to the Great Events that would preoccupy a Sewell, or even to the periodic crises that have struck Jack Goldstone as important in North American history (1980), or the cycles of protest that have attracted the attention of students of European protest events like Brand (1990), Koopmans (1993) and Tarrow (1989, 1994). In fact, Olzak's sharpest contrast with Sewell is her relative indifference to the *connections* among events or between them and the "structural" ruptures that he

---

19   Tarrow (1989) is an exception, but for a much shorter period of years. Kriesi and his collaborators, Ekiert and Kubik and their research group, and Rucht and his collaborators use one or another form of sampling.

20   To put the point more critically, as Isaac and Griffin do of a related event history study, Hannan and Freeman's (1987) analysis of trade union foundings: "their research enterprise ... is primarily grounded in the general ahistorical postulates of organizational demography rather than in the concrete history of trade unions" (Isaac and Griffin 1989: 875). Also see Abbott (1988) for a similar critique of event history analysis.

21   The procedure also allows her to analyze events and their causes at different levels of spatial aggregation - national, regional and local (Olzak 1992: 52).

tries to identify as the beginning of event-ful historical analysis. Olzak does have a concept of cyclicity, but she specifies it only as diffusion, and operationalizes the latter as the shortness of time "spells" between events.[22]

As a result of its statistical univocality and lack of attention to the connections between events, Olzak's book - like most technical event history work - is unlikely to be read by a substantial number of historians. If this is true, it will be a great pity, because beneath its forbidding statistical crust, the book is a mine of variously-demonstrated associations between different forms of ethnic collective action and the underlying structural processes that may be typical of other racially-plural or immigration-drawing societies.[23] Let us touch on some of the more striking ones.

Olzak finds that the causes of attacks on different ethnic groups appear to be remarkably similar - they are led by macro-level processes of immigration, economic contraction and growth of the labor movement (1992: 211). But their *effects* on different groups in North American society differ dramatically, with attacks on African-Americans and Chinese immigrants far more sensitive to business cycles than attacks on white immigrants. In fact, black Americans paid a high price not only for their own attempts to struggle out of poverty, but for those of white immigrants as well. Only on the final page of her book does the appalling implication of this finding raise her tone to something like outrage:

> The overriding and disturbing evidence in this book suggests that African-Americans were consistently victimized by whites when competition levels rose. The results suggest this is true *even when labor force competition was mainly from white immigrants* (Olzak 1992: 224) [emphasis added].

Even repression seems to have had different effects on black and white immigrants. The latter, faced by ethnic attacks, seemed able to create ethnic organizations - which she measures by the birth of ethnic newspapers - and to intensify their solidarity; but the latter were so battered down by the greater

---

22 This seems a questionable coding decision for the measurement of diffusion, for it would produce equally high scores for the frequent repetition of ethnic collective action by the same actor - a false measure of diffusion - as it would for separate actions by a number of different actors in close temporal proximity - which is what most people mean by diffusion. To other elements of cyclicity, such as the appearance and spread of "master frames" (Snow and Benford 1992), the centrality of particular social actors (Brand 1990), repetitive forms of collective action (Tarrow 1989), or the international diffusion of movements (McAdam and Rucht 1993), Olzak pays no attention.

23 It is no doubt this similarity that has drawn Olzak, with her former student Johan Olivier, to undertake a comparative study of racial conflict in the U.S. and South Africa (Olzak and Olivier 1995, 1996).

level of repression they encountered that their creation of ethnic newspapers remained almost constant as that of white immigrant papers rose (p. 186).[24]

The Hazards of Event History

Olzak's is a major study, one whose research design has already been replicated in other studies (see below). But it has two fundamental defects - both products of its single-minded devotion to event history methods. The first is that in specifying the variables to be examined within a linear data set model, Olzak - like other event history sociologists - is insensitive to key tipping points in history that are not directly reflected in her data.[25] Not only is it insensitive to Great Events that turned history around - like the taking of the Bastille - but even to apparently minor ones that may affect the relationships between the variables in a historical time series.

Consider the changes in the strike in North America. From a decentralized act of rebellion in the early nineteenth century, it became part of a planned campaign of putting pressure on employers by the 1980s. This shift resulted from the incremental process of unionization, but also from the decline of the conspiracy theory of labor organization and the legalization of collective action, both of which resulted from a rapid sequence of judicial decisions between the 1840s and the 1870s.[26] Once the courts had admitted the legality of strikes, the nature of the strike changed, its use spread to previously unorganized sectors, and its correlation with various structural properties of industry shifted. Without going outside of the linear progression of strikes and industrialization to institutional shifts like the judicial legitimation of collective action, we would have difficulty understanding the changing pattern of strikes in North America. Like the judicial interpretation of the strike, political change seldom complies

---

24   Alas, Olzak does not control her results by the differential literacy rates of white and black ethnic groups, a variable which surely would have affected the capacity of each group to field ethnic newspapers, and which was itself affected by a particular kind of ethnic attack - the segregation of black children into inferior schools.

25   For the development and illustration of this point in the case of event histories of labor, see Isaac and Griffin. Their general argument is that their parameter estimates are constructed to apply to long data sets of between 60 and 150 years (NB: longer than Olzak's 39 year time-period), and ignore the potential effects of non-linear variables like war and peace, depression and prosperity, the passage of pro-labor legislation and its partial dismemberment, etc. (1989: 876).

26   The key court case was Commonwealth vs. Hunt in a Massachusetts state court, an 1842 decision which gave workers the right to organize, even though it left the legal status of unions unclear. This decision was supported by a number of state courts in the years that followed. For this history, see Hattan (1993).

docilely with the linear reality of historical time series. At least to this political scientist, a paucity of attention to political events is the major lacuna in Olzak's admirable study.[27] For example, Olzak is strangely silent on the relationship of the post-Civil War American state to race, and of the lead that the dominant racist jurisprudence gave to racially exclusionary laws and practices. For example, the terms "Supreme Court" and "Plessy vs. Ferguson" do not, to my knowledge, appear anywhere in the book. How can we explain this puzzling silence on the political dimensions of racial and ethnic conflict? Olzak seems aware of the gap as she writes, in closing, that

> ... because the primary theoretical focus of this volume has been political and economic competition, this study has left unexplored the active role of legislation and government agencies (1992: 222).

But all she offers is the addendum that

> ... it seems plausible that the actions of powerful and legitimate authorities, such as the local government, police, the state militia, and other organizations affect the rate of contemporary ethnic and racial violence (1992: 222).

No student of North American social history would disagree, but why are such factors missing from the multivariate analysis in Olzak's otherwise exhaustive study? Here is one theory: If followed religiously, every methodology determines both its directions and its exclusions. In structuring her study so thoroughly around quantitative event-history techniques, has Olzak perhaps found it uncomfortable to include non-continuous variables - like particular court cases or the passage of anti-immigrant legislation - in her work: The racial segregation policies of the Supreme Court; the unopposed re-election to Congress of southern politicians whose long tenure - and thus their chairmanship of key committees - gave the South control of congressional legislation on race; the one-party, all-white electoral politics of most southern states, which turned political competition into contests between groups of white notables within the dominant Democratic party?

Unless I miss my guess, at least some of these factors could have been estimated in the form of dummy variables in the discrete-state stochastic process models that Olzak has employed (1992: 60-61). That event history methods are not incompatible with more politically-rooted analyses of collective action can be glimpsed in the work of two of Olzak's students, Johan

---

27 Some effects of political competition are indeed analyzed in the book - for example, in the correlation she uncovers between Populist strength and lynching in southern counties (Ch. 7), which were first observed by Olzak's student Sarah Soule (1992). She also hints at the effects of policy change on ethnic conflict by showing how the passage of anti-immigrant legislation lowered the rate of violence against immigrants (p. 215).

Olivier (1989) and Sarah Soule (1995, 1997).[28] Deborah Minkoff, using similar techniques to Olzak's, breaks out of the organizational ecology harness to analyze the framing of the Civil Rights and Women's movements as part of the more general political cycle of the 1960s (1996).

Susan Olzak has taken the historical analysis of series of contentious events about as far as it can be taken in the direction of causally relating structural variables to collective action, and in this her work serves as a weighty counterpart to William Sewell's. She has demonstrated clear relationships between structural changes in economy and society, and variations in ethnic conflict. But in doing so, she has left political events and historical tipping points in the background and will not satisfy historians or historical sociologists who are looking for more interpretively rounded accounts of the historical process.

How can the qualitative richness of a Sewell and the quantitative rigor of an Olzak be combined? Or are quantitative and qualitative historical studies of collective action doomed to follow diverging and mutually-indifferent paths? For an attempt to combine the richness of historical interpretation with the rigor of historical time series, we must turn to what I call "events-in-history," an approach we find in several historians of modern Europe and in the work of its foremost exemplar in sociology, Charles Tilly.

Events-in-History[29]

Charles Tilly's conception of contentions events is not as theoretically dense as William Sewell's nor is it as methodologically sophisticated as Susan Olzak's. Like Sewell, but unlike Olzak, he focuses on historical sequences of events in relation to one another in particular historical configurations. Like Olzak, and in contrast to Sewell, he has fashioned a tool for the systematic enumeration and analysis of populations of events. Over the last three decades, Tilly has striven - not always successfully or consistently - for a synthesis between sociology and history (for critiques, see Sewell 1990, 1996b).[30] I will call this synthesis "events-in-history."

---

28   Olivier investigated racial conflict in South Africa using event history methods, while
      Soule developed similar models to analyze protest tactics and success in the student
      anti-apartheid movement of the 1980s. Adapting Olzak's methods, but going beyond
      them to cross-spatial, as well as time-spell diffusion, Soule was able to model the
      diffusion of these tactics across college campuses.
29   The section that follows is a condensation of my longer paper on Tilly (1996).
30   Sewell criticized "the contentious French" for "universalizing history", that is, for using
      France as a laboratory to show how "master processes" work on collective action,
      without specifying the particularity of the French process (1990). Sewell's critique was

In the course of his career, Tilly's work has shifted between a narrative, archival-based attention to Great Events in his writing in the 1960s - in the event, *the Vendée* Rebellion (1964) - and quantitative analyses of large numbers of events in his two collaborative books in the 1970s: *Strikes in France*, written with Edward Shorter (1974), and *The Rebellious Century*, co-authored with Louise and Richard Tilly (1975). The 1980s saw him attempting a synthesis of the two approaches in a study of 400 years of French history, *The Contentious French* (1986). The book was a massive compendium of the results of decades of plowing through French archives and analyzing statistics on strikes and collective violence. In it, Tilly tried to trace how deep structural processes - mainly capitalism and statemaking - affect changes in collective action in a variety of French regions - treated separately - over four centuries. The book's major contribution was to elaborate the concept that Tilly had been playing with since his 1978 text, *From Mobilization to Revolution* - the repertoire of collective action.

The Repertoire of Contention

The concept of the "repertoire" of contention, which was laid out in a number of works, is theorized and operationalized most elaborately in Tilly's recent *Popular Contention in Britain*, where it

> ... helps describe what happens [in the ways that people act together in pursuit of shared interests] by identifying a limited set of routines that are learned, shared, and acted out through a relatively deliberate process of choice (1995: 41-42).

Repertoires are not simply ways of doing things. They are learned cultural creations that result from the history of struggle:

> People learn to break windows in protest, attack pilloried prisoners, tear down dishonored houses, stage public marches, petition, hold formal meetings, organize special-interest associations (1995 42).

What does this emphasis on repertoires mean for the event-filled study of collective action? This is as yet unclear, as Tilly's research agenda continues to evolve. But at a minimum, it means that the systematic study of events over

---

correct in one sense: that in this book, Tilly was more interested in the play of broad structural processes like state-building and capitalism on collective action than in the distinct impact of such Events as the French Revolution. But Sewell's anti-universalist critique of Tilly's book missed the mark in another sense. For while Tilly abstracted from historical narrative to trace the impact of state-building and capitalism on collective action, he also historicized and anthropologized the latter concept more thoroughly than any other contemporary theorist has done.

time - far from universalizing history and flattening it into a few master processes - becomes the mechanism for tracing the evolution of the *culture* of political struggle and the impact of structural changes upon it. The concept of the repertoire is the most ambitious attempt we have to date to historically trace the changes in the character of collective action in connection with changes in society and politics. But how to study it?

Increasingly since the early 1980s, and especially in his latest book, *Popular Contention in Great Britain* (1995), Tilly has traced the various *forms* of contentious collective action over time, which is no inconsiderable achievement, given the obduracy and partiality of the historical record. He has done this, on the one hand, by abandoning the use of official kinds of data, which seldom contain more than gross descriptions of encounters between challengers and authorities, for detailed analysis of newspaper data, and, on the other, by rejecting the economical but qualitatively questionable technique of measuring contentious events from headlines or indexes.[31]

Second, Tilly broadened the boundaries of the events he studies from "protest," "violence" or strikes to the concept of the "contentious gathering," which he defines as

> ... an occasion on which a number of people ... outside of the government gathered in a publicly-accessible place and made claims on at least one person outside their own number, claims which if realized would affect the interests of their object (1995: 63).

The definition takes in most events for which authorities and observers used such terms as "riot, disorder, disturbance, or affray" but also includes a great many "peaceful meetings, processions, and other assemblies that escaped the wrath of authorities" (p. 643). True, it ignores individual forms of resistance, as well as the routine operation of institutionalized groups, except when these spill over into visible contention in the public arena. It is also insensitive to the incremental development of collective identities and consensus mobilization which preceded contention, because the public records on which his work is based tell us little about these cultural and social-psychological processes.

Enumerating and analyzing a large number of events does not enable thick description, but it does allow Tilly to compare the nature of contention in different times and places in Britain. For *Popular Contention in Great Britain*, Tilly and his group enumerated information about roughly 8,000 contentious gatherings from seven different British press sources and from the Acts and Proceedings of Parliament for Southeast England for a sample of thirteen years

---

31   For discussion of the sample, the procedures and the instrument, see Tilly's *Popular Contention in Great Britain* (1995: Ch. 2 and Appendices).

between 1758 and 1828, and for Britain as a whole for every year between 1828 and 1834. This 76 year period included three major wars, the agitations over Wilkes, Queen Caroline and the suffrage, Catholic emancipation and suffrage expansion, and took place during the heroic phase of the industrial revolution; but also included thousands of rick burnings, machine breakings, pulling down of houses, forced illuminations, marches, petitions, demonstrations, and other less-than-Great Events, coded in standard form.[32] With such a long period to study and with so finely-honed an instrument to study it with, what has Tilly found?

Old and New Repertoires

The key assumption in the concept of the repertoire is that people act collectively in ways that they understand, but at any point in time, they learn only a rather small number of alternative ways of acting collectively. The *changes* in the repertoire are therefore an observable litmus test of the changes in the modal interactions between citizens and their opponents - and thus of the character of popular struggle and, to some extent, of popular culture.

Repertoires can vary in a variety of ways. The best known - and the most criticized dimension (Sewell 1990) - was the trichotomy between competitive, reactive and proactive collective action that Tilly developed in his 1978 textbook, but left behind as a flawed model of the historical progression of collective action in the early 1980s. Replacing it in his thinking in *Popular Contention* is the distinction between two poles, each of which is seen as an adaptation to a different type of society; the one he found dominant in mid-eighteenth century England and the one that had become more prominent there by the 1820s and 1830s.

The first pole is parochial, bifurcated and particular. It was parochial, writes Tilly, "because most often the interests and interaction involved concentrated in a single community"; it was bifurcated because "when ordinary people addressed local issues and nearby objects they took impressively direct action to achieve their ends, but when it came to national issues and objects they recurrently addressed their demands to a local patron or authority"; and it was particular because "the detailed routines of action varied greatly from group to group, issue to issue, locality to locality" (1995: 45).

The second pole is cosmopolitan, modular and autonomous. These forms of contention are cosmopolitan in "often referring to interests and issues that

---

32   Tilly's procedures differ from standard sociological practice in the extensive computer recording of textual data and the use of interactive computer technology he used to transform it into reduced word form for analysis.

spanned many localities or affected centers of power whose actions touched many localities," modular in "being easily transferable from one setting or circumstance to another," and autonomous in "beginning on the claimants' own initiative and establishing direct communication between claimants and nationally-significant centers of power" (Tilly 1995 46). These changes are not teleological, Tilly insists, but a shift to a new set of tools adopted because

> ... new users took up new tasks, and found the available tools inadequate to their problems and abilities. In the course of actual struggles, people making claims and counter-claims fashioned new means of claim-making (1995 478).

By studying real people engaged in actual struggles with others or against the state, Tilly traces the extent to which these changes show up in the historical record of contentious collective action and how they relate to his old friends, capitalism and state-building. For the secular changes in British collective action do not walk through history wholly on their own feet; they correlate roughly with the growing centralization of the national state and the capitalization of the economy, which Tilly has charted statistically and narratively in Chapter Three of *Popular Contention in Great Britain*.

But the reader will look in vain for a statistical test of the association between changes in capitalism and the timeline of change in the repertoire. Capitalism only hovers in the background of his account, in part because Tilly has not included strikes in his enumeration but in part through an explicit choice.[33] As for changes in the state, these are closer to the foreground of the analysis and can be seen operating in two directions - internal parliament-arization and external war-making - both of which show up dramatically in the changes in collective action, which, on the one hand, are increasingly directed at Parliament and, on the other, are triggered by war and by the strains of financing it. The central finding is the strong shift from the violent and parochial outbursts at the beginning of the period to the peaceful meetings and national claims towards its close, a shift which moved contention increasingly away from local and private targets and towards Parliament (1995: 104, Figure 2.10).

In arguing for the data set correlation between parliamentarization and the adoption of a repertoire that is increasingly national, modular and autonomous, Tilly stops well short of the canons of event history sociology in Olzak's mold. For these correlations are not demonstrated through statistical correlations but are only illustrated in a series of episodes for which Tilly draws both from his

---

33   "For thirty years," he writes in a personal communication to the author, commenting on an earlier version of this paper, "capitalism has dominated the discussion and I want to redress the balance."

own data and from secondary sources.[34] Once he demonstrated the overall shift in repertoires over the longish *durée* of 1758 through 1834, rather than continuing to use the entire data set for statistical analysis of the structural correlates of this change, he divided further treatment of the data into four discrete historical periods.[35] This division into roughly twenty year periods (only one of them containing full yearly records) made it impossible for Tilly to use statistical measures of association between capitalism, state-building and collective action. Why did Tilly do this? His answer helps to illuminate why I call his approach "events-in-history" and distinguish it from Sewell's strategy of "eventful history" and Olzak's "event histories" discussed earlier in this chapter.

The People's Two Rhythms

The four case study chapters shift the focus of *Popular Contention in Great Britain* from the long logic of Tilly's initial conception to another logic: that of relating the incidents of popular collective action to the broader political histories of which they are a part: to institutional processes like parliamentary conflicts; to episodes of war-making and changes in tax collection; and to the rise of private associations and their role in particular campaigns and conflicts. Tilly abandons the examination of the period 1758 to 1832 in order to construct sequences of events in the narrative tradition that Sewell would like us to revive but within the framework of a longer statistical history. In doing so, he tries to effect a synthesis between narrative event-ful history and statistical event histories and avoid the single-mindedness of each that has been noted above.

Another way of putting the same point is stated by Tilly himself. The people have two rhythms of collective action, he argues: "a jagged short-term rhythm depending heavily on shifts in the relative strategic positions and resources of connected actors" and "a smoother long-term rhythm depending more heavily on the incremental transformation of social relations in the course of such processes as proletarianization and state formation" (1995: 23). The longer-term

---

34   A major reason for this is that the small number of sample years he studied (thirteen for Southeast England from 1758 to 1834 and seven for the national sample between 1828 and 1834) did not permit Tilly to statistically analyze the relationship between the secular changes in British capitalism or state-building and the up-and-down oscillations in collective action. Tilly also writes that he decided to foreswear the modeling and estimation of causal relationships in this book to disencumber the narrative, speak to historians of Britain and give himself the discipline of laying out in words "what quantitative modeling will eventually have to represent, verify and falsify" (1995: 73).

35   These are "The Era of Wilkes and Gordon" (1758-1788), "Revolution, War, and Other Struggles" (1789-1815), "State, Class and Contention" (1816-1827), and "Struggle and Reform" (1828-1834).

changes in the repertoire described above are inscribed in the long-term rhythm of the secular changes in popular contention; but the narrative analysis of the different time periods in the book shows how these changes occurred in sequences of contentious encounters embedded in the political struggle. The shift from the people's long rhythm to their shorter one connects the story of the evolution of the repertoire to those discontinuous variables or episodic events that would escape a more rigorous event history.

There are both risks and benefits in Tilly's procedure. In rooting his event analyses in specific configurations of time and space, Tilly gains the possibility of connecting popular contention to the political opportunity structures of each epoch, to the dominant strategies of state repression and reform, and to particular campaigns and cycles of protest. (It also makes the book more likely to be read by British historians, whose fondness for historical narrative was never blemished by Braudelian structuralism.) In this respect, Tilly's work should be seen in the tradition of studies that link contention to the institutional and political opportunity structures of different countries or periods.[36]

But the shift to shorter rhythms of popular contention in particular periods of history sacrifices Tilly's ability to use the data statistically. Instead, he reinforces the original argument for period after period, leading to a certain repetitiveness and squandering opportunities to systematically analyze the overall relationships between state-building, capitalization and collective action that interest him so much.

Why then did Tilly go through the back-breaking task of assembling computerized records on over 8,000 contentious gatherings for an eighty year period and subject them to interminable interactive computing sessions? Why not, as Sewell seems to advise, select a Great Event we already know to be great and analyze it in its historical context, linking it through chains of contingent causation back to crumbling structures and forward to the cultural construction of new ones? Tilly must answer this himself, but I think there are three answers:

First, there is more than one potential book in any given data set, particularly one that has been collected with such rigor and care. Given the fecundity of his past work, Tilly may already be thinking about the next one. Second, by selecting relatively short segments of political history for analysis and adding secondary data from other sources to his own quantitative data, Tilly wants to relate contentious events to other kinds of events, to non-eventful processes, and to what we know about the period from narrative history - exactly the kind of thickening of historical accounts that Sewell calls for. Third, even for such

---

36   To cite only a few, this tradition has been carried forward by scholars like Della Porta (1995), Kitschelt (1986), Kriesi et al.(1991, 1995), McAdam (1982, 1995) and the present author (1994, 1995).

relatively short periods, the collection and analysis of records of collective events in a standard format - like Olzak, but unlike Sewell - allows us to see connections in the history of a period that may not be evident to the naked eye or even to the trained historical mind - for example the protest cycles and revolutions heretofore only analyzed with the tools of macrosociological analysis or historical narrative.

Sequences, Cycles and Revolutions

One growing implication of studying "events-in-history" is hinted at by Tilly in his chapter on the Reform period but is not fully developed - the study of "cycles of protest." Less momentous than revolutions, more connected than contingent chains of events, the concept of cycles, studied through the systematic gathering of events data during "short rhythms" of ten to twenty year periods, is a bounded way of studying the connections among events, between them and non-eventful processes and in the light of major political changes, helping to interpret history as an interactive progression between structure and action rather than - as in Olzak's version - a statistical sequence of events or in Sewell's - as the encultured outcomes of a single Great Event.

The analysis of such dense collections of events can help to study the processes of diffusion of new repertoires within cycles (Tarrow 1995). It can also help us to trace the construction and diffusion of new frames of meaning (Snow and Benford 1992) and new collective identities within sequences of collective action (Pizzorno 1978). It can help to explain why formerly inert mass publics suddenly emerge in cascades of collective action (Lohmann 1993). And it holds promise of achieving a progression from the cataloguing of contentious events to a *relational* analysis of the interactions between contending actors, their allies and enemies and the state.

For example, movement cycles may be related to changes in repertoires. First, within a given cycle, themes, symbols and tactical innovations of individual actions and groups influence one another, as when North American students borrowed the sit-in and other collective action frames from civil rights activists during the 1960s. Second, the intense interaction of a cycle generates opportunities and incentives to innovate that appear much more rarely and with greater risk outside such cycles. Third, the very movement of a cycle from an expansive to a contracting phase alters the strategic situations of all participants, thereby changing the relative attractiveness of different forms of interaction, not to mention the relative salience of other actors as models, enemies, rivals or allies. Fourth, forms of action associated with successful garnering of support, gaining of publicity or pressing of demands tend to generalize and become long-term additions to collective action repertoires, while those associated repeatedly and visibly with failure tend to disappear.

Cycles may also produce changes in the organizational dynamics of movements (Minkoff 1996). As movements crystallize into organizations, the most successful forms may be imitated and diffused across sectors and even across national boundaries (McAdam and Rucht 1993). They may also produce changes in the alignments of institutional actors, interest groups and parties, as elites jockey for position to respond to the actions of mass publics (Burstein and Freudenburg 1978). They can also produce a split between institutional collective action and the organized violence that often arrives at the end of a wave of protest (Koopmans 1993; Tarrow 1994: Ch. 9). Finally, the interactions between contentious actors and authorities can be traced through the dynamics of the course of a cycle. There is some evidence from Central America, for example, that repression varies in intensity according to the phase of the cycle in which it is used (Brockett 1995).

These relational aspects of cycles suggest surprising parallels to revolutions.[37] A revolution is a rapid, forcible, durable shift in collective control over a state that includes a passage through openly contested sovereignty (Tilly 1993). We can conveniently distinguish between revolutionary situations (moments of deep fragmentation in state power) and revolutionary outcomes (transfers of state power to new actors), designating as a full-fledged revolution any extensive combination of the two. The forms and themes of revolution vary significantly with political opportunity structures, for example, featuring dynastic contenders where succession normally supplies new rulers and taking nationalist forms where the system of rule already operates through populations claiming distinct national identities.

Revolutionary situations resemble extreme cases of social movement cycles: As the split within a polity widens, all rights and identities come to be contested, the possibility of remaining neutral disappears and the state's vulnerability becomes more visible to all parties. Just as successful mobilization of one social movement contender stimulates claim-making among both rivals and allies, revolutionary claimants on state power incite offensive or defensive mobilizations by previously inactive groups. One group's actual seizure of some portion of state power, furthermore, immediately alters the prospects for laggard actors, who must immediately choose between alliance, assault, self-defense, flight and demobilization. Consequently, rivalries, coalition-making, demand-making and defensive action all spiral rapidly upward. Because of their penchant for seeing social movements and revolutions as separate genres, each with its own immutable laws, students of contention have not yet begun to

---

37   The following passage paraphrases McAdam, Tarrow and Tilly (1996).

explore these parallels and intersections between movements, protest cycles and revolutions. By analyzing both as aggregates of contentious events and relating the latter to the political processes and structural conditions surrounding them, we may learn more about both types of historical configurations.

Contentious Events and Social Movements

A final note, which, given the length of this paper, will have to remain no more than a hint at a future analysis: None of the approaches sketched in this paper directly confronts the relationship between collective action events and social movements. Sewell does not deal with movements, but with revolutions, while Olzak, while acknowledging the importance of movements, never budges from her analytical fix on events. Tilly, who comes closest to formulating this relationship theoretically, regards movements as a form of collective action - a point on a typology consisting of the scope of action and the orientation to power holders (1983). Students of cycles regard movements as analytically distinct from, but empirically measurable through clusters, sequences and cascades of events (Lohmann 1993; Tarrow 1989).

If, as has been argued elsewhere, a social movement is "a sustained interaction between mighty people and others lacking might," then it can be studied through public actions within a movement, which "couple collective claims on authorities with displays asserting that the population in question and/or its mobilized representatives are worthy, unified, numerous and committed" (McAdam, Tarrow and Tilly 1996: 21). But if this is the case, are movements observable events, in the same sense as we observe some of the other actions in the repertoire - the forced illumination, the *charivari*, the march and the demonstration? Or is a movement an actor or coalition of actors whose presence can be traced through collective action and the combination of collective actions which typify it or them, but which is not reducible to a particular form of action? If the former is the case, then we need to understand how movements relate to the other forms of action; if the latter, then we need to theorize explicitly how we would expect movements to "look," when what we see of them is the public face of contentious events.

Kriesi et al. (1995) simply assume that their record of collective action events for four European countries during a fifteen year period constitutes in itself the record of the dynamic of the "new" social movements of that period. But are all the events they capture "movement events"? And are there not other movement events that are not captured by the record of contentious collective action? Mary Katzenstein (1996) argues that there is no inherent reason for supposing that social movements are co-terminus with disruptive behaviors or that movements do not move within institutions or utilize what are normally considered institutional behaviors. Especially given the tendency for the "normalization" of protest in Western societies since the 1960s, this is a major problem for the event-based study of social movements and one which the next generation of studies will need to confront.

Provisional Conclusions

Is there an Occam's razor-like choice between Sewell's call for thick description of temporally ordered, contingent and structurally ruptural events, Olzak's rigorous statistical modeling, Tilly's politically sensitive "short rhythms," and the event-based study of cycles of protest and revolutions? In the still young and rapidly changing state of research on contentious politics it is too soon to tell, and there is probably no reason to choose. The search for optimal methods too often descends into "right way" tests of orthodoxy, a descent of which we have seen far too much in recent scholarly fads and which is destructive of real intellectual dialogue.

"Event-ful history," "event-history" methods, "events-in-history" and the study of cycles of contentious politics offer attractive alternatives to the case study methods that have dominated the field in the past. Although these approaches are each self-contained and one of them, Sewell's, argues implicitly for the uniqueness of historical cases, all four hold promise for replicable, comparative and cumulative research on collective action in modern societies. The danger is that each of the approaches will drive those who adopt them into such different methods and perspectives that each group of specialists will proceed in blissful indifference to the contributions of the others - or worse, will reject them as epistemologically "wrong" or - even worse - old-fashioned! The optimal result of the current proliferation of approaches to event-based collective action would be the triangulation of narrative case studies, event histories and events in history, attentive to the dynamics of the cycles of political struggle within which they occur; but given the fate of past history of attempts at scholarly synthesis, that process may be as contentious as the subject on which it focuses.

References

Abbott, A. 1988. "Transcending General Linear Reality." *Sociological Theory* 6: 169-186.
Abrams, P. 1982. *Historical Sociology.* Ithaca, N.Y.; London: Cornell University Press.
Allison, P. D. 1982. "Discrete-time Methods for the Analysis of Event Histories." Pp. 61-98 in *Sociological Methodology*, ed. S. Leinhardt. San Francisco: Jessey Basis.

Appelby, J., L. Hunt and M. Jacobs. 1994. *Telling the Truth About History*. New York; London: Norton.

Ashenfelter, O. and J. Pencavel. 1969. "American Trade Union Growth, 1900-1960." *Quarterly Journal of Economics* 83: 434-448.

Baker, K. M. 1990. *Inventing the French Revolution: Essays on French Political Culture in the Eighteenth Century*. Cambridge; New York: Cambridge University Press.

Beissinger, M. R. 1990. "Non-Violent Public Protest in the USSR: December 1, 1986-December 31, 1989." Report published by the National Council for Soviet and East European Research. Washington, D.C.

Beissinger, M. R. 1991. "Ethnic-Based Mass Political Action in the USSR." Report published by the National Council for Soviet and East European Research. Washington, D.C.

Beissinger, M. R. 1993. "Demise of an Empire-State: Identity, Legitimacy, and the Deconstruction of Soviet Politics." Pp. 93-115 in *The Rising Tide of Cultural Pluralism*, ed. M. C. Young. Madison, Wis.: University of Wisconsin Press.

Beissinger, M. R. 1995a. "The State as Constructor of Nationalism: Nationalist Mobilization Before and After the Breakup of the USSR." Unpublished paper.

Beissinger, M. R. 1995b. "Protest Mobilization in the Former Soviet Union: Issues in Event Analysis." Unpublished paper.

Beissinger, M. R. 1996a. "Event Analysis in Transitional Societies: Protest Mobilization in the Former Soviet Union." Unpublished paper.

Beissinger, M. R. 1996b. "How Nationalisms Spread: Eastern Europe Adrift the Tides and Cycles of Nationalist Contention." *Social Research* 63: 1-50.

Beissinger, M. R. 1996c. "The Relentless Pursuit of the National State: Reflections on Soviet and Post-Soviet Experiences." Unpublished paper.

Bohstedt, J. 1983. *Riots and Community Politics in England and Wales, 1790-1810*. Cambridge, Mass.: Harvard University Press.

Bond, D. and J. Bond. 1995. "Protocol for the Assessment of Nonviolent Direct Action (PANDA) Codebook for the *P2* data set." Harvard University, Center for International Affairs.

Brand, K.-W. 1990. "Cyclical Aspects of New Social Movements: Waves of Cultural Criticism and Mobilization Cycles of New Middle-class Radicalism." Pp. 23-42 in *Challenging the Political Order: New Social and Political Movements in Western Democracies*, ed. R. J. Dalton and M. Kuechler. Cambridge: Polity Press.

Braudel, F. 1958. "Histoire et sciences sociales: La Longue durée." *Annales* 13: 725-753.

Burstein, P. 1995. *Discrimination, Jobs and Politics: The Struggle for Equal Employment Opportunity in the United States Since the New Deal*. Chicago: University of Chicago Press.

Burstein, P. and W. Freudenberg. 1978. "Changing Public Policy: The Impact of Public Opinion, Antiwar Demonstrations, and War Costs on Senate Voting on Vietnam War Motions." *American Journal of Sociology* 84: 99-122.

Charlesworth, A. 1983. *An Atlas of Rural Protest in Britain, 1548-1900*. London: Croom Helm.

Darnton, R. 1984. *The Great Cat Massacre and Other Episodes in French Cultural History*. New York: Random House.

Della Porta, D. 1995. *Social Movements, Political Violence and the State: A Comparative Analysis of Italy and Germany*. Cambridge; New York: Cambridge University Press.

Dumoulin, O. 1986. "Eventementielle (Histoire)." Pp. 271-272 in *Dictionnaire des sciences historiques*, ed. A. Burguière. Paris: Presses Universitaires de France.

Ekiert, G. and J. Kubik. 1995. "Protest Event Analysis in the Study of Regime Change and Democratization." Paper presented at the International Workshop on "Protest Event Analysis: Methodology, Applications, Problems." Social Science Research Center Berlin (WZB). Berlin, Germany. June 12-24.

Ekiert, G. and J. Kubik. 1996a. *Collective Protest and Democratic Consolidation in Poland, 1989-1993*. Pew Papers on Central Eastern European Reform and Regionalism. Center of International Studies, Princeton University.

Ekiert, G. and J. Kubik. 1996b. "Strategies of Collective Protest in Democratizing Societies: Hungary, Poland, and Slovakia since 1989." Paper presented at the Tenth International Conference of Europeanists. Chicago. March 14-16.

Emirbayer, M., J. Goodwin and C. Tilly. 1995. "A Symposium on Macrosociology." *Comparative and Historical Sociology* 8, No. 1&2 (Fall/Winter).

Favre, P., ed. 1990. *La Manifestation*. Paris: Presses de la Fondation Nationale des Sciences Politiques.

Fillieule, O. 1994. "Contribution à une théorie compréhensive de la manifestation: Les formes et les déterminants de l'action manifestante dans la France des années quatre-vingts." Unpublished thesis. Paris: Institut d'Etudes Politiques.

Fillieule, O. 1995. "Methodological Issues in the Collection of Data on Protest Events: Police Records and National Press France." Unpublished paper.

Floud, R. 1990. *Height, Health, and History: Nutrition Status in the United Kingdom, 1750-1980*. Cambridge: Cambridge University Press.

Franzosi, R. 1987. "The Press as a Source of Socio-Historical Data: Issues in the Methodology of Data Collection from Newspapers." *Historical Methods* 20: 5-16.

Franzosi, R. 1995. *The Puzzle of Strikes. Class and State Strategies in Postwar Italy*. New York; Cambridge: Cambridge University Press.

Gamson, W. 1975. *The Strategy of Social Protest*. Homewood, Ill.: Dorsey.

Geertz, C. 1973. *The Interpretation of Cultures*. New York: Basic Books.

Ginzburg, C. 1984. *The Night Battles: Witchcraft and Agrarian Cults in the Sixteenth and Seventeenth Centuries*. Baltimore: Johns Hopkins University Press.

Goldstone, J. 1980. "The Weakness of Organization: A Look at Gamson's 'The Strategy of Social Protest.'" *American Journal of Sociology* 85: 1017-1042.

Griffin, L. J. and L. W. Isaac. 1992. "Recursive Regression and the Historical Use of 'Time' in Time-Series Analysis of Historical Process." *Historical Methods* 25 (4): 166-179.

Gurr, T. R. 1970. *Why Men Rebel?* Princeton: Princeton University Press.

Gurr, T. R., ed. 1989. *Violence in America*, 2 Vol. London; New Delhi; Newbury Park: Sage.

Harrison, M. 1988. *Crowds and History: Mass Phenomena in English Towns, 1790-1835*. Cambridge: Cambridge University Press.

Hattan, V. C. 1993. *Labor Visions and State Power: The Origins of Business Unionism in the United States*. Princeton: Princeton University Press.

Hobsbawm, E. and G. Rudé. 1968. *Captain Swing*. New York: Pantheon.

Hunt, L. 1984. *Politics, Culture and Class in the French Revolution*. Berkeley; Los Angeles: University of California Press.

Imig, D. and S. Tarrow. 1996. *The Europeanization of Movements? Contentious Politics and the European Union, October 1983 - March 1995.* Ithaca, N.Y.: Institute of European Studies Working Papers.

Isaac, L. W. and L. J. Griffin. 1989. "Ahistoricism in Time-Series Analyses of Historical Process: Critique, Redirection, and Illustrations from U.S. Labor History." *American Sociological Review* 54: 873-890.

Jenkins, C. 1985. *The Politics of Insurgency: The Farm Worker Movement in the 1960s.* New York: Columbia University Press.

Katzenstein, M. F. 1996. "Stepsisters: Feminist Activism in Different Institutional Spaces." Paper presented to the workshop on "The Movement Society?" Cornell University. Ithaca, N.Y. March.

Kitschelt, H. 1986. "Political Opportunity Structure and Political Protest: Anti-Nuclear Movements in Four Democracies." *British Journal of Political Science* 16: 57-85.

Koopmans, R. 1993. "The Dynamics of Protest Waves: Germany, 1965 to 1989." *American Sociological Review* 58: 637-658.

Kriesi, H. et al. 1992. "New Social Movements and Political Opportunities in Western Europe." *European Journal of Political Research* 22: 219-244.

Kriesi, H., R. Koopmans, J. W. Duyvendak and M. Giugni. 1995. *New Social Movements in Western Europe: A Comparative Perspective.* Minneapolis and St. Paul: University of Minnesota Press.

Kubik, J. 1995. *Cultural Frames of Collective Protest in Post-Communist Poland, 1989-1993.* Working Paper Series, No. 4. Advanced Study Center, International Institute, University of Michigan. Ann Arbor. October.

Lloyd, C. 1993. *The Structures of History.* Oxford; Cambridge: Blackwell.

Lohmann, S. 1993. "A Signaling Model of Informative and Manipulative Political Action." *American Political Science Review* 87: 319-333.

McAdam, D. 1982. *The Political Process and the Civil Rights Movement.* Chicago: University of Chicago Press.

McAdam, D. 1995. "Conceptual Origins, Current Problems, Future Directions." Pp. 23-40 in *Comparative Perspectives on Social Movements: Political Opportunities, Mobilizing Structures, and Cultural Framings,* ed. D. McAdam, J. D. McCarthy and M. N. Zald. Cambridge; New York: Cambridge University Press.

McAdam, D. and D. Rucht. 1993. "The Cross-National Diffusion of Movement Ideas." *Annals of the American Academy of Political and Social Science* 528: 56-74.

McAdam, D., S. Tarrow and C. Tilly. 1996. "To Map Contentious Politics." *Mobilization* 1: 21-22.

McCarthy, J., C. McPhail and J. Crist. 1998. "The Emergence and Diffusion of Public Order Management Systems: Protest Cycles and Police Responses." Forthcoming in *Globalization and Social Movements,* ed. H. Kriesi, D. Della Porta and D. Rucht. Houndsmill, Hants, UK: Macmillan.

McCarthy, J., C. McPhail and J. Smith. 1992. "The Tip of the Iceberg: Some Dimensions of Selection Bias in Media Coverage of Washington Demonstrations, 1982." Paper presented at American Sociological Association Annual Meeting. Pittsburgh, Penn.

McCarthy, J., C. McPhail and J. Smith. 1993. "Up, Down, and Stable: Trends in the Number, Rate and Structure of Media Selection Bias of Washington Demonstrations, 1982, 1991." Paper presented at American Sociological Association Annual Meeting. Miami.

McCarthy, J., C. McPhail and J. Smith. 1994. "The Institutional Channeling of Protest. The Emergence and Evolution of the Demonstration Regulation System in Washington, D.C." Paper presented to the Congress of the International Sociological Association. Bielefeld, Germany.

McCarthy, J., C. McPhail, J. Smith and L. J. Crishock. 1996. "Elements of Description Bias: Electronic and Print Media Representations of Washington, D.C. Demonstrations, 1982." Paper presented at the International Workshop on "Protest Event Analysis: Methodology, Applications, Problems." Social Science Research Center Berlin (WZB). Berlin, Germany. June 12-24.

McPhail, C. and V. Husting. 1994. "Periodic Protest: The March for Life, January 22, 1994." Paper presented at the Annual Meeting of the Midwest Sociological Association. St. Louis.

McPhail, C., J. McCarthy and D. Schweingruber. 1996. "Policing Protest in the United States: From the 1960s to the 1990s." Paper presented at the Workshop on "Policing of Mass Demonstrations in Contemporary Democracies." European University Institute. Florence, Italy. October 14-16.

McPhail, C. and D. Schweingruber. 1994. "A Primer for Systematic Observation of Collective Action." Urbana: Department of Sociology, University of Illinois. (Copyrighted.)

Minkoff, D. 1995. *Organizing for Equality: The Evolution of Women's and Racial-Ethnic Organizations in America, 1955-1985.* New Brunswick, N.J.: Rutgers University Press.

Minkoff, D. 1996. "The Sequencing of Social Movements." Unpublished paper. Yale University.

Moore, S. F. 1987. "Explaining the Present: Theoretical Dilemmas in Processual Ethnography." *American Ethnologigist* 14 (1): 727-736.

Nora, P. 1974. "Le retour de l'évenement." Pp. 210-230 in *Faire de l'Histoire, I,* ed. J. Le Goff and P. Nora. Paris: Gallimard.

Olivier, J. L. 1989. "Dynamics of Ethnic Collective Action in South Africa, 1970-1984." Doctoral thesis. Cornell University.

Olzak, S. 1989. "Analysis of Events in the Study of Collective Action." *Annual Review of Sociology* 15: 119-186.

Olzak, S. 1992. *The Dynamics of Ethnic Competition and Conflict.* Stanford, Cal.: Stanford University Press.

Olzak, S. and J. L. Olivier. 1995. "Police Violence and Racial Conflict in South Africa and the United States." Unpublished paper.

Olzak, S. and J. L. Olivier. 1996. "Repression of Racial Strife in South Africa and the United States." *American Journal of Sociology.*

Perrot, M. 1987. *Workers on Strike: France 1871-1890.* New Haven; London: Yale University Press.

Pizzorno, A. 1978. "Political Exchange and Collective Identity in Industrial Conflict." Pp. 277-298 in *The Resurgence of Class Conflict in Western Europe Since 1968,* Vol. 2, ed. C. Crouch and A. Pizzorno. London: Macmillan.

Rucht, D. 1995. "Mobilizing for 'Distant Issues': German Solidarity Groups in Non-Domestic Issue Areas." Paper presented at the 90th Annual Meeting of the American Sociological Association. Washington, D.C. August 19-23.

Rucht, D. 1996a. "Forms of Protest in Germany 1950-1992: A Quantitative Overview." Paper prepared for the workshop on "Europe and the United States: Movement Societies or the Institutionalization of Protest. Cornell University. Ithaca, N.Y. March 1-3.

Rucht, D. 1996b. "The Structure and Culture of Political Protest in Germany, 1950-1992." Paper presented at the Tenth International Conference of Europeanists. Chicago. March 14-16.

Rucht, D. and R. Koopmans. 1995. "Social Movement Mobilization under Right and Left Governments: A Look at Four West European Countries." Paper presented at the 90th Annual Meeting of the American Sociological Association. Washington, D.C. August 19-23.

Rucht, D., P. Hocke and T. Ohlemacher. 1992. "Dokumentation und Analyse von Protest-ereignisen in der Bundesrepublik Deutschland (Prodat), Codebuch." Discussion Paper FS III 92-103 Wissenschaftszentrum Berlin für Sozialforschung (Social Science Research Center Berlin, WZB). Berlin.

Rucht, D. and T. Ohlemacher. 1992. "Protest Event Data: Collection, Uses and Perspectives." Pp. 76-106 in *Studying Collective Action*, ed. R. Eyerman and M. Diani. London; New Delhi; Newbury Park, Cal.: Sage.

Rudé, G. 1964. *The Crowd in History: A Study of Popular Disturbances in France and England, 1730-1848*. New York: Wiley.

Schweingruber, D. and C. McPhail. 1995. "A Methodology for Coding Field Observations and Videotape Records of Collective Action." Paper presented to the Annual Meeting of the American Sociological Association. Washington, D.C.

Sewell, W. H. Jr. 1990. "Collective Violence and Collective Loyalties in France: Why the French Revolution Made a Difference." *Politics and Society* 18: 527-552.

Sewell, W. H. Jr. 1992. "A Theory of Structure: Duality, Agency, and Social Transformation." *American Journal of Sociology* 98: 1-29.

Sewell, W. H. Jr. 1994. *A Rhetoric of Bourgeois Revolution: The Abbé Sieyes and What Is the Third Estate?* Durham; London: Duke University Press.

Sewell, W. H. Jr. 1996a. "Historical Events as Transformations of Structures: Inventing Revolution at the Bastille." *Theory and Society* 25: 841-881.

Sewell, W. H. Jr. 1996b. "Three Temporalities: Towards an Eventful Sociology." Pp. 245-280 in *The Historic Turn in the Human Sciences*, ed. T. J. MacDonald. Ann Arbor: University of Michigan Press.

Shorter, E. and C. Tilly. 1974. *Strikes in France, 1830 to 1968*. Cambridge; London; New York: Cambridge University Press.

Skocpol, T. 1994. *Social Revolutions in the Modern World*. Cambridge; New York: Cambridge University Press.

Snow, D. and R. Benford. 1992. "Master Frames and Cycles of Protest." Pp. 133-155 in *Frontiers in Social Movement Theory*, ed. A. Morris and C. McClurg Mueller. New Haven: Yale University Press.

Somers, M. R. 1992. "Narrativity, Narrative Identity, and Social Action: Rethinking English Working-Class Formation." *Social Science History* 16 (4): 591-630.

Somers, M. R. 1993. "Where is Sociology After the Historic Turn? Knowledge Cultures, Narrativity and Historical Epistemologies." *Comparative Studies in Society and History*.

Soule, S. A. 1992. "Populism and Black Lynching in Georgia, 1890-1900." *Social Forces* 72 (2): 431-449.

Soule, S. A. 1995. "The Student Anti-Apartheid Movement in the United States: Diffusion of Protest Tactics and Policy Reform." Unpublished Ph.D. thesis. Cornell University.

Soule, S. A. 1997. "The Student Divestment Movement in the United States and the Shantytown: Diffusion of a Protest Cycle." *Social Forces* 75 (3): 855-882.

Stone, L. 1979. "The Revival of Narrative: Reflections on a New Old History." *Past and Present* 85: 3-24.

Stone, L. 1982. *The Family, Sex and Marriage in England, 1500-1800.* New York: Harper Collins Publishers.

Tarrow, S. 1989. *Democracy and Disorder. Protest and Politics in Italy, 1965-1974.* Oxford: Clarendon Press.

Tarrow, S. 1994. *Power in Movement: Social Movements, Collective Action and Politics.* New York; Cambridge: Cambridge University Press.

Tarrow, S. 1995. "States and Opportunities: The Political Structuring of Social Movements." Pp. 41-61 in *Comparative Perspectives on Social Movements: Political Opportunities, Mobilizing Structures, and Cultural Framings*, ed. D. McAdam, J. D. McCarthy, M. N. Zald. New York: Cambridge University Press.

Tarrow, S. 1996. "The People's Two Rhythms: Charles Tilly and the Study of Contentious Politics; A Review Article." *Comparative Studies in Society and History* 38: 586-600.

Tilly, C. 1964. *The Vendée.* Cambridge, Mass.: Harvard University Press.

Tilly, C. 1978. *From Mobilization to Revolution.* Reading, Mass.: Addison-Wesley.

Tilly, C. 1983. "Speaking Your Mind Without Elections, Surveys, or Social Movements." *Public Opinion Quarterly* 47: 461-478.

Tilly, C. 1986. *The Contentious French.* Cambridge, Mass.: Harvard University Press.

Tilly, C. 1995. *Popular Contention in Great Britain.* Cambridge: Harvard University Press.

Tilly, C., L. Tilly and R. Tilly. 1975. *The Rebellious Century.* Cambridge, Mass.: Harvard University Press.

Tuma, N. and M. Hannan. 1984. *Social Dynamics.* New York: Academic Press.

Methodological Issues in Collecting Protest Event Data: Units of Analysis, Sources and Sampling, Coding Problems

Dieter Rucht and Friedhelm Neidhardt[1]

Introduction

Sometimes there is a striking asymmetry in the attention and sophistication that social scientists invest in various steps of their work. They usually apply sophisticated techniques of analysis that are part of their professional training and therefore well-documented in handbooks. However, they tend to invest far less energy in reasoning about, controlling for, and documenting the process of data collection. Knowledge and experience of data collection is often individualized and fragmented, and thus this wheel of research has to be reinvented from project to project. Moreover, while the quality of this wheel may not necessarily be bad, it is hard to judge for those who have not participated in the data collection. The reader has to take the quality of the data as read. Many researchers tend to be silent about the flaws and limitations of their data. Or they obscure problems in nonspecific remarks to be found in footnotes or brief methodological appendices.

We assume that all research results are largely artifacts. This in the sense that they follow from the many decisions that are made during the normal course of research. These decisions tend to prestructure and influence the research output in a way that can, at best, be seen only marginally by the recipient. Research decisions are professional to the extent that they are based upon theoretical reflection and methodological standards. But even when professional criteria are met, there will still be leeway in decision making. Here pragmatic considerations come into play, including opportunistic criteria regarding economic restrictions, social settings and the technical opportunities of field work and/or data collection.

Our conviction is that the process of data collection and its underlying reasoning deserves more attention than it usually receives. This prescription should also apply to research concerning protest events, an area which seems to have become a growth industry in the field of collective behavior and social movements. Based on our experience with a large data collection covering

1   We are grateful to Ken Kassman and Gabi Rosenstreich for their assistance in editing this text in English.

protest in Germany over more than forty years (in the Prodat project),[2] we wish here to document and discuss some key problems not only related to this particular research project but to all research of this kind.[3] Chief among these problems are: (1) defining an adequate unit of analysis, (2) choosing between the available sources of information, (3) assessing the costs and benefits of various sampling strategies, and (4) establishing and implementing some elementary coding rules. Because of their far-reaching consequences, decisions on these four problems should be made carefully and thoroughly documented. Certainly, such a strategy will make research more vulnerable to external critique. But only when researchers are conscious of and explicit about their decisions, will they have a chance to improve their work's level of validity, reliability and comparability.

The Protest Event as a Unit of Analysis

The selection of a research subject, or - in operational terms - the definition of a unit of analysis, is a crucial act on which all subsequent steps depend. As is true for all definitions, determining the unit of analysis is not a matter of right or wrong, but of adequacy regarding the research question, the available sources, the techniques of data collection, and, last but not least, the kind and amount of resources to be invested.

Even when we have a rough idea of what the core of our definition of protest should be, for instance expressing dissent by making demands and blaming somebody, we have to decide how narrowly the boundary should be drawn. All

---

2   Prodat is a German project on empirical protest event analysis ("Dokumentation und Analyse von Protestereignissen in der Bundesrepublik Deutschland"), sponsored mainly by the German Science Foundation (Deutsche Forschungsgemeinschaft) and sited at the Wissenschaftszentrum Berlin für Sozialforschung (Social Science Research Center Berlin, WZB). It includes systematic protest event data for the Federal Republic of Germany from 1950 to 1993 (see Rucht and Neidhardt 1995; Rucht 1996). For an overview of the research design and its underlying rationale, see Rucht and Ohlemacher (1992). For its reliance on content analysis, see Rucht, Hocke and Oremus (1995). The project covers protests in West Germany from 1950 and in unified Germany from 1989 onwards. At present, data from 1950 to 1993 have been collected and cleaned for the most part. Coding is underway for the period after 1993.

3   For examples of more recent work beyond that presented in this volume, see Tarrow (1989), Everett (1990), Beissinger (1992), Olzak (1992), McCarthy, McPhail and Smith (1993), Duyvendak (1994), Favre and Fillieule (1994), Fillieule (1994), Rucht (1994, 1996), Walgrave (1994), Koopmans (1993, 1995), Kriesi et al. (1992, 1995), Francisco (1993), Mueller (1994), Franzosi (1995), Tilly (1995), White (1995), Lemke (1996) and Szabó (1996).

other things - such as territory, time period, thematic focus, sources, and sample - being equal, a wide definition of protest may promise the coverage of many cases but be unrealistic because we would be overburdened by the task of covering an immense quantity of protests. Moreover, we would confront an extremely wide range of variance between protests, which, because there is no longer a true "unit" of analysis, would hardly allow general descriptions and analytically instructive explanations of the phenomenon being researched. If we wish to include all kinds of verbal protests against any other social or political group, we would have to look, for instance, at political parties that, in the normal course of daily events, oppose the government. Plus we would have to include quarrels among differing groups within parties. If we wish to include all individual protests, as expressed for example in litigation or in letters to single politicians, administrations and newspaper editors, we would have to register myriads of such activities. Thus, not only for theoretical but also for pragmatic reasons, we may restrict ourselves to a much narrower definition which includes only certain kinds of activities or actors.

Some researchers may choose to focus only on violent events - because these are smaller in number, better documented, and, very probably, a telling indicator of a high degree of discontent. Violent protests could be regarded as the tip of an iceberg. However, we cannot obtain any idea about the volume of the iceberg as long as we do not study protest in its more 'civilized' forms. Moreover, a specific kind of protest may follow its own logic in terms of its underlying causes and dynamics. Therefore, it would be misleading to apply any conclusions drawn from the specific protest under investigation to the broader phenomenon of protest. Considering these arguments, it is advisable to work with middle-range concepts that are neither too wide nor too narrow with regard to both theoretical considerations and pragmatic restrictions.

In the Prodat project we had three basic interests which were not be compromised. First, we wanted to cover all political and social protest issues; second, to cover virtually all forms of protest beyond mere verbal and quasi-routinized forms of dissent, including relatively small and "unspectacular" protests; third, to cover a long period that would allow us to study protest cycles and diffusion phenomena. The underlying idea was to get a comprehensive descriptive picture of public protest as a form of interest articulation, and at a later point to analyze its internal and external causal dynamics. A third and the most difficult goal was to analyze the impacts of protests that have a chance to influence society and politics because they are registered by mass media and thus by a wide audience. Our effort should by no means be understood as an enterprise to somehow represent the totality of protests that actually occur but, for the most part, remain invisible to the wider populace.

We preferred a relatively wide definition for our unit of analysis because the data should enable us to answer a broad range of research questions, including those of users outside our team, and allow for the option of cross-national comparisons. Nevertheless, for theoretical reasons, we decided to restrict ourselves in several ways. We ignored (1) actions undertaken by single individuals, (2) actions by governmental bodies and other state authorities, (3) actions in private contexts, and (4) forms of aggressive eruption such as vandalism, as long as these were not combined with specific demands. After checking units of analysis in comparable research and conducting preliminary tests of practicability, we finally chose the concept of protest event as the our main variable. It was defined as "a collective, public action by a non-governmental actor who expresses criticism or dissent and articulates a societal or political demand" (Rucht, Hocke and Ohlemacher 1992: 4).

We cannot specify and discuss each element of the definition here but we would like to draw attention to some of its theoretical and practical implications. First, we have added to protest the term event. By definition, an event has a beginning and an end. We regard as an event only a distinct action undertaken by the same group of actors for the same specific purpose over a continuous period of time. A protest event may last from several seconds to several months. An example of the latter case would be the occupation of a nuclear site or a university building. Even if such a longer event were to be interrupted for practical reasons (e.g. protesters leave the institute overnight and come back in the early morning), this occupation would qualify as just one event. On the other hand, a complex activity such as a revolution, which the historian William H. Sewell calls a "great event" (see Tarrow in this volume), would not qualify as such according to our understanding because it is composed of a whole set of discrete collective activities, which differ in form, concrete goal and member group. These events are often only interpreted as an interconnected process in retrospect. In our terminology, a set of discrete actions that can be subsumed under a common but specific goal or slogan is called a protest campaign.[4]

But how should one deal with a single protest event that combines different forms, for instance a rally that eventually leads to a spontaneous blockade in which the same protesters participate? One option would be to ignore one or the other part of the event. Another would be to identify two discrete events.

---

4   Our suggestion is to code events but to conceptualize a protest campaign as composed of a variable number of discrete events that are at least loosely coordinated to serve the same specific goal. Then we can analyze both events and campaigns, thus avoiding a decision on whether or not the "collective campaign" is a superior unit of analysis for the study of collective action, as Marwell and Oliver (1984) argue.

Still another option would be to code two forms of protest regarding the same event. Provided that there is no disconnection in time, location, target or participants, our decision was to allow for the coding of a primary and secondary form.[5] An additional secondary form was coded in 19.3% of all events. It still remains to be investigated which forms of protests are likely to be combined with other forms, and how such patterns can be explained.

Second, with three or more persons involved, we have set a low threshold for an event to qualify as a collective protest. This gives us a chance to analyze small events which may or may not be indicative in other respects, e.g. intensity or risk. This decision also increases the number of events to be coded. We are able to control the consequences of such a low threshold by other means. By using an inclusive definition of "collective," we can produce calculations based on more restrictive definitions if required either for specific analytical reasons or because we want to compare our results with those of other researchers who have applied higher thresholds when defining a collectivity.[6]

Another aspect of setting a threshold is deciding whether or not to rely on explicit information only. In many cases, and certainly in almost all anonymous protest actions, we can often only speculate about the number of protesters.[7] Often we do not know whether just one or more persons were involved, for example if a Jewish cemetery is desecrated during the night, or, for political reasons, someone smashes the windows of a property owner who terrorizes their tenants. Our rule was to code only those anonymous protests which, according to common sense, were likely to be result of at least three people. Such assumptions can be made if, for instance, there are complex logistics behind the act or if the nature or size of the damage indicates that a group was involved.

One may argue that most of these examples are borderline cases that do not really influence the total data set. Our experience, however, shows that there are

---

5   In most cases, in terms of planning and participation, it is clear which is antecedent but there are also arbitrary cases where no clear criteria are at hand.

6   For example, Tilly and his collaborators' notion of a "contentious gathering" refers to ten or more persons (Schweitzer and Simmons 1981: 319). Tarrow's protest events cover activities of a minimum of 20 people (Tarrow 1989: 359). Finally, in his study on collective violence, Tilly's threshold was a minimum of 50 persons (Tilly 1978: 251). The lowest threshold was set by Olzak (1992: 51) with two or more persons.

7   Olzak (1992: 55) found that "daily accounts of ethnic protests in the New York Times provide reliable counts on participants for only about half of these events." In Prodat, we only have information concerning the number of participants in 43% of all events in the 1950s and 56% in the 1980s. Since we usually have other significant information regarding events with an unknown number of participants (e.g. types of actions and area of mobilization), we have developed - similarly to Kriesi et al. (1995) - a way to extrapolate participation in events with no explicit information on participant numbers.

many such cases. The number may be so large that it could have a significant impact at the aggregate level. Moreover, some decisions which are largely irrelevant for the aggregate of all events may have a significant impact when we turn to specific fields or forms of protest. Consider, for example, aggressive acts such as arson attacks against immigrants, in which the protesters generally hide their identity and therefore cannot usually be counted. A rule that includes or excludes these activities will dramatically increase or decrease the numbers of xenophobic protests recorded.

Third, it is difficult to draw a boundary between low profile actions and purely verbal protest. In most research on protest there was a focus on "action" (mostly combined with words, slogans or written material) rather than mere "rhetoric," although it is not easy to provide theoretical arguments for this exclusion. In order to legitimize this analytical distinction, one could emphasize that action requires more in terms of individual and collective costs than speech. However, this assumption can be empirically questioned. Even if it were to generally hold, it is not so clear which theoretical aims the distinction could be fruitful for. On the other hand, one could argue that the effects of acting tend to be greater than those of mere talking. (This is also an idea that underlies some elements of constitutional and criminal law.) But this assumption may also be problematic. We can easily imagine an intense protest act appearing ridiculous to the general audience, whereas, under specific circumstances, an impressive speech may have a significant political impact. In practice, the distinction between protest acts and protest rhetoric is mainly a response to the problems of measurement. The inclusion of mere protest rhetoric would broaden the field of research in a way that could hardly be grasped using a reasonable amount of resources. Therefore, in Prodat we adopted a focus concentrating on protest acts. In quite a lot of cases, however, separating acts from mere rhetoric is difficult. Imagine a group of spectators which, in reaction to a handful of provocative demonstrators, starts to attack them verbally, forming a distinct bloc. Imagine an annual meeting of Germans who had been forced to leave their homes in the former Eastern German provinces following World War II: They basically meet to conserve their traditional culture but also demand the return of their former homes and land in what is now Poland. We have developed rules on how to deal with such cases (see the codebook), but admittedly some arbitrary decisions remain.[8]

---

8   For instance, we coded a press conference only when it was not part of the actor's routinized repertoire and included a call for a concrete protest action, e.g. to boycott.

Fourth, our seemingly clear decision to cover only protest by non-state actors is not so clear at a second glance. Are local councils that declare their town a nuclear-free zone to be excluded? How does one deal with a parliamentary group from the Green Party that initiates a blockade? Should one include or exclude an umbrella organization that litigates against low-flying military exercises and involves not only citizens' initiatives but also a number of town councils? Again, we have sought to develop and document detailed rules which, for instance, define councils and parliaments as such as state actors, but not distinct party groups within these bodies.

Fifth, we want to emphasize that our definition does not include every aspect addressed by important forerunners who have strongly influenced our research. Tarrow, who was "interested in actions that exceeded routine expectations," defines a protest event as a "disruptive direct action on behalf of collective interests, in which claims were made against some other groups, elites, or authorities" (Tarrow 1989: 359). Taken literally, however, this definition would exclude activities such as peaceful demonstrations and gatherings (explicitly recognized as legitimate action in the constitution) which can hardly be judged as "disruptive" but are included as being protest events by Tarrow. Because we also want to include these kinds of actions, we avoid definitional elements such as "disruptive," "unconventional," or "unruly." We also deviated from Tilly's definition of a "contentious gathering" because some forms of protest, such as the collection of signatures, do not necessarily require that a group of protesters physically meets at one place as the term "gathering" suggests.

These few comments and caveats should demonstrate the importance of finding an optimal definition of the unit of analysis in light of theoretical and practical considerations that sometimes contradict each other. Even when this task seems to have been dealt with (if only on the basis of arbitrary decisions), a number of subsequent problems must be solved. Let us first discuss those related to the sources of information.

Sources, their Selectivity, and how to Respond

In contrast to most other issues in protest event analysis, the problems of sources and their relative strengths and weaknesses have attracted considerable attention and therefore do not need to be discussed here in detail (see Danzger 1975; Snyder and Kelly 1977; Franzosi 1987; Olzak 1989; Rucht and Ohlemacher 1992; McCarthy et al. 1996; Mueller 1994; Koopmans 1995). Again, it is hard to give a general answer as to which sources are best suited to this kind of analysis. Many factors must be considered, such as access and the sources' selectivity, reliability, continuity over time and ease of coding.

In principle, methods as varied as participant observation, interviewing or content analysis could be used to collect information on protest events. Provided that we want to study many protest events over a large area and time period, we can hardly conduct participant observation or interviews. Moreover, such techniques would be inapplicable to or inappropriate for events that happened many years or even decades ago. Thus, for our purposes, we are dependent on others who have reported on protests in a fairly systematic and continuous way. Little of this monitoring was done explicitly for protest events, but it can be used by researchers. On the other hand, this data rarely fully meets researchers' needs.

As far as more thematically focused monitoring of protests is concerned, strike statistics and archival records, including police records covering unruly behavior, can be valuable sources. In terms of protest forms and social recruitment, however, both sources are limited. Strikes, by definition, are just one of many forms of protest. Moreover, while strike statistics may be quite accurate and relatively comprehensive (with the exception of wildcat strikes and students' strike action), they are not usually very detailed and only provide information on numbers of people and firms involved, duration and probably location (Franzosi 1989b). On the other hand, police archives may be very detailed but tend not to be accessible to researchers interested in contemporary protest. Even when access is secured in one district, this may not be the case in other areas.[9] Moreover, the criteria for documenting protest events may significantly vary from district to district, as preliminary comparisons within Germany have shown. So far the federal government has not been able to impose a standardized definition of what should be registered and counted. Finally, the use of historical police records has proven that these are often biased as far as the protesters' demands and motives are concerned.

When considering mass communication one is tempted to think immediately of radio and television as potential sources for coding protest events. National electronic media, however, tend to report only a few events, and preferably the large and/or spectacular events, thus ignoring the great bulk of other protests. Even regional and local stations tend to be extremely selective about protest events. Moreover, it would be very demanding to get access to such reports in the many regions and cities necessary to cover a whole country. Unlike the U.S., where the Vanderbild archive gathers a large collection of television news and makes these available to researchers, even nationally distributed electronic news are seldom accessible in an archive in most other countries.

---

9   So far only a few researchers have succeeded in getting access to police archives on protest events, e.g. John McCarthy et al. in Washington, D.C., Peter Hocke in Freiburg (Germany), Pierre Gentile in Switzerland and Olivier Fillieule in France.

Another promising source could be reports provided by news agencies. Again, as of yet, practical restrictions (such as a lack of access and resources) have prevented us from using these sources. These restrictions, however, may not exist in other countries, as shown by research on right-extremist protests in Switzerland (Gentile 1995) and on both violent and non-violent conflicts in many other nations (Bond and Vogele 1995).

Given the restrictions of the sources discussed above, the daily newspaper still seems to be a good choice. Newspapers "provide the most complete account of events for the widest sample of geographical or temporal units" (Olzak 1992: 57). They are, for the most part, easily accessible. Relevant information is usually grouped together in particular sections so that the coder must not look through the whole issue. Newspapers, at least in hard copy, can be perused without technical equipment. In addition, some newspapers have made searches easier by providing a conventional index and/or electronic search facility. Whereas conventional indices may have their own problems not to be discussed here, a full text electronic search, probably in combination with the use of electronic indices, is certainly an attractive option. At present, however, these new techniques are still in a nascent state and not applicable for Prodat.

We found that the clipping archives run by newspapers or other institutions are not useful for documenting protest events. These archives are organized along key words and the names of individuals and groups but never along categories such as protest, demonstration, etc. In order to single out protest events, one would have to scan virtually all the subject files. Moreover, key words are not used consistently and are frequently altered. In addition, a lack of personnel, or a change of personnel, may have an impact on the completeness and reliability of the archive. Finally, daily newspapers in Germany are neither indexed nor, with few and very recent exceptions, available as electronic data. Therefore, opportunities for quick - but not unproblematic - searches, comparable with those available in the U.S., are nonexistent in Germany.

A further consideration is that newspapers may have a bias that leads to the over- or under-representation of certain kinds of events. For example, a paper with a left-liberal leaning may be more receptive to protests events with the same political background. Another bias may stem from the fact that a journal may decide not to report specific events, for instance anti-Semitic activities, in order to avoid triggering an imitation effect. Moreover, a bias may result from changes in a newspaper's overall political orientation - it happened at least twice within four decades in the case of the German daily *DIE WELT*. Finally, newspapers' reporting on protest events may not only be selective in principle, but disproportionate over time. On the one hand, one can image that actual events concerning a new topic may first have to reach a certain number and significance before journalists identify them as newsworthy ("critical mass effect"). On the other hand, protest may continue or even expand over a lengthy period, while the reporting of these events does not simply because an inflation effect makes them no longer newsworthy (Funkhauser 1973).[10] In order to study such shifting thresholds of attention, one would have to establish a media-independent data set of events (e.g. drawn from police archives) that does not follow the logic of media attention.

It is important that the same newspapers be available for the whole period to be covered. Because each paper is likely to have its own bias, in the case of longitudinal analysis there is a high risk of producing artifacts simply by using different papers for different periods. A difficult problem not to be discussed here is comparison between countries (see Koopmans in this volume). Using the same newspaper saves resources but implies an unbalanced coverage not only of the domestic country as compared to all foreign countries but also between foreign countries.[11] Using one domestic source for each country[12] is certainly more reasonable but only works under the debatable assumption that each paper has roughly the same level of attention for the same kind of domestic protests.[13]

The use of a national newspaper is certainly advisable when one seeks to cover protests in a whole country. It should be made clear, however, that a nationally published newspaper inherently tends to apply the criterion of "nationwide relevance" for covering protests. Thus the large majority of protests to be found in regional and local newspapers will be missed.

---

10   Danzger referred to this as the "ceiling effect" (1975: 582).
11   The *World Handbook of Political and Social Indicators* essentially relied on the *New York Times (NYT)* for its documentation of protest events (see Taylor and Hudson 1972; Taylor and Jodice 1983). As far as "soft" protests are concerned, we consider the *NYT* to be worthless as a source for cross-national comparison (see Rucht and Ohlemacher 1992). Lehmann-Wilzig and Ungar make a similar judgement: "It is our impression that only after several in-depth national studies are undertaken (which take into account all the events which actually occurred) can one say anything meaningful about cross-national patterns of protest and their causes" (1985: 66).
12   This was done in the study by Kriesi et al. (1995) in four European countries.
13   Theoretically, this could be tested by using a source external to the countries under investigation - as long as we can assume that this source is not strongly biased with regard to protests in these countries. For example, in this respect the *New York Times* could serve to control for the selectivity of national newspapers in European countries provided that these do not differ very much in their overall political weighting from an U.S. perspective. Another option would be to compare the coverage of events in national newspapers with reports from the Reuters news agency. These have been available in electronic form since the early 1980s.

Consideration of these factors led to our decision not only to use two out of the four national so-called "quality newspapers" as sources[14] but also to control for their selectivity by using, among other things, a local newspaper for a period of eight years.[15] This will be done in a subproject of Prodat which, in addition, also goes beyond newspapers by using local police records on protest events in the city of Freiburg (see Hocke in this volume). Another means of controlling the selectivity and bias of our two main sources will be the coding of protest events using the left-libertarian newspaper *die tageszeitung* for selected years (1993 to 1995). Unlike the coding of the main sources, this coding will also include coverage of the local section that refers to Berlin. Finally, we have created a national data set on one particular issue, namely antinuclear protests in the period from 1970 to 1992. This data set is derived from several newspapers, scientific literature on the subject and antinuclear magazines.[16] Taken together, the data drawn from these additional sources will help us to establish some partial but systematic controls for the selectivity and reporting bias of our main sources.

When we emphasize the so far mostly underestimated need to control for selective newspaper reporting, we should also stress the fact that selectivity

---

14   Based on a pretest covering one month, we found that the two newspapers we had finally chosen *(Süddeutsche Zeitung* and *Frankfurter Rundschau)* were by far superior to the two remaining papers *(Frankfurter Allgemeine* and *DIE WELT)*. Our two sources covered more than 90% of the events reported in all four newspapers. Of this "more than 90%," only half of the events overlapped, and since only 25% were reported exclusively by either of the two papers, we had good reason to use both.

15   Among others, Snyder and Kelly (1977: 118) and Franzosi (1987) have suggested complementing data drawn from national newspapers with those drawn from local sources. For the period from 1975 to 1989, Koopmans (1995: Appendix) identified 2,351 unconventional protest events in Monday issues of the *Frankfurter Rundschau* as compared to the 2,891 protest events we found in the same period based on the Monday issues of both the *Frankfurter Rundschau* and the *Süddeutsche Zeitung.* Thus, our second source does not seem to have contributed very much. One should take into account, however, that both projects followed a different search strategy. First, Koopmans registered all events in Monday issues (including 20 to 25% which did not occur during the weekend), whereas in Prodat only those events were coded that began or continued during the preceding weekend. Second, Koopmans excluded strikes - which were included in Prodat. Third, unlike Prodat, Koopmans also covered protests reported in the regional and local section of the newspaper. Fourth, in contrast to Koopmans, in the "regular data set" we excluded events with unknown location (see Table 2). The main advantage of the second source is the possibility of controlling for a systematic bias in the first source.

16   Admittedly, this data set has been collected in a less systematic way than the others in that we followed the rule of thumb: "Get as much as you can."

differs from variable to variable. As far as the occurrence of protest events is concerned, we have indications that only a tiny percentage of the events reported in regional and local newspapers as a whole are reported in national newspapers (see Hocke in this volume). In particular, small events and/or those referring only to local issues are left out. Even if we were to code several newspapers of national stature, we would get only a very small sample of all reported events. Hence, general statements based on national sources saying that a certain number of events took place in Germany within a specific period would be misleading if we do not add that, first, these are only the events reported by newspapers and, second, they were only reported by one or a few of the national newspapers. Nevertheless, this high selectivity regarding the occurrence of "real" protests is, in some respects, not as problematic as one might think. There are in fact strong theoretical reasons, which have thus far been neglected in the literature, that suggest the use of (print) media as a source.

First, protests that remain largely unnoticed by the populace may be significant for the protesters themselves and their immediate audience, but they simply do not matter for the rest of the population, including political elites. If our interest lies in analyzing protests that are potentially relevant for social and political change, there is good reason to focus only on those events that are, or can be, registered by the wider public. In this regard, event analysis based on the mass media is not only a pragmatic choice but a theoretically grounded imperative.

Second, among those events that are potentially relevant in terms of social and political change, large-scale and/or high-intensity protests are likely to have a greater impact (Kielbowicz and Scherer 1986; Rucht 1996). We can confidently demonstrate with our subprojects that these kinds of events are well covered by all media, including the national newspapers. In the case of very large events, as in cases of violent demonstrations leading to significant damage to property and/or injuries, we can expect a total coverage even when using only one national newspaper.[17] While we estimate that probably less than 1% of all locally reported protest events may be found in a national newspaper, a large

---

17   The research done by McCarthy et al. allows for a control of media selectivity using police records (permits for demonstrations) as an independent source. The *New York Times* and the *Washington Post* reported only 4% and 8% respectively of all demonstrations that actually occurred in 1982 according to police documents. However, the authors conclude that the larger the demonstrations, the better the media coverage. All demonstrations with more than 100,000 participants in 1982 and nearly all in 1991 were covered by the several sources examined (*New York Times, Washington Post,* ABC, CBS and NBC). They found multiplicative ratios between size and coverage, "so that demonstrations in the next to largest size category (10,001-100,000) are more than 100 times more likely to be covered than those smallest in size category (1-25) for 1982 and more than 50 times more likely to be covered in 1991" (McCarthy et al. 1993: 30).

share of the total number of participants involved in all protest events will be registered by a national newspaper because of the weight of the relatively few but fully covered large events. According to our data, protests with more than 10,000 participants represent roughly 12% of all coded events but about 88% of all participants. Even the subgroup of protests with more than 100,000 participants - representing 1.8% of all coded protests - contributes to more than 56% of the total mobilization (Rucht 1996). Similar results have been found in other projects.[18] Nevertheless, we should keep the remaining (and inevitable) validity problem resulting from the use of newspaper reports in mind. We do not measure protest per se but protest covered in the media. By using this source, we rely on the "news value" logic of journalists (Staab 1990) and the production of "news as purposive behavior" (Molotch and Lester 1974) by a professional group outside the social sciences. This logic reflects the interests of the public rather than those of the protest actors. Therefore, the data is highly selective concerning the issues, motives and kind of actions the protesters use.

The value of this selective data lies in protest's potential relevance for policy-making in modern democracies. Without being perceived and transmitted by the mass media, protests are - in a Durkheimian sense - not "social facts" of political relevance. Insofar as we are interested in those protests which are an input for the political system, media-reported protests have a higher validity than the whole range of actual protests.

In quite a few cases, however, reports on protest in the media include incomplete and/or fuzzy information. Sometimes the information provided is so vague that we cannot judge whether or not the criteria of a protest event are fulfilled. In these cases, as in cases regarding most specific variables, we followed a conservative course - that of ignoring the event or the vague piece of information we have in hand. As far as the event as such is concerned, a basic decision has to be made about the core information that must be available in order for an event to become a regular case in the data set. Again, at first glance this seems to be no problem because one could simply refer to the four key elements of our definition of protest events. We came across many indications

---

18   According to Koopmans (1995: Appendix), in Germany the largest 10% of demonstrations and assemblies (with 15,000 participants or more) contributed 75% of the total number of participants registered in the source. Koopmans concludes that the total volume of participation is very insensitive to newspaper selectivity. This conclusion is also supported by McCarthy et al.'s analysis of demonstrations in Washington, D.C. Although the *New York Times* and the *Washington Post* reported only 4 and 8% of all demonstrations in 1982 respectively (see preceding footnote), the participants in the demonstrations covered by both newspapers were 61 and 68% respectively of all demonstrators mobilized in this year.

of protest events, however, where we had only very poor information. Take the following two examples drawn from our experience. One article reported in detail on a so-called "Sunday stroll" which several dozen people took along a part of the Frankfurt airport where a new runway was being built against the will of a vast majority of the local population. Clearly these "strolls" were not recreational activities but meant as a sign of protest which, among other things, was indicated by banners carried by the participants. No question about coding this event. Casually, in the same article there was also a brief mention that this kind of walk had taken place nearly every Sunday for over a year. We now have to decide whether or not we should code the other "strolls", and if so, how many? Though we were ignorant of the number of participants in all these cases and of the potential secondary actions related to these walks, we did have a rough idea of the number of walks, plus information concerning location and day of occurrence. Thus we decided to code them by following certain rules on how to get "from words to numbers" (Franzosi 1989a) regarding their occurrence.

Another example was an article on a strike wave in the machine industry. Whereas this article provided some detailed information on a strike in one particular firm in the city of Hanover, it also mentions that similar strike action had recently occurred in many other cities all over northern Germany. Again, we know about the form of these protests but have only fuzzy information about their number, the period of occurrence and location. Although we could have applied our rules as far as an estimation of number and timing is concerned, we decided not to code these events, because the locus of protest cannot be concretely defined. Therefore, in this case, only the Hanover event was coded. Instead of totally ignoring the information on the other strikes, however, we registered the frequency and forms of these protests. Although we did not integrate events without information concerning location into our regular data set, we thought that knowing the sheer number of these events would be an informative fact, helpful in qualifying the overall number of events and, more specifically, the selectivity of our regular data set. To our own surprise, the number of events with unknown location exceeds by far those of the regular data set (see Table 1). Moreover, we found that more than 50% of protests with unknown location are labor protests. Among these, strikes are by far the most important category. Therefore we can safely conclude that strikes are underrepresented in our data set.

Table 1: Frequency of Protest Events with Unknown Location, 1950s, 1980s

Time period	Regular data set		Protests with unknown location	
	All protests	Labor protests (%)	All protests	Labor protests (%)
1950-59	1,204	222 (18.4 %)	3,032	1,540 (50.8 %)
1980-89	3,825	742 (19.4 %)	8,471	4,440 (52.4 %)

Sampling Strategies

When we calculated the resources required for Prodat based on two national newspapers, several decades, many variables, and thorough coding procedures, it became obvious that, even given considerable resources, we would be unable to achieve full coverage. We would have to create a sample that would have less than half of the full coverage. The question then arose concerning a reasonable sampling strategy.

Obviously, several options are available. Each has its own costs and benefits. A natural solution would be to sample every second year, half year, month, week, or day. The longer the time unit chosen for such a 50% solution, the greater the chance of missing highly significant events or campaigns. Therefore we tended towards a reasonably continuous coverage with relatively small units.

Informed by the research project headed by Hanspeter Kriesi (which was almost exclusively relying on Monday issues) and our own pilot study, we found it wise to use at least each Monday issue as source.[19] One reason is that the two newspapers we used do not have a Sunday issue. Thus the Monday issues of our national newspapers basically cover the whole weekend. As a consequence, by scanning the Monday issue a relatively large number of events will be registered. Because not only coding but also scanning - regardless of how many events are identified - is a time-consuming task, the focus on Monday saves resources. You simply get more fish throwing out the net on Monday than on any other day.

On the other hand, we did not want to rely only on Monday issues. One reason has to do with the fact that certain kinds of activities (such as strikes, traffic blockades and various kinds of student protests) rarely happen during the weekend, and are thus unlikely to be reported in Monday issues. We definitely wanted to cover strikes as a specific and relatively common form of protest. A second reason was our interest in the immediate consequences of and reactions to protest. For some protests, consequences such as the number of wounded people or damage to property only become visible after the dust of the battle has settled. In registering such consequences, we would have to cover reports in one or several issues subsequent to the initial occurrence. A third reason for covering a sequence of several newspaper issues, rather than just the Monday issues, was our interest in specific types or chains of events, be it events that may last over several days, be it a protest campaign composed of many single events, or be it the relation between protest and counter-protests. Finally, we wanted to control for the relative number of weekend protests as compared to

---

19   When, for example because of a holiday or a strike, no newspaper was issued on the Monday, we used the first subsequent issue.

protests during the week. Although one might argue that this could be done via a highly selective sample, we preferred to allow for a more ongoing control. Technical progress or institutional decisions may result in shifting deadlines for daily production. The later the deadline for reports on the weekend, the more weekend protests will have a chance of being covered in the Monday issue. A second, though minor reason for controlling the Monday effect was that leisure time has increased over the last decades and therefore, with the exception of strikes, may have created a better opportunity for people to be mobilized.[20]

These considerations resulted in our using a combined sampling strategy. For the reasons mentioned above, we covered each Monday issue of the two main sources selected. This coding of these issues has been completed. In addition, we used the remaining issues (Tuesday through Saturday) of each fourth week as a source. The coding of these issues is still underway.[21] This latter sample not only allowed for a continuous control of the "Monday effect" but also enabled us to register the kinds of events mentioned above that otherwise tend to be missed if only a single additional day during the week is added. Overall, the combined sample of each Monday issue plus the additional issues of each fourth week comprises 37.5% of all "report days" and 46.4% of all "event days."[22] The protests in Germany coded so far (including protests in East Germany from 1989 through 1993) are shown in Table 2.

As we have mentioned above, this sample, as with any sample, has its own disadvantages. First, some weekend protests may not be reported on Monday but only on Tuesday or even later. For three out of four weeks, these events will be missed. Second, concentrating resources on each fourth week necessarily creates significant gaps during the other weeks. It is thus likely that some single outstanding protests are missed. Because we are more interested in covering all categories of events than certain weekdays, however, we consider these disadvantages acceptable.

---

20   Despite our expectation that because more people are available during the weekend, more events would occur on Saturday or Sunday than on other any day during the week, we found that this is not the case. In the periods for which comparative data are already available (1950 to 1960 and 1979 to 1992), the ratio of protests on a weekday to protests on a weekend day was 1.26 to 1. When strikes are excluded the ratio is lower.

21   At present (December 1997), we have completed coding the weekdays of each fourth week from 1950 through 1967, 1975, 1976 and 1979 through 1993.

22   Report days are those on which a newspaper issue is published (Monday through Saturday). Our sample represents 9 days (composed of four Mondays plus 5 other days) of full coverage (24 issues for each four weeks). Event days are those which precede the report day by one day. For the Monday issue only, two days (Saturday and Sunday) are event days. Our sample covers 13 event days (composed of 8 weekend days plus 5 weekdays) out of each four weeks (28 event days).

Table 2: Coded Protest Events in Germany

Period	Protests		Only weekend protests	
			Absolute	Mean per year
1950-67	2,592	(full sample)	1,284	71
1968-74	1,251	(partial sample)	887	127
1975-76	587	(full sample)	220	294
1977-78	432	(partial sample)	282	141
1979-93	6,317*	(full sample)	3,532	237
Total	11,179		6,205	141

* Including 749 protests in East Germany from 1989 to 1993

Finally, after having decided on the sampling strategy in terms of days, the question arises whether all pages of the selected newspaper issues should be coded? Mainly for reasons of economy we excluded the regional and local sections of the two newspapers to be coded. Moreover, during the pilot study we found that the sections on economy/business, culture and sports included only an extremely low number of protest events and could therefore also be ignored for our purposes.

Overall, the sampling strategy we have chosen allowed us to considerably reduce the amount of resources that would have been needed in the case of a full coverage of all newspaper issues from the first to the last page. What we are basically missing are small protests that may be reported in the local and regional sections of the papers but are not covered in the national section. This omission led us to initiate a local study in order to estimate the number and kind of protests that are not represented in the main data set.

Coding Strategy, Rules and Organization

Beyond fundamental decisions regarding the design and sources of research, the operationalization of the coding process in terms of rules and organization is another important step which, contrary to what one might assume, is not merely an executive task. Again, a series of decisions have to be made that heavily influence the quality of the data and the amount of resources required. In the following section, we present some examples of such decisions and provide reasons why they were made.

1. Nobody questions that content analysis should follow explicit, well documented and clear rules in order to guarantee a high degree of validity and reliability. Regarding resource economy, one could follow a line saying that the earlier these rules are formulated, the better. In consequence, the aim would be to establish a definite set of rules during or immediately after the pretest, and to apply these without any modification during the process of data collection. The

additional advantages of this strategy are the simplicity of further coding and a
high degree of reliability. Again, however, these advantages may be outweighed
by costs. Pretests are hardly exhaustive. That is, they do not necessarily reveal
all the problems and weaknesses that will arise during the later coding process.
New empirical facts may induce changes to existing rules and/or the creation of
new rules. In addition, theoretical reasoning during the course of data collection
may lead to changes in categories. Finally, some variables and values may occur
so seldom that it would be a waste of resources to continue with them. (As can
be seen from Table 3, it is questionable whether one should code variables such
as the second location of protest, because this only applies to very few cases.)

Table 3:   Missing Values for Selected Variables (Percentages)

Variable	Missing
Number of participants	48.2
Number of participating groups	47.5
Identification of type or name of protest group(s) - informal group/network	84.3
- formal organization	64.1
Name(s) of one or more protesters	54.4
Social composition of protesters - first option	32.2
- second option	88.3
Political position of actors (on a left/right scale)	93.5
Protest of a social movement	65.2
Form of action - second option	82.0
Unclear legal status of action	9.9
Duration of event	50.5
Second location of protest (e.g. in cases of long marches or human chains)	97.8
Level of mobilization (from local to international)	4.0
Territorial reference of protest issue (countries, continents, etc.)	0.2
Policy domain - first option	2.6
- second option	68.0
Immediate target of protest - first option	20.8
- second option	84.2
Addressee of protest	84.3
Damage to property as consequence of protest	90.6
Immediate reaction (specified in further variables)	82.1
Statements of officials in response to protest	93.0
Statements of other groups in response to protest	96.2
Court cases in response to protest	98.4
N = 11,179	

In short, several reasons may suggest a willingness to keep the coding rules
very flexible. Although flexibility of coding rules during the course of data
collection may improve the validity and usefulness of the data, it will require a

significant amount of recoding, and the task of learning and applying new and non-routinized rules. At a certain point, the costs of these tasks may become prohibitive.

Our strategy with Prodat was to seek *a compromise between laying down the coding rules early and remaining flexible*. On the one hand, we invested a lot of energy in pretests and training coders. During this period we developed a set of both elementary and detailed rules that resulted in a draft version of our codebook. One the other hand, this version was not conceived of as a "holy bible" but as a working tool. Based on our broadening experience during the first six months of the coding process, we decided on changes and supplementary rules, and on better (partially new) examples to illustrate right and wrong coding. This resulted in a first "official" version of our codebook (Rucht, Hocke and Ohlemacher 1992). The ongoing coding experience (of now more than four years) led us to additional, though minor changes, which will eventually be documented in a second edition of the codebook still to be published.

The only major revision required concerned the coding of the protests' subject matter. Relatively late, when we discovered that our coding of the protest issue was not detailed enough for several analytic objectives, we decided to replace this variable with the so-called 'issue variable.' Unlike the original subject variable based on a closed list of seventy-two main topics and subtopics, we introduced a much more detailed and open list with very concrete items such as the Gulf war, nuclear reprocessing, etc. Based on the existing subject variable and an alpha-numeric variable for a brief description of the event according to certain key questions (who, where, how, against/for what), the new issue variable has had to be coded for all events in the data set.

In some other cases we came across rules and items where, in the light of new experience, we wished to but did not make changes because the resulting recoding work would have been too time-consuming. For example, we regret not having initially introduced a movement variable - we only introduced it for data from 1992 onwards. This variable allows us to attribute (if information is available) a protest event to a particular social or political movement.[23]

2. Another important choice refers to what could be called the *overall coding strategy*. Broadly speaking, there are two basic options. According to one, only the manifest text of the source (e.g. an archive file or newspaper article) provides the information to be coded. Ideally, in this version the coder would represent a "neutral" means of transporting evident information from the source to the data file. At first glance, this strategy seems reasonable because it is

---

23   The relatively limited experience we have gained coding the year 1992 has shown that in two thirds of the protest events we cannot attribute a protest to a social movement due to a lack of information about the actor and the goals beyond the immediate demand.

clear-cut and promises to maximize reliability. The second strategy would use the coder as an intelligent and knowledgeable person who, in many cases, is able to interpret, to supplement or to correct pieces of information. Thus the coder is not considered to be only a "means of transport" but also to be a genuine source of information.

In Prodat, we have deliberately chosen the second option for several reasons. In principle we think that the image of the coder as a neutral means is an illusion. Even if we were to try to follow the first strategy, we would have to acknowledge the fact that coders often have to translate pieces information according to their own common sense on the basis of explicit coding rules. This procedure is incompatible with the idea of collecting only manifest information in its literal form. If, for example, we want to code the kind of protest action according to a list of values which imply civil disobedience, we may come across such activity which is not labeled as civil disobedience by the journalist. If we do not want to skip this case, we have to accept that coding is not a machine-like response to sharply defined stimuli. Another example would be the mentioning of a protest in "the federal capital" in the 1980s. Why should we not code Bonn as the location of this protest even though the journalist did not explicitly name the city? Beyond such simple examples, we were often confronted with cases when using or deliberately ignoring the coders interpretative knowledge was more arbitrary. Consider the case of a subtle form of protest in the former German Democratic Republic. In some cases, the inherent message or claim of the activity could only be understood by people who have been socialized in this political context. A West German coder would have dropped these events because he or she could not identify a "societal or political demand" as required in our definition. Other examples are certain actions that appeal to positive values such as human rights but which, from the vantage point of a knowledgeable person, indirectly "express criticism or dissent" against, for instance, a dictator. Including such cases in our definition immediately raises the question of how to draw a boundary between these and simple charitable activities.

Accepting the coders as intelligent readers may also encourage them to supplement missing information. For example, with the exception of a few doubtful cases, our coders responded to the question on how many people were killed during the event with "none" even when this was not explicitly mentioned. This answer can be provided because we can assume that the actual killing of one or several people would not remain unknown to and/or unreported by the journalist. Similarly, the information provided also has to be added to in cases where it is seen as so trivial for an average reader that the journalist does not feel a need to mention certain facts. For example, a coder can qualify a well-known terrorist organization as leftist or rightist even when the article does not apply one of these categorizations. Finally, there are cases when the coder is asked to correct literal information - when it is obviously wrong due to printing errors or a lack of background knowledge on the part of the journalist.

Although we are aware that this "intelligent" coding may cause problems in reliability, we think that the gains made by this strategy far exceed the costs. This is particularly true when large investments are made to secure reliability.

3. In Prodat we have tried to produce a high degree of validity and reliability by implementing a series of quite conventional measures, such as employing a person to train and supervise the coders, discussing coding problems in regular group meetings, testing inter-coder reliability several times during the coding process and developing rules on how to get "from words to numbers" (Franzosi 1989a). In addition, and independently of the preferred overall coding strategy, we sought to improve validity by other technical and organizational means, such as separating various steps of the working process,[24] securing direct data entry from the newspaper into the computer and using a comfortable data entry mask (programmed in Clipper) which, in many cases, automatically provides codes when the text in the mask is highlighted.

To some degree, reliability is also influenced by the social organization of the coding process. This is an aspect that usually seems to be neglected not only in the literature but also in the practice of data collection. Although the social climate in a research team is dependent on "human factors" that can hardly be "produced," organizational conditions and procedure may be more or less conducive to a fruitful atmosphere. In taking social aspects seriously, we tried to be very conscious of selecting coders who, among other things, would fit into the team socially. We tried to hire only coders who were prepared to work in the project for at least one year, to offer them an attractive, long-term contract, and to give them a great deal of liberty in choosing their working hours, etc. As a result, but also due to Peter Hocke's abilities as coder supervisor, we had - in contrast to predictions made by various experts - only slight fluctuation in the coder team despite the fact that the coding of thousands of events necessarily becomes a repetitive and probably even boring activity. A core of coders

---

24 The basic steps are the following: (1) scanning and copying articles that appear to be reporting protest events, (2) selecting articles that definitely refer to protest events, (3) sorting articles according to protest themes and campaigns, (4) reading articles over a period of several weeks or months, (5) coding protest events, (6) putting aside problematic cases for group discussion or a sole decision by the supervisor, (7) depositing articles in the hard copy archive. In particular, we think that if the coders read about protests occurring within a relatively long period this improves their contextual knowledge and may therefore improve coding validity.

worked in the project for three years. Aside from other advantages, this social stability also allowed for an easy integration of the new coders who came later.

Summary

What an external observer, and the scientific community in general, can usually see in quantitative research is the final outcome in terms of numbers, correlations, figures, etc. and their interpretation. While we are aware that data interpretation is a debatable and sometimes highly arbitrary matter, it often appears that the data produced is "objective" - the necessary outcome of a predetermined research interest. Why should we open the black box between interest and outcomes as long as we can assume that researchers have strictly followed professional criteria?

From the previous discussion it should be clear that the collection and coding of protest events is dependent on many decisions which, in their aggregate effect, determine the potential outcome to a great extent. Supposedly "small" decisions may have big effects. Moreover, there is often no "natural" choice and no clear methodological rule at hand. Instead, we are forced to optimize decisions with regard to several - often conflicting - ambitions and criteria.

In the Prodat project, we were not only keen to gather large numbers of cases but also to find ways to assess the selectivity of the data, based on the definition of the unit of analysis, the sources we have chosen and the sampling strategy we have applied. Only in knowing about such decisions and their implications can one use the data in a highly sensitive way. This knowledge could also help us to explain contradictions between research results, which may not necessarily be due to different realities but differences in the data collection. Moreover, knowledge about how data has been produced is particularly important when, as in our case, we have to rely on "second-hand" information not gathered by the researchers themselves but preselected by journalists who, in turn, may depend to a large degree on other journalists working in a news agency, on police reports, press releases, etc. Not only journalists, but also researchers who then selectively use, supplement and correct their information construct a "new" reality in its own right.

Unfortunately, there is no superior alternative to these social constructions as long as we want to document and analyze a large number of protest events over large territories and long periods of time. All we can do is to make conscious decisions and expose these to the scientific community for control and critique. Accordingly, our chapter should be read as an invitation not only to take note of our data (it will be presented in the future), but also to pay attention to the process of producing these data. We think that a detailed documentation of the process is a research result in its own right. Consequently, knowledge and rules of data collection should not be "privatized" within research teams but become a matter of "public" debates and institutionalized training in social science. Then, perhaps, we could reach a higher degree of standardization and create better opportunities to make comparative use of protest data generated in different contexts.

References

Beissinger, M. R. 1992. "Protest Mobilization Among Soviet Nationalities." Unpublished paper. University of Wisconsin.

Bond, D. 1994. "The Practice of Democracy: Global Patterns and Processes in 1990." Paper prepared for the XVI World Congress of the International Political Science Association. Berlin. August 25.

Bond, D. and W. B. Vogele. 1995. "Profiles of International 'Hotspots.'" Unpublished report. Center for International Affairs. Harvard University.

Danzger, M. H. 1975. "Validating Conflict Data." *American Sociological Review* 40 (October): 570-584.

Duyvendak, J. W. 1994. *Le poids du politique. Nouveaux mouvements sociaux en France.* Paris: L'Harmattan.

Everett, K. D. 1990. "Changes in the Social Movement Sector, 1991-1983: The Differentiation of Interests and the Structural Transformation of Protest Activity." Unpublished paper. Chapel Hill.

Favre, P. and O. Fillieule. 1994. "La manifestation comme indicateur de l'engagement politique." Pp. 115-139 in *L'engagement politique. Déclin ou mutation?*, ed. P. Perrineau. Paris: Presses de la Fondation des Sciences Politiques.

Fillieule, O. 1996. *Quand la France manifeste. Engagements, modes de participations et manifestations dans la France des années quatre-vingts.* Paris: Presses de la Fondation des Sciences Politiques.

Francisco, R. A. 1993. "Theories of Protest in the Revolutions of 1989." *American Journal of Political Science* 37 (3): 663-680.

Franzosi, R. 1987. "The Press as a Source of Socio-Historical Data: Issues in the Methodology of Data Collection from Newspapers." *Historical Methods* 20 (1): 5-16.

Franzosi, R. 1989a. "From Words to Numbers: A Generalized and Linguistics-Based Coding Procedure for Collecting Textual Data." *Sociological Methodology* 19: 263-298.

Franzosi, R. 1989b. "One Hundred Years of Strike Statistics: Methodological and Theoretical Issues in Quantitative Strike Research." *Industrial and Labor Relations Review* 42 (3): 348-362.

Franzosi, R. 1995. *The Puzzle of Strikes: Class and State Strategies in Postwar Italy.* Cambridge: Cambridge University Press.

Funkhauser, R. 1973. "The Issues of the Sixties: An Explanatory Study on the Dynamics of Public Opinion." *Public Opinion Quarterly* 37: 62-75.

Gentile, P. 1995. "Les trajectoires de la droite radicale, 1984-1993." Unpublished MA thesis. University of Geneva. Department of Political Science.

Hocke, P. 1996. "Determining the Selection Bias in Local and National Newspaper Reports on Protest Events." Discussion Paper FS III 96-103. Wissenschaftszentrum Berlin für Sozialforschung (Social Science Research Center Berlin, WZB).

Kielbowicz, R. B. and C. Scherer. 1986. "The Role of the Press in the Dynamics of Social Movements." Pp. 71-96 in *Research in Social Movements, Conflicts and Change 9*, ed. L. Kriesberg. Greenwich, Conn.: JAI.

Koopmans, R. 1993. "The Dynamics of Protest Waves: Germany 1965 to 1989." *American Sociological Review* 58: 637-658.

Koopmans, R. 1995. *Democracy from Below: New Social Movements and the Political System in West Germany*. Boulder, Colo.: Westview Press.

Kriesi, H., R. Koopmans, J. W. Duyvendak and M. G. Giugni. 1992. "New Social Movements and Political Opportunities in Western Europe." *European Journal of Political Research* 22 (2): 219-244.

Kriesi, H., R. Koopmans, J. W. Duyvendak and M. Giugni. 1995. *New Social Movements in Western Europe: A Comparative Perspective*. Minneapolis and St. Paul: University of Minnesota Press.

Lehman-Wilzig, S. and M. Ungar. 1985. "The Economic and Political Determinants of Public Protest Frequency and Magnitude: The Israeli Experience." *International Review of Modern Sociology* 15 (Spring-Autumn): 63-80.

Lemke, C. 1996. "Protestverhalten in post-kommunistischen Transformationsgesellschaften: Ostdeutschland im Vier-Länder-Vergleich. Komparative Dimensionen der Demokratisierung und empirische Ergebnisse." Unpublished paper.

McCarthy, J. D., C. McPhail and J. Smith. 1996. "Images of Protest: Dimensions of Selection Bias in Media Coverage of Washington Demonstrations, 1982, 1991." *American Sociological Review* 61: 478-499.

Marwell, G. and P. Oliver. 1984. "Collective Action Theory and Social Movement Research." Pp. 1-27 in *Research in Social Movements, Conflict and Change 7*, ed. L. Kriesberg. Greenwich, Conn.: JAI.

Molotch, H. and M. Lester. 1974. "News as Purposive Behavior: On the Strategic Use of Routine Events, Accidents, and Scandals." *American Sociological Review* 39: 101-112.

Mueller, C. 1994. "A Test of Synder and Kelly's Validity Model on International Press Coverage for Protest Events in East Germany, 1989." Paper prepared for the International Sociological Meeting. Bielefeld, Germany. July 18-24.

Olzak, S. 1989. "Analysis of Events in the Study of Collective Action." *Annual Review of Sociology* 15: 119-141.

Olzak, S. 1992. *The Dynamics of Ethnic Competition and Conflict*. Stanford, Cal.: Stanford University Press.

Rucht, D. 1994. *Modernisierung und neue soziale Bewegungen. Deutschland, Frankreich und USA im Vergleich*. Frankfurt/M.; New York: Campus.

Rucht, D. 1996. "Massenproteste und politische Entscheidungen in der Bundesrepublik." Pp. 139-166 in *Kommunikation und Entscheidung. WZB-Jahrbuch 1996*, ed. W. van den Daele and F. Neidhardt. Berlin: edition sigma.

Rucht, D., P. Hocke and T. Ohlemacher. 1992. *Dokumentation und Analyse von Protestereignissen in der Bundesrepublik Deutschland (Prodat). Codebuch*. Discussion Paper FS III 92-103. Wissenschaftszentrum Berlin für Sozialforschung (Social Science Research Center Berlin, WZB).

Rucht, D., P. Hocke and D. Oremus. 1995. "Quantitative Inhaltsanalyse: Warum, wo, wann und in welcher Form wurde in der Bundesrepublik protestiert?" Pp. 261-291 in *Methoden der Politikwissenschaft*, ed. U. von Alemann. Opladen: Westdeutscher Verlag.

Rucht, D. and T. Ohlemacher. 1992. "Protest Event Data: Collection, Uses and Perspectives." Pp. 76-106 in *Studying Collective Action*, ed. R. Eyerman and M. Diani. Beverly Hills: Sage.

Schweitzer, R. and S. C. Simmons. 1981. "Interactive, Direct-Entry Approaches to Event Files: British Contentious Gatherings." *Social Science History* 5 (3): 317-342.

Snyder, D. and W. R. Kelly. 1977. "Conflict Intensity, Media Sensitivity and the Validity of Newspaper Data." *American Sociological Review* 42 (February): 105-123.

Staab, J. F. 1990. "The Concept of News Factors in News Selection." *European Journal of Communication* 5 (4): 423-443.

Szabó, M. 1996. "Trends of Collective Protest in Hungary 1989-1994." Unpublished paper. Budapest, University ELTE. Department of Political Science.

Tarrow, S. 1989. *Democracy and Disorder. Protest and Politics in Italy 1965-1975*. Oxford: Clarendon Press.

Tarrow, S. 1994. *Power in Movement: Social Movements, Collective Action and Politics*. Cambridge: Cambridge University Press.

Taylor, C. and M. C. Hudson. 1972. *World Handbook of Political and Social Indicators* (2nd Edition). New Haven, Conn.: Yale University Press.

Taylor, C. and D. A. Jodice. 1983. *World Handbook of Political and Social Indicators*, 2 Vol. (3rd Edition). New Haven, Conn.: Yale University Press.

Tilly, C. 1969. "Methods for the Study of Collective Violence." Pp. 15-43 in *Problems of Research on Community Violence,* ed. R. Conant and M. A. Levin. New York: Praeger.

Tilly, C. 1978. *From Mobilization to Revolution*. Reading, Mass.: Addison-Wesley.

Tilly, C. 1993. "Contentious Repertoires in Britain, 1758-1834." *Social Science History* 17: 253-280.

Tilly, C. 1995. *Popular Contention in Great Britain 1758-1834*. Cambridge, Mass.; London: Harvard University Press.

Walgrave, S. 1994. *Nieuwe sociale bewegingen in Vlaanderen*. Leuven: SOI/KU.

White, J. W. 1995. *Ikki: Social Conflict and Political Protest in Early Modern Japan*. Ithaca, N.Y.; London: Cornell University Press.

The Use of Protest Event Data in Comparative Research: Cross-National Comparability, Sampling Methods and Robustness

Ruud Koopmans[1]

Introduction

This chapter discusses some of the central issues concerning the problems and uses of newspaper-based protest event data, referring to experiences gathered in the context of a comparative research project on the development of new social movements (NSMs) in Western Europe. The project started in 1988 and was recently concluded.[2] Principal collaborators were Hanspeter Kriesi, Jan Willem Duyvendak, Marco Giugni and the present author.[3] Data were gathered on protest events (of NSMs and other movements, with the exclusion of labor strikes, see below) in four Western European countries (Germany, France, the Netherlands and Switzerland) for the period from 1975 to 1989. For Germany and the Netherlands, data were also gathered for the years 1965 through 1974, albeit based on a smaller sample.[4] Recently, the data set has been extended to include protest events in Great Britain between 1975 and 1989, and in Spain (also based on a smaller sample[5]) between 1977 and 1989 (see Koopmans 1996a).[6]

Originally, the research design of the project was rather conventional and did not envisage the gathering of protest event data. The idea was to gather data on

---

1 I thank the participants in the workshop "Protest Event Analysis: Methodology, Applications, Problems," and in particular Friedhelm Neidhardt, for their comments on an earlier version of this paper.

2 Publications deriving from the project include Kriesi et al. (1992, 1995), Duyvendak et al. (1992), Koopmans (1993, 1995, 1996a), Duyvendak (1995), Giugni (1993), Giugni and Kriesi (1990), and Koopmans and Duyvendak (1991, 1995).
3 Other participants were Hein-Anton van der Heijden, Florence Passy and Luuk Wijmans.
4 While the 1975 to 1989 data are based on each Monday issue, the 1965 through 1974 data are based only on the first Monday issue of each month.
5 The sample for Spain was similar to that for the 1965 to 1974 periods for the Netherlands and Germany. However, because the Spanish newspaper *(El Pais)* also has a Sunday edition, the Spanish sample is based on the first Monday *and* Sunday issues of each month.
6 In addition, using a slightly adapted version of our coding scheme, Walgrave (1994) has collected data on NSM protest events in Flanders, Belgium.

some fifty new social movement organizations (SMOs) in each country through a combination of interviews and archive research. We soon became convinced, however, that such data alone would not allow us to answer the questions we wanted to address. To begin with, a focus on SMOs seemed too narrow, since many protests, especially those of the NSMs, are not organized by formal SMOs but are carried by informal subcultural and countercultural networks, or by loose, temporary coalitions of local groups. Indeed, we later found that the SMOs we had interviewed according to the original plan (the most important ones in terms of members and resources in each country) were responsible for only a small minority of protest events. Thus, data on the volume, themes and forms of protest events for the different movements seemed necessary to complement the study of SMOs. The literature did abound with statements about movements being stronger at time X than at time Y, more radical in country A than in country B, but these statements lacked any systematic empirical basis. Moreover, many of these statements seemed to us to be highly dubious. For instance, journalists and social scientists almost invariably concluded that since the late 1960s the level of protest had declined and described the 1980s as a period of political disinterest, apathy, cocooning and yuppiedom. We increasingly suspected that these conclusions were, at least for some of our countries, far off the mark.

We therefore decided to follow the example of earlier studies using protest event data (Tilly et al. 1975; Kriesi et al. 1981; McAdam 1982). I will first discuss why we chose newspapers as a data source, and not, for instance, movement or police archives. Next, I will discuss two important characteristics that distinguish our approach from that of most other projects using protest event data. First, our data include different countries, which gives rise to a number of problems and questions that are specific to the use of protest event data in cross-national comparisons. Second, we chose to draw a systematic sample from our sources, which greatly reduced the financial resources and time needed for the completion of the project. Finally, I will discuss the robustness of newspaper-based gathering of protest event data through a comparison of our data on Germany with first results from another project on protest in Germany, in which a different approach was used to gather event data.

Why Newspapers?

The gathering of protest event data on the basis of newspapers has become increasingly popular (see, for instance, Tilly et al. 1975; McAdam 1982; Tarrow 1989; Olzak 1992). This popularity is mainly the result of a negative choice. Anyone studying social movements will be aware of the fact that newspapers reflect only a selective part of reality, and that even that part is always colored by the subjective interpretations of reporters and editors. Similarly, it is one of the eternal complaints of movement activists that many of their actions are either not reported at all in the press, or are covered in a negatively biased way. Therefore, newspapers can hardly be seen as superior sources of information on protest in any absolute sense, and it is rather the deficiency of the alternatives that makes newspapers so attractive.

The most common alternative is, of course, to refrain from quantifying protest altogether and to rely solely on qualitative sources and methods. Such an approach is indeed appropriate if one's interest is limited to qualitative aspects of social movements, such as the internal structure of their organizations or the motivations and ideologies of their activists. However, most qualitative studies also aim at explaining quantitative aspects of social movements, such as the development of their strength over time or the composition of their action repertoire, and thus they cannot avoid making quantitative statements. In the absence of systematic empirical data, such statements are likely to be even more selective and biased than newspaper reports. To an important extent, the quantitative assertions in qualitative studies are themselves implicitly derived from the reflection of social movement activities in the media. Because this happens in an unsystematic way, the resulting statements are in fact the product of a double process of selection and bias, in which the subjective interpretation and selection of the social scientist are added to those of the journalist. Therefore, explicit and systematic quantification, difficult as it may be, is a necessary complement to qualitative information.

Among the possible sources for quantitative data on protest development, newspapers are generally the best choice. With the partial exception of strikes, official data on social movement activities are usually lacking, and if they exist, their criteria of selection and categorization are often vague and subject to changes over time, and anyway likely to be different from those of the social scientist. Further, the number of variables employed in these statistics is very limited; usually they are no more than counts of a specific action form. Last but not least, such listings are themselves often (partly) based on newspaper reports (see Danzger 1975).

Archives are another possible source of information. Police archives, if accessible, are one option, but for obvious reasons they are often biased toward violent or illegal events (but see McCarthy, McPhail and Smith 1996, and Hocke in this volume). Moreover, police authorities, who are often a direct party to political conflicts, can even less than the media be expected to impartially reflect even the most basic aspects of protest events. This is also true to some extent for social movement archives, which, in addition, tend to be discontinuous, incomplete, unsystematic and so disorderly as to be virtually inaccessible.

Newspapers have distinct advantages over these sources. They report a large number of news events on a regular, day-to-day basis, and because they are in competition with each other and need to maintain their credibility as reliable news sources, they - or at least those "quality" papers with an educated readership - are obliged to cover important events with some degree of accuracy (see Danzger 1975). Of course, the reliability of newspapers depends on the kind of information one wants to get from them. Here Tuchman's (1973) distinction between "hard" and "soft" news is often cited. Newspapers can be considered to be relatively reliable when it comes to reporting the "hard," factual aspects of protest events, such as their timing and locality, the number of participants, action form, the stated goal of the protestors, the number of arrests, etc. For "softer," more subjective aspects of social movements, such as whether the participants were motivated by universalistic values or merely by self-interest, or whether they were motivated by their stated goal or merely out for a riot, it is obvious that newspapers are as reliable or unreliable as anyone else's subjective judgement.

Of course, even some of the "hard" facts will sometimes be distorted to some extent. This is especially true for the number of participants and for the question whether or not a demonstration was violent. Although it is impossible to solve this problem, it should be stressed that bias as such is not always a real problem as long as we are not interested in any "absolute" truth and as long as the bias is systematic. If, for instance, a particular newspaper systematically presents only the police's estimate of the number of demonstrators, we would still be able to trace changes in the level of participation over time, because even the police estimate is a reflection of the actual size of a demonstration. Similarly, a significant increase in the amount of movement violence would be visible in the columns of any newspaper, no matter how sympathetic or unsympathetic to the protestors it may be; differences in sympathy among newspapers may affect the absolute level of violence reported in them, but they are unlikely to affect the trends.

An important conclusion that can be derived from this is that for variables that are possibly subject to bias or for which different versions of an event are presented in a report (for instance both the police's and the movement's estimate of the number of participants, and both sides' accounts of who initiated violence) the best solution is not to let the coder try to infer what "really" happened, but to create coding instructions that make the bias systematic, i.e. constant across the units - countries, movements, periods, etc. - one wants to compare.

Comparability in Cross-National Research on Protest

Anyone who has ever done cross-national comparative research has been confronted with the uncomfortable question whether he or she is really comparing like with like. This is already the case when one studies phenomena that at first sight seem relatively easily measurable, such as levels of unemployment. Each country tends to have its own definition and way of measuring and registering unemployment, and sometimes even within one country different definitions and measures coexist. Worse problems arise, for instance, with regard to the cross-national comparability of official statistics on racist violence, which display widely diverging definitions of "racism" and of "violence" and equally divergent methods of data gathering (see Koopmans 1996b).

Cross-national differences in meaning, interpretation and connotation also plague cross-national survey research. No matter how carefully one translates questions from one language to another, the problem remains that the same word often does not mean the same thing because it is embedded in different social, political and cultural contexts. What should one think, for instance, of survey results showing that the proportion of the population who "strongly approve" of the ecology movement is larger in Nigeria and China than in Switzerland and the Netherlands (Inglehart 1995: 59)? In Nigeria and China, hardly anything like an ecology movement exists and the environment is neither prominent nor polarized as a political issue. In Switzerland and the Netherlands, on the other hand, strong ecology movements exist; most people will know about one or more specific organizations or protest campaigns, and the environment is a highly prominent and contested social and political issue. Of course, this is an extreme example (though it comes from the authoritative *World Values Survey*), but similar problems also play a role when comparing Western European countries.[7]

Newspaper-based protest event data gathering is, of course, not immune to such problems. However, this method avoids some of the problems involved in using official statistics or surveys as a data source. The main advantage of using newspapers (or of any other form of content analysis) is that the researcher - at least as long as she or he sticks to the relatively "hard" aspects of protest events indicated above - has the power of definition and is independent of the definitions, categorizations and interpretations of statistical agencies or respondents, which are beyond her or his control. The fact, for instance, that

---

7   For instance, with regard to the Eurobarometer data on support for new social movements, which sometimes also produce awkward results. For a critique, see Fuchs and Rucht (1989).

blockades were until recently officially considered a form of violence in Germany does not force the researcher to code blockades in Germany as violent and blockades in other countries as a form of peaceful civil disobedience. And neither is the researcher troubled by the fact that in France survey respondents tend to identify the stimulus "peace movement" with one particular organization linked to the Communist Party, which calls itself *Mouvement de la Paix*.

Of course, there are a few borderline cases where the researcher does not have full control over definitions. With regard to our coding scheme, the most important of these problem cases concerns the distinction between legal and illegal demonstrations. In the Netherlands, for instance, the proportion of illegal and/or confrontational protests (such as blockades and the occupation of buildings) is much higher than in Germany, with the exception of illegal demonstrations, which are more frequent in Germany. In both countries peaceful demonstrations are, in principal, legal, but in both countries the possibility also exists for authorities to ban or dissolve a demonstration when public order is threatened. The problem here, of course, is that one does not know whether the larger number of illegal demonstrations in Germany is a result of a deliberate choice of German activists (who may, for instance, more frequently refuse to register or to cooperate with the police), or of a broader interpretation of German authorities of the clause "threat to public order," which would result in demonstrations being banned while similar demonstrations in the Netherlands might be perfectly legal.[8]

Nevertheless, in general, the use of newspapers as a data source allows the researcher more scope to define, operationalize, categorize and interpret the material in cross-nationally comparable ways than do the alternatives.[9] Opposing this advantage, however, is a clear disadvantage, namely that the researcher has little knowledge about and control over the selectivity of his or her sources.

This problem is not limited to cross-national protest event studies. Even if only one country is studied, the use of newspapers always implies that one works with biased sources. Only a small fraction of the total population of protest events is reported in the press, which selects those few (large, violent,

---

8   The generally lower level of tolerance of German authorities towards forms of civil disobedience as well as the fact that the tendency towards illegal demonstrations runs counter to the trend for all other forms of illegal disruption, would support the second explanation.

9   The same applies, perhaps even more strongly, to comparisons between historical periods within one country.

spectacular) events it considers "newsworthy."[10] Therefore, anyone who searches for the Holy Grail of the "true" number of protest events or the "true" distribution of protests over different themes and strategies in a certain country at a certain point in time, must be disappointed: Newspapers - *all* newspapers and *any combination* - are an extremely biased source and are absolutely unsuitable for answering such questions.

For most of the research questions that occupy our attention, however, knowledge about "true" numbers and "absolute" levels is relatively unimportant. Would it make us any wiser if we were to know, for instance, that 12.48% of all protest events in Germany are violent? In fact, it is not so much the precise levels that are interesting, but trends and differences, and these can also be inferred from biased sources, provided that the bias is more or less constant, and as long as the number of protest events reported is large enough to allow the detection of significant trends and differences. From newspaper data we may learn, for example, that the proportion of violent events is twice as high for the new social movements as for the labor movement, or that it doubled from 1980 to 1990. *These* are interesting findings, compared to which knowing whether this proportion increased from 5% to 10% or from 10% to 20% is of secondary importance.

This is not to say, of course, that comparisons of newspaper data with other sources, or comparisons between newspapers are not relevant and necessary. Particularly interesting in this respect is the comparison of newspaper data with local data on officially registered demonstrations, which is being conducted by Peter Hocke at the Social Science Research Center Berlin (WZB) for the German city of Freiburg and by John McCarthy and others for Washington, D.C. (see their respective chapters in this volume). At least for one specific set of action forms (legal demonstrations and rallies), these allow a source containing probably approximately the whole population of events to be compared with the small subset of these events reported in the media.

Nevertheless, these studies' substantiation of the fact that newspapers are highly selective in reporting protest events is in itself no argument against using newspapers to study protest. On the contrary, as McCarthy, McPhail and Smith show, the number of participants is by far the most important determinant of the chance of a particular protest event to be reported in the press. Other effects, such as those of media attention cycles around specific protest issues, can also

---

10   Thus, the German Ministry of the Interior counts several thousand demonstrations each year, of which at most some 10% are reported in the national press (see Brand 1988: 181). Similarly, McCarthy, McPhail and Smith (1996) found that of all demonstrations registered with the police in Washington, D.C., only 4 and 8% were reported in the *New York Times* and the *Washington Post* respectively.

be detected, but "are dwarfed by the consequences of size on media coverage." Moreover, the magnitude of this effect of protest size is highly similar for the two newspapers as well as for the two years compared in this study (McCarthy, McPhail and Smith 1996: 492-493). In other words, newspapers are not selective in random ways, but in highly systematic ways related to actual characteristics of protest events. Such systematic newspaper biases do not infringe in any way upon the possibilities for drawing comparative conclusions of the more/less, growth/decline type from newspaper data. Moreover, to some extent this type of bias may even be considered a blessing for protest researchers. By drawing attention to important protests and underrepresenting the far larger number of relatively insignificant protests, newspaper-based protest data may well reflect the development of the magnitude of protest in a society more accurately than more complete sources that treat huge and tiny protests on an equal basis.

While, thus, for many purposes, the fact that newspapers are a selective source of data is not really problematic when one conducts a study focusing on one country, for cross-national studies the problem of selectivity is much more aggravating. The point in cross-national studies is that one not only works with selective sources, but that one wants to compare these selective sources with one another, without knowing whether they are selective to the same extent and in the same way.

Of course, it is possible to limit the seriousness of this problem to some extent by a careful selection of newspapers in the different countries, aiming for maximum comparability. For our study, we employed the following six criteria for selecting the four newspapers:

1. *Continuity:* First, each newspaper must have appeared continuously during the whole period under study, and, second, there should be no significant changes with regard to any of the other criteria.
2. *Frequency:* Because we decided to code only Monday issues, which report news events that have taken place during the two weekend days (see below), newspapers which also appear on Sundays had to be excluded.
3. *Quality:* They should be widely recognized as a high-quality source of information.
4. *National scope:* They should cover the entire national territory.
5. *Political color:* They should be roughly comparable in their political color, and should have neither very conservative nor extremely left-wing sympathies.
6. *Selectivity:* The newspapers' selectivity in reporting protest events should be comparable and not too high.

On the basis of these criteria, we ended up choosing the following four newspapers: the *Frankfurter Rundschau (FR)* for Germany, *Le Monde* for France, the *Neue Zürcher Zeitung (NZZ)* for Switzerland and the *NRC/ Handelsblad (NRC)* for the Netherlands.

Unfortunately, as regards the important criterion of comparable selectivity, it was impossible to conduct direct tests to compare the bias of the newspapers chosen for the different countries, simply because their respective coverage is based on different facts. The only way to answer this question would be to conduct pretests and compare each newspaper with a more or less complete source (such as the police registration data alluded to above) in each of the countries. The problem here is that one would need the same kind of objective reference source, structured in the same way in each country, to conduct such a pretest. And here one runs into all the problems discussed above with regard to the cross-national comparison of official statistics (different definitions, methods of registration and classification, etc.), which is usually even more problematic than the comparison of newspapers. Thus, although the papers finally selected seemed roughly comparable as regards political color - from moderately left-wing *(Le Monde, FR)*, to the center *(NRC)* and somewhat right of center *(NZZ)* - there was no way to know beforehand whether the four papers would really be comparable as regards selectivity.

It was, however, possible to conduct a limited and indirect selectivity test a posteriori. As Snyder and Kelly have demonstrated, the chances of a protest event being reported in a particular newspaper depend on two factors, the newspaper's sensitivity with regard to protest events, and the intensity of protest. They distinguish three determinants of intensity: Size, violence and duration (1977: 110). Novelty can be added as an additional determinant (Koopmans 1993). If different newspapers are equally sensitive to protest events, there should be no differences in the likelihood of events of the same intensity being reported. Legal and non-violent demonstrations and public assemblies are particularly suited to such a comparison because their intensity varies on only one dimension. They last no longer than one day, they are characterized by the same low level of militancy and, as a particularly traditional form of protest, they are unlikely to be reported because of their novelty. In other words, the intensity of demonstrations and public assemblies is simply a function of their size. If, then, the four newspapers are equally selective, demonstrations and assemblies of the same size should have the same likelihood of being covered in the four countries. Of course, we do not have data about those actions that were not reported in the newspapers, but the question can nevertheless be answered in an indirect way by looking at the frequency distribution of the number of participants in the demonstrations and assemblies that were reported.

Table 1: Characteristics of the Frequency Distribution of Participation in Demonstrations and Public Assemblies in France, Germany (Total and Hesse), the Netherlands and Switzerland

	Mean	Mode	Median	N =
France	11,237	500	1,000	838
Germany (total)	9,483	500	1,000	1,288
Hesse	3,497	500	500	482
The Netherlands	4,845	500	500	534
Switzerland	2,073	500	500	557

Table 1 presents the mean, mode and median of the number of participants for these events in each of the four countries. For Germany, the table additionally shows these measures for those events that took place in the *Bundesland* (state) of Hesse, where the *FR* is based. The mean is the least informative of these measures, because it is strongly influenced by relatively few very large demonstrations and assemblies, which are likely to be reported in any newspaper, no matter how selective it is. In Germany, for instance, the largest 1% of these events (150,000 participants or more) contributed 33%, and the largest 10% (15,000 or more) contributed 75% to the total number of participants. Precisely because the total volume of participation is so insensitive to newspaper selectivity, it is particularly suitable for comparing levels of social movement activity among countries (provided, of course, that it is related to the population size of a country).

The mode - the most frequently reported size - and the median - the size of the average reported demonstration or assembly - on the other hand, are more likely to reflect newspaper selectivity. Both measures may be expected to be higher if a newspaper is more selective, because a higher intensity will be required to reach its columns. As it turns out, no differences at all are found with regard to the mode. In all four countries, demonstrations or assemblies with 500 participants are those most frequently reported.[11]

With regard to the median, however, there is a difference between the two larger and the two smaller countries. In France and Germany, the average reported demonstration or assembly has 1,000 participants, in Switzerland and the Netherlands 500. However, it is very likely that this difference is not due to differences in selectivity, but is related to the countries' sizes. The intensity of a particular demonstration size is likely to be lower in larger than in smaller polities; a demonstration of 300 in Switzerland may be as politically relevant

---

11 Moreover, the relative width of this category of demonstrations and assemblies is very comparable between the countries, it ranges from 12% of all events in France to 16% in the Netherlands.

and newsworthy as a demonstration of 3,000 in Germany. This argument can be checked by looking at the median for demonstrations and assemblies in Hesse. If the *Frankfurter Rundschau's* selectivity is comparable to that of the Dutch and Swiss newspapers, the median for those events taking place in the small-size polity of Hesse should be the same as that for Dutch and Swiss events. As the table shows, this is indeed the case. Thus, this indirect test suggests - though of course does not prove - that there are no large differences in the four newspapers' selectivity.

Sampling Protest Events

No researcher interested in the public's opinion on a certain subject would go door-to-door and interview each citizen individually. Of course, such a research strategy would produce very reliable results. However, provided that the sample is large enough, survey techniques can reach a level of reliability that is almost as high, with much less resource investment. Therefore, public opinion researchers agree that there are better ways of spending one's time, energy and resources than by investigating the whole population. As obvious as this may seem, sampling has not yet penetrated the field of protest event analysis, which is still characterized by "the fetish of thoroughness," as Tarrow has called it (1989: 363).[12]

Still, there is no reason why sampling could not be used equally well in the analysis of newspaper data on protest events. Our decision to sample was, to a significant extent, forced on us by the discrepancy between our ambitions and the limited resources available to us. Because we wanted to study protest events produced by any conceivable movement in four countries over a period of fifteen years, non-sampled data gathering would have required enormous investments, which we were unable to make. Moreover, the range of protest events we were interested in ensured that even a sampled data base would contain enough cases to allow for statistically relevant analyses.[13]

If one decides to sample, several options are possible. The method that is closest to the methodology of surveys, is to draw a random sample of newspapers to be coded. A similar, but more practical, method is to draw a

---

12 Tarrow regretfully remarks: "Had we sampled events, we might have had more time and resources available to devote to studying their environment, and in this way learned more about their dynamics than by recording each event" (1989: 363).

13 This implies that sampling is not always a viable option. If one is interested in a limited range of phenomena (a short period, one movement, etc.) sampling is both less necessary and less adequate, because it will probably result in too few cases to be analyzed. Our sampled data base, however, was sufficiently large, comprising 9,022 events.

sample not of individual newspapers but of months or weeks, of which all newspapers are coded (see, for example, Tilly 1978). Although such methods of random selection seem at first sight to be most appropriate, they fail to appreciate an important difference between protest events and human individuals as units of analysis. In survey research, each individual's opinion or characteristics are of equal importance, and thus a random selection method is most appropriate. Protest events, however, are not all of the same value; they have varying intensities, and their importance to politicians, to movement activists, to the media, as well as to researchers differs widely. In fact, as argued above, the coverage of newspapers already constitutes a non-random selection of protest events based to a large extent on the criterion of intensity. Thus, when sampling protest events, the question arises whether one should sample randomly, or whether the selection method should take into account differences in intensity.

Examples of the latter type of sampling can be found in the literature. Tilly, for instance, used violent events as "a biased but useful tracer of collective action in general." Within this category, he sampled on intensity as well, as only those violent events with at least 50 participants were included (1978: 245, 251).

The results of our project cast some doubt upon the usefulness of violent events as an indicator for the development of protest at large. If we had focussed on violent events we would probably have overestimated the level of protest in France and underestimated social movement activity in Switzerland, simply as a result of the fact that the share of violent events in total social movement activity differs strongly among countries (see Kriesi et al. 1992). Similarly, violence can only to a limited extent be used to trace the development of social movement activity within a country because violence often increases in periods when the general level of activity declines (see Koopmans 1993). Most importantly, this sampling method does not allow one to investigate one of the most interesting topics in protest development: Shifts over time and differences among movements and countries as regards action repertoires. In other words, violence as an indicator is not so much "biased but useful" as, for most purposes, too biased to be useful.

The main problem with choosing violence as an indicator is that it represents only one element of intensity. Theoretically, an intensity-directed sample should take into account militancy, size (possibly in combination with duration), as well as novelty. The problem, of course, is that these three elements cannot be related to each other in any meaningful way. We could, for instance, decide to include demonstrations only if their size exceeds a certain maximum, say 1,000 (cf. Tilly 1978: 247). But what is the equivalent of such a size in terms of militancy or novelty? Attempts to solve this insoluble problem will always be arbitrary.[14]

Summing up, random sampling has the advantage of methodological straightforwardness, but will also lead to the exclusion of many important protest events from the sample. Sampling on intensity has the theoretical advantage of including all important events in the sample, but is practically impossible to implement in a consistent way.

Our decision to concentrate on Monday issues constitutes a compromise between these two options.[15] A first, pragmatic, reason to choose Monday newspapers is that they cover the news from two days, Saturday and Sunday. Thus, with the same investment in time and resources, Monday issues allow one to trace substantially more information than other issues. Second, the weekend is a particularly popular time for some of the most important forms of protest mobilization. Because the political and media impact of moderate forms of mobilization such as marches and rallies depend on the "power of numbers" (De Nardo 1985), mass mobilization events are often organized during the weekend, when more people have time to protest. However, it is clear that the weekend is not the most popular time for all forms of protest. Most importantly, this is true for labor strikes, which by definition take place on workdays. To a lesser extent, the weekend may also be less suitable for detecting conventional actions - particularly juridical action, which almost never takes place during the weekend - which may be expected to follow to some extent the rhythm of conventional politics in general, i.e. to be concentrated during weekdays. Other action forms may be expected to be neither overrepresented nor underrepresented on weekend days. This will especially be the case for forms of severe violence (bombings, for instance) that depend on the involvement of very few people, and, more in general, for radical (confrontational and violent) actions, which are - at least in Western Europe - often based on a constituency of students and unemployed youth, whose availability for protest activities will not depend very much on the day of the week.

A small pretest conducted for Germany for eight weeks in 1986 confirmed these expectations. First, this test showed that the Monday issues included a sizeable share, about a third, of the total number of protest events reported. Second, strikes, conventional actions and heavy violence were relatively more

---

14   An example of a - not very selective and therefore not so problematic - attempt to solve this problem is Tarrow's decision to code only those actions with at least 20 participants or in which violence occurs (1989: 359).

15   If, for whatever reason (public holiday, strike, etc.), no Monday issue was available for a particular week, coders were instructed to code the first subsequent issue of the newspaper.

frequently reported in non-Monday issues. On this basis, we made two decisions.

First, we decided to exclude labor strikes from the sample, even in the few cases in which they were reported in the Monday paper. Although - following the above argument that a systematic bias does not preclude the detection of trends and differences - we considered a certain amount of Monday bias not to be problematic, it was clear to us that for labor strikes the representativeness of the weekend would be so low as to make the data useless for this type of mobilization. In addition, our primary interest was in the new social movements, which do not use this action form (apart from a few very exceptional cases such as a short work-stoppage organized by the German and Dutch unions within the framework of the campaign against medium-range nuclear weapons). Finally, in as far as we needed information about the level of strike activity as a context variable for new social movement mobilization, we could rely on the available official data on labor strikes.

Second, we concluded that the choice for Monday issues would not ensure that all important actions would be included in the sample. We could be quite certain to capture the vast majority of large-scale actions, such as mass demonstrations, but we would probably miss many important actions of a more conventional or more radical nature. Therefore, we decided to broaden the range of actions to be coded by including all actions that were referred to in the Monday paper, and which had taken place during the preceding week, or would take place in the following week. For instance, an action that had taken place on Thursday could be referred to in several ways: In an article that mentioned the release of those arrested during the action; in a report on a demonstration demanding the release of those arrested; in statements by politicians referring to the action; in a press release by an organization claiming responsibility for the event; in a report on the closing event of an action campaign, etc. Similarly, the Monday issue sometimes contained information referring to an event that would be taking place on one of the following days: In published announcements or advertisements by SMOs; in statements made by the authorities (who, for instance, could express their fears that the action would get out of hand); in articles on preparatory actions or meetings held by movement activists; in articles reporting the opening event of an action campaign, etc. In all these cases, the coders were instructed to consult, if necessary, the newspaper (or newspapers) in which the event (or campaign) to which the Monday issue referred was reported to find additional information.[16]

---

16   Any events which were reported in other issues, but to which no reference was made in the Monday paper, were to be ignored, no matter how important they might seem to the coder.

Although this strategy significantly increased the amount of time needed for coding (particularly for those periods in which the level of protest activity was very high), we considered this to be a worthwhile investment because it would substantially lower both the Monday bias and, more importantly, the chances that we would miss high-intensity events. Indeed, our sample seems to include the large majority of important events. For instance, of the 57 actions (for the period 1975 to 1988) reported in Rucht's listing of important protest events in West Germany (1989: 340-344), 52, or 91%, are represented in our sample.

Table 2:   Weekend and Non-Weekend Events by Action Form
           (Germany, 1982 and 1986, excluding conventional events)*

	Weekend days	Non-weekend days
Demonstrative	72.5%	52.8%
Confrontational	11.8%	25.8%
Light violence	6.1%	3.3%
Heavy violence	9.6%	18.0%
Total	100%	100%
N =	313	89
(100%)	(77.9%)	(22.1%)

*   We have presented figures only for two years of the West German sample, because the day of the week was unfortunately not included among the coded variables. The day thus had to be determined from the date, which was too labor-intensive to do for the whole sample.

Table 2 gives an impression of both the number of non-weekend events included in the sample as a result of our method of tracing references, and of the differences between these events and those actions that took place during the weekend. As the table shows, our sample contains a substantial number of events (some 20 to 25%) that did not take place during the weekend. These events were on average more radical than weekend actions, which were to a large extent of the moderate, demonstrative type.

The fact that non-weekend events are still strongly underrepresented in our sample implies that our data cannot be used to infer the "true" distribution of protest events over the different strategies (but, as argued above, this is true for all data based on newspapers). However, because this bias is systematic, it is not likely to affect trends over time and differences between countries. Again, the fact that there are substantial differences between weekend and non-weekend events is in itself not problematic for comparative purposes.[17] This

17   Thus, Rucht's conclusion that "it is likely that Kriesi et al. have underestimated the actual activity of the labor movement, and correspondingly, overestimated that of new social movements simply due to their concentration on Monday issues as a data source" (1996: 14) is probably correct. Nevertheless, it misses the point, since we never pretended - and

would only be so if we had reason to believe that the weekend bias varies over time or across countries, for instance because during an earlier period the Saturday was still a working day or because there have been significant changes in newspaper deadlines during the period under study.

The Robustness of Protest Event Data

Still, the question remains whether the pragmatic optimism that pervades the preceding pages is really warranted. The problems of selectivity and bias involved in taking newspapers as a data source make many researchers skeptical about the reliability and validity of this method. Does one not get entirely different results depending on which newspaper or newspapers one takes and on which sampling strategy one employs? This question can be addressed by comparing our data for Germany with those gathered in the context of the Prodat project at the Social Science Research Center Berlin (WZB), which also focuses on protests in Germany, and also includes the period 1975 through 1989 (see Rucht and Neidhardt in this volume). This project differs significantly from ours, both as regards the sources and the sampling method used.

1. Prodat is based on two newspapers, the *Frankfurter Rundschau* and the *Süddeutsche Zeitung*, whereas we only used the *FR*.
2. We also coded the regional and local sections of the paper, while Prodat's coding was limited to the national sections of the two papers.
3. Prodat is based on a sample of all Monday newspapers, but also all issues of every fourth week, while we relied solely on Monday issues.
4. Whereas we coded all events reported in the Monday paper and traced all references to events one week backward or forward, Prodat strictly limited itself to selected "event-days" (i.e. all Saturdays and Sundays as well as all days of every fourth week).

In spite of these substantive differences, however, a comparison of the development of the number of protest events in the 1980s in both projects yields highly similar results. The correlation between the two curves is as high as 0.94,

---

would advise anyone using newspaper data not to pretend - that our percentages are true in any absolute sense. What our data show, among other things, is that NSMs are a much more important actor within the social movement sector in Germany than in France, and that their mobilization increased in the 1980s in Germany while at the same time it deceased in France. Had we coded all newspaper issues, we would certainly have found different absolute levels than we found on the basis of Monday issues alone. However, we have no reason to believe - and comparison with other sources has thus far confirmed this expectation - that our comparative conclusions relating to differences across countries and periods would have been any different.

and every year-to-year change in the level of protest goes in the same direction in both data sets.[18] In other words, despite the fact that not only were different coders used, but also different sources and different samples, the inter-project reliability easily fulfills the methodological standard for within-project inter-coder reliability.

Similarly encouraging results can be derived from a comparison of data collected by Dieter Rucht on protest events produced by the anti-nuclear energy movement in Germany and our data (see Rucht 1994: 452). Again, Rucht's data have been gathered in a very different way than our data. Rucht aimed for a data set as inclusive as possible, and therefore used a wide variety of sources, including newspapers, the scientific literature and movement journals. As a result, the number of protests is substantially higher than in our data set (789 versus 301 [38%] for 1975 to 1989).

Figure 1: Number of Anti-Nuclear Protests, 1975 to 1989

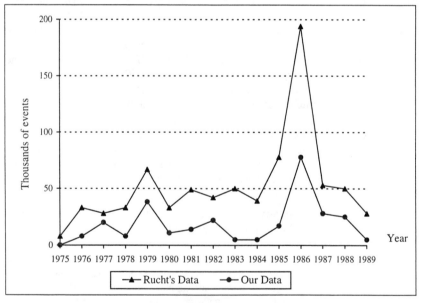

---

18   I thank Dieter Rucht for letting me use Prodat results. The correlation was computed
      excluding the labor movement. Obviously, for this movement a substantial difference
      between the two data sets exists, since we did not code strikes (as a result, labor movement
      events comprise about 19% of Prodat events and only 4% of our events).

A comparison of the number of participants in these events, shows, however, that, despite the higher total number of protests in Rucht's data set, our sample is much more inclusive when it comes to high-intensity events. Thus, the aggregate number of participants in our data is 65% of that in Rucht's data.

Figure 2: Number of Participants in Anti-Nuclear Protests, 1975 to 1989

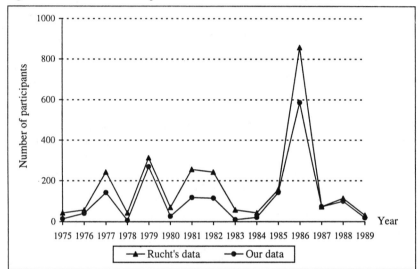

As Figures 1 and 2 above show, both for the development of the number of events and for the number of participants, the two data sets, despite the very different ways in which they have been gathered, yield highly similar results. Moreover, as Table 3 shows, the same is true for the distribution of events over various strategies, which is strikingly similar in both data sets. Thus, again, a level of reliability is reached which easily satisfies strict methodological criteria.[19]

---

19   A further example for the high reliability and validity of newspaper data is presented by Koopmans and Rucht (1996) in a study on extreme right mobilization in Germany in the early 1990s, for which two newspaper data sets using different samples and sources were used. The intercorrelation of the monthly number of acts of extreme right violence between 1990 and 1992 in the two data sets turned out to be as high as 0.98. Moreover, both data sets correlated more than 0.90 with police data on extreme right violence, despite the fact that the latter data comprised a more than ten times as high number of events.

Table 3: Distribution of Anti-Nuclear Movement Protests by Strategies

	Our data	Ruch's data
Demonstrative	70.8%	69.4%
Confrontational	20.3%	18.6%
Violent	9.0%	11.9%
Total	100.1%	99.9%
N =	301	789

We may conclude then that, despite all the problems of selectivity and bias one can think of at the theoretical level, the method of gathering protest events through newspapers seems much more robust, reliable and replicable than one might think. Moreover, these results support the idea that the field of protest studies is no exception to the rule that a sound method of sampling can produce reliable results.

In addition, these comparisons show that one does not necessarily need to use a multitude of sources to get reliable results, and that differences between sources are not as large as one tends to think. Of course, there is no denying that non-sampled data sets based on a multitude of sources will, all other things being equal, produce more reliable and valid results. The available evidence suggests, however, that for most intents and purposes the gain is relatively marginal when compared to lean designs and may not weigh up against the price to be paid for thoroughness - which not only comes in the form of time and research funds, but especially in the form of hindering the spread of an innovation that has the potential to dramatically improve the empirical foundations for research and theorizing on protest.

References

Brand, E. 1988. *Staatsgewalt. Politische Unterdrückung und innere Sicherheit in der Bundesrepublik.* Göttingen: Verlag Die Werkstatt.

Danzger, M. H. 1975. "Validating Conflict Data." *American Sociological Review* 40: 570-584.

De Nardo, J. 1985. *Power in Numbers. The Political Strategy of Protest and Rebellion.* Princeton: Princeton University Press.

Duyvendak, J. W. 1995. *The Power of Politics. New Social Movements in France.* Boulder, Colo.: Westview.

Duyvendak, J. W., H.-A. van der Heijden, R. Koopmans and L. Wijmans. 1992. *Tussen verbeelding en macht. 25 jaar nieuwe sociale bewegingen in Nederland.* Amsterdam: SUA.

Fuchs, D. and D. Rucht. 1989. "Die politische Unterstützung neuer sozialer Bewegungen: Diskussion und Kritik ausgewählter Umfragen." Paper presented at the workshop "Vergleichende Analysen sozialer Bewegungen." Berlin. October 20-21.

Giugni, M. G. 1993. "Entre stratégie et opportunité. Les nouveaux mouvements sociaux en Suisse." Dissertation. University of Geneva.

Giugni, M. G. and H. Kriesi. 1990. "Nouveaux mouvements sociaux dans les années '80: évolution et perspectives." *Annuaire Suisse de Science Politique* 30: 79-100.

Inglehart, R. 1995. "Public Support for Environmental Protection: Objective Problems and Subjective Values in 43 Societies." *PS: Political Science & Politics* (March): 57-72.

Koopmans, R. 1993. "The Dynamics of Protest Waves: West Germany, 1965 to 1989." *American Sociological Review* 58: 637-658.

Koopmans, R. 1995. *Democracy from Below. New Social Movements and the Political System in West Germany.* Boulder, Colo.: Westview.

Koopmans, R. 1996a. "New Social Movements and Changes in Political Participation in Western Europe." *West European Politics* 19 (1): 28-50.

Koopmans, R. 1996b. "Explaining the Rise of Racist and Extreme Right Violence in Western Europe: Grievances or Opportunities?" *European Journal of Political Research* 30: 185-216.

Koopmans, R. and J. W. Duyvendak. 1991. "Protest in een pacificatie-democratie. De Nederlandse nieuwe sociale bewegingen in internationaal vergelijkend perspectief." *Mens en Maatschappij* 3: 233-256.

Koopmans, R. and J. W. Duyvendak. 1995. "The Political Construction of the Nuclear Energy Issue and Its Impact on the Mobilization of Anti-Nuclear Movements in Western Europe." *Social Problems* 42: 201-218.

Koopmans, R. and D. Rucht. 1996. "Rechtsradikalismus als soziale Bewegung?" Pp. 265-287 in *Rechtsextremismus. Ergebnisse und Perspektiven der Forschung*, ed. J. W. Falter, H.-G. Jaschke and J. R. Winkler. Sonderheft 27 of *Politische Vierteljahresschrift*.

Kriesi, H., R. Koopmans, J. W. Duyvendak and M. G. Giugni. 1992. "New Social Movements and Political Opportunities in Western Europe." *European Journal of Political Research* 22: 219-244.

Kriesi, H., R. Koopmans, J. W. Duyvendak and M. Giugni. 1995. *New Social Movements in Western Europe: A Comparative Perspective.* Minneapolis and St. Paul: University of Minnesota Press.

Kriesi, H., R. Levy, G. Ganguillet and H. Zwicky. 1981. *Politische Aktivierung in der Schweiz, 1945-1978.* Diessenhofen: Regger.

McAdam, D. 1982. *Political Process and the Development of Black Insurgency.* Chicago: University of Chicago Press.

McCarthy, J. D., C. McPhail and J. Smith. 1996. "Media Bias in the Coverage of Washington, D.C. Demonstrations." *American Sociological Review* 61: 478-499.

Olzak, S. 1989. "Labor Unrest, Immigration, and Ethnic Conflict in Urban America, 1880-1914." *American Journal of Sociology* 94: 1303-1333.

Olzak, S. 1992. *The Dynamics of Ethnic Competition and Conflict.* Stanford: Stanford University Press.

Rucht, D. 1989. "Protestbewegungen." Pp. 311-344 in *Die Geschichte der Bundesrepublik Deutschland, Band 3: Gesellschaft*, ed. W. Benz. Frankfurt/M.: Fischer.

Rucht, D. 1994. *Modernisierung und neue soziale Bewegungen. Deutschland, Frankreich und USA im Vergleich.* Frankfurt/M.; New York: Campus.

Rucht, D. 1996. "Forms of Protest in Germany 1950-92: A Quantitative Overview." Paper presented at the workshop "Europe and the United States: Movement Societies or the Institutionalization of Protest." Cornell University. March 1-3.

Rucht, D. and T. Ohlemacher. 1992. "Protest Event Data: Collection, Uses and Perspectives." Pp. 76-106 in *Studying Collective Action*, ed. M. Diani and R. Eyerman. London: Sage.

Snyder, D. and W. R. Kelly. 1977. "Conflict Intensity, Media Sensitivity and the Validity of Newspaper Data." *American Sociological Review* 42: 105-123.

Tarrow, S. 1989. *Democracy and Disorder. Protest and Politics in Italy 1965-1975*. Oxford: Clarendon Press.

Tilly, C. 1978. *From Mobilization to Revolution*. Reading: Addison-Wesley.

Tilly, C., L. Tilly and R. Tilly. 1975. *The Rebellious Century. 1830-1930*. Cambridge, Mass.: Harvard University Press.

Tuchman, G. 1973. "Making News by Doing Work: Routinizing the Unexpected." *American Journal of Sociology* 79: 110-131.

Walgrave, S. 1994. *Nieuwe sociale bewegingen in Vlaanderen*. Leuven: SOI/KUL.

II.

Protest and the Mass Media

Electronic and Print Media Representations of Washington, D.C. Demonstrations, 1982 and 1991: A Demography of Description Bias

John D. McCarthy, Clark McPhail, Jackie Smith and Louis J. Crishock[1]

Introduction

Public protest has become a normal part of the politics of Western democracies during the last several decades (Dalton 1988; Tarrow 1994). Serious attempts to understand citizen preferences must now include evidence from public demonstrations as well as from elections and public opinion polls (Herbst 1993). But how do elites and mass publics come to know about public protest? Protest events may be observed directly by some citizens, and they may convey their impressions to others through networks of personal communication. But the primary way people come to know about them is through the mass media. As Michael Lipsky has noted, "Like the tree falling unheard in the forest, there is no protest unless protest is perceived and projected" (1968: 1151).

We know, however, that many public protests are ignored by news media representatives, and that only a small proportion of them are reported in large circulation media sources, thereby potentially reaching wide audiences. Of the vast assortment of public protests then, the mass media select only a few, and it is these which attentive citizens may come to know about. This small sample of actual protests serves as evidence for those who would construct images of the scope of protest and the issues raised by it. This audience includes both attentive publics and social scientists who use media reports to study protest. Many social observers suspect that media selection does not constitute a representative sample of the actual protest events. This is an issue of media selection bias.

When a mass media outlet does report some details of a protest event, however, its report is by necessity a small selection of the manifold detail of

1   We thank Allegra Foley, George Toolan and Fr. Boguslaw Augustyn for assistance in coding, David Schweingruber for spoken text transcription, and Dieter Rucht, Friedhelm Neidhardt, Barbara Pfetsch and other members of the Research Unit "Social Movements and the Public Sphere" at the Social Science Research Center Berlin (WZB) for critical comments on an earlier draft.

such a complex event, and may, in fact, distort the details it does report. The combined processes of selection of certain details over others, as well as the distortion and emphasis of those chosen for notice, together serve to shape significantly the perception of the event by those who attend to these reports, both citizens and researchers. We call this general process *media description bias* (McCarthy, McPhail and Smith 1996).

Keen observers of the mass media have long been aware of these processes, but the systematic study of them has been hampered by the lack of independent sources of information about populations of events with which media portrayals can be compared. We investigated media selection processes in Washington, D.C. by using official records of protests as one such independent source. In what follows we will (1) briefly describe the nature of protest in Washington, D.C., (2) summarize our previous media selection bias analyses of protest coverage, (3) present a more detailed analysis of media description bias of protests, including, first, an analysis of the correspondence between media and official reports of "hard news" items, and second, analyses of the demography of description bias, that is, its patterning across media source and over time, and (4) conclude by discussing the substantive implications of the interaction between the two processes of selection and description bias.

Washington, D.C. Demonstrations

Protests occur across the United States, but they are especially likely to take place at seats of power such as municipal commons, state capitals (Lofland and Fink 1982) and the U.S. National Capital in Washington, D.C. Citizens go to Washington, D.C. to stage protests in order to get the attention of the federal executive, legislators and sometimes jurists. They also do so in hope of gaining national media attention. As a result of the predominance of national government in Washington, D.C. much of the protest that occurs there includes citizens who have traveled from elsewhere to be heard and seen - a relatively small proportion of the protest is aimed at purely local issues as might be expected in other cities.

And there is a large volume of protest. By the 1990s there were approximately 2,000 protest events a year in Washington, D.C. Most of these events were of modest size, and very few of them were unruly in that they included violence, public disruption or civil disobedience. And, in recent years especially, the vast majority of protest events were formally permitted in advance. Following the cycle of protests in Washington, D.C. during the late 1960s and early 1970s a highly elaborated protest permitting system was created (McCarthy, McPhail and Crist 1998; McPhail, McCarthy and

Schweingruber 1995) in Washington, D.C. Most demonstrations require such a permit from one of the three police jurisdictions, and most of them are permitted - more than 95% by our estimates (McCarthy, McPhail and Smith 1996). It is these permit records of Washington, D.C. demonstrations that allow us to create an independent record of protests that can be compared to the media traces of them.

Selection Bias: The Problem and Results

Our effort to assess selection and description bias involves three basic steps: (1) We identified and collected an objective record of the entire population of collective action events - data from official police permit records; (2) we gathered all media traces of the protest events anticipated in those records for three years - 1973, 1981 and 1991; and (3) we compared the event records to the media records and compared the various media trace records with one another.

To estimate media biases in the coverage of collective events we generated several separate media traces of the events (those reported in *The New York Times* and *The Washington Post* along with those featured in the nightly newscasts of the three national television networks, ABC, CBS and NBC) so that different sources could be compared for the bias they might introduce in the selection of which events to cover and in their description of those events. In this way, an assessment of the biases inherent in particular traces can be evaluated.

Each of the three primary police agencies in the nation's Capitol require all groups planning to demonstrate in their respective jurisdictions to apply for permits to do so.[2] Each agency has jurisdiction over specified areas of the city, and the organizers must negotiate with all relevant agencies in order to carry out their demonstration in a given area. As a result, for very large demonstrations, protest leaders typically must secure permits from all three.

Extensive infor-mation is solicited from applicants concerning proposed demonstrations. The records provide detailed information on the individual or group sponsoring the event as well as the location, date, time, duration, form and estimated number of participants. The permit application form also indicates whether or not the demonstration is part of a multiple-day *campaign*

---

2   No permit is required to vigil or picket on non-U.S. government property or on
    sidewalks in the District of Columbia provided that the demonstration does not block
    pedestrian traffic or interfere with entry or exit to adjoining private or public properties.
    If demonstrators enter the street, they must obtain a permit from the Metropolitan Police
    of the District of Columbia (MPDC).

and whether or not organizers expect any *disruption* by counter-demonstrators. These permits are public records, and are open to public scrutiny.

Demonstration permit records from the National Park Service (NPS), United States Capitol Police (USCP), and the D.C. Metropolitan Police (MPDC) were inspected for 1982 and 1991.

The information embodied in these permit records provides the basis for our subsequent analyses of both selection and description bias in media coverage. Table 1 displays some basic features of Washington, D.C. demonstrations drawing from this record. As may be seen, most Washington, D.C. protests are quite small. Counter-demonstrating is quite rare during this time period, while protest campaigns are very common.

Table 1:   Washington, D.C. Permitted Demonstrations, 1982 and 1991

		1982	1991
Agency*	NPS	69%	62%
	USCP	25%	33%
	MPDC	5%	5%
Size	1 - 3	16%	19%
	< 12	41%	44%
	Median	20	25
	Max.	500,000	300,000
Weekend		33%	35%
Counter-demo		6%	3%
Campaign**		74%	66%
N =		1,209	1,700

 *   The three permitting agencies are the National Park Service, The U.S. Capitol Police, and the D.C. Metropolitan Police.

** A campaign is made up of multiple events held by the same organizers for the same goals over a period of more than one day.

Table 2 below summarizes the evidence we have gathered from the three media sources for our selection and description bias analyses. The entries depict the number of stories (including captioned photographs in newspapers) mentioning Washington, D.C. demonstrations by source and by year (those which have been coded and compared with the permit records).

We copied each of the newspaper stories and purchased video reproductions of each of the television stories. We created narratives of the television stories by transcribing the audio tracks of the video records for equivalent text coding. The selection bias analyses sought to determine which features of a demonstration gleaned from permit records accounted for the likelihood that any of the media sources chose to report it.

Table 2: Number of Stories, by Source, by Year Mentioning Washington, D.C.
Demonstrations

| Year | Media Source | | | |
	Times	*Post* network	National mentions	Total
1982	49	99	25	118
1991	33	101	39	126

Our analyses suggest that the structure of media selection bias appears to be relatively stable between 1982 and 1991. The vast majority of demonstrations are ignored by the mainstream media; the very large ones are covered. Demonstration size is, by far, the most important characteristic associated with the likelihood of media coverage. The next most important correlate of coverage is being in the right place at the right time in a media attention cycle. In other words, when the volume of coverage of a particular issue is large, pertinent protests receive more coverage. We demonstrated this by using a Nexis search to construct an independent measure of media coverage of the issues around which protests occurred. These patterns indicate that media agenda setting processes are a key to understanding how public dissent is filtered by media preoccupations and actions. These results are stable across all media outlets except TV in 1991. Those results demonstrate that for TV in 1991, media attention but *not* demonstration *size* predict coverage (McCarthy, McPhail and Smith 1996). Also, in general, this pattern suggests that electronic coverage of protest is increasingly driven by the issue interests of media institutions rather than by its indication of the extent of support for protest demands.

Description Bias

Mechanisms of Description Bias

There are three general mechanisms by which description bias in the reporting of events occurs: (1) by the omission of information, (2) by the misrepresentation of information, and (3) by the framing of the event with the pieces of information that are reported. Let us discuss these in turn.

Protest events are complex ones, the many details of which cannot possibly be included in media reports since the size of those reports is severely constrained by the size of the "newshole" itself. Protest events' life course typically consists of three distinct stages: an assembling phase, one or more gatherings and a dispersing phase (McPhail and Wohlstein 1983). They may be more or less well organized in advance. The gatherings themselves are typically composed of many individuals engaged in a variety of behaviors, sometimes individually and sometimes together (McPhail 1991). Inevitably, then, reporters and camera crews can observe and record only a very small portion of what happens during a protest event, even if they are committed to providing the most exhaustive description of the event possible. Consequently their reports of protests are generally based upon small, non-random samples of all possible observations of these events that might have been made over time and space. Therefore, media reports almost inevitably consist of non-representative descriptions of protest events.[3] These raw reports are then edited and packaged to be presented in finished media stories introducing another level of selection of substantive content. It is these features of media content selection that establish the parameters of the description bias problem.

The simplest mechanism of description bias constitutes which "hard news" items about the event are reported and which are not, regardless of the veracity of the reports. For instance, answers to the questions when, where, why, by whom and by how many constitute what students of journalism have called hard news. A report that focuses upon unruly demonstrators but fails to mention their goals or that there were thousands more who were not unruly may provide a vastly different impression to one that does.

Whether intentionally or inadvertently, media reports may misrepresent the features of a protest event. Journalists and/or editors may offer estimates of the number of demonstrators which misrepresent the numerical significance of the protest for its organizers and participants. This may occur by underestimating (e.g. Gitlin 1980: 28; Parenti 1993) or by exaggerating the number of people that are involved depending upon the extent of ideological correspondence between demonstrators and editorial policies (cf. Mann 1974).

Finally, the resulting combination of features included in a demonstration report and the nature of that combination can powerfully effect the impression that is conveyed. Beyond the hard news items, protest events are composed of the individual and collective actions of various categories of actors. The actions of demonstrators may include not only collective acts of marching, chanting, gesturing, applauding and the like but also individual acts of speech-making and the distribution of literature which state grievances and goals as well as interpretations and explanations of their grievances, goals and actions. Journalists' descriptions of protest may consist exclusively of reports of the actors and actions like those just noted or they can emphasize the appearance of

---

3   We have designed an schema for systematically observing protest events aimed at providing, in contrast to journalists non-random samples of observations, samples of observations that capture elements of such events across their entire time and space. Details of the schema are provided in McPhail and Schweingruber (1996).

other attributes (such as dress or lack thereof, language, lifestyle) which may trivialize, marginalize or render deviant (cf. Gitlin 1980: 27) the protesters, their grievances, goals and actions. Thus, while such accounts may be more or less factual, they may not be representative of the population of actions which occur infrequently in most demonstrations (e.g. violence against persons or property).

The work of Iyengar (1991) has called attention to another, more synthetic, dimension of the framing of protest event reports by distinguishing between those accounts which are *episodic* in emphasis and those which are *thematic*. Episodic descriptions focus upon the characteristics of the particular event or episode in question, its actors, their attributes and their actions. Thematic descriptions provide the reader or viewer with a historical and/or ideological context for the grievances raised, the goals stated and the strategies promulgated for reaching those goals. He says in this regard:

> The episodic news frame takes the form of a case study or event-oriented report and depicts public issues in terms of concrete instances (for example, the plight of a homeless person or a teenage drug user, the bombing of an airliner, or an attempted murder). The thematic frame, by contrast, places public issues in some more general or abstract context and takes the form of a "takeout," or 'backgrounder," report directed at general outcomes or conditions ... Visually, episodic reports make "good pictures," while thematic reports feature "talking heads" ... The dominance of episodic framing in television news has been documented in a number of studies. For example, television news coverage of mass-protest movements generally focuses more closely on specific acts of protest than on the issues that gave rise to the protest. This pattern characterized network coverage of the protest against the Vietnam War and of the development of nuclear energy (Iyengar 1991: 14).

Generally recognizing that the size of the "newshole," or the amount of space/ time available in any specified source/period, is quite limited, while the amount of potential material that might be chosen to fill it is vast, analysts have begun to craft several general lines of explanation for the choices that are typically made as media institutions pick and choose among events and construct the news with a few details about them. Each of these general perspectives provides clues for understanding the mechanisms of selection and description bias in the reporting of collective action events, and we have relied upon them in our analyses.

The most benign accounts of description bias argue that it is, as we have noted, an inevitable problem of sampling - only a small proportion of the detail of any complex event can be reported and those details are highly unlikely to be a representative sample of all of them no matter how they are selected. Another series of accounts focus upon how news routines affect the sampling of that detail. In other words, the routines involved with daily news gathering and copy production, the incentives (of individual reporters as well as editors) to produce stories with attractive hooks or "news pegs," and the dynamics of issue attention cycles are, to varying degrees, likely to shape the ways in which reporters describe events as well as their selection of events that are "fit to print." The behavior of unruly protesters is highly likely to be reported, for instance, even if they constitute only a tiny proportion of the participants. Other accounts, however, (particularly those focusing on the efforts of social movements to shape media agendas and reporting) view description bias as systematically influenced by news gatherers' motives (Gitlin 1980; Gamson and Modigliani 1989; Ryan 1991; Parenti 1993). The least benign accounts call attention to the structurally induced motives of media organizations, as in Herman and Chomsky's "propaganda model" (1988). We have discussed several accounts of bias in some detail elsewhere (McCarthy, McPhail and Smith 1996).

The Demography of Description Bias

Expectations. We present here a demography of description bias - that is we will describe its patterning across type of news (hard vs. soft), across type of news source (print vs. electronic), and across time (1982 and 1991) rather than attempt to account for its variability across features of protests and protesters (e.g. protest form, issue focus of protest or social characteristics of protesters). Let us briefly discuss our expectations about patterns of description bias.

We began with strong assumptions about the importance of the media logic or format rules (Altheide and Snow 1988) for the differences between print and electronic coverage of protest events. Our evidence consists of systematic coding of the texts of print stories and the transcribed texts of television stories, and as a result we are comparing the bulk of the content of print stories with only part of the content of TV stories.[4] We recognize that visuals are essential to understanding television formats. As Altheide and Snow argue,

> ... all other things being equal, the report with the most relevant visuals available will get the most air time. On U.S. TV networks, without such visuals there is little likelihood that an event will receive more than a few seconds if selected at all (1988: 201-202).

In almost every case, the TV stories reporting Washington, D.C. protests were accompanied by visuals of demonstrators. Visuals of demonstrators, then, are expected, to some extent, to substitute for actual reporting of many facts about

---

4   We are developing a systematic coding scheme designed to capture the details of TV visuals so that this content may be melded with the transcribed text. That scheme is designed to parallel the demonstration observation coding protocol described by McPhail and Schweingruber (1996).

them. As well, the size of the TV newshole is substantially smaller than that of the daily newspapers we utilize here.

Given these features of contrasting print and TV media formats, we expect substantially less detail to be conveyed by the text of TV reports than in print reports, and hence, we expect the proportion of missing hard news data in TV reports will be greater. We expect this pattern to confirm the suspicions that TV reports of protests are likely to be poor substitutes for print reports for the systematic study of protest events.

Recall our finding that television news media are more likely than print to select demonstrations to cover that address issues already receiving strong attention from them - suggesting that TV news media more often use protest visuals to enhance issue coverage than to constitute the main focus of stories. This pattern leads us to expect that TV coverage of protest will be more, rather than less, thematic than print coverage of protests.

Methods. The data presented below is based upon 766 cases of stories/demonstrations for 1982 and 1991 combined. When a story covered a single demonstration, it was coded once. When a story covered more than a single demonstration, each additional demonstration covered was coded as another separate case. Many demonstrations were covered by more than one media source. By this criteria there were 117 electronic demonstrations/stories and 649 print demonstrations/stories drawn from the five sources. For newspaper stories, coders read through copies of the story to code the features of coverage. For the electronic stories, the spoken text was transcribed and then coded.

Five hard news variables were coded: (1) the date of the event, (2) the purpose of the demonstration, (3) whether the event was part of a campaign of demonstrations, (4) whether or not the event drew counter-protesters, and 5) the number of participants. These variables were coded with equivalent schemes for both the permit and the media records. Nine soft news variables were coded: (1) the proportion of each story devoted to the demonstration, (2) the emphasis on the details of the protest itself, (3) the emphasis on protesters' purposes/goals, (4) the emphasis on incidental details about the protest itself, (5) mention of the protest's specific policy goals, (6) mention of the significance of the protesters' goals, (7) the degree of episodic coverage, (8) the degree of thematic coverage, (9) the relative weight of thematic versus episodic coverage. The coding criteria for the nine substantive description variables are described in the Appendix.

Results. Table 3 displays the level of missing data for three important hard news items concerning a protest event - its date, purpose and size.[5] We were

---

5   The other two hard news items, whether the protest was part of a campaign and whether it drew counter-protesters, were coded "yes" only if either was mentioned, and "no" if

able to establish a purpose for all of the protests that were covered in stories in any source for the three annual periods. Protest date is variably missing in newspaper coverage of these events, but can almost always be established in the electronic stories - this is because they are almost always current protests while newspaper reports more commonly refer to past protests without always specifying their exact dates. Finally, protest size is more likely to be reported in 1991 than 1982, while information about size is less likely to be reported in television news coverage of 1991 protests.

Table 3:   Missing Data for Hard News Items, by Year and Source (Percentages)

	Source			
	Print		Electronic	
Item	1982	1991	1982	1991
Protest date	30%	14%	0	4%
Protest purpose	0	0	0	0
Protest size	56%	30%	30%	74%
N =	(338)	(208)	(37)	(78)

Table 4 below displays the correspondence between permit evidence and media reports on selected hard news aspects of Washington protests for those events without missing media information. For the print sources where date is reported it is quite accurate. Protest purpose, as well, is reported quite accurately in the newspapers.[6] The relationship between the estimated size of a protest in the permit evidence and the reported size of a protest is quite strong, but variable across the years. Finally, the correspondence between whether a demonstration is part of a campaign in the two independent data sources is not so impressive. This is partially a result of the coding convention for this variable where a campaign was assumed only if there was explicit mention of it in the media report and otherwise the event was coded as not a campaign.

Table 4 also presents correspondence estimates for the electronic coverage of hard news items. As can be seen, the date of a protest and its purpose can be established with great reliability, while other details - its size and whether or not it was part of a protest campaign - are, as we suspected, less reliably established in the electronic records than in the print records.

---

they were not mentioned since reports rarely mentioned either if they were absent. As a consequence, we cannot compute a missing data figure equivalent to the those for size, purpose and date for these two variables.

6   We used a very detailed three digit code for categorizing quite specifically a protest's purpose. Because of the level of detail in that coding scheme, the magnitude of the measures of association shown in Table 4 are quite impressive.

Table 4:   Correspondence Between Substance of Hard News Reports and Official Reports for Selected Hard News Items

Item	Source			
	Print		Electronic	
	1982	1991	1982	1991
Date of protest	.981*	.999*	.999*	.999*
Protest purpose	.660*	.964*	.983*	.864*
Part of a campaign?	.563*	.265*	.383*	.167
Protest size	.616*	.872*	.101	.143

* P. < .001

The general pattern of results of our correspondence analysis for these print sources provides strong support for the belief that quality newspapers do a reasonably good job of reporting the hard news items of protest demonstrations correctly when they do report them. The major problem in using such reports remains that of non-reporting or missing data. And while the date and purpose of protests are reported by electronic sources, other hard news details of protests are less reliably reported than in print sources.

Tables 5 and 6 display the results of our analyses of substantive soft news dimensions of the description of protests. These analyses are based only on judgements of the content of the media reports of the events. There are strong and consistent patterns of description bias both across media source and across time. We review them in turn.

Table 5:   Substantive Description Bias Measures by Media News Source (Print vs. Electronic)

Substantive dimension	News source		T value
	Print	Electronic	
Proportion of story devoted to the protest	64.2%	41.7%	-6.98**
Emphasis on details of the protest	3.50	1.96	-10.20**
Emphasis on purposes/ goals of protesters	2.46	3.14	4.97**
Emphasis on incidental details of protest	0.71	0.79	0.76
Mention of specific policy goals of protest	57.3%	38.1%	-3.87*
Mention of significance of protester goals	32.5%	62.6%	6.47**
Episodic emphasis of the story	3.32	2.15	-8.24**
Thematic emphasis of the story	2.77	3.73	7.54**
More thematic than episodic coverage	0.22	0.46	5.21**
N =	(742)	(97)	

*   P. < .01.
** P. < .001.

The electronic coverage of protest events in Washington consists of stories that are, typically, devoted to broad issues, and, consequently, the proportion of the coverage and the emphasis on details of the protests is substantially less than that of print coverage (41.7% versus 64.2%). We recognize that this may be supplemented by the electronic visuals which provide additional details about protests to viewers. The electronic coverage is more likely than the print coverage to emphasize the purposes/goals of the protest than the print sources (a mean score of 3.14 versus one of 2.46) and also more likely than the print coverage to mention the significance of those goals (a mean of 0.62 versus one of 0.32 for print sources). Neither source typically places much emphasis upon incidental details of protests (both of the mean scores for this variable in Table 5 are less than one on a six point scale where 6 represents a great deal of attention to such incidental details). This finding is contrary to the claims of some analysts (e.g. Gitlin 1980; Parenti 1993). Print sources are more likely, partially as a result of the greater depth of their typical coverage, to discuss the specific policy goals of protesters (57% versus 38%), and to emphasize the actual details of the protest event (a mean of 3.50 for print versus a mean of 1.96 for electronic sources).

Finally, there are strong and consistent differences in the relative thematic and episodic emphasis of the two media source types - the electronic sources are far more thematic in their coverage of Washington, D.C. protest events by all three of our independent measures than are the print sources. In summary, the electronic coverage of protests is brief, and it is embedded in stories devoted to broader issues.[7] As a result, the spoken text of stories within which protest coverage is embedded are far more thematic than are print stories. The print stories provide substantially more detail of all kinds, and, as a result, devote

---

7   Our analyses do not capture the dimension of media bias that Fallows describes as the media's politicization of problems to the extent that the game of politics is emphasized over the nature of the issues themselves. "In the 1992 [U.S.] presidential campaign candidates spent more time answering questions from 'ordinary people' - citizens in town-hall forums, callers on radio and TV talk shows - than they had in previous years. The citizens asked overwhelmingly about that *what* of politics: What are you going to do about the health care system? What can you do to reduce the cost of welfare? The reporters asked almost exclusively about the *how*: How are you going to try to take away Perot's constituency? How do you answer charges that you have flip-flopped?" (1996: 48) (emphasis in the original). Media reports in our study have been coded in such a manner that this dimension of political coverage is included as an element of "thematic" coverage, since it does focus upon the political implications of the issue at stake in the demonstrations. We intend to recode this dimension so that we can, in future, distinguish this element of media bias from the thematic/episodic dimension we have already coded.

greater emphasis to details of the protests, and, are, consequently, less thematic in their overall presentation.[8]

Table 6: Substantive Description Bias Measures by Year of Coverage (Print and Electronic Combined)

Substantive dimension	Year		T value
	1982	1991	
Proportion of story devoted to the protest	61.5%	54.1%	3.84*
Emphasis on details of the protest	2.86	3.74	-6.43**
Emphasis on purposes/ goals of protesters	2.20	2.84	5.53**
Emphasis on incidental details of protest	0.53	1.11	-6.80**
Mention of specific policy goals of protest	45.4%	48.2%	-0.94
Mention of significance of protester goals	28.2%	39.4%	-2.90*
Episodic emphasis of the story	3.35	3.19	1.33
Thematic emphasis of the story	2.44	3.36	-7.52**
More thematic than episodic coverage	0.17	0.31	-4.18*
N =	(375)	(268)	

* P. < .01.
** P. < .001.

The results of our temporal analyses suggest several clear trends. First, both electronic and print stories that include mention of protests devote a smaller proportion of those stories to them in 1991 than they did in 1982 (54.1% in 1991 versus 61.5% in 1982).

In describing protests, there is more emphasis on the purposes and goals of the protesters in 1991 than in 1982 (a mean of 2.20 in 1982 versus a mean of 2.84 in 1991). As well, there is more emphasis on the actual details of the protests in 1991 than in 1982 (means of 3.74 and 2.86, respectively). There is also more likely to be mention of the significance of the protesters' policy goals in 1991 as compared with 1982 (39% versus 28%). Finally, the temporal trends in thematic versus episodic coverage of protest in Washington, D.C. are

---

8   It has been suggested by Friedhelm Neidhardt (personal communication) that television coverage mimics newspaper "front page" coverage. As a result, one might expect the strong source differences we have described here to be moderated if we compared only front page protest coverage with electronic coverage. We, therefore, replicated the analyses shown in Table 5 including only protest coverage that began in front page newspaper stories. Those analyses were in every case similar to the full analyses that included all newspaper stories. We conclude, therefore, that the media source differences we have uncovered here are not a result of the constricted size of the television newshole, but are, in fact, a result of their differing media logics.

consistent across our three measures - toward more thematic coverage in 1991 as compared with 1982.

The increased emphasis on details of protests and protest issues, seen in Table 6, may simply reflect the important impact of the dominance of Gulf War protest coverage for 1991. The bulk of protests covered in 1991 in Washington, D.C., by both media sources, concerned U.S. involvement in the Gulf War (see McCarthy, McPhail and Smith 1996), and they tended to be more flamboyant than has been typical of Washington, D.C. demonstrations in the last fifteen years. This may account for the increased emphasis upon protest details, and especially their incidental details, as shown in Table 6 above.

Summary and Interpretation

Our investigation of the correspondence of media reporting of hard news items of protest demonstrations in Washington, D.C., if such items are in fact reported, indicates that they are reasonably accurate representations of the basic details of protest events. As we anticipated, print coverage is more detailed, and for certain items more accurate, than electronic coverage. These findings represent a unique test of the veracity of print media reports of protest event details and provide strong justification for their use in studying protest events.

Our look at the patterning of more subjective aspects of descriptions of protests events across media source and through time reveal several clear findings. First, the electronic media, typically, utilize protest event visuals as backdrop to general issue stories to a greater extent than do newspapers. Print media equivalently use such events as minor details of broader issue coverage. This difference in how the two kinds of media cover protest events has the consequence that when events are covered by television news they are more likely to be nested in broader issue coverage than is so for newspapers. In addition, the temporal trends suggest that descriptions of protests by print sources are, in recent years, becoming more like the electronic ones along most of the soft news dimensions we have measured.

A benign interpretation of the broader patterns of description of protests we have uncovered with this systematic evidence would lean toward a heartening appraisal of the media coverage of protest in Washington, D.C. That is, the news media in general, led by patterns of electronic coverage, present more thematic accounts of protests, providing an increasing amount of detail about the issues and goals of protesters. As protest has become an institutionalized part of the democratic process in the U.S., such an account would continue, the news media has increasingly begun to focus its attention upon the substance of protest events in contrast to its irrelevant details.

We are skeptical of such an interpretation, however. Our caution stems from the findings of our earlier analyses of selection bias, and what appears to us an obvious interaction between trends in selection and description bias. Recall one of the key findings of our selection bias analyses - media attention to an issue was the most important factor in the likelihood that a protest event was covered by the electronic media in 1991. Earlier, size and other details of events were important in predicting electronic coverage, but this was no longer true for 1991. This pattern combined with the patterns of description we have displayed above lead to a very different, and less benign, account of media coverage of protest events in the recent period in Washington, D.C. It goes like this: The media increasingly choose which protest events they will cover following the logic of their own cycles of attention to substantive issues. Since very few protest events are actually covered in any source, there is always a wide variety of events that could be covered. When suitable protest events are available so that visuals of them can be used as a backdrop to stories already selected for coverage for other reasons, protest events have a far greater likelihood of being covered, if only fleetingly. This selection logic is quite different than one that focuses upon other details of protests, such as their size and form.

To the extent that such a logic governs which protests are selected to be covered, the patterns of that coverage we have shown here are quite understandable. The description of protest issues and goals can, when protests are noticed by any media source, be expected to be thematic. This is so not because media description coverage logic has shifted toward a more sensible one that honors the aims and goals of protesters, but because the media selection coverage logic has become more media-centric. Those who stage protest events in order to communicate with mass publics are subject, by this account, to far more subtle structural mechanisms of the framing of their efforts to communicate than even the most malicious accounts of description bias to date have implied.

Appendix

The following coding conventions were utilized to create our nine substantive measures of description bias.

Proportion of the Story Devoted to the Protest:

Estimate the percentage of the article that is devoted to describing this demonstration and its goals. Using a word count, find the number of words given to this demonstration, add to this the amount of words devoted simultaneously to this and any other demonstration. Divide this sum by the number of words in the article to establish the *Proportion of the Story Devoted to the Protest.*

Emphasis on Details of the Protest:

Use the following scale to indicate how much of the *proportion of the article devoted to THIS demonstration* describes *details* of the demonstration.

```
    0      1      2      3      4      5      6
  --_____--
  None   Any          About   Most          All
                       half
```

Emphasis on Purposes/Goals of Protesters:

Use the following scale to indicate how much of the *proportion of the article devoted to THIS demonstration* describes the broad purpose and goals *and/or* the narrower practical objectives of the demonstrators (e.g. description of the movement industry, details of the protest's goals).

```
    0      1      2      3      4      5      6
  --_____--
  None   Any          About   Most          All
                       half
```

Emphasis on Incidental Details of Protest:

Use the following scale to indicate how much of the *proportion of the article devoted to THIS demonstration* describes things that are *incidental* to the demonstration and its purpose (e.g. the weather, protesters' clothing).

```
    0      1      2      3      4      5      6
  --_____--
  None   Any      About half  Most          All
```

Mention of Specific Policy Goals of Protest:

Does the article state specific legislation, policy(ies) or social practice(s) which the demonstrators hope to affect (e.g. "demonstrators gathered on the steps of the Capitol to support the passage of [specified] legislation")

                    0 = No
                    1 = Yes
                    9 = Can't decide

Mention of Significance of Protesters Goals:

Does the article describe the social or political significance of the demonstrators' purpose (e.g. "protesters believe continued engagement in Vietnam will hurt social programs"; "meat boycotters argue that the price of meat now brings it out of reach of middle class consumers"; "Anti-Marcos demonstrators claim he has diverted national resources from the needs of the common people of the Philippines")?

$$0 = No$$
$$1 = Yes$$
$$9 = Can't decide$$

Episodic and Thematic Coverage:

Episodic coverage stresses predominantly the details of the demonstration itself (e.g. numbers of people, the weather, speakers or entertainers), with minimal or no attention to the issues raised by the demonstration.

Thematic coverage, on the other hand, focuses on the more general issues raised by the demo. For example, a thematic article on a homeless demonstration would provide statistics on the numbers of homeless and suggest socioeconomic reasons for this problem or it might detail pending legislation on the issue.

Evaluate the following questions independently (Your response to one question should not influence your response to the other.)

Episodic Emphasis of the Story: Given the above distinction, use the following scale to indicate the extent to which the article should be described as *episodic*.

0	1	2	3	4	5	6
Not at all episodic						Highly episodic

Thematic Emphasis of the Story: Use the following scale to indicate the extent to which the article should be described as thematic.

0	1	2	3	4	5	6
Not at all thematic						Highly thematic

More Thematic than Episodic Coverage: Given this distinction between episodic and thematic coverage, is this article:

$$0 = Primarily episodic$$
$$1 = Primarily thematic$$

References

Altheide, D. and R. P. Snow. 1988. "Toward a Theory of Mediation." *Communications Yearbook* 11: 194-223.
Dalton, R. J. 1988. *Citizen Politics in Western Democracies*. Chatham, N.J.: Chatham House.
Fallows, J. 1996. "Why Americans Hate the Media." *The Atlantic Monthly* (February): 45-64.
Gamson, W. A. and A. Modigliani. 1989. "Media Discourse and Public Opinion on Nuclear Power." *American Journal of Sociology* 95: 1 -37.
Gitlin, T. 1980. *The Whole World is Watching: Mass Media in the Making and Unmaking of the New Left*. Berkeley: University of California Press.
Herbst, S. 1993. *Numbered Voices: How Opinion Polling has Shaped American Politics*. Chicago: University of Chicago Press.
Herman, E. and N. Chomsky. 1988. *Manufacturing Consent*. New York: Pantheon.
Iyengar, S. 1991. *Is Anyone Responsible? How Television Frames Political Issues*. Chicago: University of Chicago Press.
Lipsky, M. 1968. "Protest as a Political Resource." *American Political Science Review* 62: 1144-1158.
Lofland, J. and M. Fink. 1982. *Symbolic Sit-Ins: Protest at the California Capitol*. Washington, D.C.: University Press of America.
McCarthy, J. D., C. McPhail and J. Crist. 1998. "The Emergence and Diffusion of Public Order Management Systems: Protest Cycles and Police Response." In *Globalization and Social Movements*, ed. H. Kriesi, D. Della Porta and D. Rucht. Houndsmill, Hants, UK: Macmillan. (Forthcoming.)
McCarthy, J. D., C. McPhail and J. Smith. 1996. "Images of Protest: Estimating Selection Bias in Media Coverage of Washington, D.C. Demonstrations, 1982, 1991." *American Sociological Review* 61 (3): 478-499.
McPhail, C. 1991. *The Myth of the Madding Crowd*. New York: Walter de Gruyter.
McPhail, C. and D. Schweingruber. 1996. "Unpacking Protest Events: A Methodology for Systematic Coding and Analysis of Collective Action." Revised version of a paper presented at the 1995 annual meeting of the American Sociological Association, Washington, D.C.
McPhail, C. and R. Wohlstein. 1983. "Individual and Collective Behaviors within Gatherings, Demonstrations and Riots." *Annual Review of Sociology* 9: 579-609.
Mann, L. 1974. "Counting a Crowd: The Effect of Editorial Policies on Estimates." *Journalism Quarterly* 51: 278-285.
Parenti, M. 1993. *Inventing Reality: The Politics of the News Media*. New York: St. Martin's Press.
Ryan, C. 1991. *Prime Time Activism*. Boston, Mass.: South End Press.
Tarrow, S. 1994. *Power and Movement: Social Movements, Collective Action and Politics*. New York; Cambridge: Cambridge University Press.

Determining the Selection Bias in Local and National Newspaper Reports on Protest Events

Peter Hocke

Introduction

An important goal for most political protest groups is the achievement of good media coverage. They want their aims and arguments covered by television and important newspapers. This enables protest groups to reach the broader public, to convince citizens of their goals and to conserve their (in most cases limited) financial resources, while at the same time furthering their main objective, mobilizing people to action.[1] Protest events are the main activities for achieving - with a high probability - media attention. On the other hand, the mass media are selective in reporting protest events. Not every march or vigil has an equal chance of sparking the interest of the mass media. McCarthy, McPhail and Smith (1996a) illustrate this point for Washington, D.C., where only a very small number of all political demonstrations are mentioned by the media. The question is whether the German media act in the same way. This is the focus of a case study within the Prodat project,[2] which, by using protest event data and the news value approach, centers on media selectivity and selection bias.

When speaking of the mass media, most people - whether scholars or not - understand the basic definitions. I have found through experience, however, that the concepts needed to fully understand the logic of media are not very well developed. Do the media manipulate or do they reflect reality? Are citizens informed about central societal questions or not? Is protest an issue of daily reporting? Well thought out and theoretically guided answers to these questions are rare (Gerhards 1991). The important theoretical assumption in the Prodat context is that media in liberal-democratic societies watch the public sphere continuously and report with a high degree of reliability (Gerhards and Neidhardt 1993). As the number of events in the public sphere is extremely large, the media must necessarily cover the processes they observe in a reductionist manner. In both print and electronic media the space available for

---

[1]   Raschke's definition of social movements as collective actors with the central feature of mobilizing can be used in this context. Political protest groups are organized to a great extent along the principles of social movements (1988: 77).

[2]   See Rucht and Neidhardt (1995 and in this volume), Rucht (1996), and Rucht, Hocke and Oremus (1995).

news is limited, as is the number of reporters who invest attention and time in reporting on political and especially dissenting forms of political participation. Nevertheless, spectacular protest events, like crowds of shouting people in front of the local parliament or marches against political decisions, fit the logic of the media in their search for "cheap news," because they have the character of limited events - they seldom last longer than one or two hours. This limited duration makes this type of event easy to identify in comparison with complex and lasting political or societal processes. Two further characteristics of protest events that make them effective in this sense are that they often involve striking slogans and/or spectacular actions. The search for novelty and excitement by journalists is - according to one plausible explanation - thus served by the public protesters. The "economic" interests of both actors, the mass media and the protest groups, seem to match.

Common sense tells us that this is not the whole story and that the contact between these two societal groups of actors is more complicated. Media actors have their own logic and interests. They want to inform the public audience but also seek high circulation rates and "low costs." Movement activists are also often disappointed by the low level of response they get with their protests. In this sense, the question of media selectivity and selection bias concerns an analysis of the logic behind the selection of information and thus behind the "making of news" (Tuchman 1978).

In media research, one prominent approach centers around the concept of news value (Staab 1990; Schulz 1976; Weimann and Brosius 1991). The basic argument of the news value approach is that there is a link between the characteristics of a single event and media selectivity. Schulz argues that societies, and the values connected with a certain society, cause the patterns beyond individual logic or interests (1987: 133). The news value model is thus an attempt to explain the pattern of selection as a *collective* phenomenon. The power of explanation by individual actors (such as the individual journalist responsible) is minimized with this approach. Scanning the literature concerning the news value approach, one observation is striking: The more general, and in this sense theoretical or reflective, key arguments are not very strong. Another observation is that there are many long lists of important "news factors," which constitute the news value of each event. This approach seems to be enjoying an empirical revival in the 1990s, and I will enter into this debate later in this chapter. I believe that the news value approach gives no answer to a number of questions concerning media selectivity - questions which are important to a systematic perspective. But the old acceptance and the new prominence of this approach make it worth considering in the field of protest event analysis.

In the 1980s research on political protest, especially in the European context, had in most cases focused upon "new social movements" (Brand, Büsser and Rucht 1986; Rolke 1987; Rochon 1988; Rubart 1985; Kretschmer 1988). The empirical base, i.e. the quantitative data describing the general ups and downs of movements and protest activities, was not solid (Rucht and Ohlemacher 1992). The fluid, frequently changing characteristics of protest activities and actors made it difficult to gain a precise idea of what was happening in the field of political protest.[3] All studies using data and information coming from the media had to deal with concerns that their media sources were biased. Protest event analysis is one attempt to solve these empirical difficulties within protest and social movement research. Protest events are a substantial output of active protest groups and one special form of oppositional dissent. By collecting data concerning these events, the "hard structure" of a soft and fluid form of political participation can be reconstructed. But if, and this is often the case, the protest event data are media data (see Tarrow 1989; Kriesi 1993; Koopmans 1995) their interpretation requires considerable background information about the specific and general structures of media selectivity.

In this chapter, I outline the design of the Freiburg study within the Prodat project. Prodat seeks to describe the history of mainly West German protest over time (including the different forms and demands). Within it, the Freiburg project has two aims. First, by implementing a prominent media research concept, it tries to get an idea of the logic behind the selection made by local and national print media. Second, it gives a rough estimation of the hidden events in the Prodat data base, which contains more than 10,000 protest events and covers more than four decades of German (protest) history. Because the question of the mass media's selection rate is important in evaluating the development of protest activities, the researcher needs a solid approach - one which allows comparison between the number of actual protests and those reported. If it is possible to reconstruct a highly focused, systematic and complete data base, there is a good chance of getting a solid answer concerning

---

3   There were three traditional solutions to these data collection problems. The first was the analysis of relatively stable actors, such as those social movement organizations (SMOs) which have a relatively stable membership (Leif 1985; Kriesi 1992). But there are periods of protest where they play only a subordinate role in the organization of protest events (as illustrated in the German protests against the Gulf War). The second solution was the analysis of violent forms of protest (e.g. Tilly 1970; Ohlemacher 1994). This is possible because several social institutions (police agencies, media and courts) concentrate their attention on these forms of protest. The problem here, however, is that a large percentage of protest is non-violent. The third solution was to analyze media coverage of protest events (e.g. McAdam 1982; Franzosi 1987), despite an awareness of the high selectivity of media coverage.

media selectivity. Following Rosengren (1970, 1974), I believe that comparing media independent data with "intra-media data" provides the desired perspective. For the first time in the history of German protest research we were successful in obtaining access to the local police's event-specific document files. A census was compiled of all marches, rallies, vigils and blockades that took place during a seven year period in the eighties within the city limits of Freiburg.[4] This data represents a very reliable portfolio of medium risk protest events. These data were compared with a sample of protest event data collected from the major local newspaper *(Badische Zeitung)* and reports in two national newspapers *(Süddeutsche Zeitung* and *Frankfurter Rundschau)*. This research design made it possible to code the news value of the reported and unreported protest events and to analyze media response. Aside from this empirical strength, the case study enables the study of the local manifestation of a lively protest and movement sector in the 1980s. The second section of this chapter outlines the discussion of the news value approach and its relevance to protest event analysis. The next two sections explain formal and methodological aspects of the design and combine this with questions concerning protest event analysis and social movement research. Initial empirical results are presented in the last section.

Theoretical Framework

The critique of the use of the mass media as a data source for studying movements and protest is well known (e.g. Everett 1992: 964). Nevertheless, the scientific community continues to use the mass media for data collection (Everett 1992; Koopmans 1995; Kriesi et al. 1981; Kriesi 1993; Taylor and Jodice 1983; McAdam 1982). The central argument for this decision is the lack of better alternatives. It is this argument itself which challenges us to find a solution to the dilemma.

The advice that Snyder and Kelly gave some years ago is to look for "extra-media data" - data which can be generated for specific forms of action (1977: 121). When the first pretest of this case study began in 1992, it was a mixture of trial and error. We had to find a community with exploitable sources for specific forms of action and a local press with constant reporting about local events. Empirical research concerning protest and media selectivity was still in its infancy at this time (see McCarthy et al. 1996a, 1996b; for the German discussion see Demirovic 1994; Kliment 1994). Research designs which utilized the mass media concentrated on established forms of political action

---

4   Freiburg im Breisgau is a city with ca. 180,000 inhabitants in the southwest of Germany.

(elections or electoral campaigns), and only a little (mostly explorative) work had been done on protest phenomena and media selectivity (Halloran et al. 1970; Molotoch 1979; Amann 1985; Kielbowicz and Scherer 1986). It was thus necessary to find (1) a community with enough sources covering protest events and (2) an adequate theoretical perspective as a basis for the analysis of media selectivity. Staab (1990) classifies media research's main approaches to the question of selectivity as follows: The first is called "the gatekeeper approach," the second falls under the label of "news bias," and the third is the theoretical concept of "news value."[5]

The basic argument of the gatekeeper approach is that the individual journalist acts like a gatekeeper in that he or she decides which pieces of information can pass through the gate, i.e. which become news and which do not (Schulz 1995: 328-329; Staab 1990: 15-17, 202). The decision made by the individual journalist is thus the key factor in the process of selection within this approach. The goal of the second approach is to detect the one-sidedness and political tendencies of media coverage which result from journalistic selection. This approach is backed by empirical studies, which show that journalists' political attitudes and/or editorial decisions dominate the selection of news (Staab 1990: 27-40; Kepplinger 1989: 4).[6] The striking feature in this approach is the attitude of the individual collective, comprising all journalists on the respective editorial staff. The news value concept, as a third approach, differs from both of these concepts in two major ways. First, it assumes that there are professional standards which are shared by journalists in general, and, second, it posits that these standards guide the selection of events using criteria inherent in the individual event. In this sense, Schulz maintains that - some exceptions notwithstanding - professional standards give rise to a pattern of selection, especially in the reporting of news. His explanation is that society and the values connected with a certain society cause the patterns which are observed (Schulz 1987: 133).[7]

---

5   We know that the research discussion of news selection in the media is much more complicated, and some researchers differentiate between more than three approaches. In this context it is not possible to present the various lines of discussion or to argue for the threefold distinction referred to above. One notable attempt to differentiate the different factors of influence was made by Kepplinger (1989: 8).

6   One example is a study by Leon Mann. He compared the press reporting on two marches against the Vietnam war in the sixties. His indicator was the number of participants reported for each event. His results showed that papers which held a "pro-war" position reported a lower number of participants, and papers with an "anti-war" position reported a higher number (Mann 1974: 278).

7   The news value approach has developed in Europe in particular since the 1960s. Trendsetting studies were conducted by Östgaard (1965), and Galtung and Ruge (1965).

In my work on protest events I feel a natural affinity for the news value approach as I am interested in protest events as a strong indicator of protest activities and the news value approach focuses on the selection of *events* by media. I appreciate a concept which asks for the characteristics of events and not for the characteristics of individuals or groups of individuals. My assumption is that every protest group is in competition with other (not only political) actors for the rare commodity of public attention. Specific to the average protest group is that it has very few conventional resources (money, organizational staff, etc.). Therefore, protest groups as rational actors tend to invest their resources in activities with high news value. They need publicity in order to compensate for their special weaknesses (Neidhardt 1994: 34). According to Lippman's definition, the worthiness of a report on an event depends on the existence and combination of different characteristics of the event. The "news value" of an event is also an assessment of the likelihood that an event will be reported. If the news value is high enough, the events pass through the gate of "primary selection" and will be reported. The level of news value also determines the "secondary selection," i.e. the placing of the story, the amount of space allocated, and its layout (Schmitt-Beck 1990: 646; Staab 1990: 41; Schulz 1995: 330). From this perspective news is not reality, it is always just a fragment of reality. Which fragments of reality are reported can be explained as being the result of a group of "news factors." News factors are in a causal relationship with events. If events have a high number of news factors, then they are reported, and if they do not, they are not reported.

The news value approach has the ambitious aim of constituting a theory with a high level of universality. There should be an explanation for the reporting or non-reporting of every type of event in every type of mass media. In my opinion, this theoretical approach generates a number of problems. I will mention three which were important for the Freiburg case study.

First, there is a conceptual deficiency, which has to do with the event as a stimulus for the process of selection. If the goal is to explain media selection by

---

There is also a North American discussion of this approach but it seems to lack the importance accorded it by the social sciences in Europe (Staab 1990: 42-54). A review of the literature reveals that different lines of interpretation were established, depending on the author's criticism of the classical key assumptions of the approach. In this context, Staab attempts to establish a "final model" within the approach, which gives more attention to the possibility that the news values are also instrumentalized by individual journalists according to their political positions or intentions (1990: 207). Eilders (1997) emphasizes the perspective of cognitive psychology, which can be identified in the news value studies carried out by Galtung and Ruge in particular. In the Freiburg project the aim is to stay close to the classic causal relation within this concept, which stresses the influence of event characteristics on media response.

using a concept with high universality, it becomes difficult to find or generate systematic data concerning the events comprising the input for the selection process. What constitutes the basic unit of reality? In the European debate on the news value theory (and as far as I can tell this applies to the North American discussion too) no attempt has so far been made to reflect this problem of cognition. What standard can possibly be used as an "objective" indicator of possible input? What are the general characteristics of such different events as elections, riots, statements by the president or peaceful demonstrations that would allow one to handle them as indicators of the same type?

The second problem concerns the listing of news factors within the approach. Staab presents 22 news factors (and five less for national news reporting) (1990: 120), Schulz lists 19 (1982: 151) and Emmerich mentions 18 factors (1984: 146). One may argue that the difference between 18 and 22 is not so important. But first one must examine the content of these news factors. And if - as is the case - they differ vastly, according to which dimensions are they sorted? A comparison of the dimensions referred to in various studies make the confusion apparent. And, surprisingly once again, there has been no constructive discussion about this astonishing fact within the new value approach. Table 1 shows the three to six dimensions under which news factors are arranged in four key studies.[8] Only the dimension "dynamics" is used in each of the studies. The definitions assigned to the several factors mentioned have also been found to differ greatly from study to study.[9]

Table 1: Dimensions of News Factors used in the Field of Media Research

Schulz 1976	Schulz 1982	Emmerich 1984	Wilking 1990
Time			Time
Proximity			
Status	Status		
Dynamics	Dynamics		Dynamics
Valence	Valence		
Identification	Identification		
	Relevance	Relevance	
	Consonance		
		Workability	
		Entertainment	
			Personalization

Sources: Schulz (1976: 32-34, 1982: 151-153), Emmerich (1984: 46), Wilking (1990: 113). Compiled by P. H.

8   The significance of Wilking's study (1990) lies in his attempt to test the news value approach with regard to local press.

9   This aspect was discussed in a previous paper of mine (Hocke 1994: 9-14).

A third problem with the news value approach is that there is no clear argumentation as to whether the news factors (as indicators of news worthiness) depend on the event and its characteristics or are derived from the news which is published about the event. For example, the news factor "duration" is a characteristic of the event itself. The news factor "personalization" is an indicator that depends on the manufacturing or creation of the news. In general, the listings of news factors mix these two types of indicators. My solution to these problems is to reformulate the question that the news value approach seeks to answer.

If media selectivity is the topic, the question must be: Which events, with what characteristics, pass through the filter of primary selection? First, it makes sense to answer this question only for a special group of comparable events - the sample of the media input can be explained, for example, and the news factors as event characteristics can be discussed theoretically. Second, the event characteristics used as indicators should not be allowed to be connected with the "news-making" process itself. The basic idea must be that there is an event as a "stimulus" and media coverage as a "response."[10] If this causal relation is the subject of a study, the process of selection itself must be handled as a black box. The indicators to be tested must be found in the direct context of the event and not within the unseen processes happening in the black box of journalistic news-making.

In taking this position I concur with Rosengren, who argues in a similar vein.[11] He is still right in his criticism that media bias is often specified by other media sources (Rosengren 1979: 31-33). Only extra-media data about the media in question allow anything to be said about the selection filter. Remembering the difficulties encountered in gathering "objective" data (in the sense of a more or less unbiased, relatively systematic reconstruction of reality), Rosengren lists nine possibilities: (1) Indisputable historic events are analyzed. (2) The people appearing in the news are consulted. The team of researchers (3) plants observers or uses (4) photos, (5) protocols or (6) white books. Other alternatives are (7) surveys originally undertaken for other purposes or (8) carried out specifically for the purpose. The use of (9) official statistics is also mentioned. In general, Rosengren prefers published material (1970: 6). The

---

10   At this point I argue against Staab and the integration of a "final model" into the news value approach (1990:203, 214). In my opinion he abandons the central idea of a collective pattern that works as a filter of news selection when he stresses the importance of decisions made by individual journalists.

11   "Most news studies have been report oriented. In such studies it may be difficult to differentiate between bias inherent in reality and bias inherent in reporting" (Rosengren 1979: 33).

problem with all nine options is that all may be biased. Rosengren's valid argument is that the nine possibilities enable very complete and systematic extra-media data to be generated. Nevertheless, in practice, published documentation of event-specific information compiled over time is not available in the vast majority of cases.

The Design of the Freiburg Case Study

News Factors Related to the Media Coverage of Protest Events

The main idea behind the Freiburg study was the analysis of multiple sources covering a special group of protest events within one city. The data collection had to contain a large number of characteristics relating to each event. In addition, these characteristics had to be capable of being transformed into news factors. The assumption underlying this approach is that there are protest events in any community; two examples are shown in Figure 1 (Protest Event (PE) 1 and PE 2).

Figure 1: Modeling Newsworthiness and Media Selection Bias

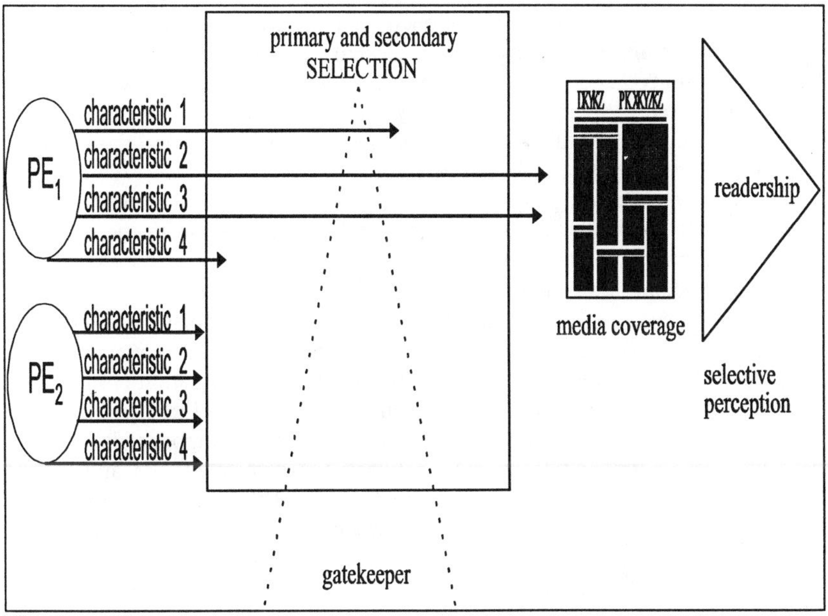

PE = Protest Event

Protest Event 1 is successful in getting media coverage and passes through the selection filter; Protest Event 2 is not reported. The large box in the middle symbolizes the process of news-gathering (sending reporters to the place of action, etc.) and the process of completing the individual report about the single event (this often includes multiple stages). Although Protest Event 1 is published, not all of its characteristics are reported. The first and the fourth characteristics (i.e. the message of the speaker at the rally and the number of participants) are filtered out in the secondary selection. The individual journalist, who gives the beat reporter the order to go to a rally or who decides about layout, headlines, and photo requirements, takes on the role of gatekeeper. Many differences in reporting are caused by the decisions made by these gatekeepers, however, if many events are tested, and the theory of news value is the primary approach, these gatekeepers do not need to be taken into account in the research design.

Within the German branch of protest research, important news factors for studying the selection bias of protest and/or protest events can be identified (Schmitt-Beck 1990: 649; Luhmann 1991: 151; Neidhardt 1993: 770). After a critical analysis of this and other relevant literature within the field of media research, the news factors shown in Table 2 were chosen for the Freiburg case study. They refer to three aspects of a protest event: The concrete action, the message of the action and the location of the protest event. For these three aspects a list of nine news factors was created. Two of these nine (the news factors "proximity" and "locality") are stable. As every protest event in the sample took place within the Freiburg city limits, there are no differences in the status of the region. The distance between the publication site and the location of the action is also the same for every event.

Five of the remaining seven news factors ("temporal setting," "size," "prominence," "established institutions," and "conflict") relate to the concrete action of the protest event. The sixth belongs to the message of the event, and the last factor combines elements of both.

News factor 5 ("conflict") is more complicated than the others as the degree of conflict it expresses is the product of two components: (1) The intended form of action with its special level of risk (component 1a) and duration (component 1b), and (2) the course of the protest event, which is one of conflict in every case (component 2). The indicator used for the second component is whether there was escalation and interaction between the protest groups and others (police or spectators). Binding these characteristics of the single event together to form one news factor has a special theoretical significance which concerns the definition of an event. The Prodat protest event definition has four distinguishing elements: (a) A distinct form of action, which must be more than rhetoric, (b) a societal or political demand, (c) the locality must be part of the public sphere and (d) the action must be made by a collective non-governmental actor.[12]

Table 2: News Factors of Protest Events in the Freiburg Study

Protest event sub-dimension	Character	Indicator	Name of the news factor
Action	Temporal start of the event	Temporal setting in relation to the copy deadline: very good / acceptable / unacceptable	News factor 1: "temporal setting"
Actor	- number of participants - individuals - collective actors	Number of participants: high / medium / low Prominent persons: strong presence / presence / no presence Established institutions as collective actors: strong presence / presence / no presence	News factor 2: "size" News factor 3: "prominence" News factor 4: "established institutions"
Degree of conflict	- level of conflict > level of risk > duration - course of conflict	Level of risk: intervening /uncooperative / cooperative Duration of the primary form of action: high / medium /low Escalation: strong interaction between protest groups and others / some interaction / no interaction	News factor 5: "conflict"
Message	Degree of concreteness	Degree of concreteness of the demands: high / low / nonexistent	News factor 6: "concretization of the demands"
(Locality)	(status of the region)		<stable>
(Proximity)	(distance between place of publication and place of action)		<stable>
Action + message	Newness of the articulated dissent and the action form	Degree of innovation: high / low / nonexistent	News factor 7: "surprise"

12 The Prodat protest event is defined as "a collective, public, activist incident by a non-governmental actor who expresses criticism or dissent and articulates a societal or political demand" (Rucht, Hocke and Ohlemacher 1992: 4).

Not every aspect of a protest event influences the news value, this only occurs if there is theoretical backing behind its selection and if it is acceptable in a model of empirical testing. The theoretical argument at this point is that protest events are forms of dissent within the democratic process, and in this sense they are forms of conflict. The form of dissent chosen by the individual protest group is collective action of a certain strength, and the argument used in the democratic discourse is the message of the respective protest event.

Strength or the "degree of conflict" means a combination of the chosen level of risk, the duration of the protest event and the course of the event itself. The second point here is that the news factor "conflict" should not be emphasized in comparison to factors like "temporal setting" or "prominence of participants." The suggestion in this study is to count this factor as equivalent to the others. In the case of the components of the single protest event related to the collective actor (and the people who constitute it), our study chooses a different approach: Because the size of an event, the prominent actors and the institutions involved are generally named in the news value approach and its news factor listings, each of these characteristics is used as a separate news factor in this model. When one considers the results of the latest research, this approach must be accepted as preliminary and open to discussion. In the following subsection the formal design and the sources of the different data types are described.

Extra- and Intra-Media Data for Freiburg

After testing access to different sources and different cities, the city of Freiburg was chosen as the model for testing the media selectivity of protest reporting over a seven year period. Two types of data could be generated: One set of extra-media data and one structured set of intra-media data.

(a) The extra-media data were collected from documents from the Freiburg local police department. German legislation governing public gatherings requires a special bureaucratic application procedure. If someone wants to organize a political march, a rally or a vigil in a public place, they must obtain a special license or registration from the authorities, specifically, from the "Ordnungsamt."[13]   What surprised us was that they had good documentation

---

13   The "Ordnungsamt" is part of the non-uniformed police in Germany. In Baden-
   Württemberg, the state (Bundesland) that Freiburg is in, this authority is also part of the
   local administration with the mayor as head of staff. It is responsible for the registration
   of residents and weapons, controls the hygiene in restaurants and issues foreigners with
   residency permits. One of their other central tasks is to manage the registration and
   public security of political events. In this context, they have to find compromises
   between the interests of traffic, private interests (i.e. economic interests) and the civil

not only for those protest events where the organizers had applied for registration, but also for those events which were not announced and therefore "unauthorized."[14]

Since 1983 the police have used a special logbook to register every march, rally, vigil, blockade and similar events which utilized - from their perspective - the right of assembly. We were able to examine this logbook and the Ordnungsamt's archives. Within the archive's complex filing system we discovered a special type of telex containing a report written by the rank and file police officer responsible at the event, dealing with protest events within the city limits.[15] This telex, with the characteristics of a follow-up report, gave the best historical documentation that could be found for single protest events within Freiburg over time. None of the other institutions that were contacted had collected event-specific data with a lower rate of missing information regarding the level of single protest events.[16]

The time span for data collection was limited by the establishment of the aforementioned police logbook in 1983, and by the originally planned end-date of data collection for Prodat (1989). As the police archives are not computerized and the police's definition of a protest event is orientated towards the juridical framework used by the Ordnungsamt, the transformation of information into the special type of protest event data required had to be done by the researchers themselves.[17]

Since the police do not work with explicit rules or codebooks for this kind of documentation, a two-step process of data gathering was necessary. The first step was to gather all event-specific information from the logbook, the telex and

---

right to gather in public (the right of assembly). The juridical task is to secure this right and not to allow or forbid it in line with the interests of the political elite (Beckord 1993; Dietel, Gintzel and Kniesel 1991).

14   The second surprise was that the police officers gave me permission to use their archives following a series of negotiations. One central condition was that no personal data was to be used.

15   This telex is distributed to different police agencies. The Ordnungsamt is one these agencies and incorporates this document in their event specific files.

16   Alternative access to event-specific local or regional data was tested at different institutions. Relatively promising sources were found in the regional office of the "Deutsche Gewerkschaftsbund" (DGB), the umbrella organization of the German trade unions, for strikes, and in the "Archiv soziale Bewegungen in Baden." This archive was founded in 1985 and publishes a special report ("Archiv Soziale Bewegungen") four times a year with protest documentation covering the wider area of Freiburg.

17   For many of the cases, only the logbook enabled me to find the document files in the department's archives. The crucial point was, however, to identify the relevant coding unit afterwards.

the document files. These pieces of information were then selected and interpreted according to the Prodat protest event definition (see Footnote 12) and comparable rules for differentiating aspects (such as how to handle estimations, mention of the number of participants, the differentiation between events in one protest context, etc.) before the single event was coded.[18] As the goal was to gather event data - documented as completely as possible - two more key decisions about the collection of data must be mentioned:

1.   During the collection of the police event data, by following the entries in the logbook and referring to the relevant document files in the police archives, it became obvious that the police documentation was systematic for only four forms of action - defined as "march," "rally," "vigil" and "blockade."[19]

2.   In Freiburg, the squatter movement had very large and often violent conflicts with private property owners, the state and the police. Because of this, the logic surrounding documentation covering this movement differed from the event-specific documentation for all other segments of protest. As resources for our research were scarce, and because the police document files about this special type of conflict were voluminous and not ready for examination, all types of protest events tied directly to messages of solidarity with squatters and the direct demands of the squatters, unfortunately had to be excluded from the quantitative analysis (see Figure 2 below).

To summarize (a), the extra-media data form a controlled and systematic set of event-specific information obtained from police logbooks and telexes. The total coverage includes four types of action (march, rally, vigil, blockade) over seven

---

18   Besides the protest events, the notes in the logbook included public events within electoral campaigns and also religious gatherings and celebrations, which had to be excluded. The number of these events was around 5%. Therefore, it was necessary to identify the political demand connected with the public appearance and the form of action the organizers of the event chose. The accompanying telex often showed that two entries of the logbook belonged to one primary form of action. In this case, they were coded as one protest event within the police data. In other cases, the description given by rank and file police officers in the telex allowed one to identify - according to the Prodat rules - a second protest event organized by a different group with a different primary form of action. Thus, the number of cases and the limits of the action units differ in some cases between the statistics within this study and those compliled by the local police. For the rules used see the Freiburg codebook (Hocke 1995). Examples of the relevance of these forms of identification are given in Rucht, Hocke and Oremus (1995).

19   All the other primary forms of action such as riots or the occupation of buildings (squatting) were excluded.

years. It is the first analysis of event-specific data from German police sources utilized in this manner.[20]

Figure 2: Coding Procedure of the Freiburg Case Study

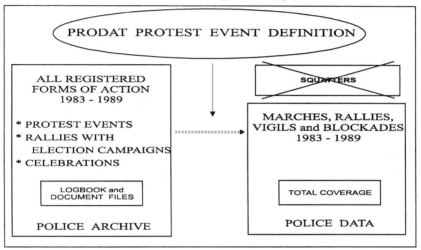

(b) The *intra-media data* were collected by using three sources on two levels. The first level was local, constructed by collecting data from the local issues of the *Badische Zeitung* in Freiburg.[21] Each edition of this newspaper contains three to five separate pages of local reporting.[22] As the local paper's archive's keyword system was not compatible with the interests of protest event analysis, and electronic files unavailable for a computer-aided search, the gathering of articles about protest events had to be done by coders.

---

20 In the meantime a study with similar French police data has been conducted by Oliver Fillieule (see Fillieule 1996 and in this volume).

21 As the resources for local data gathering were small, and the largest amount was invested in intensive extra-media data gathering, we chose the option of using only one local media source. The criteria were that the chosen medium reports constantly and with a certain amount of quality and space, has no changes in ownership and no competition with other print media in the local market. In July 1976, the *Badische Zeitung* accounted for 96% of the local papers sold in Freiburg - a rate which is approximately the same in the eighties (Kronenberg 1986: Ch. 4). All other criteria were also fulfilled.

22 Special tests showed that all Freiburg protest events reported on the front page, or on the other pages of the national or regional section of the *Badische Zeitung* were also mentioned in the local section.

The sample (46% of the year) used for the national papers, *Süddeutsche Zeitung* and *Frankfurter Rundschau*, within Prodat was the same as that used for the local newspaper (see Rucht and Ohlemacher 1992: 97). The data for the Freiburg protest events with national media coverage were identified within the Prodat "key project" (see Rucht and Neidhardt in this volume). One difference with the extra-media data was that the entire spectrum of forms of actions, ranging from the collecting of signatures or distribution of leaflets to strikes or assassinations, were coded (see Figure 3).

After coding, the extra- and intra-media data were combined in one data base. The central data set for all events was the extra-media coding, based on the police sources. All other information from media sources was linked to this set. For the coding of the news values for single events, only data from the extra-media data were used. Every piece of information (e.g. event-specific number of participants, etc.) was coded separately. By viewing this overall design, it is possible to see the "input" of protest activities as compared to the "output" presented to the broader public, which has obviously passed through the filters of media selection. The type of input formed by the protest sector in Freiburg, the context of the protest events and the media response is outlined in Figure 3 below.

Freiburg and its "Social Movement Activities"

Freiburg can be classified as one of the smaller cities in the Federal Republic of Germany. It has an active protest sector dating back to the fifties. There had been protests against neo-fascist tendencies in 1952 (Adolph and Kamp 1992: 482). The local student movement started with the campaign "students for the countryside"[23] in the early sixties. Some years later students protested against the Vietnam war and the conservative structure of German universities.[24] The first action organized by squatters took place in the early 1970s. As Roth mentions, the central conflict which structures the local left-libertarian social movement family is ecological - especially the opposition to the nuclear power plant in Wyhl (1994: 419). The Wyhl conflict, with a successful anti-nuclear movement, established civil disobedience in the action repertoire of German movements and changed the political culture in the local area as well as nationwide (Rucht 1994: 447; Koopmans 1995: 122).

---

23   "Studenten aufs Land!"
24   There was a famous discussion between the prominent student leader Rudi Dutschke and the social scientist Ralf Dahrendorf in January 1968, and a campaign against increasing fees for the public transport system in the same year (Haumann 1992: 460).

Figure 3: The Data Base of the Freiburg Protest Event Analysis (1983-1989)

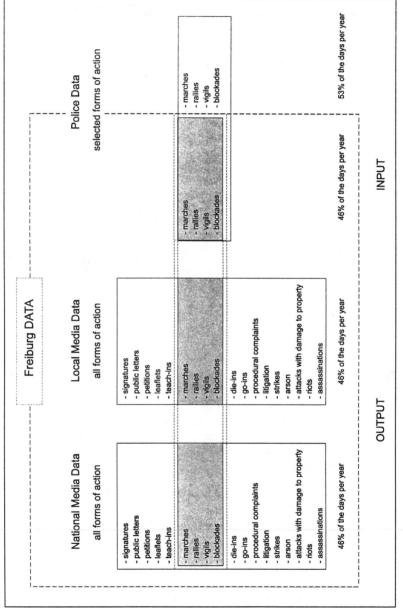

Freiburg DATA

National Media Data
all forms of action

- signatures
- public letters
- petitions
- leaflets
- teach-ins
- marches
- rallies
- vigils
- blockades
- die-ins
- go-ins
- procedural complaints
- litigation
- strikes
- arson
- attacks with damage to property
- riots
- assassinations

46% of the days per year

OUTPUT

Local Media Data
all forms of action

- signatures
- public letters
- petitions
- leaflets
- teach-ins
- marches
- rallies
- vigils
- blockades
- die-ins
- go-ins
- procedural complaints
- litigation
- strikes
- arson
- attacks with damage to property
- riots
- assassinations

46% of the days per year

Police Data
selected forms of action

- marches
- rallies
- vigils
- blockades

- marches
- rallies
- vigils
- blockades

53% of the days per year

46% of the days per year

INPUT

One of Roth's central findings was that all of the relevant trends evident in new social movements (ecology, the new women's movement and the new peace movement) are and were present in Freiburg. These tendencies are more or less connected in special networks.[25] Even in the nineties, the movement sectors are classified as homogeneous and integrated (1994: 418). Since the late eighties, a great continuity of local and regional mobilizing has been recorded. In the left-libertarian social movement family there were campaigns against the 1987 national census ("Volkszählung"), the conference held by the International Monetary Fund in Berlin in 1988 and the Gulf War. At the same time, the maturation of a new right-wing movement could also be observed.[26]

A left-libertarian and sometimes militant movement (the "Autonomen") was also established in Freiburg; nevertheless, the quota of militant confrontation is lower there than Frankfurt (am Main), as Roth reports (1994: 424). From the historical perspective, the protest sector in Freiburg lives up to the common assumptions about the ups and downs of campaigns and movements (ibid.). The protest against acid rain beginning in 1983 (lasting until 1985) is one example. Events with national mobilization were highly unusual. This is an effect of Freiburg's geographical position within Germany. Freiburg is near to the French and Swiss borders, is not the site of any important statewide administration or authorities and possesses an ingrained independent and liberal local identity. Traditional inter-city connections and personal networks run between Freiburg, the Swiss city of Basel and the French towns of Colmar, Mulhouse and Strasbourg. This "international" orientation was strengthened by the conflicts that arose from attempts to bring ecologically risky technologies to the area between these five towns (nuclear power plant projects such as Kaiseraugst in Switzerland and Fessenheim in France, or chemical industries in Basel and France).

The case of Freiburg is thus extraordinary when comparing the levels of protest and movement activities in relation to the city's size. On the other hand, it is an ideal type in the sense that protest and movement issues that were dominant in the German protest culture of the 1980s are now reflected in the issues surrounding local protest mobilization.

---

25   They had their own media (one local radio station, which was initially illegal, and an alternative magazine with a large circulation), three centers run by alternative groups and various other attempts to organize - especially left-libertarian interests in the form of parties. The Greens were also successful (in the left-libertarian "Linke Liste/ Friedens- liste"). There was also a working network of communist groups and parties (the so- called "K-Gruppen") (Langguth 1983).

26   Right-wing protest events in 1988 and 1989 show that this old German form of movement had already been revived before the German "revolution" of late 1989.

Protest events are "concrete forms of political activity" (Kriesi et al. 1981: 7), reflecting the calculated public output of oppositional dissent. The Freiburg study of media selection and media bias thus allows more than the testing of the news value approach. This is largely due to the unusual access to the police data set (used as an extra-media data set), which is highly systematic as regards time, broadness of mentioned issues and comprehensiveness.

On a second level, the Friburg study allows some specific forms of protest action to be observed. These are instructive in that they describe the local microcosm of protest activities in Freiburg during an important phase of German history - before the reunification in 1989. Beyond this, on a third level, it is possible to describe "images" constructed by the local and national print media for a limited number of events.

One question in this context is whether the assumption of high quality reporting by national papers holds true for single protest events occurring in a more or less randomly chosen town. On a fourth level, the case study allows us to obtain an idea of the "under-reporting" of protest by utilizing the nationwide study, Prodat, which is based only on reporting by the aforementioned national newspapers.

Empirical Results

The data base utilized for this research consisted of 845 individual protest events over a seven year period (1983 until 1989), if all sources are taken together. Each protest event found in one source (the police files, the *Badische Zeitung,* or the two national newspapers) was coded on a separate code sheet. For the next step, all protest events starting on days covered by the media sample and the police data were compared, cleaned up, and if the media response to them was identified, connected.

Since not all the collected protest events, as documented by the police, could be used for the test of media selectivity (due to the exclusion of events linked to squatters and the unsystematic documentation of some forms of action, like "die-ins"), the subsample of all marches, rallies, vigils and blockades for the test decreased. In fact, only 83.4% of all protest events coded within the extra-media data fulfilled the temporal criteria qualifying them for the test of selectivity.

Table 3 below presents an overview of the number of events coded from the police source before the data cleaning, and compares it with the number of events belonging to the sample for measuring possible media response. One hundred and ninety-six protest events with the specified types of action were sampled. The total coverage of this group of events was 417 (see the second and fourth columns).

Table 3: The Sample of Protest Events in the Freiburg Case Study (1983-1989)

Total coverage of protest events collected by the police	Total coverage of all marches, rallies, vigils and blockades	All marches, rallies, vigils and blockades within the sample (incl. squatters)	All marches, rallies, vigils and blockades within the sample (excl. squatters)
515	417	235	196

The first astonishing finding was the extremely low number of marches, rallies, vigils and blockades mentioned by the two national newspapers (see Table 4). Only nine Freiburg protest events with these types of actions were reported. This is only 4.6% of all events coded within the sampled police data. Five of these events were reported only in the *Frankfurter Rundschau,* two were mentioned in both national papers, and the two remaining events were mentioned only in the *Süddeutsche Zeitung.* The reporting of protest events by the *Badische Zeitung* is not nearly as incomplete. Nevertheless, 62.2% of the events found in the extra-media source received no response in the *Badische Zeitung.*

Table 4: Number of Marches, Rallies, Vigils and Blockades within the Freiburg City Limits and the Media Response, 1983-1989 (Prodat Sample)

Year	Police data	Local news coverage	National news coverage
1983	33	12	2
1984	12	4	0
1985	29	13	2
1986	21	8	1
1987	15	6	0
1988	33	14	2
1989	53	17	2
Sum	196	74	9

A second astonishing result was that every protest event reported by the national press also received media coverage in the local newspaper. Since none of the so called "quality newspapers" reported any of the local events exclusively, and the local paper missed over 60% of these events, the question arises whether the quality of national reporting has any influence on "primary selection" in comparison with the "lower quality" orientated local press. On the one hand, local newspapers certainly do not cover all oppositional happenings in their districts. On the other hand, the fact that every march, rally, vigil and blockade reported by a national newspaper was also mentioned by the local press suggests that the standards of selection for both, local *and* national press, follow similar patterns. Since the space available for reporting local events in the local press is much larger, the higher rate of reporting by the *Badische Zeitung* is easy to explain.

Since my central theoretical argument is that media selectivity is steered by the news value of single events, an interesting question is whether the protest events reported in the national newspapers are characterized by extraordinary news value. Because the news value of every tested event can be expressed by the sum of the seven coded news factors (temporal setting, size, prominence, established institutions, conflict, concretization of demands and surprise), the comparison between the strength of those events with national coverage and those with only local media response can be instructive. As every news value is coded within the categories "strongly present," "weakly present," and "nonexistent," the strength of their existence can be estimated by simple addition.[27] As was expected, the average news value of the nine events with a national media response is the highest (with a news value of 5.69, see Table 5).

Table 5: Difference in the News Value of Protest Events - Local, National and without Media Response

Type of data	Average news value	Cases with news value higher than 6 (%)	Cases with news value 0 (%)	Std. dev.	No. of cases	Median	Maximum
PE with national media coverage	5.69	55.6	22.2	3.4	9	7.55	8.67
PE with only local media coverage	3.11	12.3	43.1	2.9	65	3.67	8.33
PE with no media coverage	1.90	7.4	53.3	2.4	122	0	7.80
(All PE)	(2.49)	(11.9)	(39.5)		(196)	(1.33)	(8.27)

PE = Protest Event

The average value of events with only local media response is placed about two and a half points lower. Events without media response have the value of 1.9. Considering that the maximum value possible is 14, only a very small number

---

27   "Weakly present" is coded with the value 1, "strongly present" with 2. As there are seven news factors, the maximum value is thus 14.

of cases reached 50% of the theoretically possible news value. There are also a remarkable number of events without any news factor (news value = 0).[28] However, half the events with national media coverage have a news value over 6, while the percentage for events with only local response is 12.3%. The interpretation of these rough measurements - especially with regard to national events - is that the absolute news value of events with media response is higher, but the news value is not at all extraordinary.

Since the Freiburg study reflects a protest and movement sector that, under the circumstances in Germany in the 1980s, can be qualified as well developed and differentiated, the distribution of issues and forms of actions can be described as typical of those which press reporting and news selection has to deal with.

The forms of action are dominated by marches and rallies. These two action forms are well established in German culture as legitimate ways of articulating political dissent. Together, they constitute 83.1% of all analyzed "primary forms of action" (see Figure 4 below).[29] Blockades, with 3.6% of all primary forms, are still a small segment within the repertoire of protest groups and social movements (seven cases within seven years in contrast to 163 marches and rallies).

One reason for this may be the level of risk involved in blocking important traffic arteries like bridges or intersections. German police and politicians are generally not willing to tolerate this form of "civil disobedience." So, blockades are often met with direct force. The risk of personal injury or juridical consequences is not to be underestimated. The probability of these types of actions occurring is thus low, as activists are rational actors who calculate the risk of being beaten or punished.

Vigils, in contrast, are an absolutely peaceful form of action. They do not intervene in public life in the same way as marches do. They do not disturb the flow of traffic or occupy public space in the inner city or in front of criticized institutions. The relatively low number of vigils shows that protest groups wish to intervene to an extent which disturbs public life in one or another way.

---

28   Two cases out of nine (22.2%) with national media coverage have the lowest possible news value as do 28 of the only locally reported protest events (43.1%). Especially this last percentage is not so far away from the 53.3% of the events without media response - a rate which can be explained within the theoretical assumptions.

29   Prodat differentiates between one "primary" and a number of possible, but not necessarily existing "secondary forms of action." The primary form of action is the dominating form, chosen by the collective actors to transport their claim to the public (see Rucht, Hocke and Ohlemacher 1992: 4). A secondary form is, for example, distributing leaflets during a march; the march would be the primary form.

Figure 4: Forms of Action Tested for Media Response

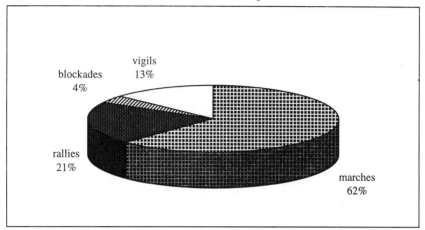

The dominant issues of the seven years studied were peace and ecological issues, and the complex issues of internal and external "solidarity" (see Table 6 below). Peace protests dominated in the Freiburg sample (19.9%). If the protests against nuclear energy (4.1%) and for better environmental conditions (8.7%) are combined, their total rate of 12.9% shows that ecological issues are another important field of protest. The group of solidarity issues (17.9%) is very diverse.

The biggest single issue (almost as big as the protest against nuclear energy) was the solidarity of the people of Freiburg with Nicaragua and its struggle for independence in the eighties (4.1%). A special case in this category involves a number of political groups which were engaged in programs of local development. The local government of Freiburg also founded a citizen partnership with the Nicaraguan community of Wiwili, a small town near the border of Honduras (Schneider 1989).

Not only in this specific block of solidarity issues, but in general, the surprising fact was the wide range of demands articulated by protesting groups. They protested against acid rain, the lack of progress in collective bargaining concerning wages, sports car races within the city limits, for the demands of the peace movement on September 1st ("anti war day") and against the right-wing parties that were elected to the local parliament. Critics of the foreign politics of other nations (like those of the Soviet Union) stood side by side with those struggling for human rights within Germany and those struggling against the apartheid system in South Africa. The structure of issues thus has to be characterized as very diversified.

Table 6:   Issues Addressed in Freiburg Protest Events and Selected Single Demands, 1983-1989 (excluding squatters)

Issue*	Sample		Total coverage	
Pro alternative military politics (peace)	39 (19.9%)		86 (20.3%)	
- against atomic bombs and pro pacifistic aims		25 (12.8%)		62 (14.6%)
- against Soviet Troops in Afghanistan		5 (2.6%)		5 (1.2%)
Solidarity	35 (17.9%)		64 (15.1%)	
- with Sandinista movement		8 (4.1%)		11 (2.6%)
- against apartheid		4 (2.0%)		13 (3.1%)
- for human rights in general		6 (3.1%)		10 (2.4%)
More ecology	17 (8.7%)		34 (8.8%)	
- against acid rain		4 (2%)		10 (2.4%)
Pro students' and pupils' interests	15 (7.7%)		47 (11.1%)	
Against racism and neo-fascism	13 (6.6%)		19 (4.5%)	
Pro women	9 (4.6%)		19 (4.5%)	
Pro workers	9 (4.6%)		17 (4.0%)	
Against civil nuclear power	8 (4.1%)		22 (5.2%)	
- against nuclear energy in general		7 (3.6%)		14 (3.3%)
Other left-libertarian campaigns***	8 (4.1%)		17 (4.0%)	
Counter mobilization	7 (3.6%)		17 (4.0%)	
Others	36 (18.4%)		62 (14.6%)	
	196 (100%)		424 (100%)**	

*   The number of cases and their corresponding percentage is a subgroup of the percentage of the total issue.

**   The 91 events connected with squatters are excluded here. Their rate is 17.7%, if they are included (n = 515).

*** For example, "for the 'free radio network' Dreyeckland."

The number of marches, rallies, vigils and blockades per year is compared with the temporal series of events under the same forms of action in the Prodat key project (see Table 7/Figure 5).

If the minimum of the Freiburg protest events is compared within this period, it is obvious that in 1984 and 1987 the lowest level of activity was documented by the police. In general, this fits with the graph presented by the national protest event data produced by Prodat for the same forms of action. The phases of increase and decrease are relatively similar.

The general pattern, which is outlined by the two graphs, shows a development which starts at a relatively high level in 1983, has a sharp reduction shortly afterwards, and seems to recover in the middle of the eighties before it drops again. After this second decrease, an enormous increase of protest activity is identified for the last two years of the sample - an increase to a level which is the highest in the whole period.

Table 7: Marches, Rallies, Vigils and Blockades (1983-1989, excl. squatters)

Year	Nationwide	Freiburg
1983	201	33
1984	151	12
1985	145	29
1986	186	21
1987	137	15
1988	143	33
1989	261	53
	1224	196

Figure 5: Nationwide Data versus Local Data

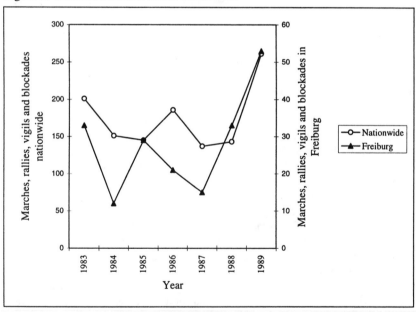

Two further observations (one about the sample and one about the completeness of the police data) are worth mentioning: (1) The difference between the rates of the four selected forms of action tested in the sample are comparable with the distribution within the total coverage of the police data. Only the number of marches in the sample is underestimated (see Figure 6).

Figure 6: Selected Forms of Action and their Number of Cases
(Sample and Total Coverage/Police Data 1983-1989)

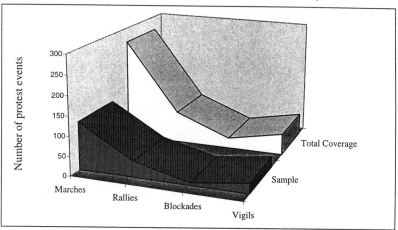

(2) As there was no opportunity to test the primary selection (which was done by the police) by direct means, a crucial and instructive aspect was the number of events mentioned only by media sources. If the number were to be high, the reliability of the police sources used would be in doubt. After excluding all protest events related to squatters, only 13 protest events remained. In five cases the chosen form of action, identified by the Prodat event definition, explained the difference. We can only speculate about the missing six cases (coder errors, imprecise entry in the police logbook, etc.). In total, these six media-exclusive cases within seven years (or 1,183 evaluated days) as compared with 196 identified cases from the police data indicates a slight lack of reliability, which is unfortunate but not worrying.

These basic pieces of information illustrate only the framework within which the question of selection bias is tested in the Prodat case study. The possibilities for analysis beside the overall interpretation of media selectivity in the case of a special class of protest events, can be sorted into three dimensions: Time, issue and form of action. Never before has local protest event data with a similar degree of comprehensiveness been gathered for a West German area. The seven years of the sample present the opportunity to study temporal shifts of selection bias for this recent period. As the media reports are available for all events, shifts within the description bias will also be analyzed. Because the protest events within these years can be separated into different groups of protest issues, the media selection according to different issues (e.g. peace issues compared to issues concerning women) can be studied; this will only be possible in an explorative sense, as the number of cases is relatively small. The third dimension of analysis belongs to the four types of events analyzed and the media response they found within local and national press. Are the demands of protest groups which organize blockades better reported than demands articulated by groups choosing the less disruptive and demonstratively peaceful protest form of the vigil? Is the message of a rally, communicated by speeches, reported in a manner similar to the slogans shouted by the participants of a militant march? Questions like these can also be analyzed and interpreted within the limits of a local case study.

Discussion

The aim of this contribution was to describe the framework of a more comprehensive study I am undertaking as a Prodat subproject and my dissertation. Here I focus on the selection bias of media coverage of protest events while in the broader study description bias (secondary selection) is also considered. In this sense this chapter explains the chosen theoretical approach, the structure of the local case and gives initial empirical results. Reading the relevant literature it became obvious that the connection between media research and protest event analysis is absolutely necessary. The strongest argument for this "project" is that in protest event analysis, which is accustomed to working with media data, more awareness is required about the selectivity of the mass media - especially of the print media. Interdisciplinary research should make the goal of learning more about the quality of commonly used empirical sources a priority.

The empirical analysis within my dissertation focuses on two aspects: (a) The "primary selection" done by mass media - meaning, which marches, rallies, vigils and blockades are reported and which are not; (b) the "secondary selection" - meaning, which characteristics of the reported protest events (e.g. goals) receive media coverage and which do not. The central unit, which is relevant within the news value approach, is the single event, which also structures the field of protest event analysis. The prominence of the news value approach within communi-cation studies made it easy to choose this concept. Though communication studies is not my traditional field (I began my academic work as a social movement researcher), I was fascinated by one of the central assumptions of the causally orientated tradition of the news value approach. Within this assumption, the strong indicators for the "news value" of events, which steers mass media selection, are "news factors" derived from the characteristics of events. The disadvantage of this approach is that some plausible intervening factors are not integrated. One example is inter-media agenda setting effects. Another example is the phenomenon of gatekeeper effects, which are the results of editorial politics, the competition between electronic and print media and the individual preferences of beat reporters or journalists on the editorial staff.

Interpreting the two questions of selection (primary and secondary) and thinking in logical terms, knowledge about the input of any selection process is one direct and plausible way to find answers about selectivity and bias. It makes sense, especially for social movement researchers and media sociologists, to follow Rosengren's often cited advice to look for high quality extra-media data and connect them with news factors. In my opinion, the most serious problem with the existing lists of news factors coming from communication studies is their "consensus orientation," which does not fit to event characteristics. It is especially difficult in cases of societal conflict to evaluate the degree of (for example) the news factor "relevance" or "personal influence" in connection with a single event (see Staab 1990: 109). This shows that the news value concept needs more general and theoretical discussion concerning the central premises and units of analysis. One first step in this direction is to develop event-specific lists of news factors and test them for their power of explanation. This "detour" provides a chance to strengthen the theoretical concept and discuss the advantages of the different branches within the news value approach.

Within the argumentation of my dissertation the news value concept is also discussed in the context of secondary selection. At this point I can only offer a few comments regarding this second mechanism of selection. One dimension of analysis is whether the news value influences the space allocated to the coverage of single protest events. A second dimension is whether detailed and event-specific interpretations about the demands and messages of protest groups gained a response? Does this type of collective actor or action have any influence? Have grassroots organizations the same chances of their messages being reported as established groups (i.e. trade unions)?

In one respect it sounds very simple to ask for extra-media data in the context of tracing the process of selection. Knowing the difficulties of reconstructing "reality" (see Schulz 1989), realizing an intra-/extra-media design depends on the access to sources and sociological fantasy. Under certain circumstances, police data are a high quality source which allows one to reconstruct patterns of the results of mass media selection in the form of an input/output comparison. The low level of protest event reporting, which is exclusively documented in the analysis of media data, and the documentation produced by other actors (local archives, trade unions, etc.) mean that it makes sense do this research with extra-media police data in the case of the German city of Freiburg. This was one of the first surprising results within Prodat.

A second and more empirical finding is the enormous selection bias caused by the strong filter of the local newspaper and the much stronger filter of the two national papers. Only a very small group of all marches, rallies, vigils and blockades within Freiburg city limits received a media response. The filtering stopped 95.4% of the protest events from reaching one or both of the national newspapers *(Süddeutsche Zeitung, Frankfurter Rundschau)*. The paper with high local attention *(Badische Zeitung)* also filters out 62.3% of the four selected forms of action before they can reach the broader public sphere via media coverage. This clear result matches that of the study by McCarthy et al., which used a larger number of media sources for their local case study, but found comparable rates of primary selection, 13% in 1982 and 7% in 1991 (McCarthy et al. 1996a). The difference between McCarthy et al.'s data and the extra-media data gathered in the Freiburg case study was due to the follow-up reports we had access to and which enabled us to include marches, rallies, vigils and blockades where the organizing actor did not ask for permission from the official police agencies. This was not the case in McCarthy et al.'s study. In Washington, D.C. this difference may not be so significant, as the U.S. capital is protected by a well developed system of internal security, which requires permits. Knowing this, every collective actor calculates the costs of their protest, and as they want to enter the public sphere without conflicts with police troops, the probability that they will ask for permission will be higher. As a phenomenon, the number of political public gatherings held without permission is a regular part of protest, which happens year after year. Whether this factor influences the dynamics of press reporting will be discussed at a later point of time.

References

Adolph, T. and U. Kamp. 1992. "Die Universität - Unruheherd und Wirtschaftsfaktor." Pp. 469-484 in *Geschichte der Stadt Freiburg, Vol. 3: Von der badischen Herrschaft bis zur Gegenwart*, ed. H. Haumann and H. Schadek. Stuttgart: Theiss.

Amann, R. 1985. *Der moralische Aufschrei. Presse und abweichendes Verhalten am Beispiel der Hausbesetzungen in Berlin.* Frankfurt/M.; New York: Campus.

Archiv Soziale Bewegungen in Baden, Chronologie. Unpublished source (quarterly since 1986). (Archiv Soziale Bewegungen in Baden, Wilhelmstr. 15, D-79098 Freiburg/ Breisgau.)

Beckord, W. 1993. "Demonstration." Pp. 122-124 in *Handwörterbuch des politischen Systems*, ed. U. Andersen and W. Woyke. Opladen: Leske+Budrich.

Brand, K.-W., D. Büsser and D. Rucht. 1986. *Aufbruch in eine andere Gesellschaft. Neue soziale Bewegungen in der Bundesrepublik.* Frankfurt/M.; New York: Campus.

Demirovic, A. 1994. "Öffentlichkeit und die alltägliche Sorge um die Demokratie." *Forschungsjournal Neue Soziale Bewegungen* 7 (1): 46-59.

Dietel, A., K. Gintzel and M. Kniesel. 1991. *Demonstrations- und Versammlungsfreiheit. Kommentar zum Gesetz über Versammlungen und Aufzüge.* Köln: Carl Heymanns.

Eilders, C. 1997. *Nachrichtenfaktoren und Rezeption. Eine empirische Analyse zur Auswahl und Verarbeitung politischer Information.* Opladen: Westdeutscher Verlag.

Emmerich, A. 1984. *Nachrichtenwertfaktoren: Die Bausteine der Sensationen. Eine empirische Studie zur Theorie der Nachrichtenauswahl in den Rundfunk- und Zeitungsredaktionen.* Saarbrücken: Verlag der Reihe "Saarländische Beiträge zur Soziologie" (Vol. 5).

Everett, K. D. 1992. "Professionalization and Protest: Changes in the Social Movement Sector, 1961-1983: The Differentiation of Interests and the Structural Transformation of Protest Activity." *Social Forces* 70 (4): 957-976.

Fillieule, O. 1996. *Police Records and the National Press in France: Issues in the Methodology of Data-Collections from Newspapers.* EUI Working Paper RSC No. 96/25. European University Institute. Badia Fiesolana, San Domenico. Florence. Italy.

Franzosi, R. 1987. "The Press as a Source of Socio-Historical Data: Issues in the Methodology of Data Collection from Newspapers." *Historical Methods* 20 (1): 5-16.

Galtung, J. and M. Holmboe Ruge. 1965. "The Structure of Foreign News: The Presentation of the Congo, Cuba and Cyprus Crisis in Four Norwegian Newspapers." *Journal of Peace Research* 2: 64-91.

Gerhards, J. 1991. *Die Macht der Massenmedien und die Demokratie: Empirische Befunde.* Discussion paper FS III 91-108. Wissenschaftszentrum Berlin für Sozialforschung (Social Science Research Center Berlin, WZB). Berlin.

Gerhards, J. and F. Neidhardt. 1993. "Strukturen und Funktionen moderner Öffentlichkeit - Fragestellungen und Ansätze." Pp. 52-88 in *Politische Kommunikation - Grundlagen, Strukturen, Prozesse,* ed. W. R. Langenbucher. Wien: Braumueller.

Halloran, J. D., P. Elliot and G. Murdock. 1970. *Demonstrations and Communication: A Case Study.* London: Penguin.

Haumann, H. 1992. "Studentendemonstrationen, "IG Krawall" und Häuserkampf. Soziale Bewegungen in den sechziger und siebziger Jahren." Pp. 460-463 in *Geschichte der Stadt Freiburg, Vol. 3: Von der badischen Herrschaft bis zur Gegenwart,* ed. H. Haumann and H. Schadek. Stuttgart: Theiss.

Hocke, P. 1994. "Nachrichtenfaktoren und lokaler Protest. Zur Theorie einer empirischen Fallstudie über Medienselektivität in einer westdeutschen 'Bewegungshochburg.'" Unpublished paper. Berlin.

Hocke, P. 1995. "Dokumentation und Analyse von Protestereignissen in Freiburg/ Breisgau. Codebuch der Prodat-Lokalstudie." Unpublished paper. Berlin.

Kepplinger, H. M. 1989. "Theorien der Nachrichtenauswahl als Theorien der Realität." *Aus Politik und Zeitgeschichte* B 15: 3-16.

Kielbowicz, R. B. and C. Scherer. 1986. "The Role of the Press in the Dynamics of Social Movements." Pp. 71-96 in *Research in Social Movements, Conflicts and Change 9,* ed. L. Kriesberg. Greenwich, Conn.: JAI.

Kliment, T. 1994. *Kernkraftprotest und Medienreaktionen. Deutungsmuster einer Widerstandsbewegung und öffentliche Rezeption.* Wiesbaden: Deutscher Universitätsverlag.

Koopmans, R. 1995. *Democracy from Below: New Social Movements and the Political System in West Germany.* Boulder, Colo.: Westview.

Kretschmer, W. 1988. "Wackersdorf: Wiederaufarbeitung im Widerstreit." Pp. 165-218 in *Von der Bittschrift zur Platzbesetzung*, ed. U. Linse et al. Berlin; Bonn: Dietz Nachf.

Kriesi, H. 1992. "Organisationsentwicklung von sozialen Bewegungen." *Forschungsjournal Neue Soziale Bewegungen* 5 (4): 85-93.

Kriesi, H. 1993. *Political Mobilization and Social Change: The Dutch Case in Comparative Perspective*. Aldershot: Avebury.

Kriesi, H., R. Levy, G. Ganguillet and H. Zwicky, eds. 1981. *Politische Aktivierung in der Schweiz, 1945-1978*. Diessenhofen: Rüegger.

Kronenberg, A. 1986. *Die Tagespresse in Südbaden nach 1945. Dargestellt am Beispiel der Badischen Zeitung*. Freiburg: Badischer Verlag.

Langguth, G. 1983. *Protestbewegung. Entwicklung - Niedergang - Renaissance. Die Neue Linke seit 1968*. Köln: Verlag Wissenschaft und Politik (Bibliothek Wissenschaft und Politik, Vol. 30).

Leif, T. 1985. *Die professionelle Bewegung. Friedensbewegung von innen*. Bonn: Forum Europa Verlag.

Luhmann, N. 1991. *Soziologie des Risikos*. Berlin; New York: Walter de Gruyter.

McAdam, D. 1982. *Political Process and the Development of Black Insurgency*. Chicago: University of Chicago Press.

McCarthy, J. D., C. McPhail and J. Smith. 1996a. "Images of Protest: Dimensions of Selection Bias in Media Coverage of Washington Demonstrations, 1982, 1991." *American Sociological Review* 61: 478-499.

McCarthy, J. D., C. McPhail and J. Smith. 1996b. "Selektionskriterien in der Berichterstattung von Fernsehen und Zeitungen. Eine vergleichende Fallstudie anhand von Demonstrationen in Washington D.C. in den Jahren 1982 und 1991." *Forschungsjournal Neue Soziale Bewegungen* 9 (1): 26-37.

Mann, L. 1974. "Counting the Crowd: Effects of Editorial Policy on Estimates." *Journalism Quarterly* 51: 278-285.

Molotoch, H. 1979. "Media and Movements." Pp. 71-93 in *The Dynamics of Social Movements*, ed. M. N. Zald and J. D. McCarthy. Cambridge, USA: Winthrop Publ.

Neidhardt, F. 1993. "Öffentlichkeit." Pp. 775-780 in *Lexikon der Wirtschaftsethik*, ed. G. Enderle et al. Freiburg: Herder.

Neidhardt, F. 1994. "Öffentlichkeit, öffentliche Meinung, soziale Bewegungen." Pp. 7-41 in *Öffentlichkeit, öffentliche Meinung, soziale Bewegungen*, ed. F. Neidhardt. Kölner Zeitschrift für Soziologie und Sozialpsychologie (Special Edition).

Ohlemacher, T. 1994. "Public Opinion and Violence Against Foreigners in the Reunified Germany." *Zeitschrift für Soziologie* 23 (3): 222-236.

Östgaard, E. 1965. "Factors Influencing the Flow of News." *Journal of Peace Research* 2: 39-63.

Raschke, J. 1988. *Soziale Bewegungen. Ein historisch-systematischer Grundriß*. Frankfurt/M.; New York: Campus.

Rochon, T. R. 1988. *Mobilizing for Peace: Antinuclear Movements in Western Europe*. Princeton, N.J.: Princeton University Press.

Rochon, T. R. 1990. "The West European Peace Movement and the Theory of New Social Movements." Pp. 105-121 in *Challenging the Political Order*, ed. R. J. Dalton and M. Kuechler. Cambridge, USA: Polity Press.

Rolke, L. 1987. *Protestbewegungen in der Bundesrepublik: Eine analytische Sozialgeschichte des Widerspruchs.* Opladen: Westdeutscher Verlag.

Rosengren, K. E. 1970. "International News: Intra and Extra Media Data." *Acta Sociologica* 13: 96-109.

Rosengren, K. E. 1974. "International News: Methods, Data and Theory." *Journal of Peace Research* 11: 145-176.

Rosengren, K. E. 1979. "Bias in News: Methods and Concepts." *Studies in Broadcasting* 15: 31-45.

Roth, R. 1991. "Proteste und soziale Bewegungen im Odenwald." *Forschungsjournal Neue Soziale Bewegungen* 4 (4): 60-72.

Roth, R. 1994. "Lokale Bewegungsnetzwerke und die Instiutionalisierung von neuen sozialen Bewegungen." Pp. 413-436 in *Öffentlichkeit, öffentliche Meinung, soziale Bewegungen*, ed. F. Neidhardt. Kölner Zeitschrift für Soziologie und Sozialpsychologie (Special Edition).

Rubart, F. 1985. "Neue soziale Bewegungen und alte Parteien in Schweden: Politischer Protest zwischen Autonomie und Integration." Pp. 200-247 in *Neue soziale Bewegungen in Westeuropa und den USA*, ed. K.-W. Brand. Frankfurt/M.; New York: Campus.

Rucht, D. 1994. *Modernisierung und neue soziale Bewegungen. Deutschland, Frankreich und USA im Vergleich.* Frankfurt/M.; New York: Campus.

Rucht, D. 1996. "Forms of Protest in Germany 1950-92: A Quantitative Overview." Paper prepared for the workshop "Europe and the United States: Movement Societies or the Institutionalization of Protest." Cornell University, Ithaca, N.Y., March 1-3.

Rucht, D., P. Hocke and T. Ohlemacher. 1992. *Dokumentation und Analyse von Protestereignissen in der Bundesrepublik Deutschland (Prodat). Codebuch.* Discussion Paper FS III 92-103. Wissenschaftszentrum Berlin für Sozialforschung (Social Science Research Center Berlin, WZB). Berlin.

Rucht, D., P. Hocke and D. Oremus. 1995. "Quantitative Inhaltsanalyse: Warum, wo, wann und in welcher Form wurde in der Bundesrepublik protestiert?" Pp. 261-291 in *Methoden der Politikwissenschaft*, ed. U. von Alemann. Opladen: Westdeutscher Verlag.

Rucht, D. and T. Ohlemacher. 1992. "Protest Event Data: Collection, Uses and Perspectives." Pp. 76-106 in *Issues in Contemporary Social Movement Research*, ed. R. Eyerman and M. Diani. Beverly Hills: Sage.

Schmitt-Beck, R. 1990. "Über die Bedeutung von Massenmedien für Soziale Bewegungen." *Kölner Zeitschrift für Soziologie und Sozialpsychologie* 42 (4): 642-662.

Schneider, R. 1989. "Fallbeispiel für kommunale Entwicklungszusammenarbeit: Freiburg/ Wiwili." Unpublished paper. Freiburg.

Schulz, W. 1976. *Konstruktion von Realität in den Nachrichtenmedien.* Freiburg; München: Karl Alber Verlag.

Schulz, W. 1982. "News Structure and People's Awareness of Political Events." *Gazette* 30: 139-153.

Schulz, W. 1987. "Politikvermittlung durch Massenmedien." Pp. 129-144 in *Politikvermittlung*, ed. U. Sarcinelli. Bonn: Schriftenreihe der Bundeszentrale für politische Bildung, Vol. 238.

Schulz, W. 1989. "Massenmedien und Realität: Die 'ptolemäische' und die 'kopernikanische' Auffassung." Pp. 135-149 in *Massenkommunikation*, ed. M. Kasse and W. Schulz. Kölner Zeitschrift für Soziologie und Sozialpsychologie (Special Edition).

Schulz, W. 1995. "Nachricht." Pp. 307-336 in *Fischer-Lexikon Publizistik und Massenkommunikation*, ed. E. Noelle-Neumann et al. Frankfurt/M.: Fischer.

Snyder, D. and W. R. Kelly. 1977. "Conflict Intensity, Media Sensitivity and the Validity of Conflict Data." *American Sociological Review* 42: 105-123.

Staab, J. F. 1990. *Nachrichtenwerttheorie. Formale Struktur und empirischer Gehalt.* München: Karl Alber.

Tarrow, S. 1989. *Democracy and Disorder: Protest and Politics in Italy 1965-1975.* Oxford: Clarendon Press.

Taylor, C. L. and D. A. Jodice. 1983. *World Handbook of Political and Social Indicators*, Vol. 1-2 (3rd Edition). New Haven, Conn.: Yale University Press.

Tilly, R. 1970. "Popular Disorders in 19th-Century Germany." *Journal of Social History* 4: 1-40.

Tuchman, G. 1978. *Making News. A Study in the Construction of Reality.* New York; London: The Free Press.

Weimann, G. and H.-B. Brosius. 1991. "The Newsworthiness of International Terrorism." *Communication Research* 18 (3): 333-354.

Wilking, T. 1990. *Strukturen lokaler Nachrichten. Eine empirische Untersuchung von Text- und Bildberichterstattung.* München; New York; London; Paris: K.G. Saur.

Unpacking Protest Events:
A Description Bias Analysis of Media Records with Systematic Direct Observations of Collective Action - The 1995 March for Life in Washington, D.C.

Clark McPhail and David Schweingruber

Introduction

Despite the extensive use of newspaper archives to study protest events over past two decades, three methodological problems remain. We do not know if descriptions of the large protest events the media report accurately represent the actors and actions of which those events are composed; we do not know if the large events that the media report differ from the more frequent smaller events that are not reported; and, until recently we have not had a methodology by which to generate the basic descriptive information about protest events necessary to address and resolve the first two problems.

In this chapter we briefly discuss the history of efforts to unpack protest events so as to make these problems more empirically accessible. We describe a taxonomy of collective action used to develop an observation and recording system with which we have trained and deployed observers to systematically sample collective actions in protest events. We then report on extensive data generated by this system in the study of one large protest event, the 1995 "March for Life." We compare our empirical representation of this protest event with newspaper and television news reports of the same event. We briefly discuss the implications of our data for "the illusion of unanimity" which surrounds much theoretical and empirical work on protest events. Finally, we advocate both further research with our observation and recording system as well as more education of media workers on the complex and social nature of the protest events which are of interest to both social science and the media.

Protest Event Analysis

Over the past quarter century social scientists have designed and produced, from national daily newspaper archives, machine-readable data sets on the issues, actors and forms of collective action making up protest events, as well as their orderly or disorderly nature, number of arrests and the like. This has enabled the mapping of repertoires of collective action as well as the examination of waves and cycles of protest events in relation to various archival measures of social, political and economic conditions which provide obstacles to or opportunities for collective action in Europe (Shorter and Tilly 1974; Tilly 1986, 1993, 1995) and the U.S. (Jenkins and Perrow 1977; McAdam 1982). Over time this methodology (Franzoni 1990; Olzak 1989; Rucht and Ohlemacher 1992; Diani 1992) has become standardized and widely employed by sociologists and political scientists in the United States (Jenkins and Perrow 1977; Everett 1992; Olzak 1992;) and in Europe (Tarrow 1989; Rucht 1991; Koopmans 1993; Kriesi et al. 1995; Della Porta 1995; Fillieule 1996). It is difficult to exaggerate the important contri-butions of this methodology to the volume and quality of our empirical knowledge and theoretical understanding of protest events.

However, until recently two questions have remained unanswered. First, how representative of the population of all protest events that take place are the events reported in the media. Second, of those events selected for reporting, are media characterizations representative of event actors and their actions within and regarding the protest events. The first question is one of selection bias, the second of description bias. Until recently there was no method for establishing the population of protest events and thereby systematically addressing the question of selection bias. McCarthy, McPhail and Smith (1996) addressed this methodo-logical problem by compiling archival records of demonstration permits granted by the three major police agencies in Washington, D.C. This allowed them to establish the population of Washington demonstration events for 1982 and 1991. They compared this population against the sample of Washington demonstrations reported in the *Washington Post* and *New York Times* and those reported in the nightly news telecasts of the three national networks. Their results have significant bearing on the many empirical and theoretical protest event analyses over the past quarter century which have been based on newspaper archives. Of the nearly 2,000 demonstrations which occur each year in Washington, less than 10% are reported by the print or electronic media. There are two significant correlates of selection bias. First, the media are much more likely to cover demonstrations which address or illustrate issues to which they are already giving attention. Second, larger demonstrations are far more likely to be reported than smaller ones even though the latter are far more frequent. Thus, news media reports of protest events represent only "the tip of the iceberg." A similar pattern is reported in several European countries.

The Washington, D.C. permit records have also been used to investigate description bias. The results, reported elsewhere in this volume (McCarthy, McPhail, Smith and Crishock 1995), yielded high correlations between newspaper accounts and information found in permits records, such as date, purpose and size of the event. The correlation between television reports and the permit records varied; e.g. they were high for date and purpose of protest but low for protest size and for whether the protest was part of a campaign. These media-permit comparisons also have great significance for protest-event theory and research based solely on media records. A limitation of the permit records, however, is that they are created before the event and thus contain very limited information about the range of collective actions occurring during the permitted events. Thus, we do not know the extent to which the description bias patterns identified in the media-permit comparisons by McCarthy, McPhail, Smith and Crishock apply to the collective action composition of demonstrations.

These recent investigations of selection and description bias raise two major questions. First, to what extent do the large protest events reported in the media differ from the more frequent smaller protest events that are not reported? Second, what is the nature of the description bias of media accounts of collective action at demonstration events? Both of these questions require a method for "unpacking" demonstrations and identifying their constituent actions. Those actions could then be (1) compared across small and large demonstrations and (2) compared with actions which are reported in news media accounts of these demonstrations. Until recently social scientists have lacked a method for generating this "basic information in the field of social protest" (Rucht and Ohlemacher 1992: 91-92).[1] In this chapter we present our system for unpacking demonstration events and a preliminary illustration of how it can be used to study description bias. Although this system has been used to investigate collective action at large protest events and has yet to be used at small ones, we hope to illustrate how the system can be used to address this question in the future.

Unpacking the Protest Event

The problem of unpacking protest events has been addressed in one way or another by a variety of scholars over the past twenty-five years. As the 19th century paradigms of "the crowd" crumbled in the face of both historical research (e.g. Rude 1967) and contemporary field research (Berk 1972; Fisher 1972; McPhail 1972; Lofland 1981), a more empirically accessible picture of crowds in general, and demonstrations in particular, began to develop. At the micro-level of analysis, scholars examined various phases in the life course of

---

1   Charles Tilly's coding of newspaper records and other chronicles of contentious gatherings is an exception. He has systematically coded type of gathering, type of gathering issue, type of acting unit and verbs used to describe type of collective action taken (Tilly 1995).

temporary gatherings: the assembling processes which form gatherings (Quarantelli and Hundley 1969; Aveni 1977; McPhail and Miller 1973; Johnson 1984; Klandermans and Oegema 1987), and the dispersal processes which terminate gatherings (Sime 1980; Johnson 1987).

Research on collective action within the gatherings themselves proved more difficult to carry out given the initial absence of conceptual frameworks and methodological procedures with which to proceed (cf. Milgram and Toch 1968; Marx and Woods 1975; McPhail and Wohlstein 1983). Blumer attributed social science ignorance of what occurs in crowds to the absence of "a well thought out analytic scheme which would provide fruitful hypotheses and lead to more incisive observations" (1957: 135). But this offered a paradox rather than a solution. Incisive observations presuppose some conceptual scheme or criteria specifying the phenomena to be observed; but a plausible conceptual scheme must build upon at least minimal observations of the phenomena to which the scheme is addressed. Not until we are familiar with the phenomena to be explained can we develop viable explanations from which fruitful hypotheses can be derived for empirical testing.

Turner's (1964) seminal discussion of "the illusion of unanimity" within crowds and his alternative characterization of "differential expression" provided McPhail (1969, 1972) with a partial solution to Blumer's paradox. McPhail argued that crowds might better be construed as temporary gatherings within which two or more people occasionally engaged in collective actions of various types or forms. Rather than the blanket of uniform behavior implied by the concept of "the crowd," the more appropriate metaphor might be a patchwork quilt of alternating and varied individual and collective actions within these temporary gatherings. The challenge was to identify and describe those collective actions. McPhail (1969) took up this challenge by training and deploying multiple observers with pen and paper to describe any and all instances of two or more persons acting with or in relation to one another. Recording gradually shifted to film and then to slides and videotape. Over the next ten years McPhail repeatedly reviewed and analyzed those varied, rich and extensive records and inductively identified approximately forty recurring elementary forms of collective action. McPhail and his colleagues developed criteria and procedures for using this taxonomic scheme to make field observation records and to code film and video records of collective actions in prosaic, religious, sport and political gatherings (McPhail 1972; Wohlstein and McPhail 1979; McPhail and Pickens 1981; McPhail and Wohlstein 1982, 1986; McPhail 1991).

McPhail's taxonomy of elementary forms is organized around four parts of the body and can be summarized by answers to four questions: Which direction are people facing? What noises are people making with their mouths? What are people doing with their arms, hands and fingers? What are the positions and movements of people's torsos and legs in relationship to the ground? The four dimensions were selected because of the meaningfulness attached to these body parts for understanding human communication, purpose, movement and action. They are called facing, voicing, manipulation and body positioning. In turn, the variations on each of these four dimensions yield approximately 40 elementary forms of collective action.

> *Facing* includes facing in the same, i.e. parallel, direction (e.g. same facing as a function of walking in the same direction or as a function of looking at a common object) and facing in converging directions (e.g. conversation clusters, arcs and rings).

> *Voicing* includes vocalization (e.g. cheering, booing, laughing, whistling) and verbalization (e.g. talking, singing, chanting). Talking can be further divided on the basis of substantive content (praying, conversing, pledging, etc.)

> *Manipulation* may involve things (e.g. carrying, striking, throwing), other people (e.g. embracing, restraining, striking), one's own body (e.g. clapping, snapping), or gesturing (making symbols, e.g. #1, peace, clenched fist).

> *Body positioning* here refers to horizontal motion (e.g. walking, running, marching), vertical motion (e.g. standing up, sitting down) and the resulting place or position of the body (e.g. upright, seated, prone). For the observations reported here we have collapsed the vertical motion/place categories.

Not every collective action which might occur in a gathering is on our list of forms. However, the taxonomy and the list of forms is empirically generated from observing hundreds of gatherings. If any collective action at all is observed in a gathering, it will likely be one or more of these forty elementary forms. However, (1) all these forms do not appear in all gatherings; (2) the forms may appear separately or in various and sometimes complex combinations; (3) the forms may vary in direction, tempo, substantive content, and in the proportion of the gathering participating in any simple or complex sequence of collective action. The taxonomy itself is exhaustive since forms which are empirically rare could be placed into it. Ten "other" categories (e.g. other facing, other carrying/lifting things) were included on the code sheet to allow coding forms of collective action which were not expected to frequently occur in political gatherings.

Levels and Units of Analysis

At first glance it may appear that there is an enormous gulf between the macro-level of analysis which has to date prevailed in protest event analysis and the micro-level of analysis with which we have proceeded to study purposive action within gatherings. On the contrary, we believe that the units of analysis at these disparate levels are not only related to one another, we think of them as nested units. Other students of collective action advance similar continua of levels and units of analysis with elementary units of analysis accumulating to form more complex units (cf. Lofland 1985: 1-25; Olzak 1989; McPhail 1991; Tilly 1993).[2]

Figure 1 illustrates our conception of a cumulative sliding scale of micro- to macro-units of analysis. As the scale moves from micro to macro, the spatial area increases over which the phenomena occur as does their temporal duration. The various elementary forms of collective action by individuals alternate with actions those same individuals take alone.

Figure 1: Units of Analysis by Spatial and Temporal Levels of Analysis
        (after McPhail 1991)

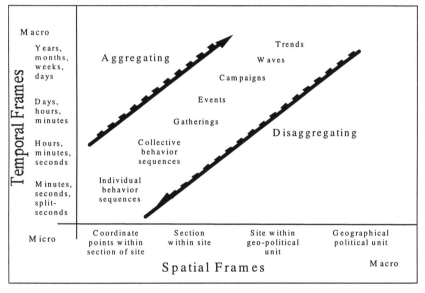

---

2   Tilly construes social movements as clusters of political performances at multiple levels of analysis, e.g. individual or collective actions and interactions, the sequences of these that make up a performance (e.g. a demonstration), the cluster of performances that constitute a campaign, the set of campaigns that make up the shared narrative history of a social movement, the repertoire of all contentious collective actions, and, "the array of all repertoires [of collective actions] ever available within given limits of time and space" (1993: 8-9).

Taken together, the aggregation of all those individual and collective actions constitute what has traditionally been termed "the crowd," but which McPhail calls a temporary gathering.[3] In turn, two or more gatherings (e.g. a rally followed by a march to some destination where dispersal or other actions occur) make up what is termed an "event"; and the aggregation of two or more events (e.g. daily rallies followed by marches to picket line sites) make up a campaign. Forms of collective action, of gatherings, or of events may spread across multiple geographical locations in a relatively brief period of time resulting in a wave, e.g. the 1960 sit-in campaign in the U.S. civil rights movement (McAdam 1982; cf. Koopmans 1993). The frequency of any or all of these collective phenomena also rises and falls across time resulting in cycles (cf. Tarrow 1989; Tilly et al. 1975; Olzak 1992; Della Porta 1995).

A Method for Observing and Recording Collective Action

Having placed the taxonomic scheme for collective action within the larger context, we will now briefly describe the translation of that taxonomy into a systematic method for observing and recording collective action. This method consists of multiple observers, distributed throughout a gathering, who record their observations on a field coding form based on our taxonomy of collective action. The objective is to systematically sample collective actions across space and time, not to produce a comprehensive record of all collective (let alone all individual) actions.

Our current field recording form (see Appendix) has as its primary element a matrix allowing observers to record each of 43 forms of behavior by actors in any of six categories. The 43 forms, each corresponding to a row, were derived from our taxonomy of collective behavior, but were tailored to include those forms we expected to find in political gatherings.[4] Ten additional "other" categories are used to code forms which are not specifically named. The six

---

3   The concept of the crowd implies a uniformity of action and a homogeneity of actors which is empirically false. In view of the problems with this antiquated concept we will use the term "temporary gathering" here to refer to a collection of two or more people in a common place in space and time. Gatherings are opportunities for two or more people to act collectively; they do not guarantee it (McPhail 1991: 153).

4   Our taxonomy of collective actions was inductively generated from observation records of hundreds of gatherings, including but not limited to political demonstrations. Thus, while the taxonomy can contain all the collective actions in which we have observed two or more persons engage, some are more likely in prosaic, sport or religious gatherings than in political gatherings. In short, the taxonomy can be expanded or contracted to fit the type of gathering under observation.

columns correspond to the five categories of people who are most often present at demonstrations (MacCannell 1973) and an "other" column. Like the elementary forms, the particular actor categories were selected because of the type of gathering being coded. For other types of gatherings in other places, different categories would be appropriate. The six actor categories are:

Demonstrators - those in the gathering whose visible and identifying actions support the stated purpose of the demonstration.

Onlookers/passersby - those at or near the gathering venue for purposes unrelated to the demonstration.

Police - any law enforcement officials at the gathering.

Media - reporters, photographers and video camera operators from newspapers or broadcast news agencies.

Counter-demonstrators - those at or near the gathering whose visible and identifying actions oppose the stated purpose of the demonstration.

Others - includes vendors, other service workers, pickpockets, sociologists and people demonstrating for purposes unrelated to the demonstration.

Coders are instructed to consider such factors as actions, words, clothing, relationships, locations and artifacts when deciding to which category an actor belongs.

Beneath each of the actor category column headings is a cell in which the observer is asked to estimate the number of actors in each category who are present in the observer's area of responsibility and who are visible to the observer. Many people in the area may not be visible to the observer because they are behind other people. The observer has no way of judging to which actor category they belong or in what elementary forms they are participating. The judgments about participation in elementary forms are based only on those actors who are visible to the observer. We do not consider this a major problem because the collective action observed and recorded represents only a sample of the collective action in the gathering.

The remaining 53 rows on the central matrix are used to record the observer's estimates of the proportions of actors in each category who are participating in one or more of the 43 elementary forms of collective action plus the 10 residual "other" categories. Each cell corresponds to the intersect of an actor category and an elementary form of collective action. For each cell the coder estimates what proportion of the visible actors in the category are participating in the elementary form. The lower case letters (a-g), from the proportion of actors key, are used to indicate seven ranges of proportions. An "a" entered in the box indicates that although the action is observed, only one person is acting so no collective action is present. The letters "b"-"g" indicate increasingly higher levels of collective action with "g" indicating 100% participation. Although making these calculations for 318 cells in a few seconds appears both complex and difficult, most of the cells are left empty (due to the absence of many of the actions at any particular sampling interval). Coders need only read down the list of actions under the categories of actors present in his or her area and record those actions which are present.

A complete description of our system is found in *The Collective Action Observation Primer* (McPhail and Schweingruber 1995), which was used to train the observers. The *Primer* contains instructions on the coding process and detailed criteria for identifying each elementary form and actor category. For instance:

> *Facing in the same direction* is when individuals' lines of sight are roughly parallel. This may result because they are moving in the same direction or because they are looking at the same thing.[5]

> *Function of monitoring* describes actors facing or orienting in the same (parallel) direction as a function of looking at (monitoring) the same thing, e.g. a passing delegation in a march. This often occurs when actors are positioned to look at something big enough to see without forming an arc.

> *Disparate pedestrian cluster(s)* describes clusters of two or more actors moving together. These people may touch, talk and/or look toward each other as they move. Although the actors within each cluster move together in the same direction, the clusters move in disparate directions. This frequently occurs when large gatherings are forming or breaking up (and sometimes on the fringes of large focused gatherings) and is described by the term "milling."

> *Chanting* is verbalizing the same words in unison, usually repeatedly, and often in rhythm.

> *Placarding/bannering* is bearing placards, banners, signs, flags or large photographs which carry visual messages in words and/or pictures.

> *Striking things* is hitting something forcefully, either with the hands or with something held with the hands such as a stick or bat. *Striking* may break something (such as striking a car window) or make noise (such as striking a drum). If the *striking* damages or destroys property, also code as *violence against property*.

---

5   The primer also indicates that "facing ... is important because it is a crude indicator of what a person is giving attention." Similarly, chanting and placarding/bannering are means by which persons state their interests and contentions (McPhail and Schweingruber 1995: 2).

Implementation

Implementing the method required recruiting observers, training them to use the code sheets correctly, positioning them throughout the gathering venue, debriefing them, and entering their records into a quantitative data base for analysis. This section briefly summarizes how we accomplished this for the two demonstrations we have so far observed with this method.

Most of our observers were Washington-area university undergraduate students recommended to us by colleagues. (The other coders included one of the authors, a professor and several graduate students involved with the project.) The undergraduate observers were paid for their time involved in group training, observing/recording and debriefing. They were also paid for studying *The Primer* and whatever practice they did on their own.

The observers were furnished with *The Primer* to study several days before their first training session. They were instructed to study it, to become familiar with it before their group training began and to prepare questions to ask during the training. The group training took place during a day-long session two days before the demonstration. The sessions consisted of (1) a brief lecture on temporary gatherings, the history of observing them and the purpose of the project, (2) a brief history of the March for Life, (3) an illustrated overview of the elementary forms and coding procedures, (4) practice using the coding forms, and (5) practice estimating the number of actors and density of gatherings. The history of the March for Life, the overview of forms and coding procedures and the practice coding forms all made extensive use of 35mm color slides. All of the forms were illustrated with slides while they were being explained.

The observers practiced using the criteria and procedures in *The Primer* by coding slides of elementary forms in various demonstrations. After each slide was coded, the authors and trainees discussed, compared and corrected the results. The training on estimating the number of actors and the density included the use of slides, but also included taking the trainees outside and arranging some of them in various formations for the other trainees to observe. The trainees were encouraged to study their codebook and practice coding the day between the group training and the demonstration.

Essential to the method is the distribution of observers throughout the demonstration venue such that each observer is responsible for a clearly delineated area. Before each demonstration took place, the authors visited the venue and divided it into a matrix. The boundaries of the various sections include sidewalks, trees, lampposts, stages, audio speakers, buildings in the background, and sightlines connecting these various markers. The entire demonstration venue was then mapped, including markers and sightlines, so that each observer had a map of the complete venue, with his/her specific observation area indicated. Depending on the size of the demonstration venue, the number of observers and the number of cells or areas in the matrix, observers might be placed in every area or in a subset of areas.

Upon arriving at the demonstration location, the observers synchronized their watches to ensure that they were coding during the same sample period. They were each given a spiral-bound pad of code sheets and a map with their area marked. Because we anticipated people questioning the observers about their identity, the code sheet books had the project name on their bright green plastic covers, each observer wore a project name tag and each observer carried business cards of the project's co-investigators. Observers were told they could answer demonstrators' questions about their coding as long as this didn't interfere with their duties. However, they were encouraged not to be drawn into discussions about demonstration-related issues.

Each observer was led to his or her area by one of the authors, who indicated the boundaries of the area. The observers were instructed to walk around these boundaries and study the area. Observers were directed to stand at a spot where they could observe the faces of most of the people in the area. At the March for Life rally venue, where we put multiple observers into some of the sections, we had the observers stand apart from each other.

Beginning at 11 a.m. (a half hour before the official start of the March for Life rally) each observer was instructed to fill out a code sheet to indicate what was taking place in their area during a one-minute sample. The observers were told to scan their area for approximately 30 seconds of the one-minute sampling period and to then begin filling out their code sheets. They could look up from the sheets to observe the area again, but they were not to code any new behavior which took place after the one-minute observation sample was completed. For the March for Life, observers repeated the observation and recording every 15 minutes. (The interval between observation samples was reduced to 10 minutes for the Rally for Women's Lives.) The March for Life observers moved, at specified times, to their second position, either along the march route or at the march destination at the Supreme Court.

Collective Action at the March for Life

The following analysis is based on data collected at the 1995 March for Life, the first demonstration we observed using this method. The code sheet was slightly different from our current version, which appears in the Appendix. We note two important differences. First, the code sheet had five fewer elementary forms. Second, at the March for Life, observers recorded the proportion of actors engaging in collective action on a six-point scale, which we subsequently re-scored into a five-point scale (cf. Table 5, below) where 0 = no one or only one person acting (thus, no collective action), 1 = two or more persons acting but less than 25%, 2 = 25-49%, 3 = 50-74%, 4 = 75%-99%, and, 5 = 100% participation (mutually inclusive collective action).[6]

Although we had multiple observers in some observation areas, the data and analysis discussed here are based on just one coder per observation area. The rally site contained 15 observation areas, which covered the entire rally site. The march had six observation areas along the route, three each on the north and south sides of the street. March observers were responsible for the one-half of the street through which the demonstrators processed as well as the adjoining sidewalk. The area in front of the Supreme Court was divided into nine areas. Across these 30 areas, the number of observer records per area ranged from 6 to 12 with a mean of 7.7. The total number of observer records was 232.

Recapitulation of the Protest Event. The first segment of the March for Life protest event consisted of a 1 hour and 20 minute rally on the Ellipse, south of the White House grounds, and bordering Constitution Avenue. From this location demonstrators walked along Constitution Avenue, then up to Capitol Hill, where they turned onto First Street SE. They then dispersed in front of the Supreme Court, which is located across First Street from the east front of the U.S. Capitol.

The procession from the Ellipse rally to the Supreme Court termination point took approximately one hour and thirty minutes. A small pro-choice counter-demonstration was held at the Supreme Court but most of the counter-demonstrators left before the majority of the pro-life "marchers" arrived. However, the pro-life demonstrators did encounter a large number of media workers and police.

Actor Categories. We had a total of 232 observation records made in the 30 observation areas across the three locations comprising the protest event. Table 1 reports the percentage of those records in which at least one individual in a particular actor category was visible to our observers. These numbers are not proportions of the total number of visible actors; we cannot generate those proportions from our data. However, we can get a sense of it from observers' estimates of how many actors were visible in each category. These estimates range from one actor to over one thousand actors.

---

6   In the scale used by the observers, a = one to six actors (with the exact number specified); b = at least seven actors but less than 25% of the total visible; c = 25-49%; d = 50-74%; e = 75-99%; f = 100%. We recoded all "a" responses with two or more actors into one of the proportional categories.

Table 1: Proportion of Observer Records Reporting Each Actor Category

Actor categories	Event		Rally		March		Destination	
	N	%	N	%	N	%	N	%
Demonstrators	219	94.4	140	100.0	26	72.2	53	94.7
Police	55	23.7	1	0.7	14	38.9	40	71.4
Media	46	19.8	26	18.6	4	11.1	16	28.6
Onlookers/passersby	27	11.6	0	0.0	15	41.7	12	21.4
Counter-demonstrators	8	3.4	0	0.0	0	0.0	8	14.3
Missing	3	1.3	0	0.0	3	8.3	0	0.0
Total	358	154.3	167	119.2	62	172.2	129	230.4
Samples	232		140		36		56	

Overall, and at each of the three separate sites, demonstrators were the most frequently observed actor category (94.4% of records); police (23.7%) were the next most frequent category, followed by media workers (19.8%), then onlooker/passersby (11.6%) and counter-demonstrators (3.4%).[7] However, the percentage of reported actors differed significantly from site to site for the latter four actor categories. Police were the second most frequently reported actors at the destination site (71.4%) and third most frequently observed along the march route (38.9%), but they were not a visible presence at the rally site (0.7%).

Media workers were most frequently reported at the destination site (28.6%), where many of them waited for the demonstrators to arrive. Media workers were also present at the rally site (18.6%), where they were accommodated by a large media platform, designed for photographers and video crews, positioned in the middle of the site and facing in the direction of the rally stage. Media workers were less frequently reported along the march route (11.1%). None of our observers reported onlookers/passersby at the rally site. Perhaps this is because all the observation areas were located within the rally site, while non-demonstrators walked along the sidewalks bordering that site. Along the march route, however, onlookers/passersby were the second most frequently observed category (41.7%), as many were using the sidewalk for non-demonstration purposes. The same was true for the march destination site where onlookers/passersby were also noted.

Counter-demonstrators were not noted in observers' records at the rally site or along the march route (although some counter-demonstrators were scattered along the route but not within the purview of our observers' assigned locations). Before the march arrived at the Supreme Court, counter-demonstrators held a

---

7   The overall rank ordering of frequency of actor categories corresponds to the only earlier report available (MacCannell 1973).

small pro-choice vigil with singing and guitar playing on the sidewalk in front of the Court. Since the March for Life has taken place each year since the 1973 Court decision - Roe vs. Wade - which legalized abortion, this is a symbolic site for both pro-choice and pro-life demonstrators. During some previous years, there had been confrontations between pro-life and pro-choice demonstrators at this site. However, at the 1995 March for Life, most counter-demonstrators left the destination site before the pro-life demonstrators arrived. They were observed in only 14.3% of the records taken at the destination site. Table 2 shows the minimum, maximum and modal range for each actor category, by site.

Table 2:   Range in Number of Actors by Category and Site

		Demonstrators	Onlookers	Police	Media	Counter-demos
Event	min	1	1	1	1	2-5
	mode	51-100	6-10	2-5	2-5	26-50
	max	501-1000	11-25	51-100	11-25	51-100
Rally	min	6-10	-	2-5	1	-
	mode	51-100	-	2-5	1	-
	max	501-1000	-	2-5	6-10	-
March	min	1	2-5	1	2-5	-
	mode	51-100	2-5	2-5	2-5	-
	max	101-250	11-25	11-25	2-5	-
Destin.	min	1	1	1	1	2-5
	mode	11-25	6-10	11-15	2-5	26-50
	max	251-500	11-25	51-100	11-25	51-100

The estimates of the number of actors in each category gives a complementary picture, but shows more clearly how much more prevalent demonstrators were than other types of actors. When demonstrators were reported, the modal estimated frequency range was 51-100 with a maximum range of 501-1000. Counter-demonstrators, when visible, had a modal range of 26-50 and a maximum range of 51-100. With one exception - a sighting of between 50 and 100 police at the destination site - none of the other actors were ever reported at a frequency higher than 11-25. Police and media both had modal frequency ranges of 2-5, while onlookers/passersby's modal range was 6-10.

Observed Collective Actions

In this section we will discuss which collective actions were observed during the 1995 March for Life; in the following section we will discuss the extent of observed demonstrator participation in those actions. Space limitations prevent the discussion of individual or collective action by other actor categories in the present paper. Thus, we will take up in turn two different units of analysis: the first will be the observers' records of the presence of collective action; the second will be their estimates of the proportion of actors in their areas of responsibility engaged in various forms of collective action.

Observer Records of Collective Action

Every fifteen minutes observers scanned their areas of responsibility for one minute and noted which categories of actors were engaged in which categories of action. We will briefly summarize the categories and extent of collective action which observers recorded. Table 3 below summarizes those types of collective actions our observers reported seeing most frequently at each of the three sites. Before turning to that table, several caveats are in order.

First, we noted earlier that actions on each of the four dimensions (facing, voicing, manipulating and locomoting) are more or less mutually exclusive. Normally people can face but one direction, can make but one noise with their mouth and are in but one body position at any one point in time. However, since people have two sets of arms/hands/fingers, their manipulation actions are less mutually exclusive.

Second, demonstrators can simultaneously engage in multiple actions across these four dimensions. Demonstrators are always facing some direction whether they are sitting, standing or walking (body position/locomotion). In addition, while demonstrators are facing in a common direction (e.g. toward a platform from which a speech is emanating), they may be holding aloft placards or banners (manipulation) and simultaneously cheering or booing the speaker's remarks (voicing). While it is unlikely they will be both raising their placards and applauding at the same time, it is not impossible. We have yet to devise an efficient means of recording all combinations of actions; thus, we report each of them separately. The reader should always bear in mind that demonstrators can engage in two or more actions at once.

Third, while our taxonomy provides us with an almost exhaustive list of all the actions in which two or more actors can engage collectively, we have not always observed all of these actions in every gathering we have observed. The March for Life was no exception. A rather long list of actions were observed at one but not at all three locations: Queuing, booing, oohing/ohhing/ahhing, the (non-violent) striking of a person, and lying down were observed at the rally but not along the march or at the destination site; neither praying nor striking of inanimate objects were observed at the rally; exchanging was not observed at the destination site; and neither arcs, rings, shouting, speech making, gesturing nor clapping were observed at the march sites. At the 15 minute intervals when observers systematically recorded one-minute samples of individual and collective actions, they reported *no instances* of restraining a person, violence against a person or against property; nor were there any instances of finger snapping or jogging/running at any of the three sites. Neither pledging/reciting, throwing things or marching were observed at the rally or march site.[8] Finally, it should be noted that while these individual or collective actions were observed on occasion, they were not frequent at any location. Consequently, we have elected to display in Table 3 only those collective actions that observers recorded in double-digit frequency at one or more sites.

Table 3:   Mean Percent of Collective Actions Reported by Site

Collective actions		Rally	March	Destination	Mean
Facing	Same-f monitoring	86.4	34.6	49.1	56.7
	Conversation clusters	61.4	23.1	73.6	52.7
	Disparate pedestrian clusters	40.0	30.8	58.5	43.1
	Same-f inclusive loco.	7.9	80.8	34.0	40.9
	Arcs	9.3	0.0	17.0	8.8
	Rings	7.9	0.0	18.9	8.9
Voicing	Conversation	61.4	65.4	56.6	61.1
	Chanting	2.1	34.6	34.0	23.6
	Cheering	30.7	3.9	11.3	15.3
	Singing	5.7	15.4	9.4	10.2
	Praying	0.0	3.9	24.5	9.5
	Shouting	0.7	0.0	13.2	4.6
	Pledging/reciting	0.0	0.0	11.3	3.8
Manipulation	Placarding/bannering	97.9	84.6	75.5	86.0
	Embracing/clasping person	7.1	15.4	13.2	11.9
	Carry/dragging person	12.1	7.7	1.9	7.2
	Leafleting	12.1	11.5	5.7	9.8
	Other carrying/lifting things	12.1	7.7	5.7	8.5
	Clapping	22.9	0.0	1.9	8.3
Locomotion/Position	Standing/upright	94.3	61.5	86.8	80.9
	Walking	66.4	96.2	83.0	81.9
	Sitting/seated	27.1	30.8	26.4	28.1
Matching Clothing		11.4	7.7	11.3	10.1
# of Observer Records		140	26	53	

The *most frequent collective action* reported overall and at all three protest event locations was collective *placarding/bannering*. While this peaked during the rally (reported in 97.9% of samples), it diminished only slightly during the

---

8   Notwithstanding the label, "March for Life," these demonstrators walked to their destination, i.e. they did not march "in step" as do military units or marching bands.

march and at the destination site. Throughout the entire protest event, many demonstrators raised their placards and banners high.[9]

Standing/upright (80.9%) and *walking* (81.9%) were the second and third most frequent forms of collective action reported by our observers. Not surprisingly, standing was more common at the rally (94.3%) and walking at the march (96.2%), while the forms had similar frequency levels at the destination.

The fourth most frequent form of collective action reported by our observers was collective or interactive voicing in the form of *conversations*; this was the case overall (61.1%) and at each of the protest venues (61.4%; 65.4% and 56.6%). We know from other research (McPhail 1994b) that conversation clusters typically involve from two to five or six persons. Thus, note here that the sixth and seventh most frequent forms of collective action overall reported by our observers involved (stationary) *conversation clusters* (reported in 52.7% of samples) and *pedestrian clusters* (reported in 43.1% of samples).

Other research (Aveni 1977; McPhail and Miller 1973; Clelland et al. 1974) suggests these are companion clusters of two to five members who assemble together, remain together throughout the duration of the protest event, and then disperse together. They intermittently participate in more inclusive forms of collective action (monitoring, chanting, cheering, singing, praying, clapping) and acting alone or interacting with their companions, e.g. engaging in conversation. These companion clusters are the most common and in our judgment the smallest but most fundamental units of social organization in all temporary gatherings. While our observers report that clusters were very much in evidence during the rally as well as at the destination site, they diminished in visibility during the march itself when a large proportion of the demonstrators were proceeding shoulder to shoulder; clusters, if observed and reported during this phase of the protest event, were likely to have been among the demonstrators standing along the march route.

The fifth most frequent overall form of collective action was *monitoring* (56.7%), which reached its peak at the initial rally (86.4%) when demonstrators were standing and facing the platform from which they were addressed by a series of rally speakers.[10] This dropped dramatically during the march and there indicates demonstrators standing along the route facing in the direction of the procession in the street; this increased slightly at the destination site.

---

9   Many placards were mass-produced statements of opposition to abortion or images of aborted fetuses; others were hand-made and expressed a variety of anti-abortion or pro-life sentiments. Banners identified their bearers as members of delegations from pro-life chapters, or parochial schools or churches in various eastern U.S. cities.

10 These included event organizers, some clergy, and many newly elected Republican congressmen and congresswomen who vowed to vote pro-life throughout their tenure.

Under the heading of facing, note that facing in a common direction as a function of *inclusive collective locomotion* was not frequently observed during the rally; however, it increased dramatically during the march because that is what the majority of demonstrators were doing.[11] This remained comparatively high at the destination because most of the demonstrators continued their "march" into the destination area before dispersing.

Under the heading of voicing, note that *chanting* is virtually absent during the rally but is reported by as many as one-third of the observers during the march and destination segments of this protest event. Conversely, under the heading of manipulation, *clapping* is reported by one-fifth of the observers during the rally but is virtually absent during the march and at the destination.

Several manipulation categories warrant comment. *Embracing/clasping* includes linking arms and holding hands; it was observed and reported in comparable frequencies at all locations. *Carrying/dragging a person* is reported with comparable frequencies at the rally and march sites and typically indicates adults lifting and carrying infants and children throughout the rally and march. *Other carrying/lifting things* refers to any inanimate object other than a placard or banner. The most frequent object reported by our observers was some piece of audio-visual equipment (e.g. camera, video camera, microphone). *Leafleting* was a frequently reported activity at the rally site and along the march route.

Demonstrator Participation in Collective Action

Collective action varies by form, by complexity, by substantive content, as well as by direction, frequency, tempo and velocity. Perhaps most importantly for this discussion, it varies by the proportion of the total gathering participating in any particular sequence of collective action. Mutually inclusive collective action is rare and this fact was once again confirmed in the records yielded by the systematic sampling of the protest event under examination.

Mutually Inclusive Collective Action. Of the forty-seven activities observers could have recorded, mutually inclusive participation by all demonstrators in an area was highly unlikely for twenty-one of those actions (e.g. speech making, restraining another person, leafleting). We gave careful scrutiny to observers' records to see if any of them reported any instances of participation by all the demonstrators in their areas in any of the remaining twenty-six actions. The frequency of recorded instances at each site was divided by the product of the

---

11   The few occasions of inclusive locomotion reported at the rally site were in all
      likelihood delegations of demonstrators moving together from the large buses in which
      they arrived into the rally venue itself, or in some instances moving together at the end
      of the rally to take positions within the line of "march" to the Supreme Court.

number of observation records at each site times the twenty-six actions in which mutually inclusive participation was possible (see Table 4).

Table 4: Demonstrator Participation in Unanimous Collective Actions by Site

Proportion participating	Rally (f)	March (f)	Destination voicing (f)
50–74%	49	19	19
75–99%	259	44	51
100%	83	14	137
# of observer records	140	26	53
# of possible actions	26	26	26
Potential collective actions	3640	676	1378
Inclusive collective actions	Rally %	March %	Destination %
Unanimous	.013	.028	.014
Three-quarters or more	.085	.093	.051
One-half or more	.107	.114	.099

Mutually inclusive collective action was rare. Slightly less than 3% (0.028) was reported by observers along the march route. Considerably less unanimous participation was reported by observers at the rally and destination sites.[12] Thinking that perhaps unanimous participation was too exacting a standard, we reduced the cut-off point to participation by three-quarters or more of the demonstrators. This lesser standard increased collective participation to near 9% at both rally and march sites and to 5% at the destination site. When we dropped the cut-off point to one-half or more of the demonstrators, collective participation increases to 10% or more at all three sites.

This is a further illustration of our earlier reminder of the "illusion of unanimity" which frequently surrounds assumptions and discussions of "protest events." They are neither homogeneous, continuous nor mutually inclusive phenomena; to the contrary, they are variegated and diversified.

Extent of Demonstrator Participation in Collective Action. In Table 5 we have summarized the extent of demonstrator participation in collective actions

---

12   Mutually inclusive actions on at least one occasion at all sites were standing and walking; at two sites, monitoring; and, at one site, inclusive collective locomotion, pedestrian clusters, singing, conversing and sitting. Collective actions by three-quarters of the demonstrators on at least one occasion at all sites were monitoring, inclusive collective locomotion, conversation clusters, conversing, placarding, standing and walking; at two sites, disparate pedestrian clusters and chanting; at one site, arcs, cheering, pledging, clapping, sitting and marching. Collective actions by half the demonstrators on at least one occasion at all sites were monitoring, chanting, conversing and placarding; at two sites, monitoring, inclusive collective locomotion, conversation clusters, disparate pedestrian clusters, chanting, singing, praying, standing and walking; and, at one site, arcs, cheering, shouting, clapping and marching.

across the entire protest event and at each of the component sites making up that event. We calculated the mean estimated proportion of demonstrators part-icipating in collective action (ranging from "0" for no collective action at all to "5" for unanimous participation) at each site and over the course of the overall protest event.

Table 5:   The Frequency of Collective Actions: Mean Values of Estimates of the Proportion of Actors in Collective Action by Protest Site

Estimated proportion	Value
None or 1 actor	0
> 2 actors but <24%	1
> 25% but < 49%	2
> 50% but < 74%	3
> 75% but < 99%	4
100%	5

Elementary forms of collective action		Rally site	March route	Destination site	Protest event
Facing	Same-f monitoring	3.13	0.54	1.09	1.59
	Same-f inclusive locomotion	0.29	3.39	1.23	1.63
	Conversation clusters	0.99	0.31	1.43	0.91
	Disparate pedestrian clusters	0.57	0.65	1.00	0.74
	Arcs	0.13	0.00	0.19	0.11
	Rings	0.08	0.00	0.21	0.10
	Queues	0.05	0.00	0.00	0.02
Voicing	Conversation	1.36	1.19	1.23	1.26
	Chanting	0.04	0.62	0.70	0.45
	Cheering	0.71	0.04	0.15	0.30
	Singing	0.13	0.27	0.11	0.17
	Praying	0.00	0.12	0.30	0.14
	Shouting	0.01	0.00	0.23	0.08
	Pledging/reciting	0.00	0.00	0.17	0.06
Manipulation	Placarding/bannering	2.51	2.46	1.57	2.18
	Clapping	0.50	0.00	0.02	0.17
	Embracing/clasping person	0.07	0.23	0.15	0.15
	Leafleting	0.13	0.12	0.06	0.10
	Other carrying/lifting things	0.14	0.08	0.06	0.09
	Carrying/dragging person	0.12	0.08	0.02	0.07
	Other manipulating things	0.03	0.08	0.02	0.04
Locomotion/Position	Standing/upright	3.76	1.58	2.74	2.69
	Walking	1.11	4.08	2.26	2.48
	Sitting/seated	0.31	0.31	0.34	0.32
# Observations		140	26	53	

The actions in which the greatest amount of demonstrator participation occurred included the collective locomotion form of walking during the "march" phase of the demonstration (mean = 4.08) and the concurrent activity of facing in a common direction as a function of inclusive locomotion (mean = 3.39). Similarly, the body position of standing/upright was highest during the rally (mean = 3.76) along with the concurrent collective facing activity of monitoring in the direction of the rally platform (mean = 3.13). Whereas each of the preceding activities varied according to demonstration site, the collective manipulation activity of placarding/bannering remained relatively constant throughout the entire protest event (mean = 2.18), although it was highest during the rally (mean = 2.51), declined slightly during the march (mean = 2.46) and then fell to a low (mean = 1.57) during the destination phase.

Conversation was also consistent overall (mean = 1.26) and at each of the three demonstrations sites (means = 1.36, 1.19 and 1.23, respectively), although at a lower level than the other collective activities just considered. Again, this activity complements the collective facing in conversation clusters at the three sites (means = 0.99, 0.31 and 1.43, respectively).

During the rally phase, cheering (mean = 0.71) and clapping (mean = 0.50) are respectably high, and chanting increases slightly during the march phase (mean = 0.62) and destination phase (mean = 0.70).

One final table provides yet another picture of the patchwork variation in collective action across the spatial distribution and temporal duration of one phase of a protest event: the opening rally. Eighty-six percent of our observer records reported demonstrators engaged in collective monitoring during the rally. Other than standing or walking, the next to the highest extent of collective action was facing in the direction of the platform during the rally (mean = 3.13). But this too varied in space and time. Table 6 provides a multivariate representation of this variation.

The first variable is what we call "depth" and refers to three swaths cutting across the width of the rally: the front cross-section (nearest the platform); the middle cross-section; and the back cross-section. The means for collective monitoring for those cross-sections were, respectively, front (3.38), middle (3.38) and back (2.53).[13]

The second spatial variable - centrality - is orthogonal to the first. The section directly in front of the rally platform was designated "the center"; the two adjoining sections, combined here, were designated "the margins"; the next

---

13　An analysis of variance was performed on the dependent variable proportion of demonstrators engaging in facing with three independent variables: depth, centrality and time. Depth and time were statistically significant at a .001 level. Centrality was statistically significant at a .10 level.

two adjoining sections, also combined, were designated "the fringes." The means for collective monitoring for those areas were, respectively, center (2.83), margins (3.31) and fringes (3.00).

Table 6:   Collective Facing as a Function of Onlooking, by Location and Time within a Rally Gathering

Depth*	Centrality			Time*
	center	margins	fringes	
front	1.50	2.75	0.00	first half hour
	4.00	4.50	3.75	second half hour
	4.00	4.00	4.00	third half hour
	4.00	4.00	4.00	fourth half hour
middle	1.00	2.00	2.00	first half hour
	2.00	4.25	2.75	second half hour
	4.00	4.50	4.00	third half hour
	4.00	4.75	4.00	fourth half hour
back	0.50	0.75	0.50	first half hour
	2.50	2.75	3.00	second half hour
	3.50	2.75	4.00	third half hour
	3.00	2.75	4.00	fourth half hour
Overall mean = 3.09				
Depth means: front = 3.38; middle = 3.38; back = 2.53				
Centrality means: center = 2.83; margins = 3.31; fringes = 3.00				
Time means: 1st half hour = 1.27; 2nd = 3.37; 3rd = 3.87; 4th = 3.87				
0 = none or 1 actor; 1 = ≥ 2 but <25%; 2 = 25–49%; 3 = 50–74%; 4 = 75–99%; 5 = 100%				
* Independent variable is significant at .001 level.				

The most dramatic differences in Table 6 involve variations across time. Our fifteen-minute intervals between observation samples were pooled into half hour periods. The means for monitoring across time were: first half hour (1.27), second half hour (3.37), third half hour (3.87) and fourth half hour (3.87). The significant differences are evident in the distribution of bold means in the table. The first half hour of observations covers the period of time preceding the start of rally; the majority of demonstrators are still standing and milling in clusters within the rally venue but occasionally facing in the direction of the platform where a musical group is providing pre-rally entertainment. The rally is fully underway in the next three half hour periods and this is evident in the front and middle cross-sections (depth). The back cross-section is only sparsely filled with demonstrators during the first two time sections and unevenly filled during the final two time sections, at which points collective facing increases.

In sum, the extent of participation in collective action is a variable, not a constant. The most characteristic feature of the sequence of demonstration gatherings making up this protest event, like the many we have observed less systematically in the past, is alternation between and variation within individual and collective actions across time and space.[14]

Media Records of Collective Action

The primary way that most citizens and most scholars learn about protest events is through the mass media. But, as noted at the outset of this paper, the media report only a small fraction of all the protest events which are held. Of those events the media do select, they report "a small selection of the manifold detail of such a complex event, and ... may, in fact, distort the details [they do] report" (McCarthy, McPhail, Smith and Crishock 1995: 1). While permit records are invaluable for answering questions regarding selection bias and some regarding description bias (ibid.; see also their contribution to this volume), they do not contain the detail to address the question of media description bias in reporting the collective actions which make up protest events. The collective action data generated with the criteria and procedures described in this paper can be used to conduct such an investigation.

The discussion which follows is based upon network news coverage of the January 23, 1995 March for Life and the related anniversary of Roe vs. Wade, as well as extended video coverage of the rally which opening the 1995 protest event by C-SPAN, a public affairs channel. While we read newspaper stories from a number of metropolitan papers, this account is based on those from _The Washington Post_, _The Washington Times_, _The New York Times_ and _U.S.A. Today_. The network television news story visuals were coded using the same system our coders used on site. The television audio track and the newspaper stories and photographs were also examined for mention of collective action. Here we report three findings. First, a small proportion of the coverage was devoted to describing collective action in the March for Life protest event. Second, those elementary forms which were reported by the media were also coded by our observers. Third, those forms which we found most prevalent at the demonstration were reported by the media. We treat each of these findings for television and then for newspaper reports.

---

14   While the primary objective in this chapter is one of describing collective actions in protest events, the alternating and varied individual and collective actions that make up any protest gathering present a formidable challenge to existing explanations of human behavior. The challenge of developing an alternative explanation is one to which we have given considerable attention elsewhere (McPhail 1991, 1994a, 1994b; McPhail and Wohlstein 1986; McPhail and Tucker 1990; McPhail, Powers and Tucker 1992; Schweingruber 1995, 1996).

Television News. All three networks ran stories on January 23 about the March for Life. Additionally, CBS and NBC ran stories on January 22, the actual anniversary of the Roe vs. Wade decision.[15] These stories totaled just over five minutes with 57 shots. For approximately two minutes of this time (33 shots) visuals of demonstrations were on-screen, but March for Life visuals accounted for only 34 seconds and nine shots. The information for each of the five stories is summarized in Table 7.

Table 7:   Length in Time (and Shots) of Television Stories Regarding the Roe vs. Wade Anniversary, the Visuals of any Demonstration and Visuals of the March for Life

Network and date		Entire story		All demos		March for Life	
CBS	1/22/95	1:55	(23)	0:44	(15)	0:00	(0)
NBC	1/22/95	0:33	(5)	0:18	(4)	0:00	(0)
ABC	1/23/95	1:58	(18)	0:42	(6)	0:12	(1)
CBS	1/23/95	0:19	(6)	0:11	(4)	0:11	(4)
NBC	1/23/95	0:17	(5)	0:11	(4)	0:11	(4)
Total		5:02	(57)	2:04	(33)	0:34	(9)

Two of the networks, CBS and NBC, constructed their March for Life stories similarly: An anchor introduced the story from the studio and continued a voice-over during four shots of people marching, each sequence of shots lasting a total of 11 seconds. The major difference was the camera position: CBS's is high above the march, with one shot showing easily over a thousand demonstrators and the others showing at least a hundred each. NBC's camera was at ground-level and showed fewer demonstrators. One shot focused on two signs, while another showed little more than a man carrying a crucifix.

Both CBS and NBC had run abortion-related stories on January 22, which were longer than their January 23 stories. NBC's story (5 shots, 0:33) included a pro-choice march-rally in Washington, D.C. (2 shots, 0:07) and a pro-life motorcade (2 shots, 0:11). CBS's story (23 shots, 1:55) included a pro-life vigil outside a church attended by President Bill Clinton (9 shots, 0:28), an unidentified pro-life vigil (2 shots, 0:03), a National Organization of Women (NOW) pro-choice march in Boston (2 shots, 0:06) and the "Deadly Dozen" press conference, in which the American Coalition of Life Activists released a list of abortionists (2 shots, 0:07).

---

15   Over the 20 plus years of the annual March for Life, the principal organizer has insisted on holding the protest event on the anniversary of the Roe vs. Wade decision (January 22) unless that date falls on a Sunday; when this occurs, as it did in 1995, the demonstration is held on the following day (cf. McPhail and Husting 1994).

ABC combined coverage of the two days' events into one January 23 story, which contained just one ten second long shot of marching March for Life demonstrators. The story focused on the "Deadly Dozen" list and reported that some of the people responsible for it believed that "killing of abortion doctors [is] justifiable homicide." ABC's story included thirty seconds (5 shots) of a vigil outside the house of one of the targeted abortionists.

From the four CBS shots, three elementary forms are visible, but they are the three forms - inclusive locomotion, walking and placard/bannering - which were engaged in by the highest proportions of demonstrators during the march. The NBC shots show the same three forms, but others - gesturing and carrying other things (crucifix and bouquet) - are also visible. ABC's shot shows the same three major forms as well as chanting. All of these forms were coded.

While the networks' March for Life visuals were entirely of the march portion of the demonstration, C-SPAN, which devoted far more time to the event than any of the networks, broadcast the rally. C-SPAN focused on the speeches in its one hour, 22 minute long coverage. For the majority of the coverage the only individuals visible were on the stage. The audience was visible for approximately 11.5 minutes. The coverage began and ended with wide shots showing the stage and audience. During the speeches, the camera zoomed out 12 times to show audience members and sometimes panned from side to side. The longest the audience was on-camera continuously was just over two minutes. When the audience is visible, peoples' backs are to the television viewer. However, several forms of collective action are visible. First, from an overhead vantage point, the orientation of the demonstrators forms a wide and shallow arc around the main stage. (Our observers at ground level, who saw smaller sections of this arc, coded it as monitoring.) However, demonstrators forming conversation clusters or walking are also visible. Demonstrators can also be seen carrying placards, banners and crosses, and sometimes waving them. The C-SPAN coverage does contain an unedited sound track of the rally. The most audible voicing is cheering, although one speaker led the demonstrators in chants. Clapping is also sometimes audible. During the pledge of allegiance, though, whatever verbal pledging the audience did was drowned out by the leader. Again, these forms were all coded by our observers and the most frequent forms they coded were visible on C-SPAN.

Newspaper coverage. The newspaper coverage shows a similar pattern to the television coverage. Minimal descriptions of individual and collective actions are present in newspaper stories covering the March for Life but are not their largest elements. The stories may also include descriptions of speech content, reporting on the political issue of abortion and quotes from demonstrators and politicians. They may also report on other demonstrations, including those by more "radical" pro-life groups and by pro-choice groups.

The collective action which is reported in the media was also recorded by our observers. *The New York Times'* account of the March for Life mentions three elementary forms (speech making, singing and placarding), *The Washington Post* four (marching, chanting, placard/bannering and singing), *USA Today* three (praying, singing and marching) and *The Washington Times* four (placard/ bannering, other carrying things [wooden crosses], carrying a person and marching). Other forms could be inferred from the newspapers' mention of gathering forms - rally and march.

Additional collective action data can be gleaned from newspaper pictures. Two types of forms occur in almost every picture: (1) some form of facing in the same or convergent directions and (2) placarding. We believe that these two elements are chosen by news photographers because they convey that many people acted together for a cause, which is pictured on the placard.

Summary and Implications

The extensive protest event research done in the last two decades has drawn almost exclusively on newspaper archives as a data source. Both newspapers and television news cannot and do not cover all protest events; there is evidence of a bias in the ones they select. Those which address or illustrate issues already the focus of media attention are more likely to receive attention than those that do not, and, very large, if infrequent, protest events ($\geq$ 100,000) are far more likely to be covered than small events which are in fact far more frequent.

To date there has been no method for ascertaining whether, first, media descriptions of large events accurately represent the actors and actions of which those events are composed, and, second, if there are any differences between large and small protest events beyond their actual size.

This chapter describes and illustrates a method for addressing the first of these problems and one which is capable of addressing the second. Because protest events are complex but nested phenomena, a systematic record of the collective actions of which demonstration gatherings are composed provides one means of unpacking those events. A taxonomy of elementary forms of collective action, inductively generated from the observation of hundreds of gatherings, was used to develop a training primer and a field observation/ recording form (see the Appendix). Observers were trained and deployed to record two large protest events; the event reported here involved an initial rally site, a procession route, and a termination/dispersal site.

Observers took one minute observation samples every 15 minutes of all the collective action by various categories of actors taking place in their assigned areas of responsibility. This paper reports the actions of demonstrators, the most frequent actor category observed during this event. The most frequent category of collective action reported throughout the event was placarding/bannering, walking, standing and conversations, followed by collective monitoring (particularly at the rally site), and both (stationary) conversation clusters and pedestrian clusters. The extent of demonstrator participation was quite mixed. There were few instances of mutually inclusive or "unanimous" collective action. When it occurred it was relatively simple, e.g. collective monitoring or "facing" in the direction of the platform during the rally, or collective inclusive locomotion during the course of the march. Even so, it was seldom that as many as one-half of the demonstrators were engaged in any form of collective action during any one minute observation sample.

There is clear evidence that collective action varies across the spatial distribution and temporal duration of protest gatherings, lending further credence to the notion that they are more likely patchwork quilts of alternating and varied individual and collective action than they are uniform blankets of mutually inclusive collective action. The "mean" levels of demonstrator participation in even the most prevalent forms of collective action (e.g. placarding/bannering) were below 50%. Prototypical protest event activities, such as chanting, cheering and singing, fell well below 25%. We found particularly noteworthy the recurring reports of conversation and pedestrian clusters which, based on other research, we take as evidence of the companion clusters (family, friends and acquaintances) that assemble together, remain together throughout protest events and then disperse together, in all likelihood the most elementary unit of social organization in protest events. In short, protest events are made up of collective actions but not continuous or mutually inclusive collective action. Researchers need to remain sensitive to the "illusion of unanimity" as they design their research and interpret their results.

Nonetheless, the results of this systematic observation of one protest event suggest that the collective actions reported by the media are also regularly reported by trained observers, and that media reports include the collective actions in which demonstrators most frequently engage. The media do not look for, note or report all the collective actions in which demonstrators engage, nor are they sensitive to the social organization composition of protest events; however, this may well be a function of social science's failure to educate media workers about the complex nature of protest events. That failure, in turn, may be due to social scientists' "lack [of] basic information in the field of social protest" (Rucht and Ohlemacher 1992: 91-92). The method we have described and illustrated here may provide one tool for altering this information base and increasing both social science knowledge and media reporting of a phenomena in which we both have a significant interest.

Appendix: The Code Sheet

initials:	coder #:		location:					time:

		Dem	O/P	Pol.	Med	Cdem	Other
Number of actors visible in category (A-J)							
FACING	*f* monitoring						
same	queuing						
direction	incl. collect. loco.						
	disp. ped. cluster(s)						
converging	convrs. cluster(s)						
directions	arc(s)						
	ring(s)						
other	other						
VOICING	cheering						
vocalization	booing						
	ooh/ohh/ahhing						
	other						
verbalization	chanting						
	singing						
	shouting						
	praying						
	pledge/reciting						
	conversing						
	speech making						
	other						
MANIPULATING gestures	gesturing						
things carry/lifting	placard/banner						
	AV equipment						
	other						
passing	leafleting						
	exchanging						
	other						
striking	striking things						
throwing	throwing						
push/pulling	pushing/pulling						
other	other						
another person	embrace/clasping						
	restraining						
	carrying/dragging						
	striking person						
	other						
self	clapping						
	snapping						
	other						

# of actors key
A = 1
B = 2 to 5
C = 6 to 10
D = 11 to 25
E = 26 to 50
F = 51 to 100
G = 101 to 250
H = 251 to 500
I = 501 to 1000
J = over 1000

Est. # Total Actors
(circle one)

A B C D E
F G H I J

Density (circle one)
Free passage
Must slow/turn
"Excuse me"
Difficult movement

Proportion of
Actors
Key
a = 1 person
b = ≥ 2 people & < 20%
c = ≥ 20% & < 40%
d = ≥ 40% & < 60%
e = ≥ 60% & < 80%
f = ≥ 80% & < 100%
g = 100%

Confidence Scale
(circle one)

0 1 2 3 4 5 6
low medium high

BODY POSITION	standing/upright									Record details of the
vertical	sitting/seated									following on back
position or	kneeling/knelt									1. "Other" categories
motion	lying/prone									2. Vehicular motion
	other									3. Violence
horizontal	walking									4. Clothing in common
motion	marching									5. Dramaturgy
	jogging/running									6. Civil Disobedience
	dancing									7. Other noteworthy
	vehicular motion									actions occurring
	other									during your coding
VIOLENCE	vs. persons									interval
	vs. property									8. Any noteworthy
CLOTHING	clothing									actions which occurred

between coding intervals (specify as such)

References

Aveni, A. 1977. "The Not-So-Lonely Crowd: Friendship Groups in Collective Behavior." *Sociometry* 40: 96-99.

Berk, R. 1974. "A Gaming Approach to Crowd Behavior." *American Sociological Review* 39: 355-373.

Blumer, H. 1957. "Collective Behavior." Pp. 127-158 in *Review of Sociology*, ed. J. B. Gittler. New York: Wiley.

Clelland, D., T. Hood, C. M. Lipsey and R. Wimberly. 1974. "In the Company of the Converted: Characteristics of a Billy Graham Crusade Audience." *Sociological Analysis* 35: 45-56.

Della Porta, D. 1995. *Social Movements, Political Violence and the State.* Cambridge: Cambridge University Press.

Diani, M. and R. Eyerman, eds. 1992. *Studying Collective Action.* London: Sage.

Everett, K. 1992. "Changes in The Social Movement Sector, 1961-1983: Differentiation of Interests and Structural Transformation of Protest Activity." *Social Forces* 70: 957-976.

Fillieule, O. 1996. "Police Records and the National Press in France: Issues in the Methodology of Data Collections from Newspapers." EUI Working Paper RSC No. 96/25. European University Institute. Florence, Italy.

Fisher, C. 1972. "Observing a Crowd: The Structure and Description of Protest Demonstrations." Pp. 187-211 in *Research on Deviance*, ed. J. D. Douglas. New York: Random House.

Franzoni, R. 1990. "Strategies for the Prevention, Detection and Correction of Measurement Error in Data Collected from Textual Sources." *Sociological Methods and Research* 18: 442-472.

Jenkins, C. and C. Perrow. 1977. "Insurgency of the Powerless: Farmworker Movements (1946-1972)." *American Sociological Review* 42: 249-268.

Johnson, N. 1987. "Panic and the Breakdown of Social Order: Popular Myth, Social Theory, Empirical Evidence." *Sociological Focus* 20: 171-183.

Johnson, N., D. Choate and W. Bunis. 1984. "Attendance at a Billy Graham Crusade: A Resource Mobilization Approach." *Sociological Analysis* 45: 383-392.

Klandermans, B. and D. Oegema. 1987. "Potentials, Networks, Motivations, and Barriers: Steps Towards Participation in Social Movements." *American Sociological Review* 52: 519-531.

Koopmans, R. 1993. "Dynamics of Protest Waves: West Germany, 1965-1989." *American Sociological Review* 58: 637-658.

Kriesi, H., R. Koopmans, J. W. Duyvendak and M. G. Giugni. 1995. *New Social Movements in Western Europe: A Comparative Perspective.* Minneapolis and St. Paul: University of Minnesota Press.

Lofland, J. 1981. "Collective Behavior: The Elementary Forms." Pp. 411-446 in *Social Psychology: Sociological Perspectives*, ed. M. Rosenberg and R. H Turner. New York: Basic Books.

Lofland, J. 1985. *Protest: Studies of Collective Behavior and Social Movements.* New Brunswick, N.J.: Transaction Books.

McAdam, D. 1982. *Political Process and the Development of Black Insurgency.* Chicago: University of Chicago Press.

MacCannell, D. 1973. "Nonviolent Action as Theater." *Nonviolent Action Research Project Monograph No. 10.* Haverford College Center for Nonviolent Conflict Resolution. Haverford, Penn.

McCarthy, J., C. McPhail and J. Smith. 1996. "Images of Protest: Estimating Dimensions of Selection Bias in Media Coverage of Washington Demonstrations, 1982 and 1991." *American Sociological Review* 61: 478-499.

McCarthy, J., C. McPhail, J. Smith and L. Crishock. 1995. "Elements of Description Bias: Electronic and Print Media Representations of Washington, D.C. Demonstrations, 1982." Paper presented to the Conference on Protest Event Analysis. Social Science Research Center Berlin (Wissenschaftszentrum Berlin für Sozialforschung, WZB). Berlin, Germany. June 12-14.

McPhail, C. 1968. "Training for Collective Behavior Sequence Recording." Research proposal funded by the National Institute of Mental Health. Department of Sociology, University of South Carolina at Columbia.

McPhail, C. 1972. "Theoretical and Methodological Strategies for the Study of Crowd Behavior." Paper presented at the annual meeting, American Sociological Association, New Orleans, La.

McPhail, C. 1991. *The Myth of the Madding Crowd.* New York: Aldine de Gruyter.

McPhail, C. 1994a. "The Dark Side of Purpose: Individual and Collective Violence." *The Sociological Quarterly* 35: 1-32.

McPhail, C. 1994b. "Social Behavior in Public Places: From Clusters to Arcs and Rings." Pp. 35-57 in *The Community of The Streets*, ed. S. Cahill and L. Lofland. Greenwich, Conn.: JAI Press.

McPhail, C. 1994c. "A Perception Control Theory of Individual and Collective Action: Problems, Resolutions and Evidence." Invited Presentation to the Workshop on Theoretical Analysis, University of Iowa. Iowa City. November.

McPhail, C. and V. Husting. 1994. "Periodic Demonstrations: The Washington, D.C. 'March for Life,' January 22, 1974-1993." Paper presented at the annual meeting of the Midwest Sociological Society. St. Louis. March.

McPhail, C. and D. L. Miller. 1973. "The Assembling Process: A Theoretical and Empirical Examination." *American Sociological Review* 38: 721-735.

McPhail, C. and R. G. Pickens. 1981. "Variation in Sport Spectator Behavior: The Illusion of Unanimity." Paper presented at the annual meeting, American Sociological Association. Boston, Mass.

McPhail, C., W. T. Powers and C. W. Tucker. 1992. "Simulating Individual and Collective Action in Temporary Gatherings." *Social Science Computer Review* 10 (1): 1-28.

McPhail, C. and D. Schweingruber. 1995. *The Collective Action Observation Primer.* Urbana, Ill.: Department of Sociology. University of Illinois at Urbana-Champaign.

McPhail, C. and C. W. Tucker. 1990. "Purposive Collective Action." *American Behavioral Scientist* 34: 81-94.

McPhail, C. and R. T. Wohlstein. 1982. "A Film Methodology for the Study of Pedestrian Behavior." *Sociological Methodology and Research* 10: 347-375.

McPhail, C. and R. T. Wohlstein. 1983. "Individual and Collective Behavior within Gatherings, Demonstrations, and Riots." *Annual Review of Sociology* 9: 579-600.

McPhail, C. and R. T. Wohlstein. 1986. "Collective Locomotion as Collective Behavior." *American Sociological Review* 51 (August): 447-463.

Marx, G. and J. Woods. 1975. "Strands of Theory and Research in Collective Behavior." *Annual Review of Sociology* 1: 363-428.

Milgram, S. and H. Toch. 1968. "Collective Behavior: Crowds and Social Movements." Pp. 507-610 in *Handbook of Social Psychology,* Vol. 4 (2nd Edition), ed. G. Lindzey and E. Aronson. Reading, Mass.: Addison-Wesley.

Olzak, S. 1989. "Analysis of Events in the Study of Collective Action." *Annual Review of Sociology* 15: 119-141.

Olzak, S. 1992. *The Dynamics of Ethnic Competition and Conflict.* Stanford: Stanford University Press.

Quarantelli, E. L. and J. Hundley. 1969. "A Test of Some Propositions about Crowd Formation and Behavior." Pp. 538-554 in *Readings in Collective Behavior,* ed. R. R. Evans. Chicago: Rand-McNally.

Rucht, D., ed. 1991. *Research on Social Movements: The State of the Art in Western Europe and the USA.* Boulder, Colo.: Westview.

Rucht, D. and T. Ohlemacher. 1992. "Protest Event Data: Collection, Uses and Perspectives." Pp. 76-106 in *Studying Collective Action,* ed. M. Diani and R. Eyerman. London: Sage.

Rudé, G. 1967. *The Crowd in History.* New York: Wiley.

Schweingruber, D. 1995. "A Computer Simulation of a Sociological Experiment." *Social Science Computer Review* 13 (3): 351-359.

Schweingruber, D. 1996. "Managing Demonstrations: Social Science Theory and Police Practice." Paper presented at the annual meeting of the Midwest Sociological Society, Chicago.

Schweingruber, D. and C. McPhail. 1995. "A Methodology for Coding Videotape and Field Observations of Collective Action." Paper presented at the annual meeting of the American Sociological Association, Washington, D.C., August 20.

Shorter, E. and C. Tilly. 1974. *Strikes in France, 1830-1968.* Cambridge: Cambridge University Press.

Sime, J. D. 1980. "The Concept of Panic." Pp. 63-82 in *Fires and Human Behavior*, ed. D. Canter. N.Y.: John Wiley.

Tarrow, S. 1989. *Democracy and Disorder: Protest and Politics in Italy 1965-1975.* Oxford: Clarendon Press.

Tilly, C. 1983. "Speaking Your Mind Without Elections, Surveys or Social Movements." *Public Opinion Quarterly* 47: 461-478.

Tilly, C. 1986. *The Contentious French.* Cambridge: Harvard University Press.

Tilly, C. 1993. "Social Movements as Historically Specific Clusters of Political Performances." *Berkeley Journal of Sociology* 38: 1-30.

Tilly, C. 1995. *Popular Contention in Great Britain, 1758-1834.* Cambridge: Harvard University Press.

Tilly, C., L. Tilly and R. Tilly. 1975. *The Rebellious Century: 1830-1930.* Cambridge: Harvard University Press.

Turner, R. 1964. "Collective Behavior." In *Handbook of Modern Sociology*, ed. R. E. L. Faris. Chicago: Rand-McNally.

Wohlstein, R. T. and C. McPhail. 1979. "Judging the Presence and Extent of Collective Behavior: A Theory and Method for Producing and Analyzing Film Records." *Social Psychology Quarterly* 42: 76-81.3

III.

Applications:
Protest in Different Contexts

"Plus ça change, moins ça change." Demonstrations in France During the Nineteen-Eighties

Olivier Fillieule

Introduction

Over the past two decades quantitative studies have become increasingly important in the works of historians and political scientists as a systematic source of historical data. Most empirical studies in the field analyze conflict events collected within spatial and temporal units and attempt to isolate longitudinal trends of data, using newspaper accounts as sources.[1]

However, at the same time, literature has also developed which attempts to demonstrate bias in such sources, and most scholars recognize that newspapers neither fully catalogue nor accurately describe conflict events (Dantzger 1975; Snyder and Kelly 1977; Glasgow Media Group 1976, 1980; Kielbowicz and Scherer 1986; Franzosi 1987; Rucht and Ohlemacher 1992). To date, as the introduction to this volume puts it, the extent and exact nature of inaccuracies in newspapers remain largely unknown.

One way to avoid these inaccuracies is to rely on more exhaustive sources. In this respect, in France the archives of the national police contain useful material on protest events.[2] This material served as the basis for my research on changes in forms of political activities in France during the eighties. From these archives, I have compiled a data base of almost 5,000 protest events occurring between 1979 and 1989 in the cities of Marseille, Nantes and Paris (Fillieule 1993, 1997; Favre and Fillieule 1994). This number, while considerable, does not represent all of the protest events which took place in France in this period. Based on various press and police sources, I estimate that in this period, for cities with 200,000 or more inhabitants, an average of 10,500 protest events took place per year. In the city of Nantes, for example, there were 1,766 events between 1979 and 1991, which means an average of one event every three and a half days. In Paris, in the same period, there were nearly 1,000 protest events a year, which means an average of three events per day. And starting in the late

---

[1] For a critical review of protest event analysis see Olzak (1989).

[2] That does not mean that police archives are not biased, but only that they are more accurate, cover many more protests, and document them in a systematic way. However, even if we have never found any concrete evidence, one may doubt whether all events are covered by the police.

seventies, the pattern is one of increasing frequency. In other words, the construction of a truly comprehensive data base on protest events has only just begun.[3] Nevertheless, the approximately 5,000 events already recorded permit us to draw certain tentative conclusions.

In this chapter, I hope to demonstrate the usefulness of data bases built on police archives by offering certain insights into the question of the changing forms of protest in contemporary France. I begin by defining what I mean by a protest event. This first step in my analysis is a crucial one upon which all subsequent steps depend.[4] I then discuss briefly some of the methodological advantages of police archives over press data, before dealing with the morphological characteristics and political evolution of protest in France. In that discussion, I will focus on the hypotheses raised by new social movement (NSM) theorists about the supposed changes in contemporary political participation.

Definition and Methodological Problems

The Definition of a Protest Event

The French national police have developed a very broad definition of a protest event. A protest event, for them, includes any type of gathering of people, either in public or private space. Hence, included in the term are events as diverse as soccer matches, rock concerts, May Day parades, religious processions and, from time to time, picket lines. For both practical and theoretical reasons which constraints of space prevent me from going into here, I define a protest event much more narrowly, using the following criteria:

The Number of Participants. I have excluded events involving only one individual. Beyond this, I do not set a minimum on the number of participants, for we cannot say what number of people is required before a protest event can be said to have occurred.[5] The police, whose records I use, paid as much

---

3   All protest events which occurred between 1979 and 1989 in Marseille (the second largest city in France) and Nantes have been fully coded and entered into the data base. Only a portion of Paris events from this period have so far been coded and entered.

4   I do not argue that this definition is superior to others. On the contrary, a plurality of definitions seems inevitable since any given definition is a reflection of the specific question posed and the nature of the materials informing the research.

5   The threshold most commonly used in the literature on social movements is ten. The Lemberg Center for the Study of Violence, however, used a threshold of four people in the 1970s. At the higher end of the scale are Spilermann (1976), whose threshold is

attention to small gatherings as they do to mass demonstrations. Nevertheless, it should be noted that only a minuscule number of events contained in the police records involved less than ten people. In addition, the data base I have constructed from police records is flexible; participant thresholds can be reset should we, in the future, wish to compare our results to those of other researchers whose definitions include higher minimums.

The Expressive Dimension. All protest events have an expressive dimension both for the participants themselves and for their audience, by the public assertion of pre-existing or newly-formed groups, by the presentation of vague or precise demands. This second criterion allows us to eliminate those gatherings of people brought together by something other than a common goal (for example, the people in a market place, the crowd which gathers in Times Square on New Year's Eve to watch the ball drop).

The Political Nature of the Event. This third dimension of the definition is difficult to formulate, but is the most important. Should we count as a protest event the celebration of Joan of Arc in the city of Orléans, with its "folkloric" parades, alongside the annual march of J. M. Le Pen[6] on the same occasion in Paris? Is there an accurate sociological criterion to use in this instance, or should we be guided by the significance that the participants themselves attach to their actions? Things become even more complicated if we consider that many events which, at first glance, appear to be apolitical, may in fact be the sign or expression of a socio-political crisis. Lacking a perfect answer to these questions, I have included here all events characterized by or leading to the expression of demands of a political nature. The political nature of the protest event can be either manifest or latent, i.e. partially or completely unknown to the protagonists.

The Nature of the Organizers. This dimension of the definition is even more difficult to ascertain, since almost all social actors today, including governmental actors, can resort to protest as a strategy. Certain social movements become institutionalized even to the extent of becoming political parties, while certain parties are quite marginal to electoral politics and have less access to institutional arenas than do certain powerful social movement organizations. Moreover, some social movements do not target the state or elites, but rather other groups or movements (for example the anti-racist and anti-Le-Pen movements). Because of this, we need to set aside such distinctions as institutional versus non-institutional groups, elites versus challengers, insiders versus outsiders. In addition, protest actions are often the result of

thirteen, and Tarrow (1989), who sets the minimum at twenty, except for actions involving violence. Finally, Rucht and Ohlemacher (1992) set the threshold at three.

6   J. M. Le Pen is the leader of the Front National, the French extreme-right political party.

political work done by changing configurations of actors; this heterogeneity makes the selection of events by virtue of their organizers even more difficult. Finally, as we all know, despite the legal forms and names attributed to various groups (unions, parties, interest groups, social movement organizations, etc.), the frontiers are constantly shifting depending on circumstances and various interests.[7] In light of these issues, the only events excluded from my data base are those which were clearly initiated by government actors. For example, in June 1989, the local government of a small town in the suburbs of Paris organized a rally in Paris to protest against the problems created by a stone-pit. (Fortunately, there were only seven such government-initiated events among the 5,000 events recorded thus far.)

The Form of the Event. Now I come to the question of whether or not to include the form of an event as a criterion. Scholars have taken just about every position possible on this question. Some studies concentrate on one particular type of action (strikes, violent actions), others focus on all forms of non-institutionalized public action (this is the catch-all approach of Tilly's "contentious gatherings"). Then there is Tarrow's approach - what he calls a middle way - which includes strikes, demonstrations, petitions, rallies and violent action, but excludes protest events which do not involve collective demands directed at other actors (1989). My own definition is not far from Tarrow's, and I include public marches, rallies, occupations, obstructions of public thoroughfares (e.g. barricades), sit-ins and "operation rescue" style actions. Eliminating certain of these modes of expression would be methodologically unwise, since it would prevent us from investigating the relationship between contesting groups and these different forms of action.

More precisely, in any given event, modes of action intermingle and overlap. An event can start as a march and often ends as a rally or a blockade (planned or unplanned). Moreover, in certain cases - for example the anti-war movement during the Gulf War - it often happens that, over a period of several days, action shifts from one mode to another (march, occupation, rally, blockades, etc.). In such cases using an overly-narrow definition forces one to ignore the fact that often many modes of action are practiced during a single event. Moreover, if only one form of action is coded - for instance a march going from point A to

---

7   In France, when considering the way public space has been constructed, one should note that parties, unions and non-profit organizations developed simultaneously, during the Second Empire (1850-1870). It was only later that they were treated by the law as different entities. So, for example, unions and non-profit organizations were assigned a separate legal status at the end of the nineteenth century, 1884 for the former and 1901 for the latter. As a result, during this intermediary period, numerous non-profit organizations adopted the legal status of a union.

point B - one loses the ability to think in terms of repertoires of action. That is why in my data base when an event includes multiple modes of action, it is recorded under up to three such modes.[8]

In conclusion, given that the unit of analysis here is the protest event, I define an event as a distinct action undertaken over a continuous period of time, with no interruption exceeding a day. Hence, the occupation of a building, for example, which continues uninterrupted for several days is entered as one event. On the other hand, if demonstrators protest for two hours every day for several days in front of an embassy, each two-hour protest will be counted as one event. In the latter case, although we may know that the purpose of the embassy demonstration has not changed from day to day, we do not know whether the actors may change. Thus the decision to record such events separately, although to some extent arbitrary, nevertheless helps reduce the problem of uncertainty about actors. Finally, I should note that I do not count strikes as protest events since these do not fulfill certain of the criteria of my definition of such events. I also exclude terrorist acts (bomb attacks, kidnappings, etc.) since they are not systematically tracked by the police records I use. The disadvantage of excluding terrorist acts is that it then becomes impossible to follow the full process of radicalization of some movements. The potential distortion this creates in a study of protest events in France, however, is limited by the fact that very few French social movements have adopted terrorist modes of action, at least since the end of the 1970s. There are basically only two such groups, the Front de Libération national Corse (FLNC) and Action directe.

In one sentence then, I define protest events as follows: An event in which a non-governmental actor occupies a public space (public buildings, streets) in order to make a political demand, to experience in-process benefits, or to celebrate something, which includes the manifest or latent expression of political opinion.

Police Records, Press Data and Methodological Problems

In France, protest events result in the production of substantial police archives.[9] In order to select the most appropriate, a comparative test was conducted on all

---

8   Protest events including only one mode of action are by far the most common. They represent 74% of those in Marseille, 63% in Nantes and 78% in Paris. Rallies and marches are the most commonly used modes of action. Events including three or more modes of action are rare (5 to 10% of the total, depending on the city).

9   There are five different archives: (1) The archives of the Office of Public Security cover protest events in Paris (collected at the Prefecture of Police in Paris). (2) Records

but one of these types of documents over a total period of six months (January to March and June to July 1991) to determine which were the best for my purposes. I conducted the test by analyzing the most important of the non-national French newspapers, *Ouest-France*, which covers Brittany and the Loire region. I draw two conclusions from this accuracy test. First, in cases where events are tracked by the police, both the dates and the location of the event are accurately noted.[10] Second, by far the most complete sources are the archives of each local subdivision of the urban police and, for Paris, those of the Police Department.[11] In Nantes, for example, of the 147 events listed in 1991, 50 are listed in no other source. Hence, I decided to concentrate on these archives, which normally exist in cities with more than 200,000 inhabitants (although there are some exceptions).

The Ministry of the Interior has actually set guidelines detailing the kind of information about events it would like to see recorded in police reports, called *main courantes.*[12] Hence, each *main courante* contains the same type of information with respect to each event: date, location and duration of the event; modes of action; description of the event as it unfolds (these descriptions always include the route taken, mention of any protestors being granted a meeting with the public authorities *(délégations)*, and the public appearance and actions of any public officials); the nature of demands made; the identification of organizing groups; the identification of the people taking part in the event (mostly in terms of their job); and, finally, any possible intervention by the police (arrests, court trials, etc.). This last category of information is particularly

---

concerning events occurring in cities with over 10,000 inhabitants are located at the National Office of City Police and, for each local subdivision, at the urban police headquarters. (3) Records concerning events occurring in small towns (less than 10,000 inhabitants), where the police militia *(la gendarmerie nationale)* are responsible for public order, are concentrated in Paris. (4) Records concerning events which fall under the jurisdiction of the Republican Security Forces (CRS) are stored at their central office in Paris. Most of these documents cover violent protest events. (5) Finally, also at the national level, the archives of the central administration office of the General Intelligence Service of the Ministry of Interior. If we had some access to these sources, we decided not to make use of them because of their lack of reliability (the data we wanted to work on were systematically collected by the police officers themselves, so that it was impossible to check their value).

10   About one hundred events are reported by these different sources. In none of them have we noticed any difference concerning the date, location and identification of demonstrators.

11   These archives, in Paris as well as in the rest of the country are called the *"main courantes."* The *main courante* is a document where all events termed "a police intervention" are recorded.

12   See preceding footnote.

important since it allows one to know, in most cases, under what conditions violence erupts, and whether it is initiated by protestors or the police.[13]

Compared to press data, the main advantage of the *main courante* is that the information reported does not vary, no matter how unimportant the event might be politically and no matter how few participants it had. This allows for a systematic study of small events and means that it is not necessary to exclude a whole category of events due to insufficient information.

In a systematic comparison, I have contrasted the data derived from a sub-sample of my data base with data pulled from our surveys of articles in two newspapers, *Le Monde* and *Libération*, for the six-month period between January and June 1989 (Fillieule 1996). The results of this comparison are striking. First, newspaper accounts report on a very small number of the protest events documented in police sources. *Libération* and *Le Monde* report on only 2% of events, and even if we combine the data from both papers, the total arrived at is only 3% of events. Second, "hard" news is not so well reported, especially as concerns the number of participants and information related to violence (e.g. description of the violent incident, number of people injured or arrested, whether charges were filed, whether protestors were brought to trial, etc.). Noteworthy here is not so much the differences between police records and press records but rather the total lack of systematization involved, both between papers and within each paper. Third, two features of events explain the bias of the majority of press accounts, location (Paris/provinces) and number of participants. *Le Monde* and *Libération*, respectively, report on 6.2% and 11.2% of events occurring in Paris, but both report on only 1% of those occurring in Marseille and on 0% of those occurring in Nantes. This almost total neglect of events outside Paris may be an artifact of the extreme centralization of the French state. Such centralization means that a large majority of the state agencies to which movement actors address their demands are located in Paris. Thus, non-Parisian organizers of protest events, conscious of this fact, attempt whenever possible to demonstrate in Paris. On the other hand, however, this finding should be tempered in part by the fact that the most determinant

---

13 In fact, given that these documents were never meant to be made available to the public or to researchers (they are not deposited in the local or national archives), the temptation to present police activities in an overly favorable light is not always as great as it might seem at first glance. However, one should note that the police generally tend to downplay their errors and use of violence in general. But, due to the internal "war" between the different police corps (CRS/*Gendarmes* and Urban Police), the *main courante* are full of criticism aimed at *gendarme* and CRS action in the field. Because we have also worked with CRS archive material from the 1980s, which is often very critical of the Urban Police, we have acquired a good understanding of the hidden meaning of the *main courantes'* bureaucratic style.

variable is the number of participants, and the average size of events covered by the press is much greater than the average size of all events documented in police records. Fourth, media sensitivity to political issues is an equally important determinant of the likelihood that an event will be covered by the press. It is necessary to distinguish between two cases. First, when an event involves a theme which is, at that moment, already the focus of media attention, its chances of receiving coverage increases. Second, when political events of great importance (such as elections or international events like the Gulf War) occur, there is a reduction in the number of events covered by the press. This dynamic was evident, for example, during the local elections at the end of March 1989 and during the elections for the European Parliament in mid-June 1989. It is tempting to simply conclude that protest events receive less coverage when certain national or international events move to the forefront of the political scene. Things, however, are not quite that simple. I have in fact shown elsewhere that during certain elections or international events, the actual number of protest events which take place diminishes (Favre and Fillieule 1994; Fillieule 1996).

In a similar vein, some have argued that when a protest campaign becomes exceptionally large, the press appears to report almost exclusively on protest events organized by this movement.[14] Here again, however, what in fact happens is that the overall number of actual protest events diminishes.

This finding is extremely important because it shows that the variation in the number of protest events indicated in the data drawn from newspapers sources are perhaps not determined primarily by changes in the actually number of events, but rather by the shifting focus of newspapers on particular protest campaigns. The problem here is that this type of bias is not systematic, but rather varies depending on the public events at the time. One conclusion to draw from this is that any medium or long-term "trends" in numbers of events that might appear in newspaper data may in reality be simple artifacts of media inattention during certain periods. In that respect, our evidence seems to indicate that the temporal and spatial patterns of newspaper reporting do not correspond to real-life patterns. The problems this poses for research are even more serious when the research in question involves cross-national comparisons, since political life (e.g. election cycles) vary from country to country.

---

14   Unfortunately, this does not mean that big protests campaigns are well reported by the press. On the one hand, the press begins to pay attention to protest campaigns in so far as these campaigns have already reached a certain degree of mobilization (this is what is usually called the "critical mass effect"). On the other hand, when these campaigns last a long time, media attention begins to decrease even if protest remains at a light level of mobilization (this is the "ceiling effect" referred to by Dantzger 1975).

It is in part to avoid such bias that for some years now attempts have been made to build up data banks drawn from administrative sources.[15] In the remainder of this chapter, I hope to show that this type of data produces a fairly complete and accurate picture of the morphology and the evolution of demonstrations.

Morphology and Evolution of Demonstrations in the 1980s

In this section, dedicated to the morphology of the French demonstration and to its recent evolution, I will first determine the "rhythmology"[16] of the phenomenon in order to then move on to the analysis of an ensemble of morphological characteristics (types of participants and organizers, and the nature of their claims). This will allow me to examine the question of the transformation of the forms of non-conventional political participation in contemporary France.

Rhythmology of Demonstrations

The "time of the protest" is the first of the morphological determinants requiring analysis. It can be understood according to two modalities, the development of the demonstration over time - that is to say, the temporal evolution of a social practice - followed by the actual time of the demonstration - in other words, the periodization produced by the phenomenon itself. In effect there exists a socially constructed time of protest in the same way as for work, family and leisure, a time marked by the existence of protest seasons according to each social group as well as by significant and stable weekly variations.

Since our data covers a decade, it is possible to determine the evolution of recourse to protest action from the beginning of the 1980s in Nantes and Marseille. We compare our data with that collected by Duyvendak (1994) using a survey of *le Monde's* Monday edition between 1975 and 1989 (see Figure 1 below).

The first thing that strikes one on looking at Figure 1 is the trough during 1981, particularly noticeable in Nantes. In subsequent years, the number of demonstrations grows. In Nantes the rise continues from 1982 to 1985, before

---

15   See research currently being undertaken by McCarthy and McPhail on police permits in Washington, D.C. (in this volume), Della Porta on Florence (1993), Wisler and Kriesi on Geneva and Zurich (1996), Hocke on Freiburg/Breisgau, Germany (in this volume) and Gentile on Switzerland (in this volume).

16   I allow myself a neologism here which I understand to mean the temporal evolution of a practice, as well as the rhythms and periodization produced by the phenomenon itself.

stabilizing at a high level. In Marseille, the increase is more or less strong but steady from 1983 to 1989, seeing a small drop in 1991 then resuming its upward growth up until 1993.

Our sources thus indicate an increase in the number of demonstrations during the 1980s. In contrast, the figures collected by Duyvendak indicate, after 1981, a consistent decrease in the number of protests (notwithstanding a slight rise in 1982) until 1985 when the number of events stabilized at just around a hundred per year. Duyvendak concluded from this that there was a strong demobilization after the socialist victory in 1981, especially when compared with the levels seen between 1975 and 1980, and never since matched. This difference stems from the bias which press sources introduce into the analysis. In particular it underestimates "micro-mobilization," which brings together small numbers of demonstrators, but which, as we have found, *Le Monde* never mentions, especially when they take place in the provinces.

Figure 1: Average Number of Demonstrations per Year, Marseille and Nantes

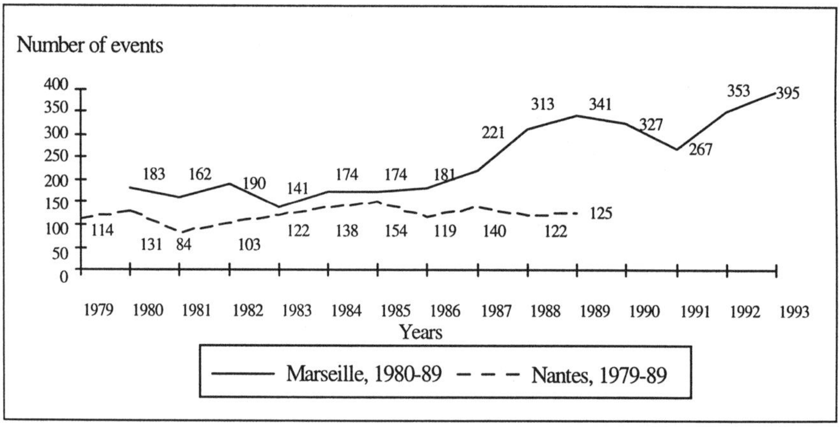

If one compares the evolution of the number of demonstrations in Marseille and in Nantes with the total number of persons marching on the streets, one sees (Figure 2 below) that the average number of demonstrators decreased after 1981, rising again with the occasional blip, first in Nantes during the medical students' mobilization against the government's reform program, then, in both towns, during the student demonstrations of 1986 alongside the rail (SNCF) employees. The size of protest actions would therefore have a tendency to diminish, which would go some way towards explaining the divergence in results: If the number of demonstrations indeed rose during the 1980s, they would nevertheless fail to match the levels reached in the 1960s.

Figure 2: Average Number of Demonstrators per Event and per Year, Marseille and Nantes

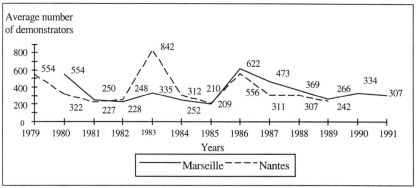

If the time of the protest can be understood through its development along a chronological axis, it is still necessary to look at the actual timing of the protest, that is to say at the rhythm and the periodization produced by the phenomenon itself. Figure 3 demonstrates the existence of protest seasons.

Figure 3: Number of Events per Month, Marseille, Nantes and Paris

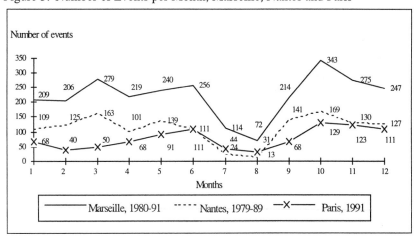

One can see three fairly distinct seasons: From January to March the number of events is high and goes on rising, then, after a trough in April, the number of protests rises again over the spring before dropping sharply from June to

August so as to all but disappear. Finally, between September and December, street protests rise again to a very high level in October before slowly diminishing towards January. In the capital city, the situation differs little if one looks at the data for the year 1991, except that the April peak in the provinces shifts to February in Paris. Note that these seasonal variations correspond to those of strike action.

If one looks at some of the available works written on urban uprisings or strikes, these seasonal rhythms have not always been the same. Michèle Perrot (1973) demonstrated that between 1871 and 1890 strike action increased in France in springtime, and was scarce between November and February. Winter saw a rise in the cost of living (due to the cold) and factories produced less. Thus people were less able or willing to be militant about their demands. A clear persistence of social rhythms from the countryside can also be seen, given the rural origins of most urban workers of the period. In the rural setting, winter is traditionally a period of withdrawal into oneself, whereas spring sees a blossoming explosion of demands. But above all, May is a month of respite from work in the fields, after the toil of sowing time and before haymaking in early summer.

By the beginning of the 20th century, this seasonal pattern of protest had changed. The spring peak became more and more pronounced over time. During the period from 1919 to 1935, the number of disputes was at its highest in March and April, while February and March were the peak times for strikes. But it was the advent of paid holidays in 1936 that overturned the seasonal patterns of protest. August, the month when most workers go on holiday, became the least active month after a "hot spring," as our own work on protests suggests. The summer break is followed by a *"rentrée sociale"* in the fall. This three-period model determines the current pattern of industrial strike action as well as that of protest demonstrations.

Moreover, if one compares the number of demonstrations to the number of demonstrators so as to measure the seasonal variations working within the size of demonstrations, the three protest seasons are observable in the same way. On average, large demonstrations begin to appear from September, rising through October and November, declining steadily from December to January, picking up again from March to May and then gradually falling off until the end of August (see Figure 4 below).

The rhythms determined here apply generally to all social categories. However, it is possible to say of certain protest groups that they have their own preferred time for action. The discrepancies between Figures 3 and 4 can be explained in this way. For example, if in Figure 3 the number of demonstrations rises considerably from September whereas in Figure 4 large-scale mobilization only really begins from October, it is essentially because the calendar of the *"rentrée sociale"* varies from group to group. Organized demonstrations by the "educational community" (teachers, parents, students) follow exactly the rhythms of the school year with the "low-water mark" during the summer months, and a strong September mobilization at the time of the new school year for primary and secondary establishments and the last enrollments for university. So, protest action in these categories is generally routine and bring together few people (except in time of crisis such as the demonstrations of 1983, 1986 and 1990).

Figure 4: Average Number of Demonstrators per Event and per Month,
Marseille and Nantes

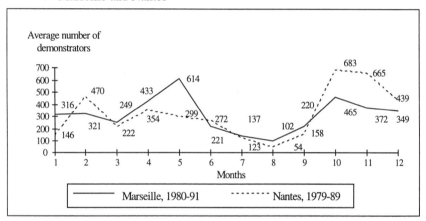

On the other hand, demonstrations by blue and white-collar workers in industry follow a similar pattern to that of demonstrations in general: a first cycle from January to March, from the start of the civil year, a second cycle in springtime and a third, the most marked, at the beginning of the fall. Differences with the global curve of demonstrations are all but non-existent, as far as Marseille or Nantes are concerned.[17]

Taking account of the high number of demands focusing around work, and in particular job losses, one may ask whether there is any correlation with seasonal variations in unemployment rates. In effect, the total number of unemployed is highest from October to January and lowest in the month of June. Of course fluctuations occur according to the age of the unemployed population, the

---

17   The similitude of the protest rhythms of workers and employees in Nantes and Marseille
      is explained by the numerical importance in both cases of salaried staff in the naval
      workshops.

youngest being controlled by the influx at the end of the school year (with a boom in the fall), 25 to 49 year-olds having more chance of finding themselves out of work in January, but having the lowest risk of loosing their work in the height of summer. Finally, job losses regularly rise from November to January, peaking in December, because the business cycle leads to a general drop in orders at that time. Now, it is in this same month of December that job offers are scarcest, which explains the high unemployment rate found in January. Seasonal variations in worker demonstrations are thus explained, given the nature of the demands, by fluctuations in the job market.

In the agricultural sector, one can distinguish two protest seasons, with strong activity at the start of the civil year which then steadily decreases over the summer months, which are a period of trough. Activity then resumes, though weakly, in November and December. One can assume that these variations very much depend on the nature of the region under consideration. Patrice Mann (1991) demonstrated that the seasonal distribution in the wine-producing south allowed one to distinguish the February/March peak from that of June/July, the dead season corresponding to the months of September and October. However, variations in the social unrest of farm-workers has not always been linked to the rhythms of work. Yves-Marie Bercé (1974, 1976) surveyed peasant revolts in the seventeenth century for the south-western quarter of France. The biggest protest movements there always developed in the spring, only to die out in summer, in time for the harvest. Bercé explains the concentration of disturbances during the months of May and June by the difficulties associated with the gap between two harvests (the period when the price of grain rises the most), but also by the passage of armies on the march having left behind their winter billets. Nowadays, the seasonal variation seems to correspond quite simply to the months in which professional activity is at its weakest.

If I emphasize this point it is because an understanding of these seasonal cycles is vital if one seeks to measure the variations in activism observable when collected data are plotted longitudinally. This was well demonstrated by Briët, Klandermans and Kroon (1987) in their study of variations in militant activism within the Dutch feminist movement.

Following on from seasonal variations, finally, are very distinct weekly variations. In contrast to the seasons, the week is a purely conventional and cultural division of time, but its rhythm takes general effect. Tartakowsky (1994) notes that between 1919 and 1934, 17% of union demonstrations and demands from union members (totaling 464 events) took place on a Sunday. Those using this day of rest most often to take to the streets are civil servants (who organized 113 of their 206 marches on this day) bearing in mind that they have no right to strike. But more than two-thirds of street demonstrations take place during the week, with a equal spread between Monday and Saturday. On the other hand, politically-inspired demonstrations make up 50% of those taking place on Sundays over the same period (totaling 853), 72 events being held on a Saturday and thirteen on a public holiday.

In the eighties, protest events are clearly not distributed equally over the week. Figures 5 and 6 below show that there is a larger number of events during the working week.

Figure 5: Average Number of Events per Day, Marseille and Nantes

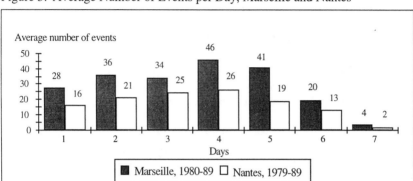

Figure 6: Average Number of Demonstrators per Day, Marseille and Nantes

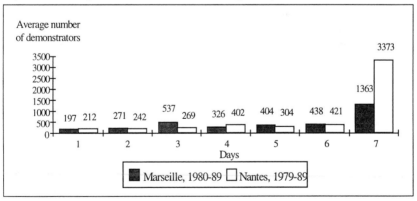

Beginning on Monday, the number of events steadily rises until Thursday, when it peaks; it then declines steadily from Friday through to Sunday. The pattern differs, however, when we compare Paris to the provinces. A greater proportion

of Paris-based events occur on Fridays and Sundays than is the case for Marseille and Nantes. In contrast, the number of participants at the weekend events is considerably higher in all three cities than on other days (see Figure 6 above). How can we explain this situation?

Table 1 (below) seems to show that events which take place on Sundays are different from those during the rest of the week, involving mainly, as in previous periods, demands which are tied more closely to "generalist" issues than to "corporatist" problems (unemployment, wages, etc.). In short, there would seem to be some link between the day on which an event occurs and the type of demand made during the event or the type of group organizing it. As shown in Table 1, the majority of events which occur between Monday and Friday (69%) are organized by unions, and revolve around generally "corporatist" issues (wages, layoffs), whereas on Saturday and Sunday, the type of event which dominates involves more "political" themes (anti-racism, diplomacy, etc.). This can be clearly seen through the type of organizers involved in protest events held on Saturdays and Sundays.

Table 1: Paris Police Records, January to June 1989 (N = 499)

Weekend		%	Rest of the Week		%
International groups	33	43%	Unions	287	68%
Political parties	14	18%	International groups	66	16%
Unions	11	14%	Political parties	24	6%
Religious groups	5	7%	Anti-racist groups	10	2%
Anti-racist groups	4	5%	Religious groups	8	2%
Other groups	9	8%	Other groups	28	7%
Total	76	100%	Total	423	100%

Table 1 also helps in building sampling strategies: In focusing on weekend events it is reasonable to assume that one is capturing most of the so-called new social movement events. This approach allows one to explore a particular category of events and movements, but it prevents one from comparing, say, the rate or pace of this type of movement with other movements, like the labor movement. In addition, when one's research involves cross-national comparisons, since the "week" is a culturally constructed category, one should inquire into the cultural meaning of the weekend in the different countries under research.

Evolution of Non-Conventional Action Forms: Stability and Identity

I would like now to test the common notion suggested by theories about new social movements (NSM) according to which protest action witnessed over a decade a profound mutation, with the disappearance of traditional activities in favor of new actors - "new social movements." This is, for example, what Nonna Mayer and P. Perrineau (1992) suggest when they put forward the idea that, in France, protest action would henceforth be a privileged modality of the salaried, and especially the urban middle classes (see also Jennings and Van Deth 1990: 37), and that at the same time partisan and union mediation would become increasingly disparate; "in these new forms of action, a civil society seems to have resurged with it's own capacity to regulate and organize itself" (Mayer and Perrineau 1992: 148).[18] Finally, it has been suggested that the nature of demands is strongly influenced by the defense of post-materialist values (Inglehart 1990). I intend to show here on the contrary at what point the 1980s in France were marked by a great stability of actors in demonstrations (as far as participants or organizers are concerned), and their claims.

The *main courantes* pose the difficult problem of the accuracy of "soft" data. Some types of information on the *main courantes* may not be accurate - specifically, information pertaining to "organizing groups," "participants" and "demands." The police officers who fill out the information on "organization groups" and "participants" get this information from several sources, for instance banners (from which information about participants can often be gleaned, for example about their jobs, the groups they belong to) and/or flyers collected throughout the course of the event (which may list the precise demands).[19] For small events, the police may get the relevant information by simply meeting with the organizers, since in most cases the police know the leaders of the protest event (except in Paris). As a consequence, the information given in the *main courantes* about organizers, participants and demands is not a reflection of categories established by the police, but is rather a reflection of the self-definitions of the groups involved in the event.

I am aware of the limits inherent in any attempt to create categories and topologies, given that both individuals and collective actors may claim many identities simultaneously. These dynamics are even more present during events which represent the acting out of a political opinion, because individuals and

---

18   This and all other translations from French in this chapter are by the author.

19   In Marseille, for example, for almost all the big events, records contain a very systematic account of the texts written on the banners and slogans. This constitutes an invaluable source of information because through it one can establish which groups participated in the event. It would, of course, be a mistake to think that these records are exhaustive. The fact that they represent only a partial record became clear during a class Nonna Mayer and I taught at the Institute for Political Studies. One of the class assignments we gave students was to attend an anti-racism march which took place that semester and to note down the kind of information recorded in the *main courantes*. The march was called by more than forty organizations; although the information gathered by the different teams was very similar, it nevertheless differed on some points.

collective actors attempt to present themselves as representatives of larger categories. Moreover, the demands expressed during an event do not correspond to the full range of goals held by organizations and participants.[20] The meanings which make up the action can take multiple forms, a reality impossible to capture in a longitudinal study and which would require an in-depth, even ethnographic study of each event. Using direct action can be a means of challenging the "State" in order to gain recognition and/or concessions of some kind. It can also be a means of offering participants the image of a unified group, to increase the legitimacy of the leaders (hence the need to turn out in large numbers); a means of appealing to various publics, spectators, media, commentators and ... why not? ... sociologists. Nevertheless, if police records do not allow us to identify all of the goals which motivated our 5,000 or so events, it is still possible to measure, based on the demands put forward by the social movement organizations themselves - as these were communicated during the event (via flyers, banners, etc.) - whether protest events of the 1980s in France embody materialist or non-materialist values, radical or more limited "corporatist" demands, etc.

Information collected on the participants call for two remarks. First, in almost all cases, the identities put forward by demonstrators are expressed in terms of professional status and/or profession, except for categories such as "pupil's parents," "anti-racists," "women" and "foreigners/immigrant workers." One can deduce from this that protest action essentially makes reference to professional occupations, to work. Moreover, the categories of identified demonstrators cover almost all socio-professional categories of the INSEE. It is clear that the classification of the professions and socio-professional categories is far from being sufficiently detailed to allow us to affirm that all categories of French people have recourse to demonstrating. It is known, for example, that airline pilots, air traffic controllers, prison officers, university professors, customs officers, notaries, high-level sporting professionals - the list is by no means exhaustive - rarely, if ever, resort to street demonstrations to defend their professional status.[21] The reasons for this are many - social and political means are more effective, class ethos, etc. However, one can legitimately conclude from our results that the end of a long process of naturalization of street demonstrations has been reached, even if certain action forms remain little used

---

20   Who has not, when attending a demonstration, seen a lone individual carrying a sign
      with which they attempt to attract attention for their cause? For a humorous illustration,
      see Sempé's picture of the protestor brandishing a sign which reads: "Will exchange a
      charming, 3-room apartment, kitchen, bathroom, for a 5-room apartment Tel. 1274123."
21   Which does not mean that these same people do not demonstrate as much as parents or
      activists for such and such a generalist cause.

by most groups (occupation of buildings, obstruction of public highways, etc.).[22]

Amongst the groups that have most often taken to the streets, workers come way out ahead, since they were present at 11% of protests in Marseille and 15% of those in Nantes. Next come teachers (with 9% of Marseille demonstrations and 12% in Nantes), followed by parents of students (5% in Nantes, 7% in Marseille) and students (7% in Marseille, 8% in Nantes). These results clearly indicate that the educational community has a highly developed "protest culture" which not only manifests itself in times of crisis, but also at the most routine of times. In fact, their level of mobilization remains consistently high throughout the period and their place in our files does not, for the most part, keep to the peaks of 1983 and 1986. On the other hand, for all other groups, a divergence of attendance is not so noticeable: Farmers, white-collar workers, civil servants and public employees within state-owned industries, craftspeople and shop-keepers, the liberal professions, retired people, are hardly less well represented at demonstrations.

One can therefore estimate that the salaried middle classes effectively constituted the great battalions in demonstrations during the 1980s, which is no doubt explained first by the size factor, given their large numbers in France. However, two facts attack the hypotheses about new social movements: Workers are those that most often take to the streets and the acknowledged identities of protestors are almost always professional, corporatist, and thus linked to earnings, and to the job.

According to the hypothesis of changed modes of political engagement, participation in protest activity is increasingly characterized by an extreme fluidity; individuals engaging and disengaging according to circumstances and, above all, outside traditional movements. Our data radically contradicts this vision and leaves no doubt that the street was dominated, during the 1980s, by

---

22   We do not wish to imply with this that demonstrations are "naturalized" as part of a continuing process. This was what Danielle Tartakowsky (1994) showed for the period 1918 through 1968. This explains well that, until 1934, all social groups demonstrated, but with an unequal propensity. In effect, protest was then strongly linked to the practice of striking, the reserve of workers. It is only since the war that the practice of demonstration seems to have taken root in new circles. In the 1950s, protest events became the occasional and possible expression of all social and political components of the country. At the same time, during these years, the independent role of young people, particularly students, became a constant in the demonstrations linked to Algeria, but equally in numerous rural demonstrations, then during the metalworkers' strikes of 1955 and November 1956. Finally, the most marked phenomenon of the 1960s from the point of view of the extension of recourse of groups to protest is the entry of farmers onto the protest scene.

the traditional organizations: More than 90% of demonstrations were called by one organization or more, as opposed to less than 7% spontaneous demonstrations. Moreover, spontaneous expressions of protest are not only channeled through demonstrations that were not formally organized, but also in events that no organization claims to have called.

The organizations that most often have recourse to strategies of street demonstrations are the unions. These were present at 77% of demonstrations in Nantes, 70% in Marseille and 43% in Paris during 1991. More precisely, the Confédération Générale du Travail (CGT, of communist persuasion) seemed to be by far the most active organization in calling demonstrations, since it is involved in more that half of the union calls to protest in Nantes and in Marseille, and a quarter of those in Paris.

In contrast to the unions, political parties very rarely call for demonstrations, with the notable exception of Marseille, where the Communist Party is strong (6% of calls, 8% if one takes into account satellite organizations). From this point of view, a change from previous decades can be noted, especially in the post-war period which saw the streets dominated by leftist parties (mainly the Communist Party). As for the right-wing parties - whether mainstream or extreme - they resort much less to street protests than their left-wing counterparts. Amongst these, the mass of the Communist Party surpasses most other groupings, and especially the Socialist Party which only attended 1% of demonstrations over a ten year period.

Associations played an equally important role in calling protests during the 1980s. However, only certain sectors resorted extensively to protest action. These primarily include, though according to a hierarchy which differs somewhat in the towns considered, parents' associations, anti-racist movements, associations in support of international causes (groups against such and such a problem abroad, e.g. remembering the Armenian genocide, supporting the PLO, the Chinese student protestors, etc.).

This distribution of the most active protest organizations corresponds broadly with their respective weight amongst the associate sector, as Héran suggests:

> Participation levels amongst parents' associations, on the one hand, and single professional unions, on the other, remain particularly high. This is because, in both cases it is a question of defending interests linked to one's personal situation, or to that of people close to you, and not of embracing a general cause which, belonging to everyone, at the same time risks being impersonal. On a quantitative level at least, forms of so-called new associations are far from posing a threat to traditional organs (1988: 21).

If one is to believe the NSM authors, the "old" movements mobilize around long-established objectives (class struggle, religious differences, the rift between the center and the periphery, etc.), whereas the "new" movements tend to become active on behalf of causes founded on new cleavages. Once again, data shows that, in the case of France, it is a question of a received idea.

The first thing to note concerning the analysis of demands during the 1980s is the high concentration on a small number of issues since two thirds of events in Marseille and Nantes revolve around nine demands. Moreover, there is an astonishing homogeneity amongst the most recurring demands from one town to another. Opposition to job losses was the focus of around 14% of demonstrations. More generally, between 18 and 19% of events targeted the problem of jobs (if one includes action against unemployment, for jobs and opposition to redundancies). Equally noteworthy is the considerable importance of demands linked to earnings, which precipitated 23% of demands in Nantes, 19% in Paris and 16% in Marseille (if one puts together claims linked to consumer power, to the value of salaries, to price rises, pensions and retirement, and agricultural matters of which almost all have direct bearing on farm revenues, disputes about pricing or the policies of Brussels). Also of considerable importance are problems linked to school (more than 15%) and to international affairs - which come first in Paris (23%), third in Marseille (12%) and sixth in Nantes (6%). The respective places taken by demands of an international nature could here be explained at once by the presence of easy targets (e.g. embassies, consulates) and by the population structure of the metropolis (implantation of communities of foreign origin).

The division of causes in our three cities does not serve to corroborate the hypothesis that there has been a modification in those values defended by protest action. "Materialist" causes in effect remain to a very large extent dominant, with jobs, earnings and the standard of living, problems linked to the schools (stemming from underfunding of school buildings and teaching posts, and from universities selection procedures during the 1980s). As for so-called post-materialist causes, including actions linked to moral issues, to the environment, to the right to abortion, anti-militarists or even to politics in general, they do not really come into play. Alone amongst causes which might be labeled more or less post-materialist, international issues and in particular anti-racist/anti-fascist groups surface. The latter make up 4% of Marseille protests, 3% of Parisian and 2% of those in Nantes.

It is therefore necessary to qualify the ideas developed by Ronald Inglehart with regard to the radical novelty of protest movements in the 1980s.[23] As far as protest action in France is concerned, our results clearly contradict these conclusions for the years 1979 through 1989. One of the possible reasons for

---

23   In fact, while Inglehart's first study was published in 1977, a second study on the 1980s was published in 1990 and thus covers the same period as ours (see Inglehart 1977, 1990).

this is that the Eurobarometer surveys measure the propensity to mobilize and not effective actions. From this point of view, our results confirm the notion according to which the extent of the propensity to participate in collective action does not produce the same results as that of effective participation. The latter alone permits the identification of protest groups at a given moment as well as their motives.

Nevertheless, Inglehart's works cover both the 1970s and 1980s while our research only covered the last decade. One might therefore suppose that the worsening of the economic crisis, with rising unemployment, the drop in salaried earnings and deflation, would have had the effect of durably braking the growth of post-materialist values in our society in favor of a return to the problems of jobs and wages. However, the latest results put forward by Inglehart suggest that the backlash of the crisis was felt, but was ephemeral. Based on a collection of surveys by Eurobarometer, undertaken in six European countries between 1970 and 1988, the author shows that the indices of post-materialism steadily increase when one passes from the oldest to the youngest members, each new member being a little more post-materialist than their predecessor. He also argues that the two oil crises of 1973 and 1979 were accompanied by a drop in the indicators of post-materialism, but from the beginning of the 1980s the growth in these indicators took hold again steadily throughout the membership.

Is this development over time confirmed in the development of the corresponding share the most important types of demands put forward in demonstrations during the 1980s?

To answer this question, we differentiated the causes on behalf of which people protested in Marseille and Nantes into two very broad categories: those linked to unemployment (against redundancies, for jobs in general, against unemployment in general) and to wages (wage reviews, consumer power, retirement and pensions, price rises, drops in farm prices) are defined as materialist causes; those linked to anti-racism/anti-fascism, regionalism, morals (abortion, violence against women and moral issues in general), certain international political issues (world peace, disarmament, third world aid, etc.) and anti-militarism are seen as reflecting post-materialist values (see Figures 7 and 8 below).

In these two graphs presented in Figures 7 and 8, the similarity in evolution of the two curves is remarkable, which tends to show that our data is not reducible to a regional specificity. When one examines the evolution of materialist demonstrations, one notices in both cases three stages: their relative weakness at first until 1983, their drop up to 1986 in Marseille and 1985 in Nantes, then their very perceptible growth from 1986 in Nantes and 1987 in Marseille.

Figure 7: Materialist and Post-Materialist Claims, 1980 to 1989, Marseille

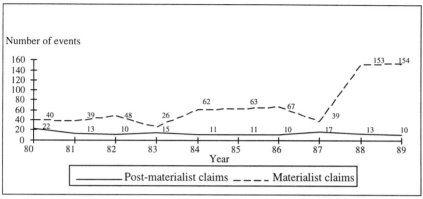

Figure 8: Post-Materialist and Materialist Claims, 1979 to 1989, Nantes

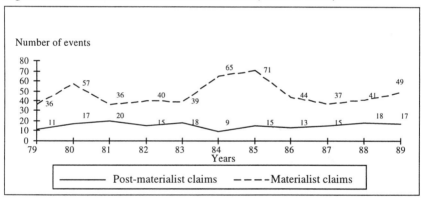

It is noteworthy that the two periods of growth in demonstrations for materialist causes corresponds to two great changes in political orientation during the decade: the socialist government's radical conversion to liberalism in 1983, with the dismissal of the communist ministers from the government and the return to protest activities by the CGT from the end of 1984 onwards;[24] then the change

---

24 From 1984, in fact, one witnesses a rebirth of national interprofessional protests. The communists' departure when the Fabius government took office brought an end to the resoluteness of the right within the unions and fired up that of the CGT which sought to regain its capacity to mobilize. It mobilized first the civil servants who had not reached any wage package agreement. On October 25, 1984, the CGT proposed a strike to civil

in political direction in 1986, with the return to power of the right in the general elections. If the *"cohabitation"* saw no change in terms of economic policy (other than symbolically in the debate over denationalization), nevertheless a strong union demobilization, notably with the insistent presence of the FEN in the streets, took place. Furthermore, FO held its first interprofessional demonstration since its creation on the 3rd October 1987 in Paris.

If one now considers post-materialist causes, one is struck by the great stability of the period. One might even say, though our data does not go so far at the moment, that there was a certain drop after the elections of 1981 and the arrival of the left in power. In order to fill the gap in the oldest data, one might turn once again to the results found by Duyvendak (1994) for the period 1975 through 1989, which seem to show that post-materialist demonstrations effectively saw a sharp drop after 1980, never to return to the levels reached in the 1970s. This seems to have subsided before Mitterrand's presidential victory, which suggests that a change in government and a drop in new social movements might not be as directly related as might have been thought. Finally, it seems that materialist activism is far more susceptible to being influenced by a change in political climate - in other words, by electoral cycles - than is post-materialist activism. This was clear in 1981 and 1986.

Conclusion

To conclude, I would say that police sources have made it possible to evaluate the hypotheses of NSM theories applicable to the French situation more precisely. It is undoubtedly the case that, contrary to the received wisdom, traditional channels of representation remain acceptable to the people as far as organizing protest action is concerned. A decline in union and party militancy has all too readily been used to infer that these organizations no longer play their role as social movement activists. Such an inference is wrong, as shown by the crucial role of the pre-existence of one or more organizations structured for mobilization activity.

I will end by discussing two points: Can one first of all say that resorting to protest action applies in all social classes? What can one then conclude from recent developments in protest action?

First, the extent of protest action and its spread across almost all social categories seems to indicate the completion of a process of institutionalization, of naturalization of the demonstration, in the sense that recourse to it has

---

servants in the PTT, EDF, SNCF, RATP and on October 24, 1985, it organized its first national interprofessional day of action since 1980.

become natural. Thus, on top of the strong mobilization of workers and of those involved in schooling (teachers, parents and students), demonstrations touch all social categories equally.

Three remarks stem from the notion of a naturalization of the demonstration. First, if in the number of demonstrations, one effectively notes equal recourse to protest of numerous socio-professional groups, this is not altogether the case when one takes the total number of people who took to the streets, especially looking at figures concerning the part taken by each group within society.

Next, certain categories never, or very rarely, have recourse to protest, whether they possess limited resources, or have none at all. Finally, this naturalization of protest is perhaps not such a recent phenomenon after all. It is true that since the Second World War, and up to the late 1960s, taking to the street remained the reserve of the "working classes," notably under the wing of the Communist Party. However, the conflicts at the start of the century - a period of intense protest activity if ever there was one - drew men and women of all backgrounds and professions into the streets as they marched on the First of May for the eight hour day, to bring General Boulanger to power, to support or barrack Captain Dreyfus, to defend religious congregations or oppose the nationalization of church properties. One encounters here an epistemological constraint: The chosen time scale is essential to understanding any phenomenon and it is retrospective projection that permits the voluntary restructuring of the object of analysis.

Second, the analysis of the *mains courantes* brings us closer to understanding what the social and political determinants of protest are thanks to the disposition of a homogenous and complete series over more than ten years. This fact is fairly rare so that one should stop there. Most of the time, statistical data without chronological and homogenous breaks go no further than a few years and the sociologist is forced to reconstitute the data on the basis of exogenous information. The retrospective projection thus gives some pace to the development of the phenomenon being studied, but the sense given resides essentially in the intentions of the researcher, which represents a firm limit, which I have here avoided.

However, one must be attentive to the fact that the developments brought to light in this work stem from our corpus. To be in a position today - which was never possible previously - to assess in a more or less exhaustive way the state of protest in certain French towns, automatically leads one to reveal a new image of protest action. This is simply because one is in a position to take into account hundreds of events which were previously known only to a few people (other than the (often very few) demonstrators themselves, and one or two onlookers).

But, above all, the epistemological problem of the timescale used is raised again. In effect, a research object takes on particular temporal characteristics depending upon the scope of the study.

> One can by analogy take a familiar example, that of sealing wax, of which the physical properties modify themselves without the need for a great change in timescale; observed over a minute, the sealing wax obeys the laws of distortion of brittle solids with a breaking- or shearing-point, which is easy to measure numerically. But, observed over the space of a month or a year, this same wax is a viscous fluid subject to plastic distortion under the sole action of its own weight (Meyer 1954, cit. Gras 1979: 24).[25]

The scale is therefore decisive in drawing conclusions on the pace of change or absence of change; in the long term, there is no demonstrable reason why a strong observable increase or decrease should not be a simple accident. An aberrant point in an otherwise gentle curve, or even moments in a cycle which the statistician does away with by paring.

It is in the light of these epistemological precautions that one must consider the question of a change in the nature of political participation, such that one might measure it in particular by replacing the materialist values by post-materialist values and by modifying the sociology of the groups involved in organizing protest actions (disappearance of parties and unions in favor of ad hoc associations).

Should one therefore assume from our results that Inglehart's work should be rejected? One might in fact put forward the hypothesis that materialist values grew strongly during the 1970s (especially in comparison with the 1950s and 1960s), only to decrease once again under the effects of the recession, and, in such a case, nothing in our ten-year survey permits us to conclude that there has been a long-lasting abandonment of post-materialist values or indeed anything other than merely a simple "blip" in the long-term trend.[26] However, given the impossibility of our being able in any way to establish a homogenous and complete series over a long period of time, this limitation does not undermine

---

25   Meyer, F. 1954. *Problématique de l'évolution.* Paris: PUF.
26   One finds a good example of this problem in *Civilisation matérielle et capitalisme* by Fernand Braudel (1967). According to Braudel there was a long-term progression in cereal yields in Europe (from 60% to 65%) during the years 1200 to 1820. But, it must be noted, "this progression does not exclude the fairly long-lasting drop in yields between 1300 and 1350, 1400 and 1500 and between 1600 and 1700" (Braudel 1967, cit. Gras 1979: 65). Alain Gras, adds that "if one takes into account the fact that there was a drop over 250 years, that is to say over half the period in question, the preceding proposition could be turned on its head (drop with limited increases) but one can take a definitive, though arbitrary, stance on the direction of the long-term trend in recent history" (ibid.).

the usefulness of our results, inasmuch as in the years to come, it will be possible to continue the process of establishing a series, derived from the same sources used so far.

The analysis of organizing groups, on the other hand, does not present the same problems, insofar as one knows better at what point political and union organizations have been involved in initiating protest actions in the preceding decades. In recent years, the feeling has spread in the media and informed discourse that political parties and unions no longer play as great a role as before in advancing certain interests. Our results largely contradict this analysis as far as the union presence in particular is concerned, and to a lesser extent, for political parties.

References

Bercé, Y. M. 1974. *Histoire des croquants. Etude des soulèvements populaires au XVIIième siècle dans le sud-ouest de la France*, 2 Vol. Geneva: Droz.

Bercé, Y. M. 1976. *Fête et révolte*. Paris: Hachette.

Briët, M., B. Klandermans and F. Kroon. 1987. "How Women Become Involved in the Women's Movement." Pp. 44-63 in *The Women's Movement in the U.S. and Western Europe: Consciousness, Political Opportunity and Public Policy*, ed. M. Katzenstein and C. Mueller. Philadelphia, Penn.: Temple University Press.

Dantzger, M. H. 1975. "Validating Conflict Data." *American Sociological Review* 40 (October): 570-584.

Della Porta, D. 1993. "Police Operational Practice and Knowledge. A Comparative Research on the Police in Contemporary Europe, Research Report for 1993 and Research Proposals for 1994." Unpublished paper.

Duyvendak, J. W. 1994. *Le poids du politique. Nouveaux mouvements sociaux en France*. Paris: L'Harmattan.

Favre, P. and O. Fillieule. 1994. "La manifestation comme indicateur de l'engagement politique." Pp. 115-139 in *L'engagement politique, déclin ou mutation?*, ed. P. Perrineau. Paris: Presses de la Fondation des sciences politiques.

Fillieule, O. 1993. "L'Emergence de la violence dans les manifestations de rue. Eléments pour une analyze étiologique." Pp. 267-291 in *La violence dans les démocraties occidentale. Cultures et conflits*, No. 7-8, ed. P. Braud. Paris: L'Harmattan.

Fillieule, O. 1996. "Police Records and National Press in France. Issues in the Methodology of Data-Collections from Newspapers." Working Paper of the Robert Schuman Centre, No. 96/25. European University Institute. Florence.

Fillieule, O. 1997. *Stratégies de la rue. Les manifestations en France*. Paris: Presses de Science Po.

Franzosi, R. 1987. "The Press as a Source of Socio-Historical Data: Issues in the Methodology of Data Collection from Newspapers." *Historical Methods* 20 (1): 5-16.

Glasgow University Media Group. 1976. *Bad News*, Vol. 1. London: Routledge and Keagan.

Glasgow University Media Group. 1980. *More Bad News*, Vol. 2. London: Routledge and Keagan.

Gras, A. 1979. *Sociologie des ruptures*. Paris: PUF, Le sociologue.

Héran, F. 1988. "Un monde sélectif, les associations." *Economie et statistique* 208: 1-14.

Hocke, P. 1995. "Determining the Selection Bias in Local and National Newspaper Reports on Protest Events." Paper presented at the workshop "Protest Event Analysis: Methodology, Applications, Problems," Wissenschaftszentrum Berlin für Sozialforschung (Social Science Research Center Berlin, WZB). June 12-14.

Inglehart, R. 1977. *The Silent Revolution: Changing Values and Political Styles Among Western Publics*. Princeton, N.J.: Princeton University Press.

Inglehart, R. 1990. *Cultural Shifts in Advanced Industrial Societies*. Princeton, N.J.: Princeton University Press.

Jennings, M. K and J. Van Deth, eds. 1990. *Continuities in Political Action: A Longitudinal Study of Political Orientations in Three Western Democracies*. Berlin: de Gruyter.

Kielbowicz, R. B. and C. Sherer. 1986. "The Role of the Press in the Dynamics of Social Movements." Pp. 71-96 in *Research in Social Movements, Conflict and Change 9*, ed. L. Kriesberg. Greenwich, Conn.: JAI.

Mann, P. 1991. L'Activité tactique des manifestants et des forces mobiles lors des crises viticoles du midi (1950-1990). Unpublished contribution to a report for IHESI (French Ministry of the Interior).

Mayer, N. and P. Perrineau. 1992. *Les Comportements politiques*. Paris: Colin, coll. Cursus.

Olzak, S. 1989. "Analysis of Events in the Study of Collective Action." *Annual Review of Sociology* 15: 119-141.

Perrot, M. 1973. *Les Ouvriers en grève, France, 1871-1890*. Paris: La Haye, Mouton. (Partially republished in 1984 as *Jeunesse de la grève*. Paris: Le Seuil.)

Rucht, D. and T. Ohlemacher. 1992. "Protest Event Data: Collection, Uses and Perspectives." Pp. 76-106 in *Studying Collective Action*, ed. R. Eyerman and M. Diani. Beverly Hills, Cal.: Sage.

Snyder, D. and W. R. Kelly. 1977. "Conflict Intensity, Media Sensitivity and the Validity of Newspaper Data." *American Sociological Review* 42 (February): 105-123.

Spilerman, S. 1976. "Structural Characteristics of Cities and the Severity of Racial Disorders." *American Sociological Review* 41 (5): 771-793.

Tarrow, S. 1989. *Democracy and Disorder. Protest and Politics in Italy, 1965-1975*. Oxford: Clarendon Press.

Tartakowsky, D. 1994. "Les manifestations de rue en France, 1918-1968." Unpublished thesis. Paris.

Wisler, D. and H. Kriesi. 1996. "Decisionmaking and Style in Protest Policing. The Cases of Geneva and Zurich." Working Paper of the Robert Schuman Centre. European University Institute. Florence.

Radical Right Protest in Switzerland

Pierre Gentile[1]

Introduction

November 1988: After a meeting whose location had to be changed at the last moment because of a leftist counter-mobilization, a group of right extremist skinheads went on to have beers in a Zurich disco. By the end of the night an altercation occurred between some skinheads and participants at a Brazilian party taking place in the same building. As he was running upstairs to enter the party, a foreign resident was hit by a young skinhead and fell back onto his head. He never recovered and died two months later, apparently due to AIDS. His death was the starting point of a mobilization against racism in Zurich. He was also the first person to die in the wave of radical right violence that had spread all over Switzerland by the end of the eighties. Unfortunately he was not the last.

A month after this event, Swiss citizens rejected an anti-immigrant initiative launched by the National Action/Swiss Democrats (AN/DS) - in 1967 the first radical right party to enter the federal assembly since World War II. This initiative demanded a drastic reduction of the proportion of foreign residents and workers in the country. Despite all other parties and economic associations rejecting the nationalist proposition during the campaign preceding the vote, 32.7% of voters still favored this very extreme initiative.

Since the mid-eighties, Swiss authorities have been confronted with waves of protest initiated by radical right parties, extra-parliamentary organizations and single activists.[2] Immigration and refugee policies, the attempt in some cantons[3] to decriminalize drug consumption, reforms of the federal government,

---

1   This contribution is partly based on a master's thesis presented at the University of Geneva in March 1995, supervised by Hanspeter Kriesi. I would like to thank Simon Hug, Ruud Koopmans, Maya Jegen and Matthias Brunner for their help on this chapter.
2   I classified all parties sharing the following characteristics in their programs as "radical right": an emphasis on identity (defined as cultural or national); condemnation of cosmo-politanism; anti-immigrant or anti-refugee speeches (from discreet xenophobia to open racism); strong inclination towards law and order; valorization of a man's work and not of capital.
3   Switzerland is a small state with approximately seven million inhabitants and an enormous cultural heterogeneity. This heterogeneity, deeply rooted in history, is reflected in the federal structure of the state which is divided into 26 cantons (six are mainly French speaking regions, one Italian and the rest German). Each of these cantons has its own party system and governing coalition. They have wide ranging jurisdiction in many areas, including justice, health policies, education and housing.

the desire to develop closer economic links with the European Union all came under sharp criticism from the right spectrum of political forces.

There are indications that these criticisms found an increasing echo in the population. The radical right parties gained almost 10% of the vote in the general elections of 1991 and 1995; their highest result. Since the early nineties, these parties have proven that they are not only able to launch initiatives and referenda but also to win some of them. They could, for example, successfully oppose a change to a federal law aimed at making it easier for foreigners to buy property, or even an international treaty concerning Swiss participation in UN troops. Referenda and initiatives are some of the most crucial institutions characterizing the Swiss political system (Kriesi 1995a; Linder 1994). They represent a political opportunity for the challengers from the radical right to put pressure on the elite.[4] Finally, the criticisms mentioned above are increasingly to be found in the discourse of some sections of established right-wing parties in the federal coalition government,[5] especially the Democratic Union of the Center (DUC).

Radical right protest is, however, not limited to the institutionalized democratic arena. The two incidents related at the beginning of this chapter show that contemporary radical right protest took different forms and involves different actors. Jaschke (1992) argues, with regard to Germany, that the success of a nationalist party (in this case the Republikaner) in several regional elections and the direct actions taken against homes for refugees are part of the same social and cultural trend. Nevertheless, the radical right is far from being a united family in any European country. What its members have in common is their will to preserve a national identity (characterized in Switzerland by political institutions such as neutrality, independence, direct democracy, and not by cultural dimensions) from external influence. This leads them to reject any loss of autonomy of the national state in supranational institutions. They also share an aversion towards any form of cosmopolitanism. In Switzerland the radical right is a mosaic composed of divergent ideological tendencies, mobilizing around different issues and using distinct action repertoires. A distinction must be made between the different parties represented at one or more of the three levels of Swiss political life and extra-parliamentary groups.

---

4   By collecting the required number of signatures (100,000 for an initiative proposing the adoption or the change of a constitutional article and 50,000 for a referendum to oppose a federal law or an international treaty) Swiss citizens can compel the government to organize a popular vote. The same institutions exist at the regional and local level.

5   The government has been an all-party coalition since 1959. Five of the seven members are from the three main right-wing parties and two from the Swiss socialist party. In order to ensure representation of the linguistic minorities, four members come from the German, two from the French and one from the Italian part of the country.

There are parties defending an ideology of social nationalism in which the state is the main social force, whereas others are fighting against state interventionism in the name of national liberalism (Gentile and Kriesi 1996).

When I decided to study the radical right in Switzerland, I had little knowledge about the real magnitude of this social and cultural trend and the activities of the different tendencies composing it. A specialized literature on the contemporary radical right was nearly non-existent (with the exception of some books and articles by a Swiss German journalist on the development of a skinhead and neo-nazi scene). By that time I was also aware of the existing counter-mobilization, without knowing how efficient it really was. Consequently, I decided to spend a year creating a data set on the whole range of radical right mobilization (including both the parties' activities and the illegal actions of non-organized groups) in order to gain an overall view of radical right protest. McAdam proved that to understand the mobilization of a particular movement (such as the skinheads for example), attention must be shifted to "the broader 'movement family' or 'cycles of protest' in which they are typically embedded" (1996: 2). I also decided to take into account the reaction of the other political actors, such as unions, the church or the governing parties.

In this chapter, I will present the results derived from this data set. I will first turn to the radical right parties' mobilization between 1984 and 1993. Then I will discuss the activities of the extra-parliamentary groups during the same period of time. Under this label I classified all organizations and individuals sharing radical right points of view and acting outside the party system. Finally, I will turn my attention to the counter-mobilization. After describing these three types of mobilization, I will look for links between them. But before going into detail, it is necessary to provide some information about the sources I used.

Methodology

To highlight the recent evolution of radical right mobilization and measure the actual public activities of the different groups and parties between 1984 and 1993, all political events[6] initiated by an identified radical right organization as well as events clearly attributable to radical right sympathizers even if nobody claimed responsibility for them (an attack against a home for refugees for example) have been registered in the data set. The only actions I did not take into account were those taking place within the parliamentary arena. Collecting

---

6   It is clear that events without a political objective (such as the wedding of a well-known radical right activist) were not registered. Furthermore, events had to be publicized (directed to media or to people outside the group initiating them).

data on events initiated by the radical right is not only useful concerning non-conventional activities, but also to gain an overall view of the conventional activities of institutionalized organizations.[7]

I first decided to refer to at least two journalistic sources on a day by day basis.[8] A newspaper tends to cover events that have occurred in the region where the potential readers are living. It was thus clear that I should avoid using two Swiss German sources, even if the newspapers with the better journalists are located in this area. I tested eight journalistic sources: six newspapers, the Swiss Press Agency and the Documentation Center that is part of the University of Bern and works with more than 20 newspapers. The test covered a period of one and a half month pre-selected because of the high number of known events initiated by the radical right that took place in the 45 days from 1st August to 15th September 1991 (Bähler 1994). Four criteria were used to evaluate the eight tested sources: complementarity, constancy over time, reliability and low cost access to data.

The Swiss Press Agency and the Documentation Center proved to be the most complete sources as well as the most complementary ones.[9] Both cover the whole territory (the Press Agency has offices in 16 towns and some of the newspapers that the Documentation Center collects are printed in the French or Italian speaking parts of Switzerland). It took less time to identify the pertinent events from these two sources than would have been the case if the primary sources had been newspapers.[10] In addition, as Veron (1981) explained, a press agency passes essential information on to its clients in a precise, clear and concise way. A newspaper is much more selective in its decision to print the

---

7   The data set was set up under the supervision of Hanspeter Kriesi and follows approximately the same guidelines (same variables with similar categories can be found) as an international research project on New Social Movements carried out by Kriesi, Koopmans, Duyvendak and Giugni (1995). We did so in order to allow further comparison between the actions of the New Social Movements and the radical right in Switzerland. So far, with the help of Maya Jegen and Marco Giugni, I have attempted to compare the action repertoires of the diverse movements (Gentile and Jegen 1996).

8   In contrast to Kriesi et al. (1995), I did not limit myself to the Monday issues. Some of the actions, such as press conferences, usually take place during the week, while others are more often held on Saturdays (e.g. festivals or demonstrations).

9   It is interesting to note that the most complete source in the test (the Documentation Center) covered only 35 out of the 70 events that were referred to in at least one of the eight tested journalistic sources. Four sources covered less than 20 events.

10   The Documentation Center categorizes the articles into approximately 350 files, twelve of them concerning the radical right. In the Press Agency all the news from 1984 onwards is available on electronic file. To pick out the news dealing with radical right activities, I had to enter a list of key-words (such as attack/refugees or Lega). If one of these words was used in the report it is automatically selected.

news it has received than a press agency is in the decision to pass information on to its clients. A press agency covers more events than any newspaper. No journalistic source is free from bias. The decision to keep an article or to release information will partly depend on conjectural factors. For example, one might expect that after an unexpected electoral success by a radical right party, journalists will be more interested in collecting information on the party's activities.

The test showed that the two journalistic sources selected only covered a small proportion of the disruptive events initiated by the radical right, as long as they did not involve human casualties (Gentile 1995). Therefore, I decided to construct my data set using, in addition to the two journalistic sources mentioned, a Federal Police working list dedicated to radical right violence and a compilation of racist events compiled by Swiss journalist Jürg Frischknecht, who is recognized as being an authority on the skinhead community. Unfortunately, these two sources only cover the radical right's illegal activities since 1988. Before then the Federal Police's attention had almost exclusively concentrated on the leftist opposition. Therefore, in the fourth section, dedicated to the non-institutionalized radical right's activities, I must limit my analysis to the period 1988 through 1993 at times.

Table 1:   The Importance of the Distinct Sources

Sources	Number of events found	% of those initiated by radical right
Documentation Center/Bern	1,113	84.2%
Swiss Press Agency	788	85.0%
Federal Police	362	94.8%
Journalist (Frischknecht)	227	99.1%
Final data set	2,036	87.1%

I found a total of 2,036 distinct events in all my sources; 1,773 initiated by the radical right and 263 by movements calling for a counter-mobilization. Over the 2490 events collected, only 454 were removed from the final data set because they appeared in more than one source. Four out of five events are original ones in the sense that they appear in only one of my sources. This observation demonstrates their high degree of complementarity. People working for the Federal Police do not have the same concerns as those working for the Swiss Press Agency. For example, threats against individual or groups are generally not reported in the media, unless they concern well-known politicians or artists. In conclusion, from my point of view, researchers who wish to cover a large range of action repertoires and groups must find the most complementary combination of different sources and should not limit themselves to one source.

Mobilization by Radical Right Parties

Besides ideological division, the fragmentation of the party system into 26 cantons with distinct problems and priorities partly explains the multitude of radical right parties in Switzerland. Their expectation of longevity varies greatly from one case to another. During the eighties, new radical right parties, such as the Lega dei Ticinesi or the Automobilist Party (AP) emerged beside the National Action/Swiss Democrats (NA/SD) (the oldest radical right party represented in the federal parliament) and the Federal Democratic Union (FDU) (a party created in 1975 to promote biblical values and oppose foreign influence in Swiss society).

The Automobilist Party was founded in the German part of the country in 1985, in reaction to the influence of ecologist movements and state interventionism in the social sphere. It soon became the largest radical right party. In contrast to the Swiss Democrats, it opposes the welfare state. Reducing taxes and balancing the state budget by limiting expenditures, especially in the areas of national insurance benefits and environmental protection, are among its main priorities (besides the will to keep Switzerland out of any supranational political organization, such as the European Union or the United Nations, in the name of the defense of Swiss identity). The Lega was created in the Italian speaking part of the country in 1991 by an entrepreneur and a newspaper editor whose populist speeches against governing parties on the left and the right soon made them successful public figures. During the same period other parties disappeared after experiencing electoral setbacks, for example, the Republicans.

According to the data set, the Swiss Democrats were the most active party between 1984 and 1993, initiating 509 events. The Automobilists staged 295 events, the FDU 150, the Lega 38 and Vigilance 34. The remaining radical right parties (including the Republicans) produced a total of 61 events. Of the 1,773 events I considered to be due to the radical right and registered in the data set, 1,087 were initiated by institutionalized parties; the four represented in the Federal Assembly being responsible for 992 of these events.

While some of the radical right parties limit their activities to a single canton, like the Lega or Vigilance before its dissolution, others are trying to develop new divisions all over the country. But, despite their efforts, they seem to have great difficulties taking root in the French speaking region.[11] Apart from the representatives of the Lega, all the radical right deputies at the federal level

---

11   During the eighties, the two most powerful radical right parties in this part of the country virtually lost their influence. In Geneva, Vigilance, once was the most strongly represented party in parliament, disappeared. In Lausanne successive internal crises were detrimental to the local division of the Swiss Democrats.

came from German speaking cantons. Hence, it is not surprising that looking at the regional distribution of events initiated by radical right parties, as depicted in Table 2, one sees that these parties are much more active in the German part of the country than the French in proportion to the respective population.

Table 2: Level of Party Mobilization According to Linguistic Region

Region	Events	Population*
German	84.7%	72.3%
French	10.1%	23.4%
Italian	5.2%	4.3%
Total	100.0% n = 1,085	100.0%

* Census figures (Recensement fédéral de la population) 1990.

Development of the Parties' Mobilization

In one or more of the four federal elections that took place between 1983 and 1995, four of the radical right parties have been able to send representatives to the National Council: NA/DS, AP, Lega and the FDU. Their collective score at the federal elections increased during the period covered by my data set (3.8 in 1983, 6.3 in 1987, 10.9 in 1991, 9.3 in 1995). Looking at the events initiated by the radical right parties between 1984 and 1993, one notes that they were more active in the last three years than they were during the first three years, but, as can be seen in Figure 1, the development of their activity is far from linear.

As Figure 1 below shows, during the electoral years of 1987 and 1991, the parties organized more events, especially conventional ones directed towards the media, such as press conferences or press releases. These kinds of events are low cost actions for parties with few resources, which is the case for those I am interested in.[12] In 1988 the level of activity fell drastically. This was partly due to an internal conflict that divided some of the most powerful sections of the Swiss Democrats. This occurred at the same time as the dissolution of two other parties, led by well known figures of the radical right,[13] that had failed to gain a single deputy at the federal elections in 1987. As for the Automobilist Party

---

12 With the exception of the Lega in Tecin, radical right parties have no permanent staff at the regional or local level. At the national level, the Swiss Democrats and the Automobilst Party each have an office with secretarial staff. Parties do not receive much state assistance when they are running for elections, and most of their income is spent on publications (Gentile and Kriesi 1996).

13 The Republicans, headed by James Schwartzenbach, and Valentin Oehen's Liberal Ecologist Party. Both men were former presidents of the Swiss Democrats before creating their own parties.

(founded in 1985), even if it already attracted more votes than the AN/SD or the FDU in the 1987 federal elections, it had its real political start four years later in various regional and local elections.

Figure 1: Development of the Parties' Mobilization

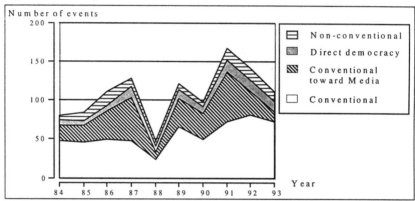

Figure 1 also emphasizes the fact that radical right parties usually limit themselves to conventional action repertoires (37.8% of their actions are voting instructions, and 9.3% are related to the use of direct democracy tools); demonstrative events represent 9.4% of their actions (mostly congresses and petitions), and illegal actions just 0.6%. If in some cases members of the Swiss Democrats were involved in illegal activities, including the use of violence, the party was not directly responsible for it. Referenda and initiatives represent an opportunity for parties in the opposition to put their claims onto the political agenda. In practice, even if they are usually unable to win initiatives, they may have a veto power when using referenda. This is especially true concerning the radical right, as a recent analysis of federal votes between 1970 and 1987 has shown (Papadopoulos 1994). According to the data set, radical right parties initiated 35 referenda and initiatives between 1984 and 1993 at the local, regional or federal level. However, even when acting through the institutions of direct democracy can be a successful way to counter the authorities, it is also very costly in terms of resources. Collecting signatures and preparing the campaign means that a movement must find activists ready to spend a lot of time and money on a single issue. In addition, if the referendum or initiative is federal, the party must be able to organize a supporting committee in the most inhabited cantons in order to reach as many voters as possible. Due to the radical right parties' lack of resources, there are only a handful of events related to the use of direct democracy each year.

Issues

Before discussing the main issue around which radical right parties mobilize, I must draw attention to the fact that when they intervene in a public debate that does not concern the defense of the Swiss identity, they do not automatically all adopt the same position. The ideology of the radical right is not homogeneous. For instance, in clear opposition to the Automobilist Party, the Swiss Democrats favored a low speed limit on highways as well as taxes on energy.

I regrouped the events initiated by radical right parties at the local, regional and federal level into ten categories. They comprise events related to:

1. National identity (struggle against immigrants or refugees, defense of myths that constitute the Swiss political identity: neutrality, independence, popular sovereignty, etc.).
2. Law and order policies (sustaining the army, opposition to the liberalization of drug laws, etc.).
3. Morality (opposition to homosexuality, etc.).
4. State budget (opposition to new taxes, or new expenses).
5. Other state policies than those listed (such as transport, education, etc.).
6. Struggle against governmental parties (taken together or separately).
7. Struggle against other political forces, including leftists, unions, punks, European institutions (if the opposition is not based on the defense of the Swiss political identity).
8. Struggle against an extreme right party or figure (in order to emphasize the demarcation between the party initiating the events and the extreme right).
9. Electoral campaigns (presentation of candidates, etc.).
10. Matters internal to the party initiating the events (revision of the program, election of a new president, etc.).

In Table 3, I excluded the instructions that a party gives before each popular vote (in such events the issue is given and does not depend upon the will of the party). Due to the high numbers of votes at each level of the Swiss political system, such events are very frequent ($n = 410$). Neither did I take into account events not clearly related to a political objective according to my sources.

In accordance with my preceding comments on the link between the volume of radical right parties' activities and the federal elections, one sees that the actions directly related to an election campaign represented a large part (22.3%) of all events between 1984 and 1993. Approximately another quarter of the radical right parties' actions concern the defense of what they consider to be the national identity. Among these actions most refer to immigration and refugee issues (13.1%).

Table 3:   Subjects of the Actions Initiated by Radical Right Parties (1984-1993)

Subject	% of the events related
Identity	22.3
Electoral campaign	22.3
Related to another state policy	19.9
Against other political forces	7.9
Related to the state budget	6.6
Internal affairs	6.0
Against governmental parties	4.9
Morality	4.4
Law and order	3.5
Against the extreme right	2.0
n = 597	100%

On the issues related to the Swiss identity, the Swiss Democrats were especially active, initiating 98 events. That they chose to be involved in the debates concerning these issues is in accordance with their programs and with the fact that these policies came under sharp criticism during this period. Between 1987 and 1991, the number of asylum seekers rapidly increased and the federal administration in charge of their registration gave the impression of being unable to cope with the increasing number of applications. This situation and the intense debate on the capacity of the country to welcome refugees was an opportunity for nationalist parties to mobilize and attract public attention for their propositions. As Kriesi (1995a) stated, pressure due to immigration in the context of an economic crisis can be a catalyst for the radical right, especially if the government does not have the capacity to avoid a politicization of the subject. As we will see in the next section, these issues mobilized not only the parties, but the whole radical right. Non-institutionalized groups, as well as non-organized citizens with xenophobic feelings resorted to heavy violence to put pressure on the authorities (Gentile, Jegen, Kriesi and Marquis 1995).

Yet the parties I am interested in are also concerned with a wide range of other political issues; and there one can distinguish some differences among them. Almost all the events related to morality were initiated by the UDF (23 out of 26); those referring to the protection of the environment were initiated by the Swiss Democrats. The Automobilist Party, which, proportionally, initiated less events related to the defense of the Swiss identity than the other radical right parties (only 4.7% of the events it initiated), was active concerning the reduction of the state budget (16.1%) and transport policy (15.5%).

It is interesting to note that only 4.9% of the radical right parties' actions were directed against one or more governmental parties. This does not correspond to the frequently voiced idea that contemporary radical right parties are anti-systemic (e.g. Ignazi 1992 concerning the AN/DS; Betz 1994 concerning the AP). With the exception of the Lega, Swiss radical right parties hardly criticize the government in a direct way. The election of the members of government by the parliament is one of the few occasions in which representatives of the AN/DS and the AP criticize the participation of the Socialist Party in the government. Although they opposed several governmental bills by launching a referendum, they never asked for resignations or new elections - not even in those cases in which they won the referenda (Gentile and Kriesi 1996).

Mobilization of the Extra-Parliamentary Radical Right[14]

Establishment of Diverse Tendencies

In the French speaking part of the country, parties like the Swiss Democrats or the Automobilists are less established than in the German part. To a certain extent the same observation can be made regarding the mobilization of the extra-parliamentary radical right. Between 1984 and 1993, 80.6% of its actions took place in the 19 German speaking cantons, 16.8% in the six French cantons, and 2.6% in the Italian part of the country. The most active organization among those that emerged in the mid-eighties during the so called "Spring of the Fronts" (Frischknecht 1991) was the "Patriotic Front," lead by Marcel Strebel.[15] It was established in a few German speaking cantons and never initiated actions outside this area. Such organizations had 10 to 70 militants, most of them young men ready to use violence. Racism and references to the thirties (especially to the "Front organizations") formed their ideology.

The skinhead community is also more developed in some German speaking cantons, but a "fanzine" edited in Lausanne *(Helvétie Blanche)* and another in Neuchâtel *(Mjolnir)* testify that the movement is also alive in the French part of the country. During the "Spring of the Fronts" some skinheads were members of explicitly racist organizations, such as the Patriotic Front or the Neue Nationale Front, most of which have since disbanded. During this period, older fascist activists tried, without a great deal of success, to instrumentalize and politicize the skinhead movement. But the skinheads' provocative life-style did not correspond to the expectations of these old fascists dreaming of a new and

---

14   As I already pointed out in the introduction, unless indicated otherwise, the analysis in this chapter concerns the period from 1988 until 1993.

15   This organization was involved in several attacks on homes for refugees. Its leader, Marcel Strebel, after having benefited from relative clemency from the justice system and the police, was finally arrested in 1994 after having shot at police officers.

disciplined advance-guard.[16] These men, whose main aim in their political struggle has always been to deny the Holocaust in order to rehabilitate the Third Reich, have nothing in common with the skinhead counter-culture except for their racist orientations. Some national meetings were organized to coordinate the activities of older activists with those of organizations founded in the "Spring of the Fronts," but, apart from a few press conferences, no action campaign was launched. The only fascist of the World War II generation to be frequently and respectfully mentioned in skinhead fanzines is G.-A. Amaudruz, the Swiss editor of European neo-nazi and revisionist books and reviews. In the early nineties, the Swiss "Hammer-Skins" became the main skinhead organization linking the remaining activists of the "Spring of the Fronts."[17] In 1995, it attracted the attention of the media and police by using heavy violence against "anti-fascists," attacking their street demonstrations and festivals (several people were injured during these events, 56 skinheads were arrested and guns were confiscated).

During the period 1988 through 1993, almost half (48.6%) of the actions which skinheads took part in had no clear political aim; 20.4% were directed against other political groups (mostly from the new social movements, such as the urban Autonomen or the Group for a Switzerland Without an Army), 25.7% aimed to "defend" the Swiss identity (about half of these actions were directed against refugees or immigrants), and the remaining 5.5% had very diverse objectives. The high proportion of actions without an identifiable political aim is, from my point of view, characteristic of a movement that is qualified as expressive and counter-cultural (Wisler 1995; Jegen 1995). In addition to the attempt to pressure the authorities on specific issues, counter-cultural movements try to reinforce their collective identity through the actions they initiate. These actions are often characterized by conflicting interactions with their opponents, including representatives of the state and counter-movements. In some cases, spontaneous action is not related to a specific political goal; action is no longer a medium to present a political point of view but instead becomes the message. In these cases "much of the benefits of collective action are produced in the action itself" (Koopmans 1990: 15). Individual physical

---

16   To gain insight into the difficulties faced by old fascists in attempting to organize a political campaign with skinheads, the reader can consult the autobiography of a former skinhead who was also the leader of an organized neo-nazi group in Berlin (Hasselbach and Bonengel 1995).

17   The Hammer-Skins, whose name refers to a sequence in the Allan Parker and Pink Floyd film "The Wall" and symbolizes for skinheads the struggling white working-class, are based in Littau, a small town in the canton of Lucerne. Their address can be found on the Internet with other divisions of the Hammer-Skin movement around North America and Europe.

violence being an integral constituent of the skinhead identity,[18] violent actions may occur to demonstrate that the local movement is still alive, that its potential to erupt has not disappeared through institutionalization or repression.

Apart from the "Spring of the Fronts" organizations and the skinhead community, new-right groups have attracted media attention during the past few years.[19] According to Altermatt and Skenderovic (1995), groups with new-right orientations have been forming one of the contemporary Swiss radical right's tendencies for a decade, essentially to be found in the French part of the country. But as shown in the data set, they initiated only a few events (1.9%). Two complementary factors explain this observation. First of all, in contrast to France or Germany, the Swiss new-right was not able to attract respected intellectuals or figures who could initiate a public debate around some of the new-right's ideas. Its capabilities only extended to organizing a handful of lectures and distributing books and reviews of the French new-right to radical right sympathizers (the indigenous production was limited in number and quality). Secondly, most of the activities of the groups composing the Swiss new-right (such as Troisième Voie, Cercle Proudhon or Avalon) were not carried out to attract public attention, so that a considerable range of their actions do not appear in my sources.

Table 4:   Most Active Groups of the Extra-Parliamentary Radical Right, 1984 to 1993

Groups	%
Skinheads	12.0
Patriotic Front	6.9
Other "Spring of the Front" related groups	5.1
New Right organizations	1.9
Other extra-parliamentary radical right groups	24.7
Events not related to an identified group	49.4
n = 686	100%

---

18   Their fanzines are full of pictures and symbols highlighting individual violence, and so is the whole "oï culture." For skinheads, fighting physically against an enemy is not only a political action but also an act of bravery. Between 1984 and 1993, 81.3% of the actions initiated by skinheads included the use of violence.

19   Under the label "New Right," I classify organizations defending anti-liberal, anti-cosmopolitan and anti-egalitarian views with references to the intellectuals of the Weimar conservative revolution. Example of such organizations are le GRECE, le Club de l'Horloge and Troisième Voie/Nouvelle Résistance in France or newspapers such as *Junge Freiheit* or *Criticon* in Germany.

Half of the events registered are not related to an identifiable radical right organization in my sources. This is not surprising given the high proportion of violent events (see Figure 2). In most cases, no organization claimed responsibility for these events; and the police never found the perpetrators. Out of 125 registered attacks, the perpetrators had been strictly identified in only 16 events. Concerning the 409 violent events to be found in the data set between 1984 and 1993, the police were able to arrest one or more persons in only 75 cases. Many events (24.7%) are attributable to a plethora of groups that each initiated only a few actions during this period.

Figure 2: Development of Extra-Parliamentary Mobilization

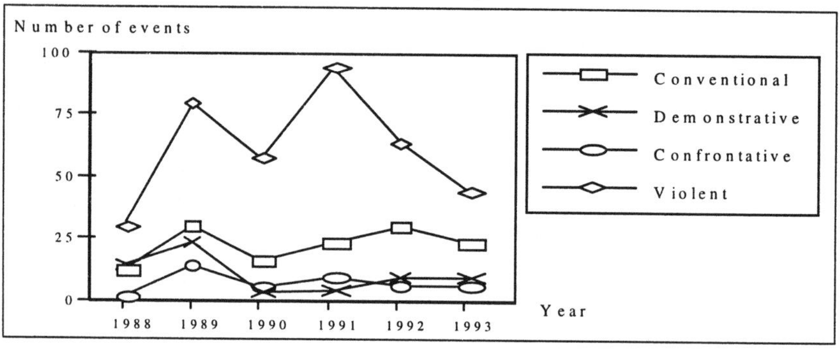

Development and Issues of the Extra-Parliamentary Radical Right's Mobilization

There is a certain similarity between the evolution of the extra-parliamentary radical right and the parties' mobilization through the period 1988 to 1993; 1989 and 1991 are the peaks of the mobilization waves (this similarity will be discussed with further analysis in the last section of this chapter).

Between 1984 and 1993, 73.7% of the events initiated by extra-parliamentary groups and having a clear political aim concerned the defense of Swiss identity. Of the 391 such events registered in this category, 222 were explicitly directed against refugees, especially those coming from non-European countries (56.8%), 40 against immigrants (10.2%) and 36 against the Jewish community (9.2%).

If one compares the main theme of the actions initiated by the extra-parliamentary radical right with those of the parties discussed earlier, one notes that while the parties are interested in diverse issues (such as ecology (SD/AN), transport (PA) or morality (EDU)), the extra-parliamentary groups are almost only concerned with the defense of Swiss identity or the struggle against their opponents.[20]

Table 5: Subjects of the Actions Initiated by Extra-Parliamentary Groups, 1984 to 1993

Subject	% of the events related to it
Identity	73.7
Against other political forces	15.1
Law and order	2.3
Electoral campaign	2.1
Related to the state budget	1.5
Related to another state policy	1.5
Internal affairs	1.5
Morality	1.5
Against governmental parties	0.9
Against extreme right	0.0
n = 531	100%

The second observation one can draw from Table 5 concerns the influence of the elections. During the federal election years the volume of conventional actions initiated by the radical right parties and directed towards the media increased. If, for the parties running for a seat, elections represent an opportunity to reach the public through the media's attention, they have no direct influence on the extra-parliamentary groups (only 2.1% of their actions were related to an electoral campaign); unless an issue around which they usually mobilize becomes salient during the campaign. This was clearly the case with the refugees in 1991.[21]

---

20 Organizations founded during the "Spring of the Fronts" and the skinhead movement are not the only ones to define themselves as anti-communist and anti-leftist. During the cold war, some groups of citizens were formed in order to register and control leftist activists. Such groups sold their information to private enterprises (for example, on request they compiled a report on the past activities of somebody having submitted an application for a position of responsibility).

21 In a recent study based on ten cases of radical right violence, Kriesi and his collaborators emphasized that when established right-wing political parties used metaphors and ideas on immigration that have been used by the radical right for a long time, activists of the extra-parliamentary radical right had the impression that they were gaining legitimacy. Even if the use of non-conventional action repertoires is still unpopular, they felt like the peak of an iceberg - their struggle becoming that of most Swiss citizens. In the study this was identified as one of the processes that can contribute to individual or collective violence against immigrants or refugees (Gentile, Jegen, Kriesi and Marquis 1995).

Extra-Parliamentary Action Repertoires

Before entering into a more detailed analysis of the evolution of the different kinds of violence initiated by the radical right, it is necessary to spend some time on the other action repertoires used by the extra-parliamentary groups. By doing so, one may be able to gain a better understanding of the nature of these groups. In the preceding section I mentioned that the parties I was interested in had only limited resources at their disposal. With the exception of a handful of organizations defending radical right ideas and having influential businessmen among their members (such as Action for Free Information, Action Freedom and Responsibility or the Union for an Independent and Neutral Switzerland, founded by Christoph Blocher, the popular DUC leader), the extra-parliamentary groups have even fewer resources than the parties. Therefore it is not surprising that they do not use direct democracy very frequently. The actions they initiated are often low-cost ones. But, as Figure 2 above shows, extra-parliamentary groups do not organize many demonstrative events (festivals, street demonstrations, public meetings, etc.). Between 1984 and 1993, these kind of events were rare.[22] In this period extra-parliamentary radical right organizations most often incited their sympathizers to disturb a leftist demonstration (for example on May 1st) rather than to demonstrate. When they did demonstrate, their aim was more to unite the militants inside the organization than to display the strength of the movement to a wider public and alert public opinion. Using demonstrations to enter the public sphere seems to be, nowadays, essentially a left-wing strategy.

Another way to attract public attention with few resources is to use the mass media. Again, Figure 2 shows that in contrast to the parties, groups from the extra-parliamentary radical right are not making many efforts to influence the public in this way (events classified as conventional). Only 5.7% of their actions are directed towards the media. Since radical right activists have hardly any privileged contact with journalists, their most effective way to use the media to spread their ideas is to organize press conferences, distribute press releases or pay for advertisements.[23]

---

22 Even among the violent events, there are few demonstrations that have turned into a direct confrontation with opponents or with the police, as is the case, for example, with the urban Autonomen (Giugni 1995). Putting together all demonstrations (legal or illegal, violent or non-violent), only 2.6% of the radical right actions between 1984 and 1993 can be classified in this category.

23 Each year, some organizations, such as L'Atout and L'Équipe in the French part of the country and the Trumpf Buur in the German part, put several dozen advertisements in newspapers in the lead up to national or cantonal votes (I did not take this kind of action into account in the data set).

Comparing the extra-parliamentary radical right's action repertoires with those used by the Swiss new social movements studied by Giugni (1995),[24] it appears that the extra-parliamentary radical right devoted little effort to attracting public attention. Instead of attempting to persuade the public, it sought to affect directly those it considers its enemies. In doing so, radical right groups try either to influence the authorities by showing their determination to oppose immigration policy, or to impress their enemies by frightening them (Gentile and Jegen 1996). The choice of the forms of violence directed against those designated as enemies is, as we will see, part of that logic.

Radical Right Violence

As Figure 2 shows, the extra-parliamentary radical right in Switzerland was especially violent. Between 1988 and 1993, out of ten actions attributable to it, six involved the use of violence. Radical right groups and activists did not hesitate to use violence directly against victims or to set fire to refugee shelters, knowing that their action might cost human lives.[25] As a result, 13 people were killed and 145 wounded during the ten years for which I have data. In an international comparison that included Germany, England, the Netherlands and three Nordic countries, Koopmans (1995) found that Switzerland was the most violent country regarding the use of heavy violence per million habitants in 1989 and 1991. If one studies the different forms of violence used by the extra-parliamentary radical right, one notes that besides the use of physical violence and attacks, other forms of violence were used to frighten those considered enemies by the radical right (see Table 6).

Slightly more than 10% of the extra-parliamentary radical right's actions is made up of threats against individuals or specific groups (Jews, Third World refugees). This massive use of threats and direct violence aiming at frightening enemies is quite new in Swiss political life and characterizes the contemporary radical right strategy.

---

24 Four movements in particular were systematically studied: the peace, ecology and solidarity movements and the "autonomous urbanites" (Autonomen).

25 In 1989 the death of four persons in a fire set by radical right sympathizers in Coire did not stop the wave of violence in Switzerland. Condemnation of the racist violence in the population was to be found, but its magnitude was limited. Studying the short term evolution of the German wave of violence against refugees, Ohlemacher (1993) found that violence decreased after the shock provoked by the fatal attack in Mölln, when German civil society reacted very strongly, showing solidarity with foreign residents and rejection of the neo-nazi ideas. The deaths in Solingen some months later did not lead to a decrease in attacks, in part because the population did not react as strongly as it had previously.

Table 6:   Forms of Violence Used by the Extra-Parliamentary Radical Right
            Activists (1988-1993)

Forms of violence	% of the extra-parliamentary radical right actions
Symbolic against objects	7.8
Symbolic against persons	0.8
Material damages	8.0
Profanations (cemetery)	1.1
Attacks / incendiary actions	18.6
Threats	10.3
Demonstration with violence	0.3
Violence against persons	12.7
Other violent actions	1.8
Total	61.4

In comparison, the new social movements have been peaceful in Switzerland, injuring, killing or frightening their opponents has never been one of their strategies. With the exception of the Autonomen movement, their violence was almost only directed against buildings or symbolic objects. And even in the case of Autonomen, the use of physical violence differs from the attacks of the radical right. As Giugni's data show (1995), violence usually occurred during demonstrations involving direct confrontation either with the police or with counter-movements. This was rarely the case with the extra-parliamentary radical right. Only 0.3% of its actions were demonstrations with violence, while this kind of action made up 20.5% of the events initiated by the Autonomen.[26]

For left-wing groups and theoreticians in the seventies, resorting to heavy violence against people (that could involve death) was a seldom taken step towards armed struggle and the militarization of organizations. Even among those that chose to act completely or partially in the underground, heavy violence resulted from a radicalization process of specific organizations that took years (Della Porta 1990; Curcio 1993). Looking at the data, it is clear that this step was not very big for radical right groups or organizations. Violence against people appeared from the beginning of the mobilization in the late eighties, it was neither a response to repression nor a radicalization of groups refusing to undergo institutionalization, trying to continue the struggle of the social movement they believed themselves to be part of (as was the case with the Italian movement in the seventies studied by Tarrow 1989).

---

26   Taking all forms of violence together, actions with violence represented 36.9% of the
      urban Autonomen actions. In other words, violence within demonstrations is the largest
      category of violent events they initiated (5.6% were damage against buildings or objects,
      6.4% attacks and 2% direct violence against persons).

The Counter-Mobilization

The increasing number of attacks against foreigners in the late eighties did not prompt the federal government, nor the leaders of the parties composing it, to publicly take a strong moral stand against radical right actions. Apart from a handful of statements condemning violence, the established political world seemed unconcerned by the radical right's activities. The same observation applies for the regional level. Only three cantons registered condemnations of radical right actions by members of the government or representatives of parties composing it. No political dike was built to contain the wave of violence.

But not all Swiss citizens were insensitive to the xenophobic arguments radical right parties used during electoral campaigns and to the increasing number of acts of violence against refugees. Numerous committees against racism and anti-Semitism were created at different levels of the political system in the period covered. These committees organized different kinds of actions in order to make the population aware of the problems refugees and immigrants face. Through these actions they also put pressure on the authorities, urging them to sign the United Nations convention against racial discrimination and propaganda. Apart from these committees, the churches, especially the Protestant ones, intervened in favor of more generosity and solidarity towards refugees. They very soon became one of the leading social forces behind the counter-mobilization. In the ten years covered, civil society's reaction against radical right actions amounted to 261 events, among them 97 demonstrations, 14 congresses, 19 events directed toward the media (press conferences or press releases), and 18 violent actions (including 6 attacks).[27] Contrary to the accusation often made by radical right politicians, left-wing organizations and the churches did not overreact to a handful of attacks against refugees by organizing dozens of demonstration after each attack against foreigners. More violent events were initiated by the extra-parliamentary radical right than were actions against racism or against violence by counter-movements.

Development of the Counter-Mobilization

In contrast to the radical right (parliamentary or not), the counter-movements were, in proportion to the number of inhabitants, more active in the French part

---

27 I did not register all the individual acts of resistance to the growing intolerance and increasingly restrictive immigration policies. Hundreds of citizens chose to express their solidarity with asylum seekers by helping them to stay in the country when they did not receive refugee status, hiding them and helping them to get a job. These acts are against the law and were therefore carried out without publicity and not reported in my sources.

of the country than in the German, as can be seen in Table 7. Across the different linguistic regions, the level of counter-mobilization is related to neither the effective level of the radical right parties' mobilization nor the level of extra-parliamentary mobilization.

Table 7: Level of Counter-Mobilization According to Linguistic Regions

Region	% of events	% of the population*
German	62.1	72.3
French	36.4	23.4
Italian	1.5	4.3
Total	100% n = 261	100%

* Census figures (Recensement fédéral de la population) 1990.

At the level of the cantons, however, there is a certain correspondence, especially in the German part of the country, between the level of anti-racist mobilization and the total number of radical right actions taking place between 1984 and 1993. Like radical right mobilization, mobilization against racism increased during the period (see Figure 3).

Figure 3: Development of Counter-Mobilization, 1984-1993

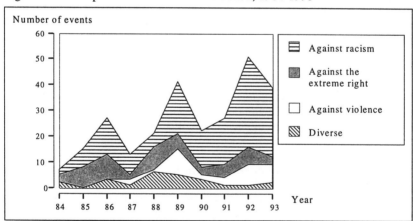

The counter-mobilization was not an immediate response to radical right mobilization as a whole. Rather, it followed the evolution of the extra-parliamentary group activities, with some months delay (see Figure 4). This observation is consistent with the analyses made by Koopmans and Duyvendak (1991). When comparing the Netherlands, France and Germany, they found a positive correlation between the actions of neo-fascist or racist groups and counter-mobilization (mostly anti-racist) between 1975 and 1989.

Figure 4 shows the evolution through time of the activities of the parties, the extra-parliamentary groups and the counter-mobilization. Each year has been divided into quarters.

Figure 4: Activities of Radical Right Parties, Extra-Parliamentary Groups and Counter-Mobilization, 1988 to 1994

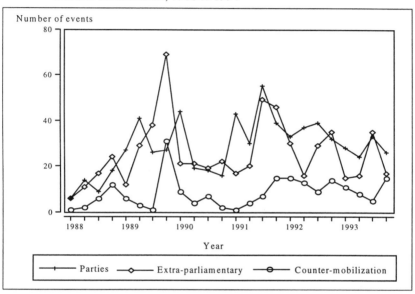

To analyze the relationship between the mobilization of extra-parliamentary groups and the counter-mobilization, a cross-correlation procedure was used, followed by a Pearson correlation. It appears that the extra-parliamentary mobilization had a positive and significant effect on counter-mobilization during four months (a extra-parliamentary mobilization of the radical right taking place in January having an effect on the level of the counter-mobilization until April). The most significant effect was a direct one (taking place the same month). In this case the correlation coefficient is 0.47 (sig. = 0.00). Accordingly, if the cantonal relationship between the level of the extra-parliamentary radical right activity, and the reaction of civil society seems to be unclear, there is undoubtedly a clear time relationship between them at the national level.

My hypothesis is that counter-mobilization responds less to the effective regional level of radical right actions, legal or not, than to the diffuse feelings in the population of increasing racism and intolerance against foreigners. The rise in extra-parliamentary actions in the country, especially those including the use of violence, reinforces this feeling. This is especially so in those cantons where counter-movements are an integral part of civil society and able to alarm the public. It is essentially through the anti-racist organizations and the regional or local media that the population was made aware of the increasing intolerance and violence against foreigners. This may explain why more events are initiated to oppose racism in general than are events expressing disapproval of specific attacks against foreigners (indeed, protests against violence are quite rare). Unfortunately, I do not have sufficient counter-mobilization events in my data set to analyze the relation between the evolution of the radical right over time and that of the counter-mobilization in the different cantons. This analysis at the regional level would have been necessary to see whether or not a reaction on the part of civil society leads to a real decrease in radical right mobilization.

Is There a Link Between the Parties and Extra-Parliamentary Mobilization?

My data set contains enough events to analyze the correlation between the actions of the parties and the events initiated by extra-parliamentary groups or individuals. In the following analysis, I took the following factors into account in each of the 26 cantons:

- The number of events initiated by the radical right parties between 1988 and 1993, per 1,000 inhabitants.[28]
- The number of events initiated by extra-parliamentary groups or individuals per 1,000 inhabitants during the same period of time.
- The percentage of voters that chose to vote for a radical right party in the 1991 federal elections.[29] This election took place in all cantons on the same date and divides my period of time approximately in two.

As each canton has its own party system, it is relevant to regard them as independent cases for my analysis. Moreover, radical right parties are not only interested in national issues. A high proportion of their activities concern the regional (35.1%) or the local level (12.8%).

The fact that the electoral success of radical right parties is to be found in those cantons where these parties are most active is not surprising. As for any

---

28   I did not use the effective volume of actions because the cantons have very different sizes and numbers of inhabitants (they range from 12,000 to 1,122,000).

29   The radical right parties' results in the federal elections were taken as another indication of their strength (in addition to the number of events they were able to initiate).

political party, to gain votes, a radical right party must capture the public's attention as much as possible. (I have already emphasized the large number of events initiated by these parties and directed towards the media during the national electoral campaign.)

More interesting is the positive relationship between the actions of the parties and those initiated by extra-parliamentary groups or activists in the 26 cantons. It proves that the existence of an established radical right party at the cantonal level did not prevent the development of violence by the late eighties in Switzerland. One must keep in mind that while the parties are almost exclusively acting within the margins of legality, the extra-parliamentary mobilization of the radical right is characterized by violence.

Table 8:   Correlation Between Party Mobilization and Extra-Parliamentary
          Radical Right Actions (Pearson)

	Extra-parliamentary actions	Radical right parties' actions	1991 federal election results
Extra-parliamentary actions	1.00		
Actions of the radical right parties	0.48*	1.00	
Results in the 1991 federal election	0.14	0.58**	1.00

sig.: * = 0.05, ** = 0.01

It is probable that in a canton where one or more radical right party tried to put their priorities onto the political agenda (and they proved to be able to do so at the federal as well as at the cantonal level through referenda and initiatives), other radical right groups became aware of a diffuse public sympathies for some of their ideas and perceived a real opportunity to act. It is interesting to note that the extra-parliamentary radical right seems to be more stimulated by the level of actions initiated by the radical right parties than by their actual electoral success. According to this observation, groups from the extra-parliamentary radical right should be more active during the electoral campaign, when the parties stressed issues they felt concerned about. To test this hypothesis, I compared the number of events initiated during an electoral campaign (the month of the election and the two months preceding it) with the number of events initiated during the other months. I considered all the elections to renew the 26 cantonal parliaments,[30] as well as the elections for the Federal Assembly. From 1988 to 1993, 75 out of 539 (13.9%) events initiated by extra-parliamentary groups took place during an electoral campaign. Since, during

---

30   In all cantons, parliamentary elections take place every four years, but the date of these
     elections varies from one canton to another.

these six years, electoral campaigns averaged 10.4% of the months (from 5.6% in the canton Fribourg to 16.6% in Intern-Appenzell), groups from the extra-parliamentary radical right were slightly more active during these specific months.[31] There is a positive correlation between party mobilization and extra-parliamentary radical right activities not only regarding their territorial location, but also regarding their evolution from 1988 to 1993.

I already mentioned that both the radical right parties and the extra-parliamentary groups became more active during the period I am interested in (1991 being the peak of both mobilizations). The correlation between the parties' activities and those of extra-parliamentary groups during the same month in Switzerland is positive and significant (0.28, sig. = 0.017).[32] On the national level there are some incentives for the radical right to mobilize, whatever the respective specific cantonal party system is. It is clear that in the early nineties the massive national debate on the country's capacity to accept refugees, as well as the debate on European integration, represented real opportunities for nationalist parties and extra-parliamentary groups to mobilize. The fact that in these two debates some prominent figures of the established right (especially in the DUC party) adopted some images usually associated with radical right parties in their own discourse, contributed to the extra-parliamentary radical right's mobilization (Gentile, Jegen, Kriesi and Marquis 1995). Indeed, sympathizers and activists of extra-parliamentary groups suddenly had the feeling that they were no longer on the periphery of the political arena, but instead they were the tip of an iceberg, a sort of "avant-garde."

Conclusion: On the Necessity of Constructing a Data Set

Thanks to a data set on all radical right mobilization, this chapter could give the reader an overall view of radical right protest in Switzerland between 1984 and 1991. It was possible to outline the effective intensity of its mobilization and to

---

31   As there is some bias beyond my control in this analysis, the result can only be interpreted as a rough indication of a tendency that confirms the hypothesis. The most important bias that underestimates the impact of electoral campaigns is that radical right parties were not present in all the elections that took place between 1988 and 1993 in the 26 cantons. In some cantons they did not even exist during this period. Another bias lay in the fact that I lacked any data on local elections.

32   Investigation of cross correlations indicated that the only significant correlation was positive, with no delay in time (an increase in the number of events initiated by the parties in January leading to an increase in the number of actions initiated by extra-parliamentary groups the same month).

highlight the similarities and differences between the parties' actions and the extra-parliamentary mobilization. Similarities concerned the linguistic area (parties and extra-parliamentary groups being more active in the German part of the country when considered proportionally to the population), the increasing number of events initiated by the late eighties, as well as the determination to limit the number of foreigners, and especially the number of refugees from non-European countries. The differences concerned the action repertoires (the parties acting almost exclusively legally, whereas extra-parliamentary mobilization was characterized by the high proportion of violent events). It was also to possible to deduce from the extra-parliamentary groups' strategy that they are not particularly interested in entering the public sphere. They attempt to directly hurt or frighten those they consider to be their enemies. This distinguishes them from the radical right parties, whose objective is precisely to reach the public and to influence public debates (through both the media and the use of institutions of direct democracy).

The results presented in this chapter emphasize the positive correlation between the parties' activities and the extra-parliamentary mobilization across time (evolution from 1988 to 1993) and in space (the level of mobilization during this period in the 26 cantons). They also underline the clear connection between extra-parliamentary mobilization of the radical right and the level of counter-mobilization initiated by the civil society. These findings demonstrate once more that, despite its limitations, event analysis is invaluable for the study of collective action over time.

References

Altermatt, U. and D. Skenderovic. 1995. "L'extrême droite: organisations, personnes et développements au cours des années 80 et 90." Pp. 1-162 in *L'extrême droite en Suisse*, ed. U. Altermatt and H. Kriesi. Fribourg: Editions Universitaires Fribourg.

Bähler, R. 1993. *Die rechtsradikale Szene in der Schweiz.* Zürich: G.M.S. & G.R.A., info-suisse ed.

Betz, H.-G. 1994. *Radical Right-Wing Populism in Western Europe.* New York: St. Martin's Press.

Curcio, R. 1993. *A visage découvert.* Paris: Lieu commun.

Della Porta, D. 1990. *Il terrorismo di Sinistra.* Bologna: Il Mulino.

Frischknecht, J. 1991. *Schweiz wir kommen - die neuen Fröntler und Rassisten.* Zürich: Limmat Verlag.

Gentile, P. and M. Jegen. 1996. "Rechtsextreme und neue soziale Bewegungen in der Schweiz: Mobilisierung im Vergleich." *Berliner Debatte/Initial* 1: 27-33.

Gentile, P., M. Jegen, H. Kriesi and L. Marquis. 1995. "La radicalisation de la droite radicale: une étude de cas." Pp. 163-287 in *L'extrême droite en Suisse*, ed. U. Altermatt and H. Kriesi. Fribourg: Editions Universitaires Fribourg.

Gentile, P. and H. Kriesi. 1996. "Contemporary Radical Right Parties in Switzerland: History of a Divided Family." Forthcoming in *New Party Politics of the Right: The Rise and Success of Neo-Populist Parties in Western-Style Democracies*, ed. H.-G. Betz and S. Immerfall.

Giugni, M. 1995. *Entre stratégie et opportunité, les nouveaux mouvements sociaux en Suisse*. Zurich: Seismo.

Hasselbach, I. and W. Bonengel. 1995. "Lettre à un père absent: 'j'étais un néonazi'." Pp. 19-129 in *Jeunesse perdue, révolte vide et vieux démons*. Paris: Autrement, Série Mutations.

Ignazi, P. 1992. "The Silent Counter-Revolution: Hypotheses on the Emergence of Extreme Right-Wing Parties in Europe." *European Journal of Political Research* 22: 3-30.

Jegen, M. 1995. "Violence de droite: une étude de cas." Paper presented at the Congress of Social Sciences, Module "Jeunesse, violence et société." Bern, 11-14 October.

Koopmans, R. 1990. "Bridging the Gap: The Missing Link Between Political Opportunity Structure and Movement Actions." Unpublished paper. Graduate School of the Social Sciences, Amsterdam.

Koopmans, R. 1995. "A Burning Question: Explaining the Rise of Racist and Extreme Right Violence in Western Europe." Paper presented at the workshop on "Racist Parties in Europe: A New Political Family" at the ECPR joint sessions. Bordeaux. 27 April - 2 May.

Koopmans, R. and J. W. Duyvendak. 1991. "Gegen die Herausforderer: Neue Soziale Bewegungen und Gegenbewegungen in der Bundesrepublik Deutschland, den Niederlanden und Frankreich." *Forschungsjournal Neue Soziale Bewegungen* 2: 17-30.

Kriesi, H. 1995a. *Le système politique suisse*. Paris: Economica.

Kriesi, H. 1995b. "Bewegung auf der Linken, Bewegung auf der Rechten: die Mobilisierung von zwei neuen Typen von sozialen Bewegungen in ihrem politischen Kontext." *Swiss Political Science Review* (1): 9-52.

Kriesi, H., R. Koopmans, J. W. Duyvendak and M. Giugni. 1995. *New Social Movements in Western Europe: A Comparative Perspective*. Minneapolis and St. Paul: University of Minnesota Press.

Linder, W. 1994: *Swiss Democracy: Possible Solutions to Conflict in Multicultural Societies*. New York: St. Martin's Press.

McAdam, D. 1996. "Initiator and Derivative Movements: Diffusion Processes in Protest Cycles." Pp. 217-239 in *Repertoires and cycles of collective action*, ed. M. Traugott. Durham, N.C.: Duke University Press.

Ohlemacher, T. 1993. *Bevölkerungsmeinung und Gewalt gegen Ausländer im wiedervereinigten Deutschland. Empirische Anmerkungen zu einem unklaren Verhältnis*. Discussion Paper FS III 93-104. Wissenschaftszentrum Berlin für Sozialforschung (Social Science Research Center Berlin, WZB). Berlin.

Tarrow, S. 1989. *Democracy and Disorder: Protest and Politics in Italy 1965-1975*. Oxford: Clarendon Press.

Veron, E. 1981. *Construire l'événement, les médias et l'accident de three mile island*. Paris: Editions de Minuit.

Comparative Event Analysis: Black Civil Rights Protest in South Africa and the United States

Susan Olzak and Johan L. Olivier[1]

Introduction

Sociologists interested in social movements and collective action have long considered the natural histories of movements and revolutions as key to understanding the underlying causes of protest.[2] Recently, researchers have begun to apply the logic of comparative historical methods to studying the emergence, peaking and decline of collective action in different countries (e.g. Koopmans 1996; Kriesi et al. 1995; Jenkins and Klandermans 1995).

Comparative analysis of state structures has been useful in developing new macro-level explanations that emphasize the significant role played by state differences in determining political outcomes (Skocpol 1975). Together, these comparative/historical strategies have suggested ways to link changes in the political system to protest movements. For example, Kriesi (1995) has suggested that the degree to which citizens have direct access to state institutions in different countries explains some of the variation in outcomes of social movements in Western Europe. Comparative research designs allow the researcher to examine the effects of different state responses to protest. New theoretical debates have been stimulated by cross-national studies that model the effects of repression and coercive measures on protest and collective violence (Lichbach 1987; Muller and Weede 1990; Moore 1995; Francisco 1995; Koopmans 1995, 1996). These comparisons become especially interesting when considering the fact that many movements - such as the ecology, animal rights, gay and lesbian, or the women's movements, have experienced varying levels of success in different state systems.

Many scholars now share the view that comparative analysis has the potential for explaining how political processes encourage or inhibit social change. Innovations in methods for analyzing the trajectories of social movements have

1   Preparation of this paper was supported by grants to Susan Olzak from the National Science Foundation (SES-9196229). Useful suggestions were provided by Michael Hannan, Elizabeth H. McEneaney, John W. Meyer, Joel Podolny, Suzanne Shanahan and S. C. Noah Uhrig.
2   For example Rule and Tilly (1965), Moore (1966), Wolf (1969), Tilly, Tilly and Tilly (1975), Paige (1975), Tilly (1986, 1995), Rucht and Neidhardt (1995).

produced advances in our understanding of protest in an international context. The ability to compare similar movements, or forms of collective action across national boundaries has led to an emphasis on *event analysis*. Analysis of events divides the history of a social movement into a series of distinct acts that can be disaggregated or aggregated into temporal or spatial units. This is helpful when attempting to adjudicate between theories that have different predictions about the trajectory of events.

This chapter compares two methods in two settings. We first compare several recent methods of event analysis that have been found useful and we then contrast two of these methods using examples from our research on racial mobilization in South Africa and the United States. In doing so, we hope to explore the advantages and disadvantages of event analysis, as well as to highlight some interesting research questions that arise in comparative research on protest in different countries.

Analysis of Protest Events

We focus here on event analysis. How should we begin to define a protest event? Most analyses of protests gather information on contentious or disruptive collective action that has claims seeking to change the system (Tilly 1986; Tarrow 1989). Others broaden the scope to include conventional collective protests if they are initiated by a social movement organization (SMO) or by a group of activists of one of these movements (Kriesi et al. 1995). Many interesting events lie on the boundary line between conventional and unconventional activity. Examples would include employee walkouts protesting against sexual harassment, press conferences announcing a new social movement organization, or a sit-in within the doors of a government agency, a university president's office or similar business settings. Some researchers also count traditional lobbying activity as a collective event if it is nonroutine (marches, protests outside of closed court sessions) and/or *if they are instigated by social movement organizations* (as in voter registration drives during the civil rights movement). Most conventional collective activities by business associations, political party officials, and government office holders (i.e. press conferences by police chiefs, mayors and presidential candidates) are usually excluded. Thus, a key feature of a protest event is that the actors instigating the events are likely to be social movement groups, organizations or quasi-organizations, or spontaneous participants acting collectively to express some claim, grievance or protest.

A second dimension of a collective event concerns the behaviors of the participants in the event. These categories involve *forms* of the collective event, which attempt to classify the predominant form of an event or the most extreme form of protest or activity (when considering violence during an event). These range from peaceful civil rights marches to sit-ins, to violent attacks and race riots. Forms are made up of one or more detailed *activity*, which is actual behavior by protesters or participants. Note that most business activities, the majority of individual crimes, individual terrorist attacks (such as the "unabomber" case), and/or vandalism (e.g. beer cans found in a Jewish cemetery) that have unidentified goals, claims, grievances or participants would be excluded. In contrast, symbolic racial attacks, such as swastikas or burning crosses in black neighborhoods, where the symbolic message is well-understood, would be considered an event by many researchers.[3]

The method of using events as key units of analysis allows researchers to consider social movements as a variable that exists along a continuum, open to empirical examination. This is in contrast to focusing on a predetermined period assumed to encompass all of the important determinants and outcomes. This strategy anticipates the possibility that events might occur after a revolution had ended or before a social movement supposedly begins. Thus, event analysis can be contrasted with traditional methods that analyze social movements only within conventional temporal boundaries defined by the history of some movement or revolution. As Tilly's analysis of contentious events in France suggested, a focus on events as the unit of analysis can uncover information on the timing of rebellions that cannot be recovered if conventional dates about the beginning and ending of revolutions are used as guidelines (1975: 56).

Event analysis uses data on events that occur within either temporal or spatial units of analysis. The actual data consists of counts, sequences of events, or the actual timing of and between adjacent events. To examine the various advantages and limitations of *event analysis*, we review and evaluate methods for using information on events - especially their timing and sequences - to analyze social movements and collective action in a comparative framework.[4]

Event analysis has an extremely broad scope for studying protest. Events form the unit of analysis for race riots (Spilerman 1970; Olzak and Shanahan 1996), strikes and industrial protests (Aminzade 1984), political violence (Tilly, Tilly, and Tilly 1975), peasant rebellions (Paige 1975), revolutionary activity (Markoff 1986), lynchings (Inverarity 1976), and coups d'état (Hannan and Carroll 1981). Studies of protest have considered North American civil rights' protests (McAdam 1982), marches against nuclear power (Walsh and Warland

---

3   See Olzak (1992) for a discussion of coding rules for ethnic and racial collective action.
4   Jenkins (1983), Marwell and Oliver (1984), Zald and McCarthy (1987), Tarrow (1989), and McAdam, McCarthy, and Zald (1988) provide recent substantive reviews of theory and research on collective action.

1983), Québécois separatist demonstrations (Olzak 1982), union organizing of farm workers (Jenkins and Perrow 1977), protests by North American Indians (Nagel 1995, 1996), and social protests in Italy (Tarrow 1989).

Event analysis allows diverse forms of collective action to be measured and compared, because each event can be characterized along numerous dimensions. For example, most existing codebooks include directions for coding duration, social categories of participants, coalition formation, size of the event, violence, police reactions, claims, actions of by-standers, and many other characteristics of a given event.[5] The advantage of gathering this amount of detail on an event means that even subtle shifts in the goals, participants and strategies of a social movement can be observed directly - because they are allowed to vary by event. This means that theories about consequences of changes in strategies, activities or the internal organizational strength of social movements can be tested empirically with event data that is collected over time.

A second advantage of event analysis is that crucial dimensions of social movement organizations, such as bureaucratic structure, use of violence, previous success, leadership roles, etc., can be analyzed with respect to distinct outcomes (Gamson 1970; Zald and McCarthy 1977; Minkoff 1993, 1994). Thus, information about social movement protest consisting of thousands of acts as well as analysis of one-time confrontations can be analyzed and compared. This feature of the strategy is important because it permits cases of unsuccessful and/or short-lived movements to be compared with successful and long-lived ones. It also allows stages that emerge during collective actions to be analyzed as a variable sequence of events rather than as one predetermined sequence. This suggests a basic analytical distinction between event analysis and social movement case studies. Event analysis allows researchers to analyze why no events occurred, while case study strategies can only follow events that did occur and were recorded by history. This leads to problems of sample selection bias, which has hampered the study of revolutions, civil wars, genocide and other dramatic events.

Methods of Analyzing Event Data

A central research question in event analysis is how much to aggregate data on events and covariates over time and place. Table 1 below classifies the four designs according to degree of aggregation of the data by time and place. An important research decision involves *which* of these methods is appropriate for

---

5   For examples, see the appendices in Tilly (1978), McAdam (1982), Burstein (1985), Olzak (1992), Tarrow (1989), and Kriesi et al. (1995).

studying the process of protest. In many cases, the research design is dictated by the availability of data. For instance, available economic data are often aggregated to the year, while census covariates are sometimes available only once a decade. Sometimes the preferred socioeconomic data are even more sparse.[6]

A key advantage of data on events is that they can usually be collected in small temporal units (such as a continuous record of daily occurrences of some kind of event from newspaper accounts). As a matter of convenience, many researchers have aggregated this information into yearly counts. For example, there have been studies of strikes aggregated to yearly counts (Hibbs 1976), and studies that have aggregated the number of lynchings to the county-level over a long period of history (Beck and Tolnay 1995). A potential cost of this decision is that it loses information about shifts in the fortunes of social movements during different periods. In particular, the effect of levels of prior mobilization cannot be taken into account in cross-sectional designs. This does not seem to be an optimal method for analyzing collective action, which by definition implies a cumulative process. By including measures of past history, researchers can examine the mechanisms underlying mobilization. The data can be analyzed in different "pieces" - by time period, by region, across countries, or by neighborhood. In this way, multiple types of analytic techniques for studying longitudinal processes can be compared and contrasted for the same set of outcome variables.

Table 1 provides an outline of four leading methods of analysis that are appropriate for analyzing event data. Cross-sectional designs aggregate completely over time and single time-series designs aggregate completely over geographical units. In the context of event analysis, this means it records the total number of events in a study period for each locality. Time-series designs record the total number of events over all localities for each period (which means that there is some temporal aggregation). Panel designs involve less aggregation on either dimension because they record event counts for each unit for each period. Count analysis aggregates event counts over some temporal period for some unit or units of analysis that can be compared across nations, regions, cities or years. Sequence analysis focuses on the specific temporal ordering of precipitating and outcome events to explain a particular event or some category of event-types, as in one lynching. Event-history designs retain exact information on timing of events and locale so that covariates can be

---

6   Table 1 is obviously not an exhaustive list. With the exception of sequence analysis, the list focuses on methods for analyzing protest that employ an underlying probability model in order to evaluate a set of arguments that can be falsified. To consult some alternative methods for using event-history data, see Griffin and Ragin (1994) and Tarrow (in this volume).

measured in natural units of time (annual levels of unemployment) or in event-time (the number of police acts in a spell preceding the beginning of a particular protest).

Table 1: Methods of Analysis Using Event Data

Data structure of independent variables	Are the events aggregated?	
	Yes	No
Cross section: Covariates fixed over time	OLS regression (Paige 1975) Poisson Regression (Spilerman 1970; Beck & Tolnay 1995) Logit regression (Markoff 1985; McAdam 1986)	Event-history analysis with fixed covariates (Olzak 1986; Hannan & Carroll 1981; Olzak et al. 1994)
Time series: Temporal variation in the covariates	Time-series OLS regression with lagged dependent variables (Jenkins & Eckert 1986; Hibbs 1976; Kelly & Isaac 1984) Logistic regression (Olzak & West 1991; Edwards & Marullo 1995) Poisson regression with aggregated event counts (Cameron & Trivedi 1986; Hannan & Freeman 1989; Minkoff 1994; Olzak & Olivier 1996a)	Event-history analysis with yearly split spells (Olzak 1992; McCarthy et al. 1988)
Panel analysis: Regular panel data	Two wave panel with lagged dependent variables (Muller & Weede 1990) Pooled-cross section and time-series (Olzak 1982; Nielsen 1980)	Event history analysis with temporal data at the unit level (Olzak et al. 1996; Minkoff 1993)
Variable timing		Event history analysis with covariates measured at the start of each spell (Strang 1991; Olzak & Olivier 1996b)
Sequence analysis: Temporal ordering of event narrative		Event structure analysis (Cosaro & Heise 1990; Griffin 1993)

Most of the methods of analysis in Table 1 vary along a second dimension: choice of an underlying probability model. For event counts, the main choices have been between (1) classical regression models which assume a normal distribution and (2) discrete-state stochastic process models. Most previous research on the occurrence of collective events has used models (such as OLS regression) that assume that the outcome is a continuous variable with a normal distribution. As noted above, counts of events, such as riots and revolutions, often have quite discontinuous distributions. Revolutions, racial violence and civil rights' campaign activity comes in bursts or cycles of protest, which then decline over time. Moreover, counts are, by definition, non-negative, and this restriction is inconsistent with the assumption of a normal distribution. Indeed, taking account of this constraint is important in analysis of counts of collective events because observed counts of zero are common. While counted data never strictly satisfy assumptions of non-negativity and continuity, in some collective action research, this does not make much practical difference when counts were large, as in the case of number of strikes per year in the U.S. (Hibbs 1976).

Cross-Sectional Analysis

Numerous studies of collective action use cross-sectional methods to estimate the effects of cross-sectional community characteristics on variations in the number of events that occurred in a set of communities. In cross-sectional applications this involves relating constant community characteristics to frequencies of events, aggregated over time to produce a total count for each community. This approach has been used in studies of lynchings (Inverarity 1976; Tolnay and Beck 1995), peasant rebellions (Chirot and Ragin 1975), organizational success (Steedly and Foley 1979), and urban protests (Eisinger 1973). Some investigators, such as Markoff (1986), have collapsed information on event counts into binary distinctions between "no event" and "one or more events" and used logit analysis. As we mentioned above, there are serious drawbacks to applying cross-sectional designs to data on events that occur over time. Specifically, this approach ignores the possibility that past experience with events affected the flow of subsequent events. For example, a protest movement's ability to gain more resources is likely to be facilitated by prior success in mobilization (McAdam 1982). If researchers ignore these effects of prior history, models of collective action are likely to be misspecified.

Time-Series Analysis

Time-series regression is a common but perhaps not always appropriate technique that has been used to analyze longitudinal data sets on events. Time-series analysis is commonly used in research on collective events in diverse settings and historical periods: French collective violence, 1830 to 1960 (Rule and Tilly 1972; Snyder and Tilly 1972; Tilly 1986); lynchings of African-Americans (McAdam 1982), North American urban racial violence, 1948 to 1979 (Kelly and Isaac 1984), civil rights movement activity, 1950 to 1980 (McAdam 1982; Jenkins and Eckert 1986), and analysis of all forms of domestic violence in the U.S., 1890 to 1970 (Rasler 1986). The key advantage of this design is that it highlights the effects of historical change. Why is this important? When there are theoretical or historical reasons to believe that effects differ among periods, or that protest counts rise and fall over time in systematic ways, then cross-sectional data on events is inappropriate. Time-series methods allow the analyst to estimate shifts in the parameters at pre-determined times. However, this approach has one important disadvantage. It loses important information by aggregating over units and by aggregating over time within periods (i.e. creating event counts within a week, month or year). This contrasts with methods using the exact timing of rare events to estimate a rate of occurrence using continuous time models (e.g. transition rate analysis).

Poission regression with aggregated event counts. Event count analysis also aggregates data on events into yearly or spatial units of analysis. Discrete-state stochastic models, such as the Poisson model, have been used to analyze data of the counts of riots, protests or revolutions in a year or in a country. This is because it is often useful to aggregate yearly occurrences of events of some kind and compare these counts with annual data on the independent or explanatory variables. Discrete-state models are useful because they take the non-negativity constraint of event counts into account. However, the assumptions of normal distribution theory are frequently violated with such data as counts in particular localities or periods are non-negative and are generally small (or even zero).

Logistic regression techniques can be used in a cross-sectional as well as time-series design (see Table 1). In a cross-sectional analysis, the dependent variable conveys information on whether or not some region experienced an event (Markoff 1986). In longitudinal analysis, the information is aggregated to a specific time boundary, indicating whether or not an event occurred within some time period. Studies of organizational mortality have used this method successfully to build in effects of individual organizational characteristics (such as age and size), as well as population-level characteristics, such as the density of particular social movement organizations in the environment (Minkoff 1993; Carroll and Huo 1988).

Poisson models have been used to analyze cross-sectional data on the propensity of cities to riot (Lieberson and Silverman 1965; Spilerman 1970). Poisson regression has also been used to estimate models of the occurrence of yearly counts of events in a single time series (Hannan and Freeman 1989).

The disadvantage of using Poisson regression with event data is that its use is likely to violate two assumptions that underlie the model: (1) that the rate at which events occur is a constant over the observation time, and (2) there is no unobserved heterogeneity (Spilerman 1971). Analysis of protest events has suggested, for example, that contagion affects the likelihood of proximate events, such that the occurrence of one protest increases the chances that another event will occur. Furthermore, evidence suggests that proximity to highly volatile regions of unrest generates higher risks of protest within that same region, when compared to more distant areas (Soule 1995). A generalized version of the Poisson model, known as the negative binomial, can estimate the effects of both unobserved heterogeneity and/or time dependence in the rate, which results from these type of examples of contagion and spatial diffusion (Hausman, Hall and Griliches 1984; Cameron and Trivedi 1986).

The negative binomial model, however, rests on the assumption that the distribution of events are *independent of the disturbance term* which is also likely to be violated in much of the protest data that sociologists might analyze. This is because autocorrelation is likely to be present, especially when using time-series of socioeconomic characteristics of countries that are causally linked to one another (for a common example that has plagued our own research, consider income and education measures of disadvantaged groups over time at the national-level of analysis). To confront this problem, Barron (1992) and Barron and Hannan (1990) applied a method of estimating autocorrelation while simultaneously building in effects of the causal variables and measures of unobserved heterogeneity. This is the generalized quasi-likelihood (GQL) method to analyze a series of count data.[7]

Panel Analysis

Regular panel data. If data over time exists for the *same* units of analysis, then there are alternatives to cross-sectional analysis. Use of both cross-sectional and longitudinal variation, or panel analysis, to analyze events over multiple units represents a third approach (see Table 1 above). When information on events is available for two or more time periods on multiple behavioral units, several estimation procedures can exploit more of the information than can done with either cross-sectional or time-series analysis alone. These more general approaches are particularly advantageous when analyzing rare events, such as

---

7   For a comparison of properties of Poisson regression, negative binomial regression and GQL methods applied to the same data on labor union foundings, see Barron (1992). Furthermore, Barron's research describes how nested GQL models can be compared using the log-likelihood ratio test statistic that has an asymptotic chi-square distribution.

deaths from collective violence (Muller and Weede 1990). Nonetheless, this approach still involves temporal aggregation (to periods) and does not employ appropriate probability models for small counts, or when there are many zero counts in the data.

Pooled cross-section and time-series methods allow the researcher to capture specific temporal effects and unit-specific effects in the same model. Thus, in analysis of Québécois separatist activity, Olzak (1982) included a measure that tested whether a "Montreal" effect existed. This indicator of Montreal location estimated the net effect of that (highly unusual) metropolitan area over and above the linguistic composition effects in the model. The disadvantage of this method is that it requires assumptions that the units of analysis over the panel period have not changed boundaries. This assumption is not often sound with data on geographical locations that merge, split, and change names over time.

In using time-series or panel designs to analyze protests, another tricky problem is likely to arise which causes problems for the estimation techniques associated with these methods. This is the problem that occurs when the numbers of some types of protests in any given year or country are zero. This is especially likely if the study has a long time frame or compares a large number of countries, many of which will not experience any events. How can we analyze event data that has large numbers of zero counts? Fortunately, event count analysis techniques, especially ones that can estimate truncated event counts, can address this question (as in COUNT software (King 1990)).

Methods that use variable timing. In contrast to panel analysis that aggregates data into temporal units, event-history analysis uses the exact timing of an event. There are two basic ways of analyzing data on the timing of events using the methods of event-history analysis. The event-history approach involves application and generalization of methods originally designed for studying events in biostatistics and industrial engineering. Recently event-history analysis has been used to study rates of occurrence of collective actions, such as riots and protests, as well as the establishment and disbanding of social movement organizations. This class of methods uses information on the timing and sequencing of events to estimate models of transition rates. Two general forms of event-history analysis are relevant to the study of collective action and social movements. The first involves study of recurrent events, such as riots, where the typical duration of an event is small relative to the waiting time between events. In this case the attention focuses on the rate of occurrence, that is the transition from an event count of N to N + 1 (Coleman 1981; Amburgey and Carroll 1984; Amburgey 1986; Hannan and Freeman 1987). The second considers transitions between enduring states, such as different forms of political regimes (Hannan and Carroll 1981). This second approach can be used for studying transitions among phases in the histories of demonstrations, revolutions and social movements (Tuma and Hannan 1984; Blossfeld and Rohwer 1995).

Event-history analysis is particularly useful for analyzing cycles or waves of protest and violence. As noted above, while the concept of cycles of social movement activity is not new, it has rarely been investigated empirically. Use of event-history analysis facilitates the study of the diffusion of events. It uses information on the amount of time that has elapsed since an event of some type can first escalate and then depress the rate of that type of event. Moreover, questions about whether contagion is restricted to particular forms or stages in collective protest can also be investigated with event-history analysis. For example, questions about whether civil rights' protests spark subsequent racial conflicts, or vice-versa, can be investigated with analysis that estimates the transition rates among multiple states (Tuma and Hannan 1984). We will explicitly analyze hypotheses about potential cross-effects of this kind below in our analysis of protest and race riots in the section that follows.

As with panel analysis, event-history analysis can use information on the timing of events in a series of localities to estimate models that take both unit-specific characteristics and the timing of events into account. In contrast to the single point process models described above, examples of this combined cross-sectional and longitudinal design commonly analyze events in a number of cities, SMSAs or some other sub-unit over a number of observation points. This approach combines the advantages of using both cross sectional and temporal variation with the appropriateness of stochastic models that analyze events as outcomes of processes that unfold over time.

The advantage of event-history analysis is that when covariates are available in (nearly) continuous time, characteristics of the units can be "updated" whenever an event occurs. Thus, changes in the social structure can be realistically taken into account at important time points, rather than averaged across yearly periods or smoothed into linear time trends. The temporal characteristics of a city or state change over time, as one more day without a race riot passes. One problem that occurs when trying to apply this method is that data on covariates are not always readily available, or are unreliable (or both).[8] Of course, this problem is shared by virtually all of the methods that analyze models which include time-varying covariates. The advantage of event history data depends in part on the ability to capture minute changes in events *and* social structure in the analysis.

---

8   Another problem that arises in analyzing event histories is referred to as time-aggregation bias in continuous-time-hazard-rate models (see Petersen 1991 for one solution to this problem).

Event Sequence Analysis

Sequence analysis represents a significant departure from other types of event analysis because the focus is on using full information on the *narrative* of events. In most explorations of this technique no attempt has been made to include social structural covariates as explanatory factors. The chronology of actions are transformed by the analyst "into a series of 'yes/no' questions where the analyst/expert is asked if a temporal antecedent ('or a similar event') is required for the occurrence of a subsequent action" (Griffin 1994: 1105).

The data are broken down into a series of repeated or non-repeated actions within an event. These unitary actions are then used to interpret some final outcome variable. In Griffin's (1993) analysis, for instance, he focuses on the sequence of events that lead up to "the point of mob formation" in a lynching. He uses a software program, ETHNO, to determine whether this particular sequence of events *requires* some prior action or not. The comparison set is either (1) other events of the same type, or (2) counterfactual sequences of events within a narrative. However, studies of collective action using this method have not yet developed any probability models for deciding on which of the hypothetical narratives is more or less likely (but see Abbott and Hrycak 1990).

In many cases of singular events, however, developing comparisons for statistical analysis would involve the use of counterfactual histories, which has well-known drawbacks to making causal inferences. Thus, although practitioners argue that the method reflects historical detail more faithfully than other methods, sequence analysis shares the same limitations as other historical methods that rely on a relatively small number of (possible) cases (Lieberson 1991). In other words, there usually are more explanations than degrees of freedom in the analysis.

One advantage that sequence analysis shares with all event-history techniques is that it is flexible in terms of participants in actions, which can be an individual ("sheriff engaged in court"), a collective group ("search party formed") or a corporate actor (such as "racist organization") (Griffin 1993: 1120). The protest activity can be recurrent events (analyzed individually) or historically unique ones.

The disadvantage of sequence analysis is that more than one interpretation is logically possible, and, given that outcome, there has been little consensus (at the time of writing) concerning methods for adjudicating between competing sequences of events. Nevertheless, this method provides a promising strategy for drawing correspondence between a narrative story and a historical explanation that can account for a particular sequencing of events.

Comparison of Two Methods of Analysis of Protest

A researcher's choice of methods for analyzing event data ideally depends on the theoretical questions guiding the research agenda. In our analysis of protest in South Africa and the U.S., two processes stand out as paramount issues: state-repression and regional diffusion of protest. We focus first on the key theoretical questions driving our research, then discuss two methods for evaluating the effects of regional experience on and state repression of protest.

Diffusion of Specific Forms of Protest

Many theoretical discussions imply that the effects of group violence (whether instigated by protesters, antagonists or the police) depend on the recent history of outbreaks of collective action (Tilly 1978). In other words, the effect of an action depends on past experience with such actions in a region, city or neighborhood. A wide variety of studies found that the occurrence of racial unrest affected the spread of race riots across (mostly urban) North America.[9] We follow this lead in our study of protest in South Africa and the U.S.

In examining the spread of riots, rebellions and other disturbances, information on the timing and sequences of events becomes particularly important. We hypothesize that diffusion intensifies the effects of declining racial barriers. A city's prior riot history means that residents as well as the police are familiar with collective violence. Recent events are even more likely to affect expectations, so that a second (or third) riot might be perceived as more likely to happen. Thus, according to this view, the *salience of unrest rises with its occurrence in a community.* We also expect that state-sponsored violence will intensify these effects. Examining these diffusion processes empirically requires data on variations in police activity, economic well-being, and unrest during periods of substantial change in racial policies.

It might be useful to explore two of the commonly used event-history methods using data from recent research on racial protest in the United States and South Africa. We will compare (1) dependent variables, (2) the structure of the data on independent variables, and (3) differences in results obtained with the two methods. In particular, we compare two methods of event history analysis: The first aggregates monthly event counts and the second uses data on the exact timing of transitions (from inactivity to a protest event). Our comparisons high-light not only some advantages of using event analysis to compare similar out-comes, but it underscores some of the main difficulties that

---

9   Spilerman (1971, 1976); McPhail and Wohlstein (1983); Olzak, Shanahan and McEneaney (1996).

researchers encounter when trying to analyze data from vastly different countries and cultures.

Black Protest in South Africa and the United States

Researchers comparing the civil rights movement in the United States with the anti-apartheid movement in South Africa have found both similarities and differences (Fredrickson 1980). For example, some conclude that the relatively high levels of racial unrest in both settings are due to the history of racial oppression and the continuation of racial inequality (van den Berghe 1967; Magubane 1979; Fredrickson 1995; Wilson and Ramphele 1989).

Despite a shared British colonial history and a history of the legalization of racial subjugation in laws, citizenship, the franchise, housing, marriage and employment, there was an interesting divergence in racial policies during the 1960s and 1970s. For example, during the 1960s, government policies regarding barriers to racial inequality in South Africa and the United States appeared to be moving in opposite directions (Fredrickson 1995). In one, a national government enforced a program of racial segregation. In the other, the national government attempted to implement policies of racial integration.

Many theoretical discussions in the social sciences imply that the effects of group violence (whether instigated by protesters, antagonists or the police) are path dependent. That is, the outbreak of collective action of some kind depends upon prior history of events of that type (Tilly 1978). In other words, the effect of racial clashes on subsequent racial events depends on the most recent set of events or non-activity. For example, Soule (1995) found that use of a specific anti-apartheid strategy diffused rapidly across elite colleges and universities in the U.S. between 1985 and 1990. Models of diffusion have been useful in testing for differences in susceptibility to risk of adoption of strategies, allowing researchers to track the spread of tactics within cycles of social movements. Information on the timing and sequences of events becomes particularly important when examining the spread of riots, rebellions and other disturbances. These observations about the centrality of diffusion suggest that we apply event-history techniques to analyze and compare the effects of state repression and three types of racial activity: diffusion of protests, violence against blacks, and race riots. These techniques explicitly model the effect of recent history on the subsequent rate of protest, holding constant a series of other factors that might also be expected to affect the rate of racial protest.

Leading political theories of protest also emphasize the importance of the role of state repression in producing a rise in subsequent protest (Rasler 1986, 1995; Francisco 1995; Moore 1995). Resource mobilization theories of collective action hold that state-sponsored violence encourages collective violence (Tilly 1978). We build on this insight and explore the notion that the form and magnitude of response by racial groups depends upon the *level* of state repression and the racial nature of the state political system. We also extend competition theory arguments, suggesting that decreased apartheid barriers will raise rates of race/ethnic conflict and protest (Olzak 1992). Examining such arguments empirically requires data on variations in police activity regarding blacks, economic well-being and changes in policies about racial groups in South Africa and the U.S. The passage of civil rights laws and school desegregation mandates in the 1960s and 1970s in the U.S. and of laws eliminating segregation in public accommodation in South Africa in the 1980s and 1990s provide a natural research design for analyzing the consequences of shifts in state policy on racial unrest.

These arguments suggest that a longitudinal account of black protest events would be appropriate to use to test several implications of these theories. Because these methods use data on periods of intense racial protest as well as periods of relative racial quiet, we can consider what other historical processes are associated with peaks and troughs in collective protest. Below we discuss how we have used event data on the occurrence and timing of civil rights' (and anti-apartheid) protest to begin to analyze these theoretical questions. We focus on urbanized areas in the United States during the period 1954 through 1993, and in all urban magistrates in South Africa between 1970 and 1986.[10]

Concepts and Measurement Issues

Table 2 below provides some substantive comparisons between measures of theoretical concepts in our analysis of protest suggested by these repression and diffusion arguments. We discuss differences in conceptualizing the dependent variables in each analysis first, followed by a comparison of the type of measures that can be used in the two methods of event analysis.

Monthly Event Counts. The event count approach aggregates event counts into temporal units (see Table 1 above). This lead us to consider several new questions: Should we count events occurring daily, weekly, monthly, yearly, or over the whole period? We settled on monthly counts in both countries because previous research found evidence that cycles of protest often peak and decline within one month (Olzak 1992; McAdam 1982). Our time spans yielded monthly counts of 468 observations for the U.S. and 192 units for South Africa. An evaluation of monthly, daily and yearly aggregate counts further revealed

---

10   Our observation period in South Africa is regrettably truncated. This is because the passage of the Emergency Act at the end of 1985 effectively cut off all public news information about racial events.

that monthly counts were more tractable in the analysis, although a comparison of the effects of daily and monthly counts showed consistent results.

Table 2:   Comparisons of Measures in Event Analysis Using Two Methods to Analyze Black Protest in the USA and South Africa

Independent variables	Count analysis	Transition rate analysis
Dependent variable:	Monthly count of events	Number of days between events
Type of prior event:		
Protest:	Not applicable	Past event was a protest
Anti-black violence:	Not applicable	Past event was anti-black violence
Race riot:	Not applicable	Past event was a riot
Prior state repression:		
Local-level police violence	Lagged no. of annual events with police violence	Scale of police violence per no. of protests
National-level repression:	Annual no. of blacks arrested	Annual no. of detentions Recent national guard presence
Contagion	Not applicable	Time dependence parameter
Economic factors:		
General indicators:	Gross national product Unemployment rate	Gross national product Unemployment rate
Country-specific measure:	Business failure rate	Change in no. of migrant laborers

Our analysis uses information on all protests or conflicts that occurred within a month in both countries.[11] This analysis uses counts of protest involving blacks that occurred each month from January 1, 1954 and ending December 31, 1992. In the U.S., the monthly totals of protests ranged from 0 to 7. In South Africa, monthly totals of protests ranged from 0 to 11.[12]

Transition Rate Analysis. The basic data structure used in the analysis of a rate of collective action consists of *spells*, calculated as the number of days between adjacent racial events (of any kind). Our data include the duration of all spells, but only events that end in the type we are interested in are treated as uncensored. A spell begins with the first event in each country and ends at the point when an event of a particular type occurs (e.g. an attack on blacks, a race riot, a protest, etc). An important research decision concerns the treatment of time that elapses between events. Should we define durations between race riots only, for instance, ignoring the fact that some other racial events occurred in the interim? Or should we calculate the duration of spells between any type of racial collective event in our entire data set? Because our previous research found that both protest and conflicts affected either type of event (Olzak 1992),

---

11   For details on estimation techniques using count analysis regressions, see King (1990).
12   As noted above, our coding rules define racial conflicts and civil rights' protest similarly in both data sets to allow us to compare the results from both countries.

we include all spells that end in an ethnic or racial event of some kind. Spells that end in an event other than the specific type we are analyzing are treated as truncated. For instance, in the protest analysis, only those spells that end in a protest are analyzed as uncensored spells. All first spells were left-truncated, because we do not observe when these spells began. That is, we began observations on a particular date: January 1, 1970 in South Africa and January 1, 1954 in the U.S.

Characteristics of Racial Events. Recall that we argued that event analysis allows researchers to compare causal sequences of different forms of ethnic/racial collective action - from riots to civil rights protests, for example - as along as the event observations were collected in commensurate dimensions (Olzak 1989). In this research we have focused upon four of these dimensions: (1) ethnic and racial identities of participants (targets and initiators) in ethnic conflicts, (2) type of event, (3) the occurrence of violence in ethnic conflicts, and (4) the size or magnitude of ethnic conflicts.

We collected information on events that were collective and racial: two or more persons collectively attack a member or members of an ethnic/racial group and this attack is reported as having been motivated by the target's ethnic identity, language or skin color. In the case of an ethnic protest, a group articulates a racial or ethnic grievance, usually to an audience consisting of a government agency or the public at large. Examples might include a march for voting rights, a sit-in against a restaurant that bans blacks, or a boycott against a company that has discriminated against blacks. Regularly scheduled events and institutionalized events such as congressional hearings were excluded, as were ordinary instances of crime between individuals from different nationalities or race groups. We err on the conservative side in the attempt to include only those incidents (reported in newspapers) that have primarily ethnic/racial motives.[13] In particular, we exclude interracial muggings, rapes, robberies, etc. that constitute everyday crime events. We also exclude public pronouncements by public figures, political speeches and editorials on racial issues.

Past research has distinguished two kinds of racial collective action (Olzak 1992; Olzak and Olivier 1998). *Ethnic/racial conflict* involves a confrontation between members of two or more ethnic/racial populations. The *target* of a

---

13 Our method of analysis characterizes the ethnic/racial grievances voiced during collective action, instead of characterizing an event based on the ethnic identity of participants. Civil rights marches in the U.S. or anti-apartheid protests (that could and did include whites and blacks, as well as other minorities) were counted as ethnic/racial collective action in our study. In both countries we define black race riots as those events in which black participants were described as the primary participants (see Olzak, Shanahan and McEneaney 1996).

conflict is one or more members of some other ethnic/racial population, i.e. when there is evidence that one group is the aggressor. Victims may also be involved symbolically, as in a cross-burning in the yard of a black homeowner in a predominantly white neighborhood. *Ethnic/racial protest* is collective action that has the general public or some government agency as its audience and seeks to present a grievance to this audience on behalf of an ethnic or racial group (in the case of protests, then, there is no victim of aggression). A civil rights march is a modern prototype.[14]

A second important distinction is between *violent and non-violent ethnic events*. Ethnic events were defined as violent if participants (not police) wielded weapons (in the form of bricks, stones, guns, knives or bats), or used weapons, fire, bombs or vehicles to harm other persons or property, such as taking hostages or taking over a public building. In this paper, we analyze only *violence directed against blacks*. Although black protests and race riots are defined similarly in terms of targets, claims and goals, anti-black violence in the two countries is somewhat different with respect to the racial identity of the instigators. In South Africa, these events were almost always instigated mainly by blacks against other black Africans, from other linguistic, political and/or homeland origins. In the United States, the instigators of anti-black violence were almost always not black, instead the majority of events were instigated by white or assailants of unknown racial origin.

Another distinction involves the category of black-instigated race riots, which were defined by the presence of racial grievances, voiced by a large mob (hundreds or thousands of persons) and contained violent activity that lasted several hours or more, in which blacks were the main participants. Nearly all South African race riots were larger in scale than those in the USA, mobilizing thousands of participants. In the U.S., race riots only rarely involve thousands of active participants. In all cases of race riots in both countries, injuries and damage to property occurred, and, in all cases, the police were a visible and active presence. In addition, in all cases that we judged to be race riots (based upon size, violence and duration), the reports label the event as a "race riot."

Our definitions allow us to create dependent variables for the analysis of black protest events. We also use information on two other types of events - riots and violence against blacks - in our analysis of hypotheses concerning the effect of a region's past experience with racial unrest. Thus, we have collected different targets, levels of violence and participants in racial events so that we

---

14   In South Africa, racial protests against apartheid also mobilized other groups. Such protests often took place at funerals, since these were the only legal form of mass assembly permitted for blacks until February 1990 (Olivier 1989). Thus, funerals would be coded as protests if they met our criteria for civil rights and anti-apartheid protest.

can evaluate the claim that violence against black significantly increases the likelihood that blacks will protest for civil rights in a nearby region.

Arguments and Hypotheses

Path Dependence: Effects of Prior Events. Sociologists have argued that a country's history of unrest is relevant to subsequent collective action - that the effects of collective violence are path dependent (Tilly 1978). Our research builds on these arguments. We are also informed by past research on race riots, which found that cities that experienced at least one race riot have higher risks of experiencing a second or third one (Spilerman 1976). In the transition rate analysis, we employ a Weibull model that includes the effects of time dependence on the rate (discussed below). Thus, our transition rate analysis (see Table 2) that uses the duration of time between protests becomes relevant to evaluating these core theories of collective action.

There is additional evidence of an independent effect of the recency of an event. For instance, the probability of another race riot occurring is most likely just after a race riot has occurred anywhere in the country. To examine this hypothesis, we modeled a "recency effect" which is event-specific. In practical terms, this implies that a country that has just experienced a racial disturbance, for example, would be expected to have a higher rate of that event, compared to adjacent periods without any racial confrontations.

We analyze a measure of prior experience with unrest (Table 2). It is calculated as a dummy variable that equals one if a specific type of event (e.g. protests, violence or race riots) had occurred at the time of the previous event (at the beginning of a spell). Hypothesis 1 expects the rate of protest to increase as a result of regional protest activity of protests. We also expect regional violence against blacks and race riots to raise the salience of racial discrimination, thus, motivating blacks to protest.

> H1: Periods that experienced recent racial protest, violence and race riots will have higher rates of protest, violence or race riots, respectively.

Prior State Repression. Our comparative research builds on several theoretically important distinctions regarding the way the two countries have applied state repression to racial unrest. Recently, theorists have suggested a causal relationship between collective violence and government repression (Muller and Weede 1990). There are two dimensions that are relevant to the comparison between South Africa and the United States: First, the level of repression employed in the two countries. The banning of various education and religious leaders, detentions (without due process), military encampment around black townships and the Emergency Act of 1986, characterized South Africa during the 1970s and 1980s. This suggests that the overall level of repression was more widespread there than most police force actions taken against blacks during the civil rights movement in the U.S. (McAdam 1982; Morris 1984).[15]

The second dimension concerns the ethnic composition of the South African and United States police forces. These comparisons are more complex because they involve the fact that representation of blacks in occupations such as the police force and state administration has changed drastically over the years, in part as a function of prior mobilization. The historic ethnic identification of the South African and the U.S. states with European whites has shaped the extent to which protests became defined as racially motivated. In this view, countries lie on a continuum, where each endpoint indicates high or low levels of ethnic monopoly over state power and authority (Enloe 1980). To the extent that state power is also perceived as white power, we believe that many forms of anti-state activity will be mobilized around claims of racial oppression. Because the South African state represented the dominance of white Afrikaners, police actions were likely to be perceived as upholding racial domination over whites (Bekker 1995). Thus, we would expect that the effect of police violence on racial events would be more potent in South Africa when compared to the U.S.

> H2: Periods that have high levels of police violence during racial unrest have higher rates of subsequent racial unrest.

> H3: Police violence will have stronger repressive effects on the rate of black protest in South Africa when compared to the United States.

Contagion and Exhaustion Effects

The effect of recency can be conceptualized as contagion. Contagion processes are those that increase the salience of some type of event. We suspect that dramatic and highly publicized events are most likely to follow this pattern. Examples include airplane hijackings, bombings and other violent events (Holden 1986; Strang and Tuma 1993). In this view, an event produces ripple effects that raise the rate just after an event has occurred, but then this effect dissipates. Such contagion effects have also been described in the literature

---

15   Scholars sometimes criticize event history analysis for omitting so-called watershed political events from the models of effects on the rate. These watershed events might include such unique historical events as the passage of the Civil Rights Act, crucial Supreme Court decisions, Martin Luther King's assassination and similar political events. Such criticism misses the point that watershed events are more accurately considered *endogenous* to the protest process (i.e. they are a function of the rate of protest). If we do include the passage of laws, court cases, etc., in event-history models, we risk serious problems related to misspecification of the models.

suggesting a strong effect of cycles of protest (Tarrow 1989). Another model suggested by Strang (1991) relates the event timing to the probability of another similar event by other actors. This salience model builds in an effect of decay, so that the probability decreases with time since the last event in the proximate region. Our event history analysis that uses a model of transition rates first explores whether time dependence affects the rate.

Negative time dependence implies that long periods of quiescence in ethnic activity generate low levels of ethnic conflict and that the rate will be highest just after an event of that kind has occurred. Why is this important? Previous research suggested that contagion or diffusion of racial strife affects the rate in this non-linear fashion (Olzak 1992). Thus, if we ignore time dependence (in the form of temporal diffusion) when it actually affects the rate of racial unrest, then we might be attributing some of its causal effects to our substantive covariates incorrectly. This seems important for the study of collective action, which may be sensitive to the timing of prior events as well as the location of these events. Thus we explore an additional measure of contagion. In other words, our model of negative time dependence examines whether or not temporal diffusion affects the rate over and above the effects of other substantive covariates.

> H4: The time dependence parameter will be negative, indicating that the rate declines sharply as time elapses since the previous event has occurred.

Economic Factors. Olzak, Shanahan and McEneaney (1996) combined arguments from competition and research mobilization theories that link changes in conditions of oppression with predictions about the timing of racial unrest. These perspectives suggest that declining inequality provides the political incentives, opportunities and resources to mobilize the disadvantaged racial population. We include two general economic indicators: (1) Gross national product (GNP) is the annual time-series of GNP in 1992 constant U.S. dollars or 1994 constant rand in South Africa, and (2) the unemployment rate, which indicates the annual rate of civilian unemployment per 100,000 persons. We have included two country-specific measures of economic fluctuation: the business failure rate in the U.S. is the number of business failures per 100,000 existing businesses, which has been used to signal a decline in labor demand, and (2) the annual change in migrant workers, which is the yearly increase or decrease in the number of black Africans from neighboring countries (such as Lesotho, Swaziland and Mozambique) or from the so-called "independent homelands" migrating to urban (white) South Africa. Virtually all migrant workers were black, and most were unskilled labor from rural areas (Central Statistical Services 1986). The change is measured in 100,000 persons annually and it measures fluctuation in demand for black unskilled labor.

Results

In the transition rate analysis, we analyzed 2,749 spells for the United States and 3,148 in South Africa. Of the 2,748 racial and ethnic events reported in the United States over the 1954 to 1992 period, 982 were black protests. In the monthly count analysis, we analyzed how these 982 protests were distributed across 468 months in the United States. There were 3,147 racial and ethnic events reported in South Africa from 1970 until 1986 and 1,411 were protests by black Africans. Thus we have 1,411 uncensored spells of black protest in the South African transition rate analysis. In the monthly count analysis, we analyzed the distribution of 1,411 black protests over 192 months.[16]

Effects of Recent Protest and Violence

Table 3:   Results of Analysis of Black Protest in the U.S. and South Africa

Independent variables		United States	South Africa
Effects of contagion:	Prior event was a black protest	+	+
	Prior event violence vs. blacks	n.s.	n.s.
	Prior event was a race riot	n.s.	+
Prior state repression:			
Scale of police violence/per no. of protests			
(duration analysis)		-	n.s.
Lagged no. of annual events with police violence			
(count analysis)		+	(not incl.)
Annual number of blacks arrested/detained			
(duration analysis)		n.s.	-
(count analysis)		+	-
National guard present at prior event			
(duration analysis)		-	(not incl.)
Effects of time dependence: Time dependence parameter		-	-
(duration analysis)			
Economic factors: *General indicators*:			
Gross national product		-	+
Unemployment rate		-	+
Country-specific measure:			
Business failure rate		+	
Change in no. migrant laborers			-

\+   = the effect of this variable was positive and significant.
-    = the effect was negative and significant.
n.s. = the effect was not statistically significant.

---

16   In South Africa, racial protests against apartheid also spilled over into other more formal occasions and gatherings (e.g. funerals, see above).

We first analyze the effects of each country's recent experience with racial unrest on the rate of black protest. Investigation of this hypothesis is appropriate only for the duration analysis. Hypothesis 1 suggested that these effects on black protest would be strongest for recent protest (compared to the effect of having a recent race riot or experiencing an recent attack of violence against blacks). The results show that this hypothesis holds for both South Africa and the United States. We also see an additional effect of recent race riots on protest in South Africa, suggesting that there is an affinity between these two forms in that country. Even though many researchers have claimed that race riots in the United States are akin to racial protest, our results show no systematic effect of recent race rioting on the rate of black protests.

Contrary to our expectations, prior violence against blacks did not significantly affect black civil rights mobilization in either country. We expected that racial grievances and the salience of racial discrimination would rise in the wake of anti-black violence. In retrospect, we can see that both grievances and repression effects might increase after a violent attack against blacks. Thus, violent attacks on disadvantaged racial groups are more complex than pure grievance-mobilization arguments would lead us to believe.

State Repression

In South Africa, the event count analysis suggests that state detentions of political activists decreased the rate of anti-apartheid protest. In the United States, the scale of police violence has a similarly negative and repressive effect on the rate of protest. Yet, in the United States event count analysis, the lagged number of annual events with police violence had a significantly positive effect on racial protest, as many case studies would have led us to expect.

At first glance, it seems like police violence in the USA has different effects on protests depending upon which of the two methods of event analysis are used. That is, the significantly positive effects of lagged police violence (for the count analysis) contrasts with the negative effect reported for the scale of police violence (in the transition rate analysis): In Table 3, we can see that the effect of the scale of police violence per number of protests is negative in the U.S. But, in the very next row we can see that the lagged number of events with police violence is positive and significant.

Are these results contradictory? Not necessarily, if one considers the fact that the independent variables indicate very different aspects of police violence in the U.S. context. Thus, the *scale* of police violence (or overreaction, indicated by the ratio of violence to protests) decreased the rate of protest but the absolute count of violent acts raised the rates of protest in the U.S. The scale of police violence and annual number of detentions had similarly repressive effects on protest in the USA and South Africa, respectively.

Yet in the count analysis, arrests during racial events and detentions of black protesters had effects that were mirror images of each other in the two countries. We believe that these results might reflect the ways that police arrests of blacks were viewed in the two countries. In the United States, these arrests during racial confrontations and protests were increasingly viewed as illegitimate acts by authorities. In contrast, in South Africa during this period, they were more likely to be interpreted in the context of ongoing political repression by the Afrikaner state.

In the United States, we find pure repression effects of police acts on the rate of protest only at the extreme levels of police mobilization. Thus, the presence of the National Guard significantly decreased the rate of protest, but ordinary police violence raised this rate in the United States. In South Africa, peak repression occurred when large numbers of well-known individuals were detained without legal recourse. Both results also suggest that state repression depends on scale and scope of activity. It appears that the deployment of federal-level repression rather than local police violence was more "effective" in containing black protest in both countries.

Now consider the evidence for hypothesis 3, which suggested that repressive state policies in South Africa would have stronger effects on the rate of protest in that country, when compared to repression in the U.S.. There is mixed evidence for and against this hypothesis. Overall, in South Africa, the effect of regional history of unrest and repression decreased the rate of protest. Thus our results show support for hypothesis 3, which expected repression to be predominant in that country during this period of peak repression and social control of protest by South African police. In the U.S., the count of prior arrests of blacks raised this rate.

Hypothesis 3 is thus supported for the detention measure of repression but not for the scale of police violence. In South Africa, both regional experience with protest and detentions of black protest leaders undermined black protest.

Time Dependence Effects

Analyses that explored the effects of time dependence on the rate of black protest had consistent and negative effects on the rates in both countries. As hypothesis 4 suggested, time dependence was negative in both settings, which suggests that the rate peaks just after a protest has occurred, and then it declines sharply. Our results show that approximately one month after a protest, the effect of recency disappears (Olzak and Olivier 1998).

Economic Factors

Finally, we note with some surprise that the economic indicators had opposite effects in the two countries: In South Africa, rising unemployment and declining demand for black laborers (indicated by a decline in the number of migrant laborers) together measure periods of economic hardship. Both indicators of economic decline raise rates of protest, indicating support for more traditional grievance theories of protest in South Africa. For the United States, economic hardship theories find some support: declining economic indicators of higher than average business failure rates and lower levels of GNP increase the rate of protest, which follows the same pattern as in South Africa. However, one indicator of economic fluctuation - that of unemployment - is consistent with the resource mobilization and competition theory arguments that economic well-being would contribute to higher rates of protest.

Comparison of Count Analysis and Duration Analysis of Events

There are several important differences in the methods for analyzing data using event counts or transition rates between event-states. The most obvious difference discernible from the results reported in Table 3 (see also this distinction in Table 2) is that count analysis does not estimate the effects of time dependence. This is because the data on events are aggregated into monthly units, and so any estimate of the effects of time dependence is constrained by the temporal aggregation of the data. In contrast, the transition rate model that includes a time dependence parameter is less constrained. Thus, the estimated effect of time dependence in the U.S. analysis can be summarized in days since the last event. The results suggest that the effect of recency of a race riot is ten times higher one day after a riot has occurred, compared to a period of three months without a riot. Thus, the transition rate analysis estimates an effect of contagion which is not as constrained as methods which aggregate events temporally.

A second difference is more substantive. Analysis of the rate of collective action has been criticized in the past for ignoring variance in the magnitude of events. For example, Rule and Tilly (1965) recommended calculating the number of person-days of an event, to capture the size and duration of an event in a single measure. Analysis of the transition rate focuses instead on the amount of time that elapses between similarly defined events. But these events are not constrained to be the same size, or magnitude, or duration. Nevertheless, these methods allow analysis of very large events compared to smaller events. To construct these distinctions, one uses various size or duration dimensions to construct a new dependent variable: the rate of events larger than 1,000 persons, etc. We acknowledge that most analysts using transition rate analysis have not emphasized all of these dimensions equally.[17]

Methods that use event counts, however, measure magnitude explicitly. They do so by aggregating the number of events that occur within a defined period of time (a month, a year, a decade). In this way, peak periods of protest that occur in South Africa and the United States can be meaningfully compared. Months with especially high counts can be compared with months with relatively few or even zero counts, within countries, across time periods, or between regions.

Models that can consider the effects of time dependence are also not without trade-offs. It is well known that unobserved heterogeneity can cause spurious negative time dependence, causing the researcher to conclude that time dependence affects the rate when this is in fact not the case (Flinn and Heckman 1982). Methods of estimating event counts, such as negative binomial estimation and generalized quasi-likelihood estimation can minimize some of the sources of unobserved heterogeneity. It is therefore often important to conduct analysis with more than one event-history method and compare the results for discrepancies.

In summary, our results inform us about how two different methods of event analysis can address arguments and hypotheses about the effects of contagion, repression and economic hardship in different ways. We can analyze events of the same type - political protest for civil rights by black Africans and African Americans, and we can begin to draw some parallels about the way that state repression worked to encourage protest in the United States and repress it in South Africa. Finally, by comparing the results from these two different methods of analysis, we see some important differences in the pattern of effects on the timing compared to the absolute number of occurrences.

Conclusion

We began with two goals: to highlight some of the useful features of event analysis without neglecting the political implications of state violence and civil rights protests that shape these ethnic events. We discussed the fact that event histories can be aggregated over a variety of temporal or spatial categories, and we suggested several methods that are appropriate for analyzing these data. We

---

17   For instance, Olzak (1992) found that the duration of ethnic and racial events did not vary much. Most events coded from the turn of the century in the United States were only between one and two hours long. In the recent period, however, race riots (which are analyzed separately) last substantially longer than most other kinds of racial protests and conflicts (Olzak, Shanahan and McEneaney 1996).

also showed that time-varying covariates can be used in analyses of events that have or have not been aggregated over time, in a variety of methods that take the sequence or timing of events into account explicitly in the analysis.

We then summarized two sets of analyses of event data from South Africa and the United States. We emphasized theories that hypothesize effects of prior experience with protest and with government repression, in order to highlight some advantages of event-history analysis. We reported that, in South Africa, the scale of police violence had little effect on protest while in the United States it decreased protest. Arrests and detention of civil rights activists and protesters encouraged protest in the United States but it decreased the magnitude of protest in South Africa. In South Africa, diffusion processes decreased the rate of protest, while in the United States, diffusion increased this rate. At the same time, we see that in the analysis of the monthly count of anti-apartheid protests, peak periods of detentions raised the magnitude of protest. One implication is that, although state violence in South Africa might have temporarily undercut protest, it might have been productive for the anti-apartheid movement in the long run. In the United States, state repression seems to have had a galvanizing effect on the civil rights movement that is reflected in our results.

Our results also imply that the relationship between state violence and collective racial unrest involves a dynamic between repression and movement activity. These dynamics were compared using both count and transition rate analysis of data on events. While count analysis allows us to make inferences about what affects periods witnessing many protests, transition rate analysis allows us to make inferences about what influences the timing of protest.

We have also suggested that a comparative analysis of protest in two countries allows us to contrast some of the theoretically relevant political differences in the two countries with regard to state-sponsored violence. In particular, repression of blacks in the United States is clearly causally connected to rising black protest, while in South Africa, the effects of state repressive powers inhibited protest in the short run.

References

Abbott, A. and A. Hrycak. 1990. "Measuring Resemblance in Sequence Data: An Optimal Matching Analysis of Musicians' Careers." *American Journal of Sociology* 96: 144-185.

Aminzade, R. 1984. "Capitalist Industrialization and Patterns of Industrial Protest: A Comparative Urban Study of Nineteenth-Century France." *American Sociological Review* 49: 437-453.

Amburgey, T. L. 1986. "Multivariate Point Process Models in Social Research." *Social Science Research* 15: 190-207.

Amburgey, T. L. and G. R. Carroll. 1984. "Time Series Models for Event Counts." *Social Science Research* 13: 38-54.

Barron, D. N. 1990. "Analysis of Event Counts: Over-Dispersion and Autocorrelation." Unpublished Masters Thesis, Cornell University. Ithaca, N.Y.

Barron, D. N. 1992. "The Analysis of Count Data: Overdispersion and Autocorrelation." Pp. 179-220 in *Sociological Methodology 1992*, ed. P. V. Marsden. Oxford: Basil Blackwell.

Barron, D. N. and M. T. Hannan. 1991. "Autocorrelation and Density Dependence in Organizational Founding Rates: Quasi-likelihood Estimation." *Sociological Methods and Research* 20: 218-241.

Cameron, A. C. and P. K. Trivedi. 1986. "Econometric Models Based on Count Data." *Journal of Applied Econometrics* 1: 29-53.

Carroll, G. R. and Y. P. Huo. 1988. "Organizational and Electoral Paradoxes of the Knights of Labor." Pp. 175-194 in *Ecological Models of Organizations*, ed. G. R. Carroll. Cambridge, Mass.: Ballinger.

Central Statistical Services. 1986. *South African Statistics, 1986*. Pretoria, South Africa: Government Printer.

Chirot, D. and C. Ragin. 1975. "The Market, Tradition and Peasant Rebellion: The Case of Romania in 1907." *American Sociological Review* 40: 428-444.

Coleman, J. S. 1981. *Longitudinal Data Analysis*. New York: Basic.

Cosaro, W. and D. Heise. 1990. "Event Structure Models from Ethnographic Data." Pp. 1-57 in *Sociological Methodology*, ed. C. Clogg. London: Basil Blackwell.

Edwards, B. and S. Marullo. 1995. "Organizational Mortality in a Declining Social Movement: The Demise of Peace Movement Organizations in the End of the Cold War Era." *American Sociological Review* 60: 874-907.

Eisinger, P. K. 1973. "The Conditions of Protest Behavior in American Cities." *American Political Science Review* 67: 11-28.

Flinn, C. J. and J. Heckman. 1982. "New Methods for Analyzing Individual Event Histories." Pp. 99-140 in *Sociological Methodology 1982*, ed. S. Leinhardt. San Francisco: Jossey-Bass.

Francisco, R. 1995. "The Relationship Between Coercion and Protest: An Empirical Evaluation in Three Coercive States." *Journal of Conflict Resolution* 39: 263-282.

Fredrickson, G. 1980. *White Supremacy: A Comparative Study in American and South African Race Relations*. New York: Oxford University Press.

Fredrickson, G. 1995. *Black Liberation: A Comparative History of Black Ideologies in the United States and South Africa*. New York: Oxford University Press.

Griffin, L. J. 1993. "Narrative, Event-Structure Analysis, and Causal Interpretation in Historical Sociology." *American Journal of Sociology* 98: 1094-1132.

Griffin, L. J. and C. C. Ragin. 1994. "Some Observations on Formal Methods of Qualitative Analysis." *Sociological Methods & Research* 23: 4-21.

Hannan, M. T. and G. R. Carroll. 1981. "Dynamics of Formal Political Structure." *American Sociological Review* 46: 19-35.

Hannan, M. T. and J. Freeman. 1987. "The Ecology of Organizational Founding: American Labor Unions, 1836-1985." *American Journal of Sociology* 92: 1210-1213.

Hausman, J., B. H. Hall and Z. Griliches. 1984. "Econometric Models for Count Data With An Application to the Patents-R&D Relationship." *Econometrica* 52: 909-938.

Hibbs, D. 1976. "Industrial Conflict in Advanced Industrial Societies." *American Political Science Review* 70: 1033-1058.

Holden, R. T. 1986. "The Contagiousness of Aircraft Hijackings." *American Journal of Sociology* 91: 874-904.

Inverarity, J. 1976. "Populism and Lynching in Louisiana, 1889-1896: A Test of Erikson's Theory of the Relationship Between Boundary Crises and Justice." *American Sociological Review* 41: 262-280.

Jenkins, J. C. 1983. "Resource Mobilization Theory and the Study of Social Movements." *Annual Review of Sociology* 9: 527-553.

Jenkins, J. C. and C. M. Eckert. 1986. "Channeling Black Insurgency: Elite Patronage and Professional Social Movement Organizations in the Development of the Black Movement." *American Sociological Review* 51: 812-829.

Jenkins, J. C. and C. Perrow. 1977. "Insurgency of the Powerless: Farm Workers Movements (1946-1972)." *American Sociological Review* 42: 249-268.

Kelly, W. R. and L. Isaac. 1984. "The Rise and Fall of Urban Racial Violence in the U.S.: 1948-1979." *Research in Social Movements, Conflict, and Change* 7: 203-233.

Koopmans, R. 1995. *Democracy From Below: New Social Movements and the Political System in West Germany.* Boulder, Colo.: Westview Press.

Koopmans, R. 1996. "New Social Movements and Changes in Political Participation in Western Europe." *Western European Politics* 19: 28-50.

Kriesi, H. 1995. "The Political Opportunity Structure of New Social Movements: Its Impact on Their Mobilization." Pp. 167-198 in *The Politics of Social Protest*, ed. J. C. Jenkins and B. Klandermans. Minneapolis and St. Paul: University of Minnesota Press.

Kriesi, H., R. Koopmans, J. W. Duyvendak and M. Giugni. 1995. *New Social Movements in Western Europe: A Comparative Perspective.* Minneapolis and St. Paul: University of Minnesota Press.

Lichbach, M. I. 1987. "Deterrence or Escalation? The Puzzle of Aggregate Studies of Repression and Dissent." *Journal of Conflict Resolution* 31: 266-297.

Lieberson, S. 1991. "Small N's and Big Conclusions: An Examination of Reasoning in Comparative Studies Based on a Small Number of Cases." *Social Forces* 70: 307-320.

Magubane, B. M. 1979. *The Political Economy of Race and Class in South Africa.* New York; London: Monthly Review Press.

Markoff, J. 1985. "The Social Geography of Rural Revolt at the Beginning of the French Revolution." *American Sociological Review* 50: 761-781.

Markoff, J. 1986. "Literacy and Revolt: Some Empirical Notes on 1789 in France." *American Journal of Sociology* 92: 323-349.

Marwell, G. and P. Oliver. 1984. "Collective Action Theory and Social Movements Research." *Research in Social Movements, Conflicts and Change* 7: 1-27.

McAdam, D., J. D. McCarthy and M. Zald. 1988. "Social Movements." Pp. 695-738 in *Handbook of Sociology*, ed. N. J. Smelser. Newbury Park, Cal.: Sage.

McCarthy, J. D., M. Wolfson, D. P. Baker and E. Mosakowski. 1988. "The Founding of Social Movement Organizations: Local Citizens' Groups Opposing Drunken Driving." Pp. 71-84 in *Ecological Models of Organizations*, ed. G. R. Carroll. Cambridge, Mass.: Ballinger.

McPhail, C. and R. Wohlstein. 1983. "Individual and Collective Behaviors Within Gatherings, Demonstrations, and Riots. *Annual Review of Sociology* 9: 579-600.

Minkoff, D. 1993. "The Organization of Survival: Women's and Racial-Ethnic Voluntarist and Activist Organizations." *Social Forces* 71: 887-908.

Minkoff, D. 1994. "From Service Provision to Institutional Advocacy: The Shifting Legitimacy of Organizational Forms." *Social Forces* 72: 943-970.

Moore, W. H. 1995. "Action-Reaction or Rational Expectations?" *Journal of Conflict Resolution* 39: 129-167.

Morris, A. 1984. *The Origins of the Civil-Rights Movement: Black Communities Organizing for Change.* New York: Free Press.

Muller E. and E. Weede. 1990. "Cross-National Variation in Political Violence." *Journal of Conflict Resolution* 34: 624-651.

Nagel, J. 1995. "American Indian Ethnic Renewal: Politics and the Resurgence of Identity." *American Sociological Review* 60: 947-965.

Nagel, J. 1996. *American Indian Ethnic Renewal: Red Power and the Resurgence of Identity and Culture.* New York: Oxford University Press.

Nielsen, F. 1980. "The Flemish Movement in Belgium After World War II: A Dynamic Analysis." *American Sociological Review* 45: 76-94.

Olzak, S. 1982 "Ethnic Mobilization in Quebec." *Ethnic and Racial Studies* 5: 253-275.

Olzak, S. 1986. "A Competition Model of Ethnic Collective Action in American Cities, 1877-1889." Pp. 29-46 in *Competitive Ethnic Relations*, ed. S. Olzak and J. Nagel. Orlando, Fla.: Academic Press.

Olzak, S. 1989. "Analysis of Events in Studies of Collective Action." *Annual Review of Sociology* 15: 119-141.

Olzak, S. 1992. *The Dynamics of Ethnic Competition and Conflict.* Stanford, Cal.: Stanford University Press.

Olzak, S. and J. L. Olivier. 1997. "The Countervailing Forces of Repression and Contagion: Racial Unrest in South Africa and the United States." Unpublished manuscript. Stanford University. Stanford, California.

Olzak, S. and J. L. Olivier. 1998. "Racial Conflict and Protest in South Africa and the United States." *European Sociological Review.* Forthcoming.

Olzak, S. and S. Shanahan. 1996. "Deprivation and Race Riots: An Extension of Spilerman's Analysis" *Social Forces* 74, March: 931-961.

Olzak, S., S. Shanahan and E. H. McEneaney. 1996. "Poverty, Segregation, and Race Riots, 1960-1993." *American Sociological Review* 61: 590-613.

Paige, J. M. 1975. *Agrarian Revolution.* New York: Free Press.

Petersen, T. 1991. "Time-Aggregation Bias in Continuous-Time Hazard-Rate Models." Pp. 263-290 in *Sociological Methodology*, ed. P. V. Marsden. San Francisco: Jossey-Bass.

Rasler, K. 1986 "War, Accommodation, and Violence in the United States, 1890-1970." *American Political Science Review* 80: 921-943.

Rasler, K. 1995. "Concessions, Repression and Political Protest: A Model of Escalation in the Iranian Revolution." Unpublished manuscript. Indiana University.

Rucht, D. and F. Neidhardt. 1995 "Methodological Issues in Collecting Protest Event Data: Units of Analysis, Sources and Sampling, Coding Problems." Paper presented at the "Workshop on Protest Event Analysis," Wissenschaftszentrum Berlin für Sozialforschung (Social Science Research Center Berlin, WZB), June 12-14.

Rucht, D., P. Hocke and T. Ohlemacher. 1992. *Dokumentation und Analyse von Protestereignissen in der Bundesrepublik Deutschland (Prodat). Codebuch.* Discussion Paper

FS III 92-103. Wissenschaftszentrum Berlin für Sozialforschung (Social Science Research Center Berlin, WZB) (1994, English translation: "PRODAT Codebook"). Berlin.

Rule, J. and C. Tilly. 1965. *Measuring Political Upheaval*. Princeton, N.J.: Center of International Studies.

Rule, J. and C. Tilly. 1972. "1830 and the Un-Natural History of Revolution." *Journal of Social Issues* 28: 49-76.

Snyder, D., and C. Tilly. 1972. "Hardship and Collective Violence in France, 1830-1960." *American Sociological Review* 37: 312-320.

Soule, S. A. 1995. "The Student Anti-Apartheid Movement on US Campuses: Diffusion of Tactics and Policy Reform." Unpublished Ph.D. Dissertation. Department of Sociology, Cornell University. Ithaca, N.Y.

Spilerman, S. 1970a. "The Causes of Racial Disturbances: A Comparison of Alternative Explanations." *American Sociological Review* 35: 627-649.

Spilerman, S. 1970b. "Comment on Wanderer's Article on Riot Severity and Its Correlates." *American Journal of Sociology* 75: 556-559.

Spilerman, S. 1971. "The Causes of Racial Disturbances: Test of an Explanation." *American Sociological Review* 35: 427-442.

Spilerman, S. 1976. "Structural Characteristics of Cities and the Severity of Racial Disorders." *American Sociological Review* 41: 771-793.

Steedly, H. R. and J. W. Foley. 1979. "The Success of Protest Groups: Multivariate Analysis." *Social Science Research* 8: 1-15.

Strang, D. 1990. "From Dependency to Sovereignty: An Event History Analysis of Decolonialization 1870-1987." *American Sociological Review* 55: 846-860.

Tarrow, S. 1989. *Democracy and Disorder: Politics and Protests in Italy, 1965-1975*. Oxford: Clarendon Press.

Tilly, C. 1978. *From Mobilization to Revolution*. Boston: Addison-Wesley.

Tilly, C. 1986. *The Contentious French*. Cambridge, Mass.: Harvard University Press.

Tilly, C. 1995. *Popular Contention in Great Britain 1758-1834*. Cambridge, Mass.: Harvard University Press.

Tilly, C., L. Tilly and R. Tilly. 1975. *The Rebellious Century, 1830-1930*. Cambridge, Mass.: Harvard University Press.

van den Berghe, P. L. *Race and Racism: A Comparative Perspective*. New York: John Wiley & Sons.

Walsh, E. J. and R. H. Warland. 1983. "Social Movement Involvement in the Wake of Nuclear Accident: Activists and Free-Riders in the TMI Area." *American Sociological Review* 48: 764-780.

Wilson, F. and M. Ramphele. 1989. *Uprooting Poverty: The South African Challenge*. New York: W. W. Norton and Co.

Wolf, E. 1969. *Peasant Wars of the Twentieth Century*. New York: Harper and Row.

Zald, M. and J. D. McCarthy. 1977. "Resource Mobilization and Social Movements: A Partial Theory." *American Journal of Sociology* 82: 1212-1241.

Zald, M. and J. D. McCarthy, eds. 1987. *Social Movements in an Organizational Society*. New Brunswick, N.J.: Transaction Books.

Event Analysis in Transitional Societies: Protest Mobilization in the Former Soviet Union

Mark R. Beissinger[1]

Introduction

The waves of mobilization that encompassed the former Soviet Union from 1987 through 1991 constituted one of the more spectacular manifestations of public contestation to emerge in the twentieth century. In Tilly's estimation, they unambiguously deserve the designation of "revolution," both in terms of their characteristics as well as the outcome which they precipitated (1993: 234-235). It is hardly exaggeration to say that these events fundamentally changed the face of our world, provoking an end to half a century of communist domination in Eastern Europe, shattering the Soviet state, and provoking new waves of mobilization with which the world is still attempting to grapple.

Yet, interpretations of the collapse of the Soviet state suffer from eclecticism and proclivity for conjecture. Both those who have argued the inevitability of the collapse of communism and those who have stressed its coincidental or contingent nature so far have done so by isolating the collapse from the larger wave of mobilization which brought it about.[2] How are we to understand these critical events, and what can the study of this massive wave of mobilization tell us more generally about the phenomena of protest, revolution, nationalism and state disintegration?

Those who study empirically waves of mobilization appreciate the painstaking effort that it involves. Event analysis is an essential tool for dissecting a mobilizational cycle, although by no means the only tool. As Sidney Tarrow observed,

> ... protest is, first and foremost, a form of action - not a set of dispositions towards, or reports of participation in collective action. Without carrying out

1   Research on protest mobilization in the former Soviet Union was carried out under the auspices of grants from the National Science Foundation, the National Council for Soviet and East European Research, the International Research and Exchanges Board, and the Graduate School of the University of Wisconsin-Madison, as well as a fellowship from the Woodrow Wilson International Center for Scholars. I gratefully acknowledge their support. I would also like to thank Ruud Koopmans, Doug McAdam and Sidney Tarrow for their comments on an earlier version of this essay.

2   See, e.g., Malia (1994), Dallin (1992), Carrère d'Encausse (1993), Lapidus et al. (1992).

systematic studies of collective action itself, it is difficult to know when, against whom, and in what collective contexts people decide to engage in protest activities (1991: 13).

Event analysis is, however, an extremely time-consuming and laborious process, particularly when dealing with a society as complex and as volatile as the former USSR.

This chapter provides a sampling of some of the methodological and substantive issues involved in studying the waves of mobilization that brought about the collapse of the USSR. Over the past six years, I have been engaged in constructing event data bases for studying the "glasnost" mobilizational cycle. In all, information was coded on 6,663 protest demonstrations, 2,177 mass violent events, and 678 strikes[3] in the former Soviet Union from January 1987 through the end of 1992. Although the Soviet Union collapsed in the wake of the August 1991 coup, analysis of protest events was extended to the end of 1992 to avoid problems of right-censoring and to allow analysis of the impact of the breakup of the USSR on patterns of mobilization. In addition, information was systematically collected for 185 protest demonstrations, 50 violent mass events and 61 strikes that occurred between 1965 and 1986[4] to avert problems of left-censoring and to provide a baseline by which to judge the development of the mobilizational cycle. The project represents one of the few attempts to extend event analysis outside of North America and Western Europe and one of the first to utilize the method to analyze the mobilizational waves that brought down the communist regimes of the Soviet bloc.

Issues of Data Collection and Source Bias

The problems presented by data collection about protest mobilization in the former Soviet Union are hardly unique; on the contrary, they are symptomatic of the broader issues involved in the analysis of mobilizational waves as we move beyond North America and Western Europe to apply our methodologies throughout the world. Most analyses of mobilizational waves have been conducted within a Western European or North American context - polities that

---

3   The strike data, which have yet to be cleaned and are coded only to the end of 1991, are not examined in this paper. In reporting the number of events, I have chosen to weight them consistently by the duration of the event.

4   In a study of protest demonstrations in the USSR from 1956 to 1983, Alexeeva and Chalidze (1985) uncovered a total of 406 events of all sizes, ranging from just a few participants to tens of thousands. Only 165 of these events qualified for inclusion in the current project. In another study, David Kowalewski (1980a) found a total of 497 protest demonstrations of various sizes that took place from 1965 to 1978.

have been relatively open to contestation in a comparative sense. When we move to the "second" or "third worlds," however, we walk upon a radically different political terrain. These are often polities which have experienced massive violent repressions, with extensive restrictions on freedom of expression and internal security bureaucracies whose purpose is to prevent any manifestation of collective action. This presents special problems of data collection and analysis - problems which make extension of event analysis beyond the advanced industrial democracies an especially demanding effort.

In the first place, police records, even if they were available, are highly politicized documents. In the communist context, they reflect the mentality and biases of a security apparatus charged with extirpating all acts of dissidence, although it was an apparatus which ultimately failed in its mission. Moreover, in the aftermath of regime change these records themselves are at the center of controversy, since they can be utilized all too easily as weapons for political compromise and intrigue (not to mention their continued security value to post-communist governments). Indeed, in the Baltic most local KGB records were transferred back to Moscow on the eve of the collapse of the USSR to prevent the unmasking of informers. While party archives have been opened throughout much of the former Soviet Union, for the most part KGB records covering the post-Stalin period have not been available for scrutiny. By the end of 1990 Soviet researchers working with the civilian police were provided with daily reports on acts of mass protest; the analyses based on these reports covered a small part of the mobilizational cycle, were usually presented in index form rather than as event-counts, and failed to differentiate between types of events.

Of course, even if these records were available to Western researchers they would still raise reliability issues. Not surprisingly, police estimates of the number of participants in demonstrations differed significantly from those found in the media, with the gap being larger during the early part of the mobilizational cycle.[5] As experience elsewhere suggests, this was most likely due not only to police bias but also to overestimation by social movement activists, given the political uses of such figures. We do know that the police during this period engaged in systematic disinformation efforts not only towards society, but also towards their own superiors. Moreover, in some of the cases for which we have information police estimates of crowds so differed from those of multiple and independent Western eyewitnesses (not to mention those of social movement activists) as to be implausible. Analysis of official Soviet strike statistics during the glasnost period similarly indicates significant

---

5   See Table 4 below.

under-reporting of strikes by official bureaucracies, perhaps an artifact of falsification of figures by local statistical collection agencies.[6]

As a result, any analysis of mobilizational cycles in these societies must rely to a great extent on the press. But press-based analysis within such a context presents special problems. As the literature on social movements tells us, cycles of contestation are conditioned by shifts in the political opportunities facing populations - the opening of previously closed polities or the closing of previously open polities. These are transitional societies. The shift from repression to contestation, which in itself involves an explosion in the possibilities of public expression, makes it extremely difficult to base an analysis of mobilization on any single press source and necessitates casting a broader net of information gathering. In the early stages of a mobilizational cycle in such societies, foreign, émigré and underground (in the former Soviet Union, *samizdat*) publications are likely to be the most accessible and reliable media sources about protest events. These, of course, contain their own biases. But they do afford extensive coverage of events in this part of the mobilizational cycle. Even in a country with the size and diversity of the former Soviet Union, extensive informational networks developed among dissident groups, fostered in part through acquaintance in the Gulag and in part through struggle against a common enemy.

The attention of individual media sources to acts of protest changes over the course of a mobilizational cycle, and the explosion of events that characterizes a cycle makes it difficult for any single media source to cover events consistently. The example of the newsletter *Vesti iz SSSR*, published from 1978 through 1990 by Kronid Liubarskii, demonstrates well the inability of any source to encompass the record of protest mobilization in a revolutionary period. After his forced emigration from the USSR, Liubarskii was approached by several human rights organizations about establishing a central collection point for information about the human rights movement in the USSR. This project eventually turned into *Vesti iz SSSR*, a bimonthly newsletter based in Munich on the human rights movement in the Soviet Union. Relying on established networks of dissidents throughout the USSR, *Vesti* reported systematically on any act of protest that came to public attention during the late 1970s and early 1980s. With these same networks in place, *Vesti* was well situated to report on protest events in the early part of the glasnost mobilizational cycle and became an outstanding news source on mobilizational acts of all kinds. But in January 1990 Liubarskii decided to cease reporting on mass events entirely and to focus

---

6   When, after the end of a strike, enterprises worked overtime to make up for lost time, this was often factored out of official statistics. On some of the problems of relying on official Soviet statistics, see Shenfield (1992).

instead on bringing individual cases of human rights abuse to light. As Liubarskii explained:

> The geography of events has broadened, their scale and tempo increased. Over the last few years the editor has tried to keep up with events, attempting to give, albeit in a condensed form, a full picture of what was going on in the country. The bulletin has been constantly expanding. More and more often the quantity of information has made it impossible to process the news quickly, meaning that we have had to put out double issues and forego the periodicity that we started out with ... It has become clear that to continue publication on the previous basis was simply physically impossible. In any case the point of doing so has to a great extent disappeared. A significant proportion of such information about events in the USSR has started appearing in numerous other publications, both *samizdat* and official, as well as in the foreign press (*Vesti iz SSSR*, No. 1, 1990: 1-2).[7]

As one Soviet journalist observed in the fall of 1989, "We are living in an extremely condensed historical period. Social processes which earlier required decades now develop in a matter of months" (*Literaturnaia gazeta*, September 13, 1989). In such times events are extremely compact; they overwhelm and overtake the media, making it impossible to rely on any single source.

Moreover, throughout a cycle of mobilization the press (like the rest of the polity) is itself undergoing radical change. Hundreds of publications of newly-emerging social movements spring up, and over the course of the cycle sources continue to emerge and die. Whereas studies of protest mobilization in advanced industrial democracies deal with an institutionalized press, making a single source study feasible, these conditions are absent in contexts where an independent press emerges concurrently with mobilization. The breakup of the USSR is also associated with the death, transformation and emergence of major news sources. Figure 1 below portrays some indicators of the development of the independent press in the former Soviet Union during the glasnost years drawn from the holdings of the *Arkhiv samizdata* at Radio Liberty[8] and a recurrent survey of the independent press conducted by the unofficial trade union, SMOT.[9] It shows how the evolution of the independent press sector followed broadly the patterns of the mobilizational cycle itself. An independent press sector in the former Soviet Union emerged by the end of 1987, before the first major explosions in protest activity in early 1988, but did not develop on a significant scale until early 1989.

---

7   This and all other translations into English are by the author. Liubarskii eventually closed *Vesti* altogether and emigrated back to Russia.
8   The data are based on Part 2 of the catalogue to the archive, published in *Materialy samizdata*, No. 13 (November 4, 1991), pp. 143-155.
9   The data come from an examination of the full press run of *Informatsionnyi biulleten' SMOTa* from 1988 through 1991.

Figure 1: Development of an Independent Press Sector and Demonstration
Activity in the former USSR, 1987 to 1991

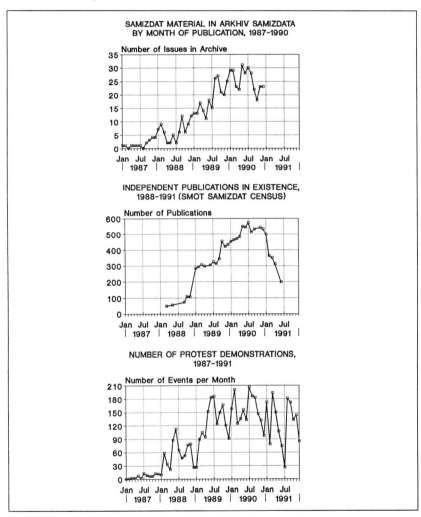

The relatively smooth rise in the number of independent publications in 1988
contrasts with the uneven development of protest activity, and the specific
contours of publishing activity do not match those of media-covered protest
events. Both the organization of demonstrations and the organization of

publications are elite activities that are strongly influenced by the openness of political order. While both followed much the same trajectory in the early part of the mobilizational cycle, closer examination reveals that independent press activity and the number of demonstrations varied independently of each other. The heyday of the independent press was in 1989 and 1990, when hundreds of publications burst into existence, with many of these fly-by-night operations run by social movements. Here again, while overall trends in publishing and protest activity were similar, the smooth rise of independent publishing contrasts sharply with the jagged profile of demonstrations. The number of independent publications peaked at about the same time as the number of demonstrations in the mobilizational cycle (mid-1990). Much like the fluidity within the social movement sector, the independent press sector was highly unstable, with publications appearing with great irregularity and, often, disappearing as quickly as they had appeared. By early 1991 the number of independent press publications began to decline sharply, due in part to financial and organizational difficulties, in part to a plaguing shortage of paper. Indeed, on the eve of the breakup of the USSR in June 1991, there were fewer independent press publications than had been in existence in January 1989, with a sharp shift away from party and social movement publications toward commercial publications. Although not covered in these figures, the drop in independent publishing activity did not alter significantly after the breakup of the USSR. This shake-out within the independent press and the growing institutionalization of the press developed well after the institutionalization of protest mobilization in the wake of the 1990 elections. Moreover, the organization of protest demonstrations largely continued apace despite the decline in independent publications.

While most scholars prefer a single set of newspaper sources that are available throughout the entire period of study to ensure coverage consistency when constructing event data, the reality is that in a transitional or revolutionary society these conditions are rarely met. Indeed, in a transitional society the best strategy available to a researcher is likely to be a "blanketing" strategy, utilizing multiple sources and types of information whenever they are available. Tarrow speaks of the "fetish of thoroughness" in event analysis (1989: 362). This obsession may be irrational within a context in which a free press is institutionalized. But within a transitional society some attempt to simulate thoroughness is a necessary condition of event analysis. In the former Soviet Union, for instance, coverage of protest events by any single source was confined to a particular part of the mobilizational cycle. Moreover, as Table 1 indicates, even the best sources of information reported on only a fraction of the events about which we know. Of the events studied for this project, only 43.3% of demonstrations and 33.3% of mass violent events were reported on in more than one source; this highlights the lack of duplication in press coverage across sources for a significant number of events and the need to use multiple and disparate sources to gain a reasonably accurate record of what occurred. In those cases in which duplication of reporting occurred, disparate news sources often added significant information about an event that otherwise would have been lost. For this project, over 150 different news sources were examined, including not only Western newspaper, wire service and U.S. government sources, but also a wide variety of émigré publications, central and local Soviet newspapers, and unofficial *samizdat* sources, including Russian-language papers produced by opposition political movements throughout the former USSR, unofficial wire services, material drawn from unofficial libraries and archives in Moscow, and from Radio Liberty's *Arkhiv samizdata* in Munich. Of course, such a strategy creates a need to develop consistent rules to reconcile conflicting information about events from different sources.

Table 1: Coverage of Demonstrations and Mass Violent Events in the Former USSR, Multiple-Source Media Sample, Commonly Used Sources

Source	Dates of coverage	Proportion of events analyzed during period that contained some coverage	
		Demonstrations	Mass violent events
Foreign Broadcast Information Service (FBIS), Daily Report (English language, U.S. government publication)	12/1/1986- 12/31/1992	34.8%	52.7%
Vesti iz SSSR (Russian, émigré publ., Munich)	12/1/1986- 12/31/1989	61.9%	51.3%
Ekspress khronika (Russian, *samizdat*)	11/1/1988- 12/31/1992	42.9%	48.9%
Yezhednevnaia glasnost (Russian, *samizdat*)	5/1/1989- 5/31/1991	32.2%	10.2%

We can get some idea of the gains in accuracy obtained from a multiple-source media sample by comparing the sample used in this study with others based on subsets of sources. Philip Roeder (1991) based a cursory examination of nationalist mobilization in the early glasnost period (September 1985 to August 1989) on a reading of *The New York Times (NYT)* and Radio Liberty's *Report on the USSR*. Excluding Russians within the Russian Republic from his analysis, he found a total of 84 demonstrations with over 10,000 participants, 45 of which had over 100,000 participants. By contrast, the multiple-source media sample used for this study includes 386 events with at least 10,000 participants that fit these criteria during the same period, 150 of which had at least 100,000 participants. Of course, for some kinds of analysis one might mind missing so many large demonstrations, particularly if one is interested in tracking protest over years and decades rather than months.[10] But our interest lies in comparing patterns of mobilization among subgroups of a population or tracking the rise of protest within a mobilizational cycle, Roeder's two-source sample becomes grossly inadequate. Table 2 presents a comparison by nationality between the Roeder sample and the multiple-source sample used in this study.

Table 2: A Comparison of Coverage of Demonstrations in Two-Source and Multiple-Source Media Samples, September 1985 to August 1989 (Number of Events Covered)

Nationality	Greater than 100,000 participants		Greater than 10,000 participants*	
	Two-source sample**	Multiple-source sample	Two-source sample**	Multiple-source sample
Armenians	25	102	30	175
Azeris	9	18	19	27
Lithuanians	4	7	9	50
Latvians	3	7	7	17
Georgians	2	10	4	25
Estonians	2	4	4	11
Moldavians	1	1	6	17
Uzbeks	1	0	1	3
"Exclave" Russians	0	0	3	17
Belorussians	0	0	1	5
Ukrainians	0	1	0	39
Kazakhs, Kirgiz, Tadzhiks, Turkmen	0	0	0	0

*   Also including demonstrations with ≥100,000 participants, as reported by Roeder (1991).
** Sources: *The NYT* and Radio Liberty's *Report on the USSR*, as presented by Roeder (1991).

As is evident, patterns of demonstrations with over 100,000 participants by nationality are not that radically different, with the exception of the Georgians, whose mobilization is underestimated in the Roeder sample. When we examine demonstrations with 10,000 or more participants, however, the samples are

10   Roeder was primarily interested in generalizing about the impact of education and the Soviet federal system on patterns of mobilization, although his sample of nationalities was too small and the time period examined too limited to draw firm conclusions. Also, no attempt was made to control for population size or other factors. Statistical analysis of patterns of mobilization during the 1987 to 1991 period for 40 nationalities (excluding Russians) shows that the Soviet federal system did have an independent effect on the number of demonstrations in which a nationality engaged, controlling for the influence of other factors, including population size. But it did not have an independent effect on the extent to which populations participated in these demonstrations, controlling for the number of demonstrations in which a nationality engaged. See Beissinger (1996).

drastically dissimilar. If we were interested only in patterns of very large demonstrations among subgroups of a population, then a single- or two-source sample might be sufficient for some purposes. Most studies of protest, however, do not limit themselves to events with over 100,000 participants.

Figure 2 illustrates some of the time-dependent biases that emerge from relying on a single-source sample of Soviet protest - in this particular case, *Foreign Broadcast Information Service, Daily Report (FBIS)*. This source is published by the U.S. government and provides extensive coverage of events in the former Soviet Union. It is probably the most accessible source to Western researchers, and one which provides considerable coverage of protest events. However, the picture one would obtain by relying solely on this source is significantly different than what one receives when using multiple sources. Using *FBIS,*[11] one would conclude that the number of demonstrations increased steadily over the glasnost period and peaked after the breakup of the USSR, whereas using a multiple-source sample the peak in demonstrations occurs in 1990. Not surprisingly, coverage of smaller demonstrations in *FBIS* was worse than coverage of larger demonstrations; whereas 33.9% of demonstrations with less than 30,000 participants covered in the multiple-source sample were also covered in *FBIS*, 44.4% of those with 30,000 or more participants were. Still, *FBIS* provided coverage of only 37.7% of demonstrations with 100,000 to 199,000 participants, 40.7% of those with 200,000 to 499,000 participants, and 45.9% of those with 500,000 or more participants that were recorded in the multiple-source sample. Moreover, coverage of the early part of the protest cycle is almost completely absent in *FBIS* (both for demonstrations and mass violent events).

As one might expect, it took some time before *FBIS* selectors began paying attention to protest activities. Indeed, by the account that one would glean from a careful analysis of *FBIS* materials, significant mass violence did not begin in the USSR until mid-1989, whereas using other sources we know that several major waves of violence had already occurred by that time. Finally, mass violent events are poorly covered in 1991 and early 1992 by *FBIS* as other events came to attract the attention of selectors; this would lead a researcher to underestimate mass violence during this critical period of the breakup of the USSR. These patterns of coverage are largely explicable by bureaucratic routine, the difficulties of news gathering from this part of the world, and the

---

11   Actually, *FBIS* was the sole source of information for only 914 demonstrations; the other 1,323 demonstrations pictured in Figure 2 about which *FBIS* reported also were reported on in other sources. The need to use multiple sources is particularly pressing if one seeks to obtain a good sense of the demands put forth, the number of participants and the reaction of the authorities, not just merely an event count.

demands for particular types of news coming from government agencies. They demonstrate once again the hazards of relying on any single source to analyze a mobilizational cycle in a transitional society.

Figure 2: Coverage of Protest Events by *FBIS Daily Reports* Versus Coverage in Multi-Source Sample

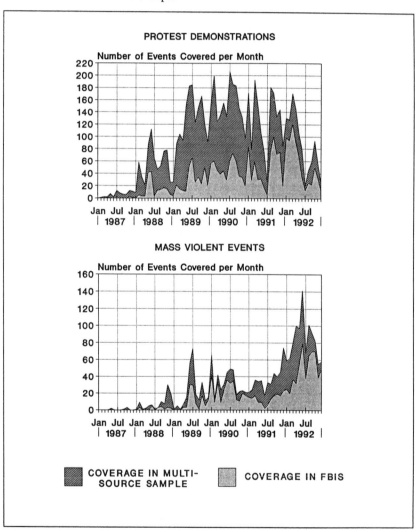

Another dimension of the Soviet context which strongly affects efforts to analyze protest events is the multinational and multilingual character of this society. Numerous Russian-language publications from all regions of the former Soviet Union (including official and unofficial publications from nearly all the union republics and from remote regions of Russia) were used in this study. However, in a country in which 127 different ethnic groups were officially recognized by the state, it is obvious that a considerable amount of important source material appeared in languages that would be inaccessible to any researcher or, for that matter, research organization, causing potential problems of bias. Of course, cultural pluralism is a condition found in most states around the world, and given the prominence of ethnic cleavages in conditioning and motivating protest, the issue of the language of source material is hardly a problem confined to the former Soviet Union.

To some degree, this problem was offset by the extensive ties that existed within the dissident community across national groups. Widely recognized informational collection points for acts of protest throughout the former Soviet Union operated for large portions of the period studied and published regular accounts of events (for instance, Radio Liberty's *Report on the USSR, Vesti iz SSSR, Ekspress khronika, Yezhednevnaia glasnost'*, and *Informatsionnyi biulleten' SMOTa*). A number of these publications maintained their own extensive networks of native correspondents throughout the country who reported systematically on protest events. Other groups attempted to create such networks over portions of the country, but many of these existed for a short time only.[12] Unofficial archives of ephemeral material also appeared and acted as collection points for social movement publications.[13] A number of Russian-language newspapers reported on protest events throughout the USSR with some regularity, although these only operated for portions of the cycle.[14] Finally, some of the more significant events of the period (such as the August 1991 coup) have received lengthy book treatments which provide systematic chronological accounts of developments throughout the country.[15]

---

12 Examples of such publications utilized for this study include *Informatsionnnyi biulleten' KAS-KOR, Sibirskoe Informatsionnoe Agentsvo* (Novosibirsk), *Center for Democracy Bulletin, EKhO, Khronika matsne* (Tbilisi), *Sluzhba yezhednevnykh novostei, DS-Inform*, and *Agentsvo novostei i informatsii*.

13 In particular, I benefited from access to the archives of the Moscow Library for Information Exchange, which attempted to act as a repository for unofficial publications throughout Russia, but which also included publications from other republics.

14 Examples of such newspapers that were utilized in this study are *Nasha gazeta* (Kemerovo), *Tartuskii kur'er* (Tartu), *Atmoda* (Riga), *Soglasie* (Vil'nius), *Panorama, Svobodnoe slovo, Nezavisimaia gazeta*, and *Kommersant'*.

15 See, for instance, Rasshivalova and Seregin (1991); Gorshkov and Zhuravlev (1992).

Source coverage of events before and after a mobilizational cycle is likely to be radically different than source coverage of events during a cycle. Before and after a cycle, very small events tend to obtain considerable coverage, while during a cycle, when it is not uncommon for protest events to attract tens and hundreds of thousands (even millions) of participants, very small events are covered poorly. In a study of 321 demonstrations by Soviet ethnic groups from 1965 to 1978, David Kowalewski (1980a) found that most demonstrations during these years were small, with 58% having had less than a hundred participants, and most of these having less than fifty. Similarly, as Table 3 indicates, during the 1987 to 1992 period the bulk of protest demonstrations were small. After examining several hundred demonstrations, it became evident that the source coverage of events with less than 100 participants was spotty. Given the sheer number of demonstrations and the poor coverage of smaller events, it became necessary to impose a minimum size of a hundred participants for demonstrations. A minimum of 15 participants was kept as a criterion for inclusion of mass violent events, so as to distinguish them from terrorist, criminal or other small-scale acts of violence. No formal size minimum was imposed for strikes, simply because the events tended to be of significant size to warrant inclusion.

Table 3:   Size of Protest Demonstrations in the Former USSR, 1987 to 1992

Number of participants	Number of events	Percent
<100	n.a.	n.a.
100-999	2,560	38.4%
1,000-4,999	2,035	30.5%
5,000-9,999	781	11.7%
10,000-19,999	402	6.0%
20,000-29,999	208	3.1%
30,000-49,999	211	3.2%
50,000-99,999	189	2.8%
100,000-199,999	122	1.8%
200,000-499,999	118	1.8%
Greater than 500,000	37	0.6%
Total	6,663	100%

Obviously, as is true of any event analysis, coverage of the actual number of protest demonstrations that took place was incomplete. Nevertheless, coverage was quite substantial. As Table 4 shows, according to official police statistics in 1989 there were 5,300 demonstrations of all sizes throughout the entire Soviet Union. The multiple-source media sample includes information on 1,496 of these protest events, or about 28.2% of those reported by the police. Coverage of demonstrations recorded by the police in 1988 was the same. According to police statistics, there were 2,328 protest demonstrations throughout the Soviet Union in 1988; information was found for 665 of these, or 28.6%. The parallel between trends in the multiple-source media sample and those in police statistics during these years is striking. Considering that the police statistics also included demonstrations and instances of picketing that were less than a hundred in size (as noted above, likely to be a large proportion of all events), the coverage of demonstrations with a hundred or more participants in the multiple-source media sample can be said to be extensive. But as Table 4 shows, the proportion of events recorded by the police that were also covered in the multiple-source media sample dropped in early 1990. Whether due to a significant rise in the number of demonstrations with less than 100 participants, an explosion in the number of events that outstripped the media's capacity to report them, or a decline in media attention to protest, the multiple-source sample covered only 19.3% of the events recorded by the police for the first 54 days of 1990 (still a quite respectable figure).

Table 4: A Comparison of Published Police Statistics on Demonstrations with Coverage in Multiple-Source Media Sample

Location	Dates	Number of demonstrations			Number of participants (thousands)		
		Police*	Sample	Percent	Police*	Sample	Percent
USSR	1/1/88-12/31/88	2,328	665	28.6%			
USSR	1/1/88-8/2/88	600	390	65.0%			
Latvia	1/1/88-12/31/88	83	37	44.6%	220	924	420.0%
Moscow	5/26/88-6/10/88	40	8	20.0%	2	3	150.0%
USSR	1/1/89-12/31/89	5,300	1,496	28.2%	12,600	30,047	238.5%
Ukraine	1/1/89-9/30/89	724	226	31.2%			
Ukraine	10/1/89-10/20/89	125	31	24.8%			
Uzbekistan	1/1/89-10/30/89	200	32	16.0%			
USSR	1/1/90-2/23/90	1,500	289	19.3%	6,400	5,100	79.7%
USSR	2/25/90	311	61	19.6%	982	888	90.4%
Moscow	1/1/91-3/31/91	180	19	10.5%	1,000	1,735	173.5%
RSFSR	3/15/92	73	22	30.1%	35	17	49.4%

* Sources: *Kommunist* (Yerevan), December 24, 1989: 1; TASS, August 2, 1988; Radio Moscow World Service, in *FBIS*, June 13, 1988: 62; *Brianskii rabochii*, February 9, 1989: 3; *Pravda*, March 26, 1990: 1; *Radianska Ukraina*, in *FBIS*, November 30, 1989: 69; Reuters, October 30, 1989; *Pravda*, in *FBIS*, March 26, 1990: 59; *Demokraticheskaia platforma*, June 1990: 1; *Izvestiia*, in *FBIS*, April 4, 1991; 51; Interfax, in *FBIS*, March 16, 1992: 58.

The regional statistics in Table 4 suggest that the proportion of events recorded by the police which were also covered in the multiple-source media sample was lower in areas of the former Soviet Union where participation in demonstrations was lower (such as in Uzbekistan) or where there was an explosion of small demonstrations (as implied by the statistics on demonstrations and participation rates for Moscow during the first three months of 1991). The shifting proportions of events in the multiple-source media sample that were recorded by the police are certainly in part a function of the size limit imposed on the sample and the shifting mobilizational capacities of social movements. But shifts and variations in media attention cannot be ruled out, and a definitive answer obviously will require detailed analysis of the police records when they become available.

Objects of Analysis

The use of event analysis to study the explosion of protest that precipitated the breakup of the Soviet Union raises a number of broader issues about the basic concepts and assumptions that lie behind our analyses. Given that the Soviet Union disappeared, even the issue of the societal parameters of a study are potentially on the decision table. In this case, what began as a comparative study of multinational protest within a single country ended as a cross-national study of protest within fifteen countries (or more, depending on who does the counting).

The variety of contentious events that scholars have taken as objects of study is quite large. Tarrow, for instance, included strikes, demonstrations, petitions, delegations and violence (1989: 359). Tilly's "contentious gatherings" included not only riots, disturbances, and disorders, but also meetings, processions, and assemblies (see Tilly 1995 for his more recent reflections on repertoires of contention). Although certainly various other modes of collective action existed in the protest repertoires of Soviet citizens, demonstrations,[16] mass violent

---

16   A demonstration was defined as an event that met the following six criteria: (1) It was a
      voluntary gathering of persons with the purpose of engaging in a collective display of
      sentiment for or against public policies; (2) it involved a minimum of 100 persons; (3) it
      was bounded by space and time (i.e. occurred in a specific location during a limited time
      period); (4) the number of participants was not restricted by the organizers of the event
      (i.e. was not a conference, convention or other restricted organized meeting); (5) it did
      not have as one of its purposes the infliction of violence by its participants (i.e. was not
      a mass violent event); (6) it was not in itself a refusal to work (i.e. a strike). The Russian
      vocabulary for events of this type is rich, including such terms as *demonstratsiia*
      (demonstration), *miting* (meeting), *protest* (protest), *manifestatsiia* (manifestation) and
      panakhida (funeral procession). Significantly enough, most Russian words used to
      described demonstrations are of foreign origin - indicative of the extent to which such
      behavior within the Russian context has been learned over the last century from
      examples of analogous behavior abroad.

events,[17] and strikes[18] comprised the most widespread forms of collective action within the former Soviet Union in the period under study and were selected as the basic units of analysis. The rise of the demonstration, the strike and the mass violent event as widespread forms of protest was closely linked with the liberalization of Soviet politics under glasnost. Indeed, in the repressive atmosphere of the 1960s and 1970s in the USSR, less confrontational forms of contention, such as the petition and the hunger strike, were more often used by dissident groups than the demonstration, strike or mass violent event. This shift in protest repertoires was one of the more spectacular changes that accompanied Gorbachev's reforms. As one Soviet author wrote in 1988:

> Several years ago we knew exactly what a rally was and what a demonstration was. The former was when we gathered together in one place to hear someone speak. The latter was when, on a holiday, we passed by a reviewing stand in an orderly column ... [But now] there has been a real explosion of social activeness (Mikhailov 1988: 7).

Ideally, information on petitioning, hunger strikes and terrorist actions should have been collected as well in order to obtain a more complete picture of how repertoires evolved over time. However, the sheer volume of demonstrations, mass violent events and strikes made it impractical to do so.

Dissecting a mobilizational cycle is an extremely complicated affair not only because of the variety of forms of mobilization used, but also because of the various dimensions by which one can analyze these forms. Some studies of protest mobilization focus solely on the number of events as a measure of protest activity, largely because events are relatively easy to identify. But what does an "event" represent? Essentially, an "event" is an attempt, an effort, by some group of people to mobilize a population and to disrupt the normalized course of affairs (see Tarrow 1985: 7; DeNardo 1985: 35-36). Counting the frequency of events tells us something about efforts to engage in protest. But it tells us relatively little about the mobilization itself - the goal for which "events" are being organized. Whenever possible both measures of frequency and measures of size or magnitude were used. In all, specific information on the

---

17   A mass violent event was defined as a mass political action whose primary purpose was to inflict violence, either in the form of an attack on people or on property. The Russian words used to describe mass violent events include the terms *besporiadki* (disorders), *pogrom* (pogrom), *drak* (fight), *volneniia* (disturbances), *stychki* (clashes), *boi* (battles), and *miatezh* (insurrection).

18   A strike was defined as a refusal by members of a work collective to engage in work in pursuit of collective aims. Hunger-strikes (meaning the refusal to ingest food as a sign of protest) were not in themselves considered strikes unless they also involved a refusal by a work collective to work. Two Russian words are used with regularity to describe strikes - *zabastovka* and *stachka*.

number of participants was available for 68.4% of the demonstrations recorded. For the remaining cases, descriptors allowed for classification into size categories, which were later translated into specific figures for analysis. In cases in which information on the size of a demonstration was still unavailable, a search was made in the sample for the closest similar events in time that occurred in the same location, were organized by the same group, and put forward the same demands; the size category of that event was used as the basis for the size category of the demonstration in question. Given the size and scope of the sample, analogous events were almost always available for comparison. Indeed, this is one of the great advantages of a multiple-source media sample; it allows one to piece together disparate bits of information, thereby gaining a richer body of data than otherwise would have been the case.[19]

Figure 3 below shows the relationship between the number of demonstrations and patterns of mass participation in them. Efforts to organize demonstrations increased steadily throughout 1988 and 1989,[20] peaking in July 1990 and continuing at a high level until March 1992, when the number of demonstrations began to decline more sharply. Although the movements seeking to mobilize populations shifted radically after the breakup of the Soviet Union in August 1991, by the end of 1992 efforts to organize demonstrations continued at a level roughly similar to that of 1988.

By contrast, participation in demonstrations was "forward-packed," occurring to a greater extent in the early part of the mobilizational cycle, peaking in 1988 and 1989, and declining significantly over the course of 1990. This demobilization was due in large part to the institutionalization of participation resulting from the republican elections of 1990 and the shift in the constellation of power that these elections produced in many republics. During 1991 partial remobilizations took place in connection with the attempted crackdown in Lithuania in January 1991 and with the August 1991 coup. The sharp drop in mobilization and in elite efforts to organize protest demonstrations that occurred from April through July 1991 was due to pact politics - in particular, the negotiations between Gorbachev and republican leaders at Novo-Ogarevo, which led to agreement to halt protest against the Soviet regime among the participating

---

19   Since estimating the size of crowds is obviously subjective, divergent estimates were recorded whenever available. In those cases in which multiple estimates existed but did not diverge, they were not recorded. Two divergent crowd estimates were recorded for 14.8%, and three divergent estimates were recorded for 3.3% of demonstrations.

20   The sharp decline in protest demonstrations in December 1988 and January 1989 was due to the impact of the Armenian earthquake of December 1988, which temporarily put an end to efforts to mobilize throughout the former Soviet Union. It took a natural disaster that killed 50 thousand people to produce a temporary decline in mobilization.

leaders.[21] With the collapse of the Soviet Union, smaller waves of mobilization were unleashed, but by July 1992 participation in demonstrations had largely petered out, even though mobilization efforts by elites continued. These patterns raise the question of how to determine when a mobilizational cycle begins and ends. For instance, December 1986 is often viewed as a starting date for the glasnost mobilizational cycle because the first major protest events of the era occurred at that time - the Alma-Ata demonstrations and riots of December 17th and 18th, when up to 10,000 participants took to the streets in response to the removal of the Communist Party leader of Kazakhstan, Dinmukhamed Kunaev, and the appointment of a Russian in his place. Olzhas Suleimenov, the Kazakh writer, later noted that "the Alma-Ata students and workers were the first in the country to conduct unsanctioned meetings" (1989: 2). However, these events were more reminiscent of earlier protest demonstrations in the pre-glasnost period and had relatively little effect on mobilization elsewhere in the former Soviet Union. They were relatively unorganized, lacked social movement organization, and only two-and-a-half years later gave birth to lasting social movement organization.[22] Moreover, the severe repression that accompanied the Alma Ata events effectively subdued further mobilization in Kazakhstan for several years after; the population did not engage again in significant protest mobilization until June 1989, when thousands took to the streets in the provincial oil town of Novyi Uzen' to engage in violent pogroms against local Meskhetian Turks.[23] Rather, the beginning of the glasnost mobilizational cycle should probably be located in 1987, when iterative attempts by dissident groupings in Moscow, Leningrad, Riga, Tallin and Uzbekistan (in this case, exiled Crimean Tatars) to test the political waters by organizing demonstrations grew regularized, thereby changing the public's expectations about the possibility of collective action.

---

21   See, for instance, Yeltsin (1994: 27). The sharp decline in mobilization on the eve of the breakup of the USSR, of course, raises the question of whether the complete disintegration of the Soviet Union would have occurred if the plotters who formed the State Emergency Committee had not attempted to seize power in August 1991. While the partial breakup of the Union would seem to have been impossible to reverse at this point in time, nine of the republics were groping their way towards a new agreement of union before the coup intervened. Whether that agreement could have saved a rump Soviet Union is unclear; nevertheless, on the eve of its breakup an odd social peace had set in, with elites groping for a common language above the heads of society.

22   For detailed accounts of what occurred, see Helsinki Watch 1990; *Literaturnaia gazeta,* in *FBIS,* January 5, 1990: 66-69; *Ekspress khronika,* no. 50, December 8-14, 1992: 5. The *Zholtoksan* (December) movement was organized in May 1989 by those sentenced for their role in the December 1986 events.

23   *Izvestiia,* in *FBIS,* June 21, 1989: 52; Radio Moscow, in *FBIS,* June 20, 1989: 45; Alma-Ata Domestic Radio, in *FBIS,* June 22, 1989: 54.

Mark Beissinger

Figure 3: Mobilization Waves in the Former Soviet Union, 1987 to 1992

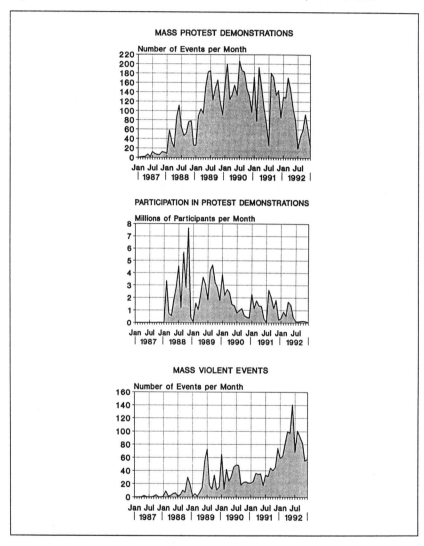

The end of a mobilizational cycle, by contrast, is much more difficult to pinpoint. The August 1991 coup is often viewed as the conclusion of the glasnost mobilizational cycle. It did precipitate a major change in authority relations and a sharp shift in the groups seeking to challenge the state. Yet, it is clear that the number of demonstrations continued at a fairly high rate after the collapse of the Soviet Union, as did mobilization in these demonstrations until March 1992. Moreover, as Figure 3 shows, violent mobilization mushroomed after the disintegration of the USSR. What defines the contours of a mobilizational cycle is not so much shifts in the locus of political power, changes in the populations seeking to challenge the state, or innovations in mobilizational repertoires, but rather whether politics grows "normalized," in the sense that challenges to the state through mobilizational acts become marginalized and/or institutionalized parts of the political process. While in some parts of the former Soviet Union this occurred after the breakup of the USSR as new states and their governments consolidated authority, in other areas the mobilizational waves evoked by glasnost and persisting challenges rooted in the politics unleashed by glasnost continued to define politics well beyond the breakup. When we talk about the essential "softness" of states in post-Soviet Eurasia, we are speaking in part about the failure of these states to normalize their authority and the perennial contestation that these polities evoke. As we know, this condition is widespread throughout much of the world and contrasts sharply with the experience of North America and Western Europe. It does, of course, raise the larger issue of why contentious politics sustains itself in some circumstances, while in others it eventually grows marginalized.

Institutions and Violent Mobilization

In their study of mass violence in Italy, Della Porta and Tarrow found that, within the protest cycle as a whole, "as mass mobilization winds down, political violence rises in magnitude and intensity" (1986: 620). In their words, mass violence "rose later, was more likely to take small group forms than to involve masses of people, and was not an important aspect of the height of the cycle" (ibid.: 627). They explain the "rear-packed" location of violence within the cycle by reference to the growth of competition and differentiation within the social movement sector, the declining ability of movements to mobilize mass followings, and a growing demand for public order on the part of authorities. As they argue, in a climate of demobilization, political violence becomes the only form of serious disruption possible, particularly for small competing groups that emerge as the social movement sector expands. In the former Soviet Union as well, mass violence tended to be concentrated in the latter portion of the mobilizational cycle. As Figure 3 above shows, mass violent events rose sharply in 1989 and 1990, at the very time when non-violent mobilization in demonstrations was declining. The level of mass violence gradually increased until the August 1991 coup and the breakup of the USSR, which unleashed a new wave of violent mobilization. Indeed, the number of mass violent events increased exponentially over the course of 1992, to levels two or three times those experienced in the Gorbachev era.

Yet, there is little evidence that the quantum leaps in violence in 1989 and 1990 and at the end of 1991 can be traced to competition or to smaller factions within the social movement sector. Indeed, in many cases violence was organized by mainstream nationalist movements, and by the latter part of the mobilizational cycle governments themselves were playing an increasing role in the organization of violence. In short, violence did not become a marginalized part of the political process, as in Italy, but instead grew partially institutionalized in state structures.

The key for understanding why and how nationalist violence spread in the former USSR is the fact that most of the violence was connected with a particular type of issue: The definition of republican borders. As Figure 4 below indicates, violence over the definition of republican borders rose significantly in 1989 and 1990, increasing exponentially in 1991 and 1992. By contrast, in spite of the widespread belief among experts that the breakup of the USSR would most likely evoke a violent struggle between supporters and opponents of the regime, violence over the issue of secession from the USSR remained minimal. The issue of secession was almost entirely contested through non-violent means - in particular, through demonstrations and strikes. Georgians, Armenians and Azerbaidzhanis, for instance, while engaging in massive levels of violence over the definition of the borders of their respective republics, for the most part did not contest the issue of secession from the USSR through violence, but through massive non-violent mobilizations. Even though in a number of cases violent repressions were carried out by the regime against groups agitating for independence from the USSR, in general these acts of violence did not precipitate larger waves of violence targeted against the USSR government.

Figure 4 makes apparent the very strong effect of the shifts in authority that took place in 1989 and 1990 on patterns of violence in the former Soviet Union. As a result of the mobilizations of 1988 and 1989 and the republican and local elections of 1990, groups formerly excluded from power gained control over portions of the state and over outcomes of particular issues at the republican and local level. This in turn mobilized additional groups into politics who feared the consequences of this new constellation of power for their own interests. Changes in authority wrought by earlier waves of mobilization within the cycle brought about a shift in the issues of mobilization and in the groups that were mobilizing. Sidney Tarrow (1991) has written about how studying protest mobilization is like aiming at a moving target. But there are really two moving targets in any revolutionary period, both society and the state. Politics in and outside institutions are constantly in interaction, and it is this interaction which defines the playing field upon which repertoires of mobilization are chosen.

Figure 4: A Comparison of Mobilization Activity over Sucession from the USSR and over Republican Border, 1987-1992*

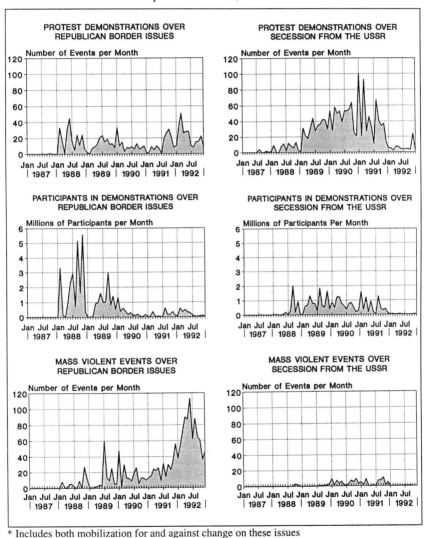

* Includes both mobilization for and against change on these issues

In 1988 and 1989, there were massive non-violent mobilizations over the issue of changing republican borders. The goal of most of these demonstrations was to pressure the USSR authorities and one's own republican or local government to engage in policies aimed at bringing about a revision or maintenance of these borders. By mid-1989, however, many of these republican governments had grown nationalized under the pressure of the crowd, and the USSR government had shown itself repeatedly unwilling to consider any alteration of republican borders and incapable of defending effectively their inviolability. The logic for appealing to the center or to one's own republic or local government dissipated, and the targets of mobilization began to focus more singularly on *other* republics, local governments and ethnic groups. But demonstrations and strikes were ineffective means for bargaining with other republics, local governments and ethnic groups at a time when these populations were often equally mobilized over these issues and where the disruptive effects of these measures were little felt. Violence became a more appealing form of contestation precisely because it could be effectively channeled against the vulnerabilities of these targets.[24]

The exponential rise in mass violence over republican border issues in 1991 and 1992 was not the result of competition within the social movement sector and the marginalization of violence, as in Italy, but was rather due to the implications of a radical shift in authority for patterns of mobilization, the broader breakdown of the USSR government and its inability to control processes over its territory, and the institutionalization of mass violence as a result of the growing role played by republican and local governments in its organization. The different explanations for why violent mobilizations occurred in Italy and the former Soviet Union, of course, have much to do with why Italy today is not the former Soviet Union (a nonexistent state with tens of thousands of people dying in ethnic wars across the expanse of its former territories). In general violent contestation in the former Soviet Union evolved over the course of the cycle away from forms of mob violence (pogroms, riots and communal violence) towards more organized and sustained forms of armed combat. By 1991 and 1992 nationalist mass violence shaded off into organized warfare; where the line stood between the state-sponsored and mass violence was impossible to tell, much as it was difficult to draw clear lines between social movements, the para-military organizations that frequently carried out these acts, and the state. Indeed, the Soviet experience shows that the divide between institutional activity and mass mobilization is often quite artificial, particularly in situations where the state itself is permeable, "soft," or unraveling. In

---

24   Gamson (1975) argued that the choice of violence is largely determined by the vulnerabilities of the target of mobilization.

circumstances of "dual power" *(dvoevlastie)* typical of revolutionary situations, who actually controls the state becomes a matter of interpretation. Certainly, these events deserve to be considered as part of a larger politics of contention, in spite of the fact that the groups that carry them out often control segments of the state or engage in violence with the encouragement and support of authority.

This is a far more typical situation in contentious politics than those studying social movements in North America or Western Europe realize. Civil wars, secessionist and irredentist violence, revolts, and guerilla and para-military warfare may be alien to (but not entirely absent from) the terrain of the advanced industrial democracies to which event analysis has been traditionally applied. They are more frequent phenomena, however, throughout the rest of the world. These conflagrations typically combine elements of movement and institutional politics. Nationalist violence, for instance, is more likely to be a tactic of groups that control segments of the state than of completely marginalized groups that lack any access to the state (Tishkov 1995: 133). It is nevertheless part of a contentious politics, involving both those seeking to challenge a given order and those seeking to defend it. One of the key factors triggering major waves of nationalist violence is the ambiguous signals sent by local authorities, which are often susceptible to interpretation that segments of the state condone the use of violence as a means for redressing problems, or at least would look the other way. The role played by government in fostering and directly organizing nationalist violence is generally under-appreciated - a conclusion shared by a recent Human Rights Watch (1995) study of violent nationalist conflicts in ten countries around the world. Indeed, what distinguishes conflicts in which mass violence grows sustained from those conflicts in which violence ultimately does not proliferate is the role that eventually comes to be played by the state as an organizer of violence. In short, the boundary between mass violence and institutionalized violence in much of the world is porous, and scholars walking on this territory need to be aware that the formal distinctions that may hold in advanced industrial democracies fail to hold given different political parameters.

Event Analysis, Framing, and the Study of Nationalism

Event analysis has been utilized by a number of scholars to study ethnic mobilization.[25] Its use to study nationalism, however, has been rarer, in large

---

25 See here, in particular, the works of Peter Eisinger, Doug McAdam and Susan Olzak. Much of the literature utilizing event analysis to study the North American civil rights movement and violence in North American cities in the 1960s falls into this category.

part because the advanced industrial societies to which event analysis has most often been applied have often been viewed (indeed, falsely viewed, as developments in recent years in Canada, Great Britain, Belgium, Germany and elsewhere demonstrate) as having transcended nationalism.[26] Nationalism is essentially activity that concerns authority over a particular set of objects in politics: The drawing of the physical, human and cultural boundaries of the state and the life chances that people believe are associated with these definitions of boundaries. In this sense, nationalism differs from ethnic political action in much the same way that an object differs grammatically from a subject. Nationalism overlaps and intersects with ethnic political action, but is defined not by the subject engaged in it, but primarily by its orientation towards a particular type of goal.

States inherently involve a bounded community, both in terms of physical territory and in terms of the population which is afforded membership (see, for instance, Brubaker 1992: 21-34). These boundaries represent, in Lustick's terms, "institutional constraints ... which advantage certain groups and rival elites within the state at the expense of others" (1993: 41). In this sense, the institutions of the state are more than merely a set of organizations; they involve a whole series of normalized practices and assumptions that stand behind the state - as Lustick calls them, "unquestioned features of ... public life" and "part of the natural order of things for the overwhelming majority of the population whose political behavior is relevant" (ibid.: 44). This includes the central issue at stake in nationalist political action and discourse: The physical, human, and cultural boundaries of the state. The naturalization and institutionalization of these boundaries inevitably involve an affective dimension. The notions of citizenship which define modern politics assume the existence of a community from which the modern state seeks its legitimacy - in short, a nation. In modern discourse, a nation refers to a community of people deserving of its own state. It is a claim, not a condition. Nations need not be based exclusively upon ethnicity, and many are not. However, ethnicity has formed the most powerful bond justifying nation status.[27] Not only do groups claiming the status of nation seek states, but polities claiming the status of state also seek nations. Recognizing the advantages that this type of legitimation grants in terms of control over citizenry and claims over territory, as well as the efficiencies of rule that cultural standardization provides, almost all states seek to impart aspects of a common culture to their citizens and to inculcate a belief in the immutability of boundaries in an attempt to rationalize, naturalize and

---

26   For a review of trends within the study of nationalism, see Young (1993).
27   Why this has occurred is the subject of considerable debate among specialists on nationalism.

legitimate their rule (see Beissinger 1995). In times of "normalized" politics, a given crystallization of state boundaries is backed by the effective authority of the state and is not subject to open challenge from within. In such conditions, there is a strong tendency for individuals to adjust their beliefs to the boundaries of the possible, accepting a given institutional arrangement as unalterable and even natural. Essentially, when we talk about the spread of nationalism, we are talking about the politics by which the hitherto impossible, implicit and inconceivable come to be viewed by large numbers of people as thinkable, necessary, and even to a great extent conventional (see Beissinger 1996).

This background must be kept in mind for understanding why event analysis is such a powerful tool for dissecting nationalism. Nationalism inherently involves contestation - contestation over the institutions of the state, and more specifically over its physical, human and cultural boundaries. In an article entitled "When Is a Nation?" Walker Connor bemoaned the fact that scholars of nationalism have focused excessively on the "musings of elites whose general-izations concerning the existence of national consciousness are highly suspect" (1990: 95). By contrast, he argues, nationalism should be understood as "a mass, not an elite phenomenon" (ibid.: 97-98), although the moment when "a sufficient portion of a people has internalized the national identity in order to cause nationalism to become an effective force for mobilizing the masses" (ibid.: 100) is not easy to identify.[28] Elie Kedourie came to recognize that

> ... [t]o narrate the spread, influence and operation of nationalism in various politics is to write a history of events, rather than of ideas. It is a matter of understanding a polity in its particular time, place and circumstances, and of following the activity of specific political agents acting in context of their own specific and peculiar conditions. The coherence of contingent events is not the same as the coherence of contingent ideas, and the historian has to order his strategies accordingly ... (1993:139).

Studying waves of nationalist mobilization through event analysis allows us to perceive the contexts in which nationalism becomes politically salient. While event data do not in themselves measure attitudes, they provide insight into the issues that resonate within populations and the changing or consistent character of issues over which populations mobilize. There are no systematic public opinion polls, for instance, which adequately capture the changing attitudes of the Soviet population to the existence of the USSR during the glasnost period; in fact, it was not until August 1989 that the first major survey on attitudes towards the existence of the USSR was taken (see "Za i protiv" 1989). This is

---

28 For a critique of the excess focus in the study of mobilizational politics on social movements rather than the ways in which they interact with and resonate in society, see Oliver (1989).

fairly typical of transformative politics more generally; revolutions rarely are accompanied by systematic surveys of public opinion, since they usually occur in polities where the expression of opinion is suppressed. Even if public opinion polling had been conducted with some regularity (not to speak of methodological rigor), it is unusual in a period of discursive transformation in society that pollsters would frame questions in such a way as to capture relevant attitudes over the span of a mobilizational cycle. By giving us a sense of the temporal relationship between mobilization and the resonance of particular frames, event analysis helps us understand the politics by which identities and the collective beliefs that underpin them are affirmed or changed.

Indeed, when one gets down to specific cases, many of the central theoretical issues which engage scholars of nationalism tend to boil down to questions of the timing of mobilization and its relationship to identities and collective beliefs, consistency in the demands over which groups mobilize, and the relationship of past cycles of mobilization to the particular wave of mobilization being studied. Primordialists stress the independent character of identities, their historical continuity, and the role played by pre-existing psychological attachments in conditioning mobilization; this would lead one to expect consistency in the demands over which individual groups mobilize, with nationalist mobilization emerging swiftly as a result of changing political opportunities. Instrumentalists, by contrast, stress the plasticity of identities, seeing them as the product of class-based or elite-led mobilization in competition for scarce resources and viewing them as resources for mobilization, not as agents of conflict. Instrumentalists tend to look for the ways in which the incidence of nationalist mobilization is related to the timing of other social processes, particularly to forms of economic competition. An emerging constructivist school focuses on the ways in which identities are constructed through acts of discourse, the actions of institutions and the state, and the transactions of everyday life.[29] Constructivists would expect to see mobilization structured by the implicit boundaries and workings of institutions prior to mobilization, national consciousness emerging out of the process of mobilization itself, and nationalism spreading in part as a result of the influence of analogy and the confluence of circumstances.

Each of these perspectives contains hypothesized temporal relationships that can to some extent be unraveled by means of event analysis. What makes the former Soviet Union so exciting a case (or set of cases) to study in this regard are the multiple nationalist mobilizations which the collapse of the USSR unleashed and the extent to which nationalism was a significant element in the mobilizational "master frames" that became dominant throughout the region

---

29   For a review of these three schools, see Young (1993) and Horowitz (1985).

during this period. Figure 5 below demonstrates the overwhelming significance of nationalist issues in the mobilizational cycle and the extraordinary power of nationalist issues to mobilize populations. Not only did nationalist issues weigh heavily in the agenda of counter-elites, but nationalist issues also seemed to possess a remarkable mobilizing capacity relative to other issues.

As Figure 5 shows, groups which mobilized around nationalist issues gained higher rates of participation in protest demonstrations than those which did not. In spite of numerous efforts to organize demonstrations around non-nationalist themes, these demonstrations exhibited relatively low mobilizational turnouts. Ethnic but not nationalist issues lost whatever mobilizational power they had shortly after the 1990 republican elections, as the shift in power that these elections produced led to changes in policies that undermined the rationale for mobilization over these issues. If nationalist issues were not on the agenda of a demonstration, it was less likely to generate a significant mobilization. Indeed, even in 1992, at a time when price liberalization and the hyperinflation that it unleashed throughout much of the former Soviet Union caused many experts to predict an explosion of social unrest, demonstrations which did not raise nationalist issues turned out to be very poor mobilizers of the population.

Why was nationalism such a potent mobilizer in the former Soviet Union, while other issues seemed to fare poorly? The "forward-packed" character of nationalist mobilization (i.e. the fact that participation was concentrated in the early part of the cycle) tells at least part of the story. "Forward-packing" of a particular set of issues within a mobilizational cycle can only be due to the fact that these were the issues that, at least in some contexts, lay most immediately beneath the surface of politics and were most readily raised once the opportunity to do so became available, requiring the least effort by counter-elites to transform popular consciousness. Soviet society as it emerged in the early 1980s was pregnant with many of the nationalist issues which found quick expression in the early glasnost period. The sudden explosion of nationalist mobilization in 1988 and 1989 provides vivid proof of the existence of a considerable store of symbolic capital among those groups that mobilized in the early part of the cycle. Like most contentious politics, nationalism has both "quiet" and "noisy" phases. The "quiet" politics of nationalism occurs in a milieu in which state institutions remain dominant and nationalist contestation turns around efforts to institutionalize behaviors and identities to prevent challenges to official conceptions of nationhood or to prepare for moments when direct challenge to official conceptions becomes possible, the latter often revolving around what Scott (1991) calls "hidden transcripts of resistance." The "noisy" politics of nationalism is precipitated by an opening of political opportunities in which the political order and its institutions come under direct challenge and contest. As the late Ernest Gellner wrote, "[n]ationalism is like gravity, an important and pervasive force, but not, at *most* times, strong enough to be violently disruptive" (1994: xi).

Figure 5: Demonstration Activity Raising Nationalist Issues, Compared with Demonstration Activity not Raising Nationalist Issues*

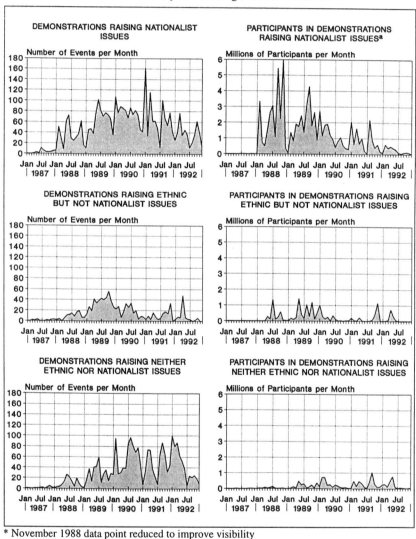

* November 1988 data point reduced to improve visibility

Figure 5 suggests that prior contestation and the "quiet" politics of nationalism are critical to understanding how the "noisy" politics of nationalism plays itself out.[30] Indeed, it is a clarion call for us to integrate history into our analyses of contentious politics by paying closer attention to the ways in which past mobilizations become embedded in collective memory (see Halbwachs 1980) and how the subtle interactions between state and society prior to mobilization shape the expectations of actors once mobilizational politics become possible.

Conclusion

As this essay has shown, scholars need to be attuned to a number of methodological and substantive issues as we move to apply techniques of event analysis beyond the advanced industrial societies of Western Europe and North America to study the transitional regimes of the second and third worlds. Transitional and revolutionary regimes have never been particularly easy to study.

The absence of an institutionalized press or access to reliable police records complicates enormously efforts to engage in event analysis of these waves of mobilization. Multi-ethnicity challenges our ability to capture acts of contention accurately in societies characterized by extreme cultural pluralism or hierarchical ethnic stratification. States that disintegrate in the wake of mobilization fundamentally alter the ground on which analysis stands. This is the stuff of which modern politics is made, and to ignore these phenomena because one cannot follow a strict code of methodological rules developed for studying radically different contexts would be absurd. Instead, one copes as best as one can, developing strategies by which to minimize inaccuracy that are appropriate for the context in which one operates. It is evident, however, that event analysis is much more difficult to operationalize within a transitional society than within a stable one. Nevertheless, it is precisely transitional societies and the explosions of mass mobilization which they experience that lie at the center of the concerns of the field of contentious politics.

The convulsions that encompassed the former Soviet Union and brought about its demise represent one of the great mobilizational upheavals of our century. As the examples in this essay illustrate, empirical analysis of these events promises to tell us a great deal about cycles of protest mobilization, as well as about the phenomena of nationalism, state disintegration and regime transition more generally. Certain patterns of protest mobilization familiar to

---

30 For more on the distinction between the "quiet" and "noisy" politics of nationalism, see Beissinger (1996).

those studying other contexts appeared in the Soviet case as well: The important structuring role played by political opportunity; the role played by elections in institutionalizing mobilization; the sequencing of waves of non-violent and violent mobilizations; and the evolution of mass consciousness over the course of the cycle.

But the Soviet experience, resulting in the breakup of the state rather than in its successful reform, sensitizes us to the variety of outcomes in contentious politics. Mobilization in the Soviet case did not lead to reform or even to the breakdown of the state, but rather to state disintegration. And violent mobilization, rather than constituting a marginalized part of the political process, became partially institutionalized in the post-Soviet era, as states came to be increasingly involved in organizing mass violence. "Soft" states and the institutionalization of conflict that is often characteristic of them defy efforts to define the boundaries of mobilizational cycles with precision. And in situations of "dual power," fundamental contest over who controls the state, or sustained violent contestation, the line between institutional and non-institutional politics grows blurred. One of the great merits of event analysis is that it is flexible enough to be fitted to these circumstances. As the Soviet experience indicates, it is not in the mechanistic application of method but in its creative adaptation that we gain meaningful comparisons which otherwise would be lost to investigation.

References

Alexeeva, L. and V. Chalidze. 1985. *Mass Unrest in the USSR*. Report No. 19, submitted to the Office of Net Assessment of the U.S. Department of Defense (OSD/NA 85-2965), August 1985.

Beissinger, M. R. 1995. "The Persisting Ambiguity of Empire." *Post-Soviet Affairs* 11 (2): 149-184.

Beissinger, M. R. 1996. "How Nationalisms Spread: Eastern Europe Adrift the Tides of Nationalist Contention." *Social Research* 63 (Spring): 1-50.

Brubaker, R. 1992. *Citizenship and Nationhood in France and Germany*. Cambridge, Mass.: Harvard University Press.

Carrère d'Encausse, H. 1993. *The End of the Soviet Empire: The Triumph of Nations*. New York: Basic Books.

Connor, W. 1990. "When Is a Nation?" *Ethnic and Racial Studies* 13 (1): 92-103.

Dallin, A. 1992. "Causes of the Collapse of the USSR." *Post-Soviet Affairs* (October - December): 279-302.

Della Porta, D. and S. Tarrow. 1986. "Unwanted Children: Political Violence and the Cycle of Protest in Italy, 1966-1973." *European Journal of Political Research* 14: 607-632.

DeNardo, J. 1985. *Power in Numbers: The Political Strategy of Protest Rebellion*. Princeton, N.J.: Princeton University Press.

Eisinger, P. K. 1973. "The Conditions of Protest Behavior in American Cities." *American Political Science Review* 67: 11-28.

Gamson, W. A. 1975. *The Strategy of Social Protest*. Homewood, Ill.: The Dorsey Press.
Gellner, E. 1994. *Encounters with Nationalism*. Cambridge, Mass.: Blackwell.
Gorshkov, M. K. and V. V. Zhuravlev, eds. 1992. *Krasnoe ili beloe? - Drama Avgusta-91: Fakty, gipotezy, stolknovenie mnenii*. Moscow: Terra.
Halbwachs, M. 1980. *The Collective Memory*. New York: Harper and Row.
Helsinki Watch. 1990. *Conflict in the Soviet Union: The Untold Story of the Clashes in Kazakhstan*. New York: Helsinki Watch.
Horowitz, D. 1985. *Ethnic Groups in Conflict*. Berkeley, Cal.: University of California Press.
Human Rights Watch. 1995. *Slaughter Among Neighbors: The Political Origins of Communal Violence*. New Haven, Conn.: Yale University Press.
Kedourie, E. 1993. *Nationalism* (4th expanded Edition). Oxford: Blackwell.
Kowalewski, D. 1980a. "Protest for National Rights in the USSR: Characteristics and Consequences." *Nationalities Papers* 8 (2): 179-194.
Kowalewski, D. 1980b. "Trends in the Human Rights Movement." Pp. 150-181 in *Soviet Politics in the Brezhnev Era*, ed. D. R. Kelley. New York: Praeger.
Lapidus, G. et al., eds. 1992. *From Union to Commonwealth: Nationalism and Separatism in the Soviet Republics*. Cambridge: Cambridge University Press.
Lustick, I. S. 1993. *Unsettled States, Disputed Lands: Britain and Ireland, France and Algeria, Israel and the West Bank-Gaza*. Ithaca, N.Y.: Cornell University Press.
McAdam, D. 1982. *Political Process and the Development of Black Insurgency, 1930-1970*. Chicago: University of Chicago Press.
Malia, M. 1994. *The Soviet Tragedy*. New York: The Free Press.
Mikhailov, K. 1988. " Proverka na dorogakh." *Sobesednik*, No. 3 (January): 7-8.
Oliver, P. E. 1989. "Bringing the Crowd Back In: The Nonorganizational Elements of Social Movements." Pp. 1-30 in *Research in Social Movements, Conflicts and Change, Vol. 11*, ed. L. Kriesberg. Greenwich, Conn.: JAI Press.
Olzak, S. 1982. *The Dynamics of Ethnic Competition and Conflict*. Stanford, Cal.: Stanford University Press.
Rasshivalova, E. and N. Seregin, eds. 1991. *Putch: khronika trevozhnykh dnei*. Moscow: Progress.
Roeder, P. G. 1991. "Soviet Federalism and Ethnic Mobilization." *World Politics* 43 (January): 196-232.
Scott, J. C. 1991. *Domination and the Arts of Resistance: Hidden Transcripts*. New Haven, Conn.: Yale University Press.
Shenfield, S. D. 1992. "The Struggle for Control over Statistics: The Role of the Central Statistical Administration within the Inclusive Statistical System of the USSR." Pp. 89-119 in *Cracks in the Monolith: Party Power in the Brezhnev Era*, ed. J. R. Millar. Armonk, N.Y.: M. E. Sharpe.
Suleimenov, O. 1989. " Vystuplenie deputata Sulemeinova, O. O." *Kazakhstanskaia pravda*, June 10: 2.
Tarrow, S. 1985. *Struggle, Politics, and Reform: Collective Action, Social Movements, and Cycles of Protest*. Ithaca, N.Y.: Cornell Studies in International Affairs.
Tarrow, S. 1989. *Democracy and Disorder: Protest and Politics in Italy 1965-1975*. Oxford: Clarendon Press.
Tarrow, S. 1991. "'Aiming at a Moving Target': Social Science and the Recent Rebellions in Eastern Europe." *PS: Political Science and Politics* (March): 12-20.

Tilly, C. 1993. *European Revolutions, 1492-1992*. Oxford: Blackwell.

Tilly, C. 1995. "Contentious Repertoires in Great Britain, 1758-1834." Pp. 15-42 in *Repertoires and Cycles of Collective Action*, ed. M. Traugott. Durham, N.C.: Duke University Press.

Tishkov, V. 1995. "'Don't Kill Me, I'm a Kyrgyz!': An Anthropological Analysis of Violence in the Osh Ethnic Conflict." *Journal of Peace Research* 32 (2): 133-149.

Yeltsin, B. 1994. *The Struggle for Russia*. New York: Random House.

Young, C. 1993. "The Dialectics of Cultural Pluralism: Concept and Reality." Pp. 3-35 in *The Rising Tide of Cultural Pluralism: The Nation-State at Bay?* ed. C. Young. Madison, Wis.: University of Wisconsin Press.

"Za i protiv" 1989. *Ogonek,* No. 43, October: 4-5.

Protest Event Analysis in the Study of Democratic Consolidation: Poland, 1989-1993

Grzegorz Ekiert and Jan Kubik

Introduction

The research project on which this chapter is based has both exploratory and theoretical goals.[1] Our first objective is to create a systematic data base on a neglected topic: collective protest in post-communist Poland. It was pre-1989 Poland, after all, that was renowned for its rebellious civil society, which engendered more protest than occurred in any other communist state. After 1989, Poles experienced a rapid political metamorphosis and comprehensive economic reforms which exacted high social costs. Given these dramatic changes, we want to know whether Poles have continued to protest after the fall of communism, and if so, how. But we also intend to contribute to the theory of democratic consolidations: We want to learn more about the role that bottom-up, popular activities on the part of civil society's organizations play in this process, focusing in particular on protest politics.

As a result of the "round table" negotiations which began in Warsaw on February 6, 1989, Poland became the first country in the Soviet bloc to initiate a peaceful transfer of political power. The semi-democratic elections in June 1989 led to the political triumph of the re-legalized Solidarity movement; the first post-World War II non-communist government was in office by the end of the summer; and the communist party had dismantled itself by January 1990. The transfer of power was followed by the comprehensive transformation of the

1   The empirical evidence for this paper comes primarily from a research project which involves systematic data collection on collective protest during the first years of democratic transition in four countries: Poland, Hungary, Slovakia and former East Germany. The project is funded by the Program for the Study of Germany and Europe administered by the Center for European Studies at Harvard University, the National Council for Soviet and East European Research and the American Council of Learned Societies. It is directed by Grzegorz Ekiert and Jan Kubik. We would like to thank Sidney Tarrow for his generous help and encouragement. For their indispensable assistance and advice, our special gratitude goes to Martha Kubik, Nancy Bermeo, Mark Beissinger, Ellen Comisso, Krzysztof Gorlach, Bela Greskovits, Anna Grzymala-Busse, Michael Kennedy, Kazimierz Kloc, Christiane Lemke, Anna Seleny, Jason Wittenberg, and Mayer N. Zald. Particularly insightful comments were provided by Dieter Rucht and Ruud Koopmans. Thank you both!!!

national political institutions and local administration, and radical economic reform. The new political elites which emerged from the Solidarity movement set Poland on the path toward liberal democracy and a market economy.

The transformation policies, however, had to be forged and implemented amidst a deepening economic crisis, regional political chaos, as well as disintegrating regional economic and political institutions. These external adversities combined with the need to institute radical macro-economic stabilization measures contributed to a sharp decline in real incomes, the rapid growth of unemployment, new social inequalities and rising insecurity. Various professional and social groups responded to this largely unanticipated situation with strikes and protests, whose intensity increased from 1989 through 1993. At the same time, the political consensus concerning the extent, speed and sequencing of institutional reforms, which initially unified the new elites, unraveled. The post-Solidarity political bloc, united for the 1989 elections and initially constituting a single caucus in parliament, split into several fiercely competing parties with contrasting programs and political agendas. Consequently, from 1989 until 1994 Poland experienced a turbulent political evolution. It had three parliamentary elections, two local and two presidential elections, as well as eight consecutive prime ministers and six governments. After its political triumph in 1989, the Solidarity-based political movement disintegrated and descendant political parties were unable to form effective electoral coalitions. Finally, as a result, in the 1993 elections the ex-communist parties were returned to power. In brief, during its first five years, Poland's fledgling democratic system faced rising popular dissatisfaction, intensifying pressure from below and governmental instability - all symptoms of the serious problems of consolidation.

Protest in Various Types of Polities

The question is often posed whether a high level of protest activities in a given society is indicative of a robust, active civil society and thus a component of a healthy democratic polity, or whether it rather implies instability and low legitimacy of the established institutions. In brief - is protest a positive or negative political phenomenon? The answer must be - it depends. Different types of protest actions, different kinds of protest strategies and demands will have different significance in different types of polities and political situations.[2] We

---

2   According to Tilly, "the different forms of collective action are part of the regular
     processes of struggle. The coherent phenomenon is a process that has an orderly side
     and a disorderly side. The central process is a process of sets of people acting together

need to ask more nuanced questions by taking into consideration both the complexity of protest politics itself and the complexity of its relationships with other types of politics.

For example, a high magnitude of protest in a country which has a set of well-functioning political institutions and *additionally* has developed a set of mechanisms through which protest activities are channeled, may be only moderately disruptive and signify the strong, vibrant public life of a well-functioning democracy. On the other hand, frequent protests may occur in a country in which the institutionalized channels of state-society interactions, such as political parties, interest groups or parliament are not functioning properly. If, additionally, this country has not developed a set of procedures to deal with protest activities, protests will be highly destabilizing.

In this chapter, we review the general features of protest in post-communist Poland and then focus on its two specific characteristics directly related to the consolidation dilemmas. They are (1) the degree of institutionalization and (2) the general function of protest, which we conceptualize as either *supplementary* or *complementary* to other forms of politics. Protest politics *supplements* other types of politics when all or most institutionalized channels of interaction between the state and its citizens are closed. Under such circumstances, collective contentious action is the citizens' only recourse for voicing their grievances and demands and the only means of genuine political participation. Such is the situation with authoritarian and totalitarian regimes. In democratic polities, citizens protest to *complement* the existing institutionalized political mechanisms (activities by political parties, referenda, elections, etc.). They usually do so to publicize newly emerged issues and identities, to inform the wider public of new organizations or to voice concerns and claims which are, in their assessment, inadequately conveyed to the authorities through the more established institutional channels.[3] In many countries, protest actions will be complementary at times and on other occasions supplementary vis-a-vis "conventional" politics. Furthermore, we need to consider the various institutional domains of the polity. In some, protest may be supplementary and in others complementary. Finally, it should be noted that the "complementary/ supplementary" variable is not dichotomous; it is rather a continuum.

With regard to the other dimension, we note that protest politics in a given country may be more or less institutionalized. It is institutionalized when it is

---

on their interests, and that is what we ought to be theorizing about" (Morris and Herring 1987: 165). Kriesi and Giugni argue similarly: "Our contention is that the mobilization of social movements is closely linked to conventional politics in the parliamentary and extraparliamentary arenas of a given country" (1995: vii).

3   See Kriesi et al. (1995), Dalton and Kuechler (1990).

predictably channeled through well-established procedures and perceived by both the authorities and the public as a legitimate form of public activity. Since institutionalization is a multi-dimensional phenomenon, we assume that a social practice (or interaction pattern) is institutionalized when one or more of the following four conditions are met:

1. Conformity with the pattern is insured and enforced by punishments and/ or rewards. Of particular importance is "official" approval, i.e. *authorization*.

2. It is carried out according to a set of pre-existing *procedures* and is used with high frequency, i.e. repeated almost always when a problem or issue it is designed to deal with emerges (it is standardized).

3. Its application involves relatively low costs (low mobilization of actors and resources)[4] and causes *less disruption* of established routines then the application of (most) alternative practices. Disruption occurs when (often unreflectedly) accepted and routinely obeyed rules which regulate the flow of everyday life are temporarily suspended, i.e. when people cease to act according to generally accepted routines.[5]

4. It is widely regarded as "normal" or "taken-for-granted," i.e. it is *legitimate*.

A cross-tabulation of the two criteria, institutionalization and supplementary/ complementary continuum, renders a four-fold typology of various situations. There are polities where protest is highly institutionalized and functions as a mechanism complementary to other robust political institutions (e.g. Israel, France, United States). There are polities where protest actions complement other political mechanisms, but they are poorly institutionalized - this may be the case in some new democracies undergoing processes of consolidation (e.g. post-1989 Romania). In authoritarian polities, where protest is by definition

---

4   According to Jepperson, practices are institutionalized when they requires "little 'action' - repetitive mobilization and intervention - for their sustenance" (1991: 146). The basic assumption behind this point is that the mobilization is inversely related to institutionalization: the higher the former, the lower the latter. However, even though an institutionalized strategy may be less costly than direct action, it may be less efficient than other institutionalized strategies. This is the problem of the "stickiness" of suboptimal institutions (higher institutionalization does not always imply the highest available efficiency). See, e.g., North (1990: 7), March and Olsen (1989: 54-56).

5   All four features are not dichotomous (absent/present) variables, but rather continua of increasing/decreasing intensity; institutionalization is thus a multi-dimensional quality of varying intensity. Accordingly, in order to answer the question "To what degree is protest action institutionalized?" we need to compare its "partial" institutionalizations along the four specified dimensions with relevant institutionalizations of other modes of interaction between the state and society.

predominantly supplementary, it is also almost always poorly institutionalized; there are no opportunities to develop institutionalization (e.g. the former Soviet Bloc). There are some exceptions, however, and Poland between 1976 and 1989 was one of them. Protest politics developed there in the late 1970s, flourished during the 1980s and contributed to the fall of state socialism. It was never authorized by the ruling communists, but it was frequent, organized according to well-developed procedures, and had a high legitimacy. It was solidly, though not completely, institutionalized as a "routine" element of the political land-scape. To summarize, protest in pre-1989 Poland supplemented non-existent or inadequate forms of democratic politics. Furthermore, protest politics were relatively well institutionalized (in comparison to other Eastern European countries).

In this chapter we focus on the role of protest in a consolidating democracy. We must therefore present our definition of consolidation.

Protest and Democratic Consolidation

We propose to analyze the consolidation of democracy as a complex process occurring simultaneously on several levels (or within several institutional domains) of the socio-political organization of society: the state, political society and civil society. The state is the realm of authoritative and bureaucratic politics. It should be considered

> ... as something more than the 'government.' It is a continuous administrative, legal, bureaucratic and coercive system that attempts not only to manage the state apparatus but to structure the relationship between civil and public power and to structure many crucial relationships within civil and political society (Stepan 1988: 4).

The most distinct characteristics of the state are its control of coercive resources, its monopoly of rule making and its capability to implement its decisions within a defined territory, regardless of public opposition or resistance. Political society is an intermediate realm within which the dual process of translation and mediation takes place. It provides channels through which various societal interests and claims are aggregated and translated into generalized policy recommendations. Civil society is defined by Schmitter as

> ... a set or system of self-organized intermediary groups: (1) that are relatively independent of both public authorities and private units of production and reproduction, i.e., of firms and families; (2) that are capable of deliberating about and taking collective actions in defense/promotion of their interests/ passions; (3) but do not seek to replace either state agents or private (re-) producers or to accept responsibility for governing the polity as a whole; (4) but do agree to act within pre-established rules of 'civil' or legal nature (1995a: 4-5).

Many divergent types of democratic consolidation exist that may have only a very basic set of generalized procedures in common.[6] Each consolidating democracy may feature a different set of principal actors, different types of relationships both within and between the state, political society and civil society, and, in particular, a different style of institutionalizing political participation, including contentious collective action.

Democratic consolidation is a process which approaches its completion when the establishment of a *political democracy*[7] is accompanied by three additional conditions.

1.   The formation of a consensus concerning the boundaries of political community. This is when the "stateness problem" facing many newly democratized societies is resolved.[8]
2.   The development of transparency and predictability at the institutional level. This condition is realized when the following elements are in place: (2.1) the basic democratic architecture, such as tri-division of powers, regularity of elections, etc., is assured by the *constitution,*[9] (2.2) *the state possesses the stability, autonomy and capacity to implement its policies;*[10]

---

6   Schmitter argues that "no single format or set of institutions embodies modern democracy." (1992: 162) See also Schmitter and Karl (1991), and Karl and Schmitter (1991).
7   Following an emerging consensus, we subscribe to a minimalist, procedural definition of democracy. Diamond, Linz and Lipset offer one: "Democracy denotes a system of government that meets three essential conditions: meaningful and extensive competition among individuals and organized groups (especially political parties) for all elective positions of government power, at regular intervals and excluding the use of force; a highly inclusive level of political participation in the selection of leaders and policies, at least through regular and fair elections, such that no major (adult) social group is excluded; and a level of civil and political liberties - freedom of expression, freedom of the press, freedom to form and join organizations - sufficient to ensure integrity of political competition and participation" (1990: 6-7).
8   Linz and Stepan (1992) offer a seminal analysis of this problem. Schmitter believes that most "considologists" would agree that: "It is preferable, if not indispensable, that national identity and territorial limits be established before introducing reforms in political (or economic) institutions" (1995b: 29).
9   The importance of early constitutional choices is emphasized by Jon Elster (1993) and Arend Lijphart (1992).
10   We define autonomy, following Michael Shafer, as "the extent to which the state is not merely an arena for conflict but is distinct from non-state actors" (1994: 6). State capacity is defined, following Barkey and Parikh, "as the state's ability to implement strategies to achieve its economic, political, or social goals in society." They argue that "the state may acquire capacity through institutions such as the bureaucracy, or through resources such as external ties to entrepreneurs and finance capital [but it is also] determined by the state's relations to society " (1991: 526).

(2.3) *the party system* has stability and autonomy vis-a-vis both the state and civil society; and (2.4) public participation by citizens, groups and organizations within *civil society* is unconstrained and institutionalized.[11]
3. The achievement of a *sufficient level of legitimacy*, i.e. a situation whereby the basic institutional set-up of the polity and political procedures must be considered legitimate by all significant social and political forces. As Mainwaring observes, "Legitimacy is every bit as much the root of democratic stability as objective payoffs, and it is less dependent on economic payoffs than Przeworski or Lipset (1959) indicate" (1992: 306).[12] To put it differently, the absence of sizable anti-systemic parties and movements that act as a disloyal opposition fosters consolidation (see Linz 1978: 27-38).

Political democracy is the necessary condition of consolidated democracy; without it consolidation is meaningless. The three additional conditions are realizable and realized to various degrees (O'Donnell 1992: 18) but their absence makes democracy weak and unstable.

In our study of protest politics during democratic consolidation, we take an important cue from Shin who argues that "consolidation and stability are not the same phenomenon" (1994: 144). A budding democracy may stabilize in such a way that the *threat* to overthrow its institutions remains a viable option for some significant actors. Samuel Valenzuela characterizes such a situation as a "vicious circle of perverse institutionalization" (1992: 68). Another possibility is an "incomplete democracy"[13] when stabilization occurs at a sub-optimal level, that is without the institutionalization of one or more elements of the fully consolidated democracy (specified above).

Event analysis of protest politics is a good method for testing democratic consolidation. By using this tool, in combination with public opinion surveys and analyses of institutional arrangements, we can determine (1) the intensity (magnitude) of protest, (2) its "direction" (increasing/decreasing), and (3) the level and main features of protest's institutionalization. Let us briefly consider these features and their impact on democratic consolidation.

A high magnitude of protest in given country may be construed as sign of incomplete consolidation. Yet there are no solid theoretical reasons to claim that a high magnitude of protest indicates serious problems of consolidation. Perhaps the opposite view is more accurate: The high magnitude of protest may

---

11 On the distinction between organizations and institutions, see North (1990: 4-5).
12 Schmitter observed, "the core of consolidation dilemma lies in coming up with a set of institutions that politicians can agree upon and citizens are willing to support" (1992: 159).
13 On "incomplete democracies" in Central Europe, see Greskovits (1996).

indicate progress in consolidation. As we indicated earlier, this dilemma can be resolved only when a model of protest politics becomes sufficiently nuanced: The devil is in details, i.e. the positive or negative impact of protest on consolidation depends on both the specific features of protest and the socio-political context within which the protest politics occur.

Three general views seem to exist on the "fate" of protest activities of the populace during the early stages of democratic consolidation. According to the first, protest activities during the post-breakthrough period should diminish since the citizens, who won their battle against an unwanted regime, "are taking a break." This argument can be seen as a part of a more general reasoning that civil society's vibrancy should decline in the aftermath of democratic victory.[14] In general, exponents of this view expect the decline of civic (both conventional and unconventional) activism, due to the contentment of the victors.

According the second view, protest is likely to intensify with the progress of transition. First, groups previously excluded from politics regain their "voice" and seek to redress long-standing grievances. Second, the populace's discontent with harsh measures of economic stabilization programs, which often follow democratic victory, leads to the increase and radicalization of protest politics (see, e.g., Walton and Ragin 1990), which stall or even subverts democratic consolidation. This view can be summarized as the *rage of the victims*.

The third view predicts that when the main elements of democracy are expediently instituted, protest quickly takes its place amongst other forms of politics (becomes complementary to them), as happens in well-established democracies. Evidence of this situation would be high or increasing incidence (or magnitude) of protest, whose demands would nonetheless be predominantly moderate and reformist and the strategies increasingly institutionalized. Under such circumstances, protest would constitute *unconventional civic involvement* of those citizens who feel excluded from conventional politics and policy-making, and will not become a serious threat to democratic consolidation.

After presenting our method and the main findings of our study, we will determine which of these three views of the post-breakthrough protest is corroborated by the Polish data.

Method: Event Analysis in the Study of Democratization - Poland

Following the pioneering work of Charles Tilly and his associates, event analysis has become accepted and an often indispensable research method in the

---

14   Karl and Schmitter claim that demobilization "of various mass publics" during democratic consolidation is "the almost universal fact" (1995: 976).

study of collective action, protest and social movements. Despite its imperfections and limitations, acknowledged by those who use it, event analysis is uniquely capable of providing researchers with the most extensive and systematic sets of data on protest activities and their different components and dimensions. Data sets constructed on the basis of specifically selected press sources as well as archival data bases, including police and municipal records, and movements' documents, allow both qualitative and quantitative aspects of protest actions to be studied over time and large geographical areas. Event analysis may be also incorporated within various research designs, focusing either on a single case or employing a comparative perspective, and it can be applied to answer a variety of questions concerning collective action, its forms and outcomes, its organizers and participants, responses of the state and broader political issues.

In our research project we adopted a broad definition of protest event to cover all types of non-institutional and unconventional public political actions.[15] We selected two national "prestige" newspapers,[16] *Rzeczpospolita* and *Gazeta Wyborcza*, and had our coders read *every* issue of each paper published during the analyzed period (1989 to 1993). In so doing we avoided the problems associated with selecting (sampling) a subset of issues to be analyzed. The papers we selected are the largest (in term of readership) and the most comprehensive dailies in Poland. Before 1989 *Rzeczpospolita* had been a governmental daily, but after a change in personnel it emerged as the country's most reliable and objective paper. Despite its formal status as a state-owned newspaper it has ceased to be the government's mouthpiece and retains its independence. *Gazeta Wyborcza* was founded in the spring of 1989 as an organ of the Solidarity movement. The paper quickly distanced itself from any explicit

---

15   Our definition of a collective public protest event includes the following elements: Public is understood to mean an action which is reported in at least one newspaper; collective action is an action undertaken by at least three people. Extreme acts such as self-immolation, hunger strikes or acts of terror - carried out by individuals as a form of political protest - are also counted as "collective acts"; A collective public event is an acts of protest if it is undertaken to articulate certain specified demands and is not a routine or legally prescribed behavior of a social or political organization, and whose form deviates from the routinely accepted way of voicing demands. If protest actions are officially (i.e. outwardly or publicly) directed or coordinated by one decision-making center, they constitute together a protest campaign.

16   An excellent, though rather forgotten, manual defines "prestige" papers in the following way: "The prestige paper has become an institution in all modern major powers. In each there is one paper, and usually only one, easily identified as being addressed to an elite audience and providing statements of public policy which are not available to readers of the ordinary papers. This paper is often, although not always, a great paper in the sense of having widespread news coverage" (Laswell, Lerner and de Sola Pool 1952: 42).

affiliation with political parties which succeeded Solidarity and has become the most popular daily in the country, with a circulation higher than that of any other paper in Eastern Europe. Its bias is clear: It sympathizes with the liberal-democratic option, most prominently represented by the Union of Freedom (formerly Democratic Union). Both newspapers have extended networks of regional offices and cover both national and local events. These two dailies were supplemented by four weeklies: *Tygodnik Solidarnosc* (the official organ of the Solidarity Trade Union), *Wiesci* (a weekly focusing on agriculture and peasant issues), *Polityka* (a prominent political weekly), and *Zycie Gospodarcze* (a major business weekly). Again, the coders were asked to read every issue printed during the analyzed period. By selecting these four weeklies we gained access to both national and regional news as well as to specific sectoral reporting. The reliance on several sources greatly increased the amount of information on protest events recorded in our data base.

Results

In this section we will (1) describe the general features of protest politics during the studied period and try to determine (2) whether it was complementary or supplementary in relation to other forms of politics, and (3) whether Polish protest politics was institutionalized or becoming increasingly institutionalized.

Protest in Post-Communist Poland: Main Features

Between 1989 and 1993 collective protest in Poland was intense. Actions ranged from single isolated strikes to nation-wide protest campaigns involving hundreds of schools, hospitals and enterprises as well as thousands of workers and public sector employees. They included hour long warning strikes as well as protracted and desperate month-long strike campaigns. The repertoire of protest was very diverse. It consisted of both violent and non-violent street demonstrations, a variety of strikes, dramatic hunger strikes, huge rallies, boycotts, occupation of public buildings, blockades of roads and public spaces, rent strikes, and various other forms of symbolic protest. Protest activities spread to all regions and involved all social groups and categories, with workers, public sector employees, peasants and youth being the most active participants. Our research indicates that Poland had the highest frequency of protest among the Central Eastern European countries we studied (Table 1).[17]

---

17 For the first presentation of the results of our four-country study see Ekiert and Kubik (1996a). In Germany our coders used two dailies and two weeklies; in Slovakia, 2 dailies and 2 weeklies; in Hungary, 2 dailies and 4 weeklies.

The most striking finding that emerges from our study is that during the period from 1989 to 1993 the number of protest actions remained relatively constant. Moreover, there was an increase in the magnitude of protest (discussed below). The picture presented by our data base is shown in Table 2.

Table 1: Post-1989 Protest Events in Poland, Hungary, Slovakia and East Germany*

	1989	1990	1991	1992	1993	1994	Total
Poland	314	306	292	314	250		1476
Slovakia		50	82	116	47	40	335
Hungary	122	126	191	112	148	44	743
East Germany	222	188	291	268	283	183	1435

* East Germany refers to the former German Democratic Republic (GDR). Data for Slovakia, Hungary, and the former GDR include only those protest actions held before the elections in each country. (Parliamentary elections were held from September 30 to October 1, 1994 in Slovakia, and on May 8 and 30, 1994 in Hungary. General elections were held on October 16, 1994 in Germany.)

Table 2: The Number of Protest Events in Poland, 1989-1993 (by category)*

Year	1989	1990	1991	1992	1993	Total
Single protest events	247 78.6%	261 85.3%	235 80.5%	256 81.5%	202 80.8%	1201
Series of protest events	41 13.1%	27 8.8%	17 5.8%	17 5.4%	6 2.4%	108
Protest campaigns	27 8.6%	18 5.9%	40 13.7%	41 13.1%	41 16.4%	167
N = Total no. of protest events	314	306	292	314	250	1476

* For the purpose of our project we assume that a protest event may include the activities of several separate groups or organizations. The activities of different groups are considered to be a part of the same protest event if (1) they relate to the same grievances and (2) take place at the same time without any considerable delays.

The number of protest events recorded in our database differs from figures found in other sources due to a specific definition of the protest event we accepted. Yet, in the Polish Statistical Yearbook, we found an independent confirmation of our crucial finding that the frequency (number of events) of protest was increasing or, at least, remained steady throughout the studied period.[18]

---

18   The Polish Statistical Yearbook *(Rocznik Statystyczny)* for 1994 reports the following figures (percentage of workers who participated in strikes in those enterprises where strikes took place): 1990 - 29.7% (250 strikes); 1991 - 41.4% (305 strikes); 1992 -

Table 3 illustrates another major finding of our study: During the 1989 to 1993 period, protests had predominantly economic character - Poles protested mostly to battle for improvements in their living conditions.

Table 3:   Types of Demands (more than one per protest event)

Type of demand	1989	1990	1991	1992	1993	Total
Economic	220	174	277	237	192	1100
	70.1%	56.9%	94.9%	75.5%	76.8%	74.5%
Political	72	151	109	127	127	586
	23.0%	48.1%	37.3%	40.4%	50.8%	39.7%
Other	38	53	61	48	36	236
	12.1%	17.3%	20.9%	15.3%	13.8%	16.0%
Data unavailable	83	23	16	24	8	154
	26.4%	7.8%	5.5%	8.2%	3.2%	10.4%
Total protest events	314	306	292	314	250	1476
Total demands	330	378	447	402	355	1912

As a detailed examination of demands reveals, "wage increases/material demands" was by far the most frequently reported category. Only a few contentious collective actions used radically polarizing symbolism and stated as one of their objectives the revolutionary overthrow of the post-1989 socio-political order. A demand to "modify/reform existing state or public institutions" was voiced in only 0.6% of protests in 1989, 4.6% in 1990, 4.1% in 1991, 1.3% in 1992, 2.0% in 1993. A more radical demand to "abolish/replace the post-1989 political order" was practically never voiced. The tenor of post-communist protest in Poland was decisively reformist. Protestors did not intend to engage in "state-re-making" or implementing radical political/ideological programs; instead they wanted to correct specific state policies or express dissatisfaction with their outcomes.

While the number of protest events was relatively constant during the five year period, a closer look at the more specific features of contentious actions reveals the growing intensity of protest. We singled out four such features for consideration: (1) Organizational complexity of protest event, (2) scope of protest event, (3) number of participants, and (4) event's duration.

43.4% (6351 strikes; 1993 - 55.2% (7443 strikes). The tremendous increase of the number of strikes between 1992 and 1993 results from the change in calculating techniques. In 1990 and 1991, the GUS (the Main Statistical Office) reported strikes using a single strike action as a unit of observation, regardless of how many enterprises actually took part in the strike. Since 1992, the new unit of observation was a strike in an individual institution, regardless of whether other institutions participated in the same strike action.

As Table 2 above illustrates, the number of large-scale, coordinated protest campaigns increased considerably. In 1990 there were 18 campaigns, but during the 1991 to 1993 period their number climbed to 40 or more each year. Since organizing a large campaign calls for considerable material, organizational and human resources, the increase in the number of campaigns indicates a higher level of *institutionalization of protest* activity during the later part of the studied period. Furthermore, the higher "saturation" of national politics with protest is confirmed by the increased number of protest actions whose scope was non-local (i.e. regional or national). In 1989, regional protests constituted 7.0% of all protest events, in 1991 - 9.3%, in 1993 - 12.6%. Protests whose scope was national, accounted for 13.7% of all protest events in 1990 and 18.4% in 1993.

Judging by the growing number of protests with large numbers of participants (above 2,000), the amount of people who engaged in contentious collective actions also increased. In 1989 we recorded nine protest events which had more than 2,000 participants (they constituted 2.9% of all recorded protest events for this year). In 1990 there were eleven such protest events (3.6%), in 1992 - 36 (11.5%), and in 1993 - 28 (11.2%). Other available data bases on protest activities confirm our results. According to GUS (Main Statistical Office), the number of workers on strike doubled between 1990 and 1991 (from 115,687 to 221,547) and the number of workdays lost due to strikes tripled (from 159,016 to 517,647). Both the number of workers on strikes and the number of lost workdays increased even further in 1992, although it declined in 1993. Our data also suggest that during the 1989 through 1993 period, protest actions involved not only more participants, but there was also a significant increase in protest actions lasting over one month.

Table 4:   Duration of Protest Events

Duration of protest	1989	1990	1991	1992	1993	Total
One day or less	71	118	94	131	77	491
	22.6%	38.5%	32.2%	41.7%	30.8%	33.3%
2-7 days	36	21	31	18	28	134
	11.5%	6.9%	10.6%	5.7%	11.2%	9.1%
8 days -1 month	37	27	39	40	38	181
	11.8%	8.8%	13.0%	12.7%	15.2%	12.3%
More than 1 month	14	21	33	35	35	138
	4.5%	6.9%	11.3%	11.1%	14.0%	9.4%
Not applicable	45	31	33	42	53	204
	14.3%	10.1%	11.3%	13.4%	21.2%	13.8%
Data unavailable	111	87	63	48	19	328
	35.4%	28.4	21.6%	15.3%	7.6%	22.2%
N = Total no. of protest events	314	306	292	314	250	1476

This growing magnitude of protest in Poland can be synthetically measured with a composite index. Inspired by Tilly's method of calculating protest magnitude, which multiplies the size, duration and frequency of collective protest (1978: 95-97), we constructed an index of protest magnitude.[19] The index's values demonstrate that during the first five years of post-communist consolidation, the magnitude of collective protest in Poland increased.

Table 5: Index of Protest Magnitude, 1989-1993

	1989	1990	1991	1992	1993
Index of magnitude	12.6	10.7	18.8	17.6	25.5
N = All valid cases	268	276	259	267	202

The most protest-prone groups in Polish society included various sections of the working class, young people and state employees (see Table 6 below).[20]

Protesting workers were usually employed by state-owned enterprises. Their "regular opponent" (see Table 10 below) was the state and its various agencies. Thus, we identified the most active cleavage of Polish protest politics between 1989 and 1993: the state versus its own employees. It is an intriguing finding, since the structure of employment changed considerably during the analyzed period the number of people employed by private firms increased dramatically, and yet the number of protests involving employees of such enterprises was consistently almost negligible.

These findings indicate that one of the "classical" cleavages of modern politics, between employees and employers (predominantly the state in our

---

19   Constructing an index of magnitude is difficult because of the number of missing values, the ordinal quality of the data and the presence of a significant number of events for which traditional indicators of magnitude, such as "duration," scope," and "number of participants," are not applicable. Since factors analysis is not an appropriate procedure for non-interval variables, our index of magnitude is a product of our three protest indicators, "duration," "scope" and "number of participants," all of which are ordinal. Their ascending values represent a higher "intensity" of a given variable. Missing data for "scope" and "duration" were recoded by substituting the lowest possible values of the variable for the missing values (e.g. in the case of duration we substituted "1" for missing values; "1" stands for "8 hours or less"). Missing values in "number of participants" were estimated using standard linear regression with "scope" and "duration" as predictor variables. A comprehensive description of these procedures is available upon request.

20   The category "public sector employees" comprises the following sub-categories used by our coders: "employees of the state-run sector," "health services/welfare," "education/ science," culture/arts," "transport/airlines/railways," "media," "state/local government/ administration/judiciary," "police/armed forces/fire fighters."

case), was salient but non-institutionalized in Polish post-communist politics.[21] Most protest actions were engendered by "group-based cleavages."

Table 6: Socio-Vocational Categories of Participants (> one per protest event)

	1989	1990	1991	1992	1993	Total
Workers	116 36.9%	35 11.5%	123 32.2%	142 45.2%	100 35.0%	516 35.0%
Farmers/peasants	15 4.8%	34 11.1%	31 10.6%	27 8.6%	34 13.6%	141 9.6%
Service sector	44 14.0%	14 4.6%	23 7.9%	31 9.9%	9 3.6%	121 8.2%
Public state sector	78 24.9%	70 22.8%	70 24.0%	79 25.2%	53 24.8%	350 23.7%
Youth/students	35 11.1%	44 14.4%	24 8.2%	34 10.8%	17 6.8%	154 10.5%
Other	34 10.8%	42 13.7%	44 15.1%	47 15.0%	51 20.4%	218 14.7%
Data unavailable	20 6.4%	80 26.1%	22 7.5%	36 11.5%	42 16.8%	200 13.6%
N = Total protests	314	306	292	314	250	1476

"Issue-based cleavages," typical of Western "new" social movements, were the cause of relatively few protests. Polish protest politics was still "traditional" in Rokkan's sense, i.e. it was driven by mostly economic demands made by well-defined social groups and it was not fluid "with participants joining and disengaging as the political context and their personal circumstances change" (Dalton, Kuechler and Burklin 1990: 12).[22] It was therefore much more similar to the class-based French pattern than the German, Dutch or Swiss "new" protest industries, revealingly analyzed by Kriesi and his collaborators.

As John McCarthy reminds us, "scholars of social movements have come to a quite broad consensus about the importance of *mobilizing structures* [original emphasis] for understanding the trajectory of particular social movements and broader social movement cycles" (1996: 141). Limited by our methodology, which did not allow us to study the process of mobilization directly, we settled for a more modest task: collection of data on organizations which were involved in protest actions, either as organizers or participants.

---

21 We employ here a specific definition of institutionalization: "The institutionalization of a cleavage does not imply that it no longer gives rise to political competition. It only implies that the competition is no longer taking place in unconventional terms" (Kriesi and Duyvendak 1995: 6).

22 On the relationship between social cleavages and (new) social movements see also Kriesi and Duyvendak (1995).

We expected that a lot of protest actions would be organized by newly formed organizations, somewhat weakly institutionalized and "spontaneous." Furthermore we hypothesized that we will find many organizations formed *as a result* of collective protest actions. Neither of these hypotheses was confirmed. As Table 7 demonstrates, most of the protest actions were sponsored or led by the "old," well-institutionalized organizations. Our data also reveal that protest actions were organized predominantly by organizations belonging to civil society, such as labor unions, peasant organizations, and social and political movements. The number of protests for which our coders were not able to determine organizers was not very high (11.3%). One of the most interesting findings of our study was the *very low* involvement of political parties in protest activities; it was *much* lower than in Hungary, Slovakia and East Germany.[23]

Table 7: Organizations Sponsoring or Leading Protest (> 1 per protest event)

	1989	1990	1991	1992	1993	Total
None	25	27	48	28	39	167
	8.0%	8.8%	16.4%	8.9%	15.6%	11.3%
Political parties	22	29	6	20	12	89
	7.0%	9.5%	2.0%	6.4%	4.8%	6.0%
Labor unions	95	84	162	205	163	709
	30.3%	27.4%	55.5%	65.2%	65.2%	48.0%
Peasant/ farmer organizations	6	16	12	24	22	80
	1.9%	5.3%	4.1%	7.6%	8.8%	5.4%
Interest groups	16	24	21	17	13	91
	5.1%	7.9%	7.1%	5.5%	5.2%	6.2%
Social/ political movements	56	65	38	37	32	228
	17.8%	21.3%	12.9%	11.8%	12.8%	15.5%
Other	6	25	12	10	27	80
	1.9%	8.2%	4.1%	3.2%	10.8%	5.4%
Data unavailable	158	88	48	47	14	355
	50.3%	28.8%	16.4%	15.0%	5.6%	24.1%
N =	314	306	292	314	250	1476

Between 1989 and 1993, of all civil society organizations, trade unions were the main driving force behind collective protest. Among trade union federations, Solidarity was the most active. In the 1991 to 1993 period we noted, however, a significant increase in protests organized by other trade unions.

We found additional support for our central argument that during the analyzed period both the magnitude and the significance of protest were intensifying. Reviewing the data we collected on the number of organizers

---

23   Political parties (co-)sponsored or (co-)led 35.5% of protest actions in Hungary, 29.6% in Slovakia and 23.3% in East Germany.

involved in each protest action, we discovered the following pattern: In 1990 12.7% of protest events were sponsored by two or more organizations; in 1991 this number went up to 14.7%; in 1992 it was 17.8%; and in 1993 it was even higher, 19.6%. We submit that this growing *inter-organizational coordination* of protest activities indicates the increasing routinization of protest, i.e. its increasing significance as a mode of interaction between the state and its citizenry or amongst various actors of the public sphere.

Post-communist collective protest in Poland was *decidedly non-violent* (see Table 8) - a startling contrast to Latin America, where the so-called "IMF riots" exacted a heavy toll in casualties (150-190 dead) and property damage (see Walton 1991; Greskovits 1994). Violence occurred most often when youth participated in protest actions - of 154 events involving youth, 36 (23.4%) included some form of violent incidents. By contrast, out of 479 actions workers were involved in, only 13 (2.7%) were violent. As far as organizations are concerned, violence most often accompanied protests including social and political movements (16.2% of events involving such groups). When political parties were involved, protest turned violent in 11.5% of cases. Only 3.5% of protest actions in which trade unions partook were violent!

Table 8: Violent, Disruptive and Non-Disruptive Protest Strategies (> 1 per protest event)

	1989	1990	1991	1992	1993	Total
Violent	21	26	20	26	22	115
	6.7%	18.5%	6.9%	8.2%	8.8%	7.8%
Disruptive	247	232	229	253	184	1145
	78.7%	75.8%	78.4%	80.6%	73.6%	77.6%
Non-disruptive	130	144	269	261	247	1051
	41.4%	47.1%	92.2%	83.1%	98.8%	71.2%
Other	5	6	7	4	8	30
	1.6%	2.0%	2.4%	1.3%	3.2%	2.0%
Data unavailable	7	25	6	10	0	48
	2.2%	8.2%	2.1%	3.2%		3.3%
N =	314	306	292	314	250	1476

The most popular strategy of protest in Poland was *striking* (including strikes and strike alerts) (see Table 9). It did not dominate the repertoire of protest only in 1990. Demonstrations, marches and rallies were the second most dominant form. Protest letters and statements followed. The next most common forms of protest were more disruptive actions, such as the occupation of public buildings and blockades of roads and public places. The Polish repertoire of protest has proven to be significantly different from the repertoires employed by Hungarians, Slovaks and Germans from the former GDR. Protestors from the first two nations most often used street demonstrations and open letters or statements; German protestors most often employed demonstrations and marches. The relatively high number of violent protest actions in Germany was largely a result of the involvement of right-wing movements.[24]

Table 9:   Protest Strategies (> one per protest event)

	1989	1990	1991	1992	1993	Total
Demonstration/	71	141	108	139	85	544
march/blockade	22.6%	46.1%	37.0%	44.6%	35.0%	36.9%
Strike	159	43	92	75	63	432
	50.6%	14.1%	31.5%	23.9%	25.2%	29.3%
Strike alert/ threat	50	53	106	100	99	418
of protest action	15.9%	17.3%	36.3%	31.8%	39.6%	28.3%
Open letters/	39	37	77	79	84	316
statements	12.4%	12.1%	26.4%	25.2%	33.6%	21.4%
Occupation of	9	43	19	29	19	119
public buildings	2.9%	14.1%	6.5%	9.2%	7.6%	8.1%
Violent	21	26	20	26	22	115
	6.7%	18.5%	6.9%	8.2%	8.8%	7.8%
Other	5	6	7	4	8	30
	1.6%	2.0%	2.4%	1.3%	3.2%	2.0%
Data unavailable	7	25	6	10	0	48
	2.2%	8.2%	2.1%	3.2%		3.3%
N =	314	306	292	314	250	1476

It is also worth noting that the "tactical versatility" (Tarrow's term) of Polish protestors improved: In 1990 three or more protest strategies were employed in only 7.4% of all events. In 1991, this was the case in 19.2% of events, in 1992 17.9%; and in 1993 20.4%. This increased versatility seems to have involved more careful planning and coordination of protest actions; hence it testifies to the increased sophistication of protest organizers and thus *higher institutionalization* of protest as a mode of interaction with the authorities. This conclusion is supported by another finding - the number of protests involving two or more organizations increased as well.

Our analysis would be incomplete without examining the targets of protest actions. As Table 10 illustrates, institutions of the state (the government, parliament and the president) were targeted by protesters more often than any other groups or institutions. Moreover, the frequency with which the state institutions were targeted (particularly the government and ministries) increased considerably during the examined period. Given the predominance of economic

---

24   In Poland, 4.9% protest events included violence; in Hungary - 1.7%; in Slovakia - 2.0%, but in the former GDR - 13.1%.

demands, this finding indicates that protest actions responded to the continuing substantial involvement of the state in the economy. The increased targeting of state institutions was coupled with the revival of the "us-versus-them" conceptualization of politics, in which the "state" is seen as the main antagonist of "society" (confirmed both by our own and other studies). This signifies the re-polarization of Polish political culture, briefly de-polarized after 1989.

Table 10: Targets of Protest Actions (> one per protest event)

	1989	1990	1991	1992	1993	Total
President	3	7	20	26	36	92
	1.0%	2.3%	6.8%	8.3%	14.4%	6.2%
Parliament	28	43	46	81	49	247
	8.9%	14.1%	15.8%	25.8%	19.6%	16.7%
Government/	88	137	185	222	201	833
ministries	28.0%	44.8%	63.4%	70.7%	80.4%	56.4%
Other state	7	26	7	15	19	74
agencies	2.2%	8.4%	2.4%	4.8%	7.6%	5.1%
Local	17	50	42	27	41	177
government	5.4%	16.3%	14.4%	8.6%	16.4%	12.0%
Management	95	54	69	45	59	322
	30.2%	17.6%	23.6%	14.3%	23.6%	21.8%
Domestic and	1	0	0	9	5	15
foreign owners	0.3%			2.9%	2.0%	1.0%
Other	19	31	12	17	18	87
	6.5%	10.1%	4.1%	5.4%	7.2%	5.9%
Data unavailable	130	88	59	90	22	389
	41.4%	28.8%	20.2%	28.7%	8.8%	26.4%
N =	314	306	292	314	250	1476

Table 10 also illustrates another intriguing phenomenon - the *growing* number of protests targeted at all branches of the government. At the same time, the number of protests directed against management fluctuated without any appreciable growth or decline, and protests against domestic or foreign owners were infrequent. The protestors seem to have been driven by an expectation shaped by the old regime, that the state is responsible for all aspects of economic and social life and, therefore, should solve all problems.

Politics of Protest in Post-Communist Poland: Supplementary or Complementary to Other Types of Politics?

In order to determine whether protest politics are supplementary or complementary to other types of politics, we need to place protest in a wider context of activities taking place within both political and civil societies. Paul Lewis

summarized prevailing views on political parties (political society) in Eastern
Europe the following way:

> ... political parties have not had a good press in post-communist eastern Europe.
> They have been seen as weak, fragmented, barely capable of sustaining effective
> government and poor at presenting themselves to the electorate, cliquish,
> divorced from the mass of society, increasingly unrepresentative of public
> interests and generally under-developed, divisive, self-seeking, antithetic to
> hopes of national recovery and harmful to state interests (1994: 5).

At the beginning of 1993 Poland had 222 registered political parties.[25]
Although the majority of these parties were not serious contenders for power,
many did actually enter the political process. The choice of the electoral system
reinforced the initial fragmentation of political forces. In its first fully
democratic elections in 1991, Poland adopted a strictly proportional electoral
law and 111 parties participated in the electoral contest. Among these parties,
69 registered their lists in only one electoral district, 42 were present in at least
two districts, and 27 registered national lists (see Jasiewicz 1992: 497). As a
result, the winner (Democratic Union) received only 12.3% of the vote and a
fragmented parliament was elected, with 29 parties holding seats. Among these,
eleven had enough seats to be considered a credible partner in a potential ruling
coalition. The electoral reforms prior to the 1993 elections reduced the number
of parties entering the electoral process and forced many to join coalitions. Still,
there were 35 parties and coalitions represented in the national elections, with
15 registering national lists. Only seven parties and coalitions won seats in the
lower chamber of parliament, but due to the existing electoral law, 35% of the
votes went to parties which did not win any seats. Given that only 52.1% of
eligible voters cast their ballots, those that did not make it to the parliament
could easily question the representativeness of this institution.

   Polish electoral politics reflected the overall weakness of political society.
The political spectrum was strongly fragmented, with larger parties plagued by
internal conflicts, divisions and frequent splits (see Zubek 1993). Moreover, the
majority of parties, including those most influential in shaping the country's
politics during the first years of consolidation, had surprisingly low membership. Most parties had only a few hundred to a few thousand members.[26] As a

---

- 25   By the end of 1995, the number of political parties increased to 297. The number of
      parties reflects a very liberal party registration procedure. In order to register a political
      party, 15 signatures must be collected on the registration form and three people must
      appear in the District Court in Warsaw. The process is free of any charge.

26   For example, the Liberal Democratic Congress - one of the most influential parties,
      whose leader Krzysztof Bielecki served as the Prime Minister - has approximately 3,000
      members. The Christian National Union - the most important representative of Catholic
      views, which had several ministers in the last three governments and a Deputy Prime

result, party activities came to be monopolized by a narrow, newly formed political class organized into a myriad of small political parties and which concentrated on national level politics, creating a political vacuum underneath.

The second problem plaguing Polish political society, common to all post-communist countries, was the absence of clear and stable political cleavages. According to Ken Jowitt, "the cleavages in Eastern Europe are neither cross-cutting nor superimposed" but "diffused, poorly articulated, psychological as much as political, and for that reason remarkably intense" (1992: 216). Multiple cleavage lines within Polish political society were not clearly delineated and often shifted, although the process of their articulation was underway (Kitschelt 1994). For example, the politically active cleavage between post-Solidarity and post-Communist forces cut across other divisions, engendered by various visions of the pace and content of economic reforms, the relationship between the state and the Roman Catholic Church, the definition of national interests, or the basic foundations of democratic politics (see Ekiert 1992).[27] These cleavages blurred other typical political divisions based on ideology (right-left), regional diversity (center-periphery) or class interests. In the 1989 to 1993 period, the unclear cleavages were additionally complicated by frequent changes in positions and programs presented by specific parties. Many observers of the Polish political scene attributed the low electoral participation to the vague and confused positions advocated by major parties.

Despite a multitude of political parties, the poll conducted by Demoskop in 1994 revealed that 67% of Poles believed that none of the existing parties represented their interests. The decline of formal political participation was also illustrated by the strikingly low membership in political parties. In 1991 only 1.1% of Poles admitted that they belonged to a political party (Siemienska 1991). The general population's knowledge and interest in politics was very low: The majority of Poles were unable to match the names of well known politicians with the parties they belonged to.

After 1989 Polish political parties became major players in parliamentary politics and the formation of governmental alliances. They also emerged as significant foci of articulation of political programs. Yet despite such successes, as well as gradual consolidation of the country's political elites (see Wasilewski 1994, 1995) and a growing clarity of political cleavages (see Kitschelt 1992,

---

Minister in Suchocka's government - has approximately 6,000 members. Seven hundred members were in Warsaw and one in every one hundred members held a parliamentary seat. See Janicki (1993: 15).

27 See also Szawiel (1993), Grabowska and Szawiel (1993), and Wesolowski (1995). For an overview of various conceptualizations of the Polish post-communist field, see Kubik (1994) and Kitschelt (1992, 1995).

1995; Marody 1995), in 1993 the gap between the newly formed political society and Poland's electorate seemed as wide as it had been in 1989.

Given this general weakness of political society and the rising magnitude of protest politics, we conclude that although the organizations sponsoring protest actions did not supplement political parties as major political actors, protest acquired a significant *supplementary political function* in Polish public life. It provided people with the means to bring their criticisms, concerns and grievances into the public forum.

In contrast to the weak political society, civil society became the strongest and most rapidly developing realm of the polity. Democratization theory acknowledges that the "revival," "resurrection" or "re-inventing" of civil society is an important part of democratic consolidation. But in the former communist countries this aspect of democratization should be described as the process *combining the resurrection with the re-configuration of civil society*, since many organizations inherited from the old regime became dominant players in the new public scene. Additionally, even if there is significant organizational continuity within all sectors of civil society, the pattern of re-configuration and re-institutionalization of various sectors differs from country to country. This in turn influences protest activities and the types of collective actors who become most active during the consolidation of new democratic regimes in the region.

In post-1989 Poland thousands of new organizations and movements sprang up locally and nationally. A comprehensive data base tracking the development of associations in Poland ("Jawor"), listed 4,515 organizations in 1993, while before 1989 there were only several hundred large, centralized organizations.[28] In a study conducted during late 1994/early 1995, "Jawor" researchers collected information on 4,328 associations and foundations (NGOs in their terminology), 6,050 local chapters of these organizations, and additionally registered 6,500 other organizations. They also estimated that two million Poles were active in these NGOs, which had some 53,000 full-time employees, 64% of their budget came from private and foreign sources while 26% came from the state budget (*Jawor* 1993). Their activities were mostly concentrated in large urban centers (68%) (see Prawelska-Skrzypek). New organizations were rapidly emerging in all sectors of civil society, especially where existing organizations were unsuccessful in adapting to the new conditions or where new spaces and issue-arenas opened after the collapse of the party-state. In general, three types

---

28   According to another source, by the end of 1992, there were more than 2,000 nation-
       wide voluntary associations registered in the Warsaw District Court, a majority of which
       existed before 1989 (*Polska '93* 1992: 148). This number did not include associations
       whose activities were limited to the regional or local level and were registered by
       provincial courts.

of organizations emerged: (1) reformed organizations inherited from the communist period, (2) spin-off organizations, i.e. those who broke away from their communist-era parent organizations, and (3) newly formed organizations.

The speed and intensity of the recovery of Polish civil society from 1989 to 1993, after four decades of communist rule, was astonishing. Civil society's organizations and actors played an increasingly visible and vocal role in the country's politics, often confronting both the parliament and the government. The most striking feature of this new civil society was its *lack of systematic linkages with the party system (political society)*. As the "Klon-Jawor" data base demonstrates (see Table 11), NGOs' relationships with political parties were much worse than their relationships with any other institutional sector.

Table 11: Relationships Between NGOs and Other Public Actors (%)*

	No contact	Willingness to establish contact	No willingness to establish contact	Sporadic contact	Mutual assistance	Cooper-ation
Government, ministries	30	21	2	23	9	15
*Voievods*** and their agencies	13	18	1	29	17	22
Territorial self-government	5	12	0	21	27	35
Political parties	41	4	35	12	3	5
The Church	14	6	5	26	15	34
Business	6	34	1	13	38	9
Local communities	9	14	1	16	28	31

* Representatives of NGOs assessed their relationships with various other public actors.
** *"Voievod"* can be roughly translated as "governor" of a province *(voievodstvo)*.
Source: Krasnodebska et al. (1996).

In short, during the examined period the re-configuration of civil society was well underway, but the new institutionalization pattern foretold a highly contentious and fragmented domain, *strongly separated* from political society. As a result, many organizations of civil society were themselves politicized although they faced serious identity dilemmas related to their unclear role in politics (see Sewerynski 1994; Waller 1994: 25-26). If fragmentation, competition and political exclusion accompanied by divisions lead to an increase in protest activities, we should expect that the most militant and protest-prone sectors of civil society will include youth organizations, the labor and social/political movements. This hypothesis was indeed confirmed by our study.

To sum up, civil society organizations were the main sponsors of protest activities, although they also engaged in more "conventional" forms of public activity and interest representation. We conclude that protest actions played an important *complementary role* in the activities of the newly reinvigorated Polish civil society.

Was Protest Becoming Increasingly Institutionalized?

The final question we posed for ourselves was whether protest was becoming more institutionalized during the analyzed period. In order to assess the degree of institutionalization we used the four criteria specified earlier. Given these four criteria of institutionalization, during the 1989 to 1993 period protest in Poland had the following features:

1. *Its authorization was high.* Initially, right after the 1989 breakthrough, protest activities were tolerated by the authorities, although no appropriate legislative acts and regulations existed. In 1992, industrial conflicts were codified; the procedures of mediation as well as the conditions for "proper" striking by labor unions were established. In stark contrast to state-socialism, protest became authorized.

2. *Its procedures were well developed.* Among all Eastern European states, Poland has the most developed tradition of protest politics. Its roots go back to the late 1970s and the first "Solidarity" period (1980-1981). Protest also played an extensive role in Polish public life during the 1980s. Moreover, it should be remembered that the transfer of power in early 1989 was accompanied by a wave of strikes and demonstrations. In brief, during the last 14 years of communist rule large segments of the Polish populace learned and mastered a varied repertoire of protest.

3. *Disruptiveness of protest was diminishing* or at least not growing. Data presented in Table 8 illustrate a dramatic change in the ratio of disruptive to non-disruptive strategies in 1991. This phenomenon may be a result of the improved quality of reporting and/or a re-definition of disruptiveness by journalists. It is, however, safe to conclude that there was no increase in the disruptiveness of protest in Poland during the 1989 to 1993 period.

4. *Legitimacy of protest was high/increasing.* After 1989, the degree of acceptance of various forms of protest politics increased (see Table 12).

In sum, our research indicates that during the period from 1989 until 1993, contentious collective action (protest) became increasingly institutionalized on all four dimensions in Poland. It is therefore a *different kind of institutionalization* to the one Pereira, Carlos, Maravall and Przeworski seem to have had in mind when they made the successful consolidation of democracy dependent on the following condition: "All groups must channel their demands through the democratic institutions and abjure other tactics." Highly institutionalized protest may be a "democratic institution" (1993: 4).

Table 12: Net Approval of Specific Forms of Protest*

Forms of protest	1981	1984	1988	1989	1990	1992
Petitions, letters	39	61	60	50	68	84
Posting posters	-8	1	15	-4	38	41
Strikes	-2	7	-12	-15	22	47
Street demonstration	-50	-3	-24	-35	7	39
Boycott of state decisions	-26	-14	1	-16	4	22
Occupying public buildings	-52	-72	-67	-71	-63	-55
Actively resisting police	-50	-41	-48	-39	-45	-47

* Net approval is the difference between those who think that citizens should have the right
  to use a specific form of action and those who think they should not.
Sources: Adamski (1989: 192-193); Jasiewicz (1993: 131); *Opinia publiczna...* (1992).

Summary and Conclusions

Between 1989 and 1993 collective protest was widespread and used by various groups and organizations to press for a variety of economic and political claims. Moreover, the magnitude of protest increased. Protests were not organized by marginal groups; rather, members of "mainstream" social categories, such as workers and state employees, were most likely to engage in protest activities.

Protest organizers most often came from civil society. Labor unions were the most active. Political parties engaged in protest infrequently. Thus, relying on our own data and other available sources of information, we conclude that Polish civil society was *not demobilized* after the downfall of the old regime. Parenthetically, the discussion on the weakening or strengthening of civil society during the transition process may be the result of a definitional confusion: Civil society under communism and civil society in democracy are two different entities. The role or meaning of civil society in the political process simply *changed*. Whereas under state socialism civil society (i.e. various illegal and semi-legal associations) was simply coterminous with political society (oppositional parties, political movements), during democratic consolidation the public domain underwent a rapid bifurcation. Two separate (at least in Poland) domains emerged - a *vibrant and growing domain* of civic associations and organizations and a more *torpid and elitist domain* of political parties and "political" interest groups.

Our data base does not provide much evidence for our initial hypothesis that through protest actions people would forge new identities and set up new organizations. The decisive majority of protest actions were organized by existing organizations, mobilizing people in the name of existing identities. The only exceptions were youth protests which spawned a large network of "counter-cultural" organizations.

The repertoire of protest was stable and predominantly non-violent. Violent strategies were used very rarely. The dominant form of protest was striking, including strikes and strike alerts. Demands were predominantly economic and reformist. Radical demands, such as calls for the abolition of the whole post-1989 order, were infrequent. Only a small minority of protestors turned to the highly polarized symbolism of militant populism, but *most* of them engaged in strikes and demonstrations to put forth demands related to their everyday (chiefly "economic") concerns. For them, it seems, collective protest was a mode of *civic* action based on an acceptance of the existing order and intended to *correct* the governmental - mostly economic - policies. The most popular targets of protest actions were top state institutions, such as the government, parliament and the presidency. During the examined period they were targeted with increased frequency. There was no increase in protest actions directed at management. Domestic and foreign owners were targeted very rarely.

Contentious collective action was an important mode of participation in public life by civil society organizations. Thus we conclude that many Poles who were uncomfortable with routine parliamentary democracy and dissatisfied with party politics turned to *contentious collective action* as a mode of public participation. This tendency may be interpreted as a growing dissatisfaction with political parties as channels of interest articulation and representation. The post-communist party system in Poland might have become more consolidated and structured, but its ability to articulate and represent people's interests - in light of our research results - did not increase.

Thus we conclude that the main functions of protest in post-communist Poland were both supplementary and complementary in relation to other forms of politics. Within the domain of civil society, protest's function was largely complementary, since the growing magnitude of protest did not hinder the development of more institutionalized channels and organizations, such as NGOs, trade unions, churches, minority associations, etc. By contrast, in relation to political society, the function of protest often seems to have been to supplement at least partially, interest aggregation and representation - important political functions poorly performed by the relatively weak party system.

As far as the question of institutionalization is concerned, our research demonstrates that during the first years of democratic consolidation in Poland, protest was becoming a routine, thus institutionalized, form of participation in politics. People's civic activities, including collective protests, were usually organized by already established organizations (mostly trade unions). But very often such civic activities occurred as *contentious collective action* rather than *inter-organizational negotiation and mediation*. Instead of engaging in well-institutionalized inter-organizational games (negotiations, lobbying, etc.), organizations such as trade unions were very quick to organize or sponsor strikes and demonstrations. In a sense, then, civil society (at least its significant segment) was specifically institutionalized, i.e. the rules of routine conflict resolution were not established and/or legitimized. This kind of institutionaliza-tion was not the result of organizations' passivity, but rather of their tendency to employ contentious forms of participation in public life. In brief, what we found in Poland was *contentious action by well-established and institutionalized organizations* which did not lead to any significant policy shifts. The effectiveness of protest - in so far as we can determine - was low. Yet, protest activities became a routine mode of interaction between the state and civil society. The emerging set of norms and rules should thus be referred to as *institutionalized contentiousness*.

Thus, given our four-fold matrix, during the period from 1989 to 1993, Poland was a country that belonged to the category characterized by strong institutionalization of protest. A brief characterization of protest's functions in the country's public life is more complicated. Protest seems to have been both complementary, for it became yet another form of public participation within civil society, and supplementary, for it often replaced underdeveloped channels of interest aggregation and articulation within political society.

Going back to our three views on the "fate" of protest in consolidating democracies, we conclude that protest politics in Poland during the 1989 to 1993 period fit neither the "contentment of the victors" nor the "rage of the victims" models. The model which best characterizes protest politics is "uncon-ventional civic involvement." This finding suggests that from the vantage point offered by event analysis of protest politics, early post-communist democratic consolidation in Poland proceeded in the "right" direction.

Our study allowed us, however, to construct a more nuanced picture of the consolidation of democracy in Poland. First, it is imperative to note that the basic components of democracy, such as competition, political participation and civil liberties, were swiftly instituted. Moreover, Poland did not have to deal with the "stateness problem," nor did it face serious legitimacy problems: Our research demonstrated that calls to abolish the new socio-political order were extremely rare and usually voiced by marginal, radical groups.

The problems of consolidation were located at the level of institution-building. As we argued elsewhere, the first five years of consolidation in Poland produced (1) a state that was bigger but not necessarily more efficient than the communist Party-state,[29] (2) a political society that was disorganized, though arguably increasingly more consolidated (structured), and (3) a civil society that

---

29   After 1989 two ministries were added to the 19 which remained after the 1987 reform; the overall number of central state agencies grew (1988: 32; 1993: 43); the number of state employees rose (1989: 161,579; 1993: 223,707) (*Rocznik Statystyczny* 1989, 1994).

was rapidly growing, but within which several sectors (e.g. trade unions) were increasingly contentious (Ekiert and Kubik 1996b).

We suspect that the pattern of gradually *intensifying* and *increasingly institutionalized* contentious collective action, occurring mostly within civil society, may have contributed to the peculiar type of democratic consolidation in Poland: The stability of the political regime and the absence of disruptive shifts in state policies coexisted with the relatively high level of contentious activities. Paradoxically, the very same pattern may have contributed to the constancy of the radical economic reforms. Opposition to the reforms was ineffective for it was either channeled through the medium of inconclusive (as our data indicate) contentious collective action or was articulated by several small parties in an uncoordinated, and thus impotent, fashion.[30]

We conclude that post-communist Poland is an excellent example of the disjointed and chaotic development of the institutional realms of the polity during a period of consolidation. The state, political society and civil society had their own transformational dynamics and the formation of institutional structures *within* each of them was far more advanced than the formation of the institutional linkages *between* them. An equivalent to the system of *"nomenklatura,"* which had very effectively coordinated various institutional orders of state socialism, did not develop. Each of the three domains had a relatively high level of *autonomy* vis-a-vis the other two, which prevented any of them from monopolizing political power. But the linkage between civil society organizations and the party system (political society) was extremely weak: The rising magnitude of protest can be construed as an indication of continual dissatisfaction with the party channels of interest aggregation and representation. In turn, the low number and weak institutionalization of links between the civil and political societies diminished the effectiveness of the whole polity.

---

30   This finding supports Geddes' conclusions that " ... labor has not been able to translate its opposition to adjustment policies into credible threats to punish the initiators of adjustment. Labor has not lacked the capacity to mount opposition; there have been numerous strikes and demonstrations. But this opposition has not routinely led to threats of regime breakdown, the defeat of the incumbents at the polls, or the wholesale abandonment of market-oriented policies" (1994: 66).

References

Adamski, W. 1989. "Afiliacje zwiazkowe, stosunek do protestow i wartosci obywatelskich jako przejaw konfliktu interesow." Pp. 159-222 in *Polacy 88. Dynamika konfliktu a szanse reform*, ed. W. Adamski et al. Warsaw: University of Warsaw Press.

Barkey, K. and S. Parikh. 1991. "Comparative Perspectives on the State." *Annual Review of Sociology,* Vol. 17: 523-549.

Dalton, R. J. and M. Kuechler, eds. 1990. *Challenging the Political Order. New Social and Political Movements in Western Democracies.* New York: Oxford University Press.

Dalton, R. J., M. Kuechler and W. Burklin. 1990. "The Challenge of New Movements." Pp. 3-20 in *Challenging the Political Order. New Social and Political Movements in Western Democracies*, ed. R. J. Dalton and M. Kuechler. New York: Oxford University Press.

Diamond, L., J. Linz and S. M. Lipset, eds. 1990. *Politics in Developing Countries. Comparing Experiences with Democracy.* Boulder: Lynne Rienner.

Ekiert, G. 1992. "Peculiarities of Post-Communist Politics in Poland." *Studies in Comparative Communism* 25 (4): 341-361.

Ekiert, G. and J. Kubik. 1996a. "Strategies of Collective Protest in Democratizing Societies: Hungary, Poland, and Slovakia since 1989." Paper presented at the Tenth International Conference of Europeanists, Chicago, March 14-16.

Ekiert, G. and J. Kubik. 1996b. "Collective Protest and Democratic Consolidation in Poland, 1989-1993." Pew Papers on Central Eastern European Reform and Regionalism. Center of International Studies. Princeton University.

Elster, J. 1993. "Constitution-making in Eastern Europe: Rebuilding the Boat in the Open Sea." *Public Administration* 27: 167-217.

Geddes, B. 1994. "Challenging the Conventional Wisdom." *Journal of Democracy* 5 (4): 104-118.

Grabowska, M. and T. Szawiel. 1993. *Anatomia elit politycznych. Partie polityczne w postkomunistycznej Polsce 1991-93.* Warszawa: Instytut Socjologii UW.

Greskovits, B. 1994. "Is the East Becoming the South? Where Threats to Reforms May Come From?" Paper presented at the XVIth World Congress of the International Political Science Association in Berlin, August 21-25.

Greskovits, B. 1996. "Good Bye Breakdown Prophecies, Hello Poor Democracies." Paper presented at the Tenth International Conference of Europeanists, Chicago, March 14-17.

Janicki, M. 1993. "Czysto i ubogo." *Polityka,* February 27: 15.

Jasiewicz, K. 1992. "Poland." *European Journal of Political Research* 22: 489-504.

Jasiewicz, K. 1993. "From Protest and Repression to the Free Elections." Pp. 117-140 in *Societal Conflict and Systemic Change. The Case of Poland 1980-1992*, ed. W. Adamski. Warsaw: IFIS PAN

Jawor 93. Informator o organizacjach pozarzadowych w Polsce. 1993. Warsaw: Fundusz Wspolpracy, Program Dialog Spoleczny-NGOs.

Jepperson, R. L. 1991. "Institutions, Institutional Effects, and Institutionalism." Pp. 143-163 in *The New Institutionalism in Organizational Analysis*, ed. W. W. Powell and P. J. DiMaggio. Chicago: University of Chicago Press.

Jowitt, K. 1992. "The Leninist Legacy," Pp. 207-224 in: *East Europe in Revolution*, ed. I. Banac. Ithaca, N.Y.: Cornell University Press.

Karl, T. L. and P. C. Schmitter. 1991. "Modes of Transition in Latin America, Southern and Eastern Europe." *International Social Science Journal* 128: 269-284.

Karl, T. L. and P. C. Schmitter. 1995. "From an Iron Curtain to a Paper Curtain: Grounding Transitologists or Students of Postcommunism?" *Slavic Review* 54 (4): 965-978.

Kitschelt, H. 1992. "The Formation of Party Systems in East Central Europe." *Politics and Society* 20: 7-50.

Kitschelt, H. 1994. "Emerging Structures of Political Representation in Eastern Europe." Paper presented at the conference on the Social and Political Bases of Economic Liberalization, organized by the SSRC and funded by the Pew Charitable Foundation. Warsaw, September 23-26.

Kitschelt, H. 1995. "Formation of Party Cleavages in Post-Communist Democracies" *Party Politics* 1 (4): 447-472.

Krasnodebska, U., J. Pucek, G. Kowalczyk and J. J. Wygnanski. 1996. *Podstawowe statystyki dotyczace dzialan organizacji pozarzadowych w Polsce*. Warsaw: Klon/Jawor, Phare Program.

Kriesi, H. and J. W. Duyvendak. 1995. "National Cleavage Structures." Pp. 3-25 in *New Social Movements in Western Europe: A Comparative Perspective*, H. Kriesi, R. Koopmans, J. W. Duyvendak and M. Giugni. Minneapolis and St. Paul: University of Minnesota Press.

Kriesi, H. and M. Giugni. 1995. "Introduction." Pp. ix-xxvi in *New Social Movements in Western Europe: A Comparative Perspective*, H. Kriesi, R. Koopmans, J. W. Duyvendak and M. Giugni. Minneapolis and St. Paul: University of Minnesota Press.

Kriesi, H., R. Koopmans, J. W. Duyvendak and M. Giugni. 1995. *New Social Movements in Western Europe: A Comparative Perspective*. Minneapolis and St. Paul: University of Minnesota Press.

Kubik, J. 1994. "The Role of Decentralization and Cultural Revival in Post-Communist Transformations. The Case of Cieszyn Silesia, Poland." *Communist and Post-Communist Studies* 27 (4): 331-55

Laswell, H., D. Lerner and I. de Sola Pool. 1952. *The Comparative Study of Symbols. An Introduction*. The Hoover Institute Studies, Series C: Symbols, No. 1. Stanford, Cal.: Stanford University Press.

Lewis, P. 1994. "Civil Society and the Development of Political Parties in East-Central Europe," Pp. 5-20 in *Parties, Trade Unions and Society in East-Central Europe*, ed. M. Waller and M. Myant. Portland: Frank Cass.

Lijphart, A. 1992. "Democratization and Constitutional Choices in Czechoslovakia, Hungary, and Poland, 1989-91." *Journal of Theoretical Politics* 4 (2): 207-223.

Linz, J. 1978. *The Breakdown of Democratic Regimes; Crisis, Breakdown, and Reequilibration*. Baltimore: Johns Hopkins University Press.

Linz, J. and A. Stepan. 1992. "Political Identities and Electoral Sequences: Spain, the Soviet Union, and Yugoslavia." *Daedalus* (Spring): 123-139.

McCarthy, J. D. 1996. "Constraints and Opportunities in Adopting, Adapting, and Inventing," Pp. 141-151 in *Comparative Perspectives on Social Movements*, ed. D. McAdam, J. D. McCarthy and M. N. Zald. Cambridge: Cambridge University Press.

Mainwaring, S. 1992. "Transitions to Democracy and Democratic Consolidation: Theoretical and Comparative Issues," Pp. 294-341 in *Issues in Democratic Consolidation: The New South American Democracies in Comparative Perspective*, ed. S. Mainwaring, G. O'Donnell and J. S. Valenzuela. Notre Dame: University of Notre Dame Press.

March, J. and J. P. Olsen. 1989. *Rediscovering Institutions. The Organizational Basis of Politics.* New York: The Free Press.

Marody, M. 1995. "Three Stages of Party System Emergence in Poland." *Communist and Post-Communist Studies* 28 (2): 263-270

Morris, A. and C. Herring. 1987. "Theory and Research in Social Movements: A Critical Review." Pp. 137-198 in *Annual Review of Political Science*, Vol. 2, ed. S. Long. Norwood: Ablex Publishing.

North, D. C. 1990. *Institutions, Institutional Change and Economic Performance.* Cambridge: Cambridge University Press.

O'Donnell, G. 1992. "Transitions, Continuities, and Paradoxes." Pp. 17-56 in *Issues in Democratic Consolidation,* ed. S. Mainwaring, G. O'Donnell and J. S. Valenzuela. Notre Dame: University of Notre Dame Press.

Opinia publiczna o roznych formach protestow spolecznych i skierowanych przeciw nim represjom. 1992 (February). Warsaw: CBOS.

Pereira, B., L. Carlos, J. M. Maravall and A. Przeworski. 1993. *Economic Reforms in New Democracies.* Cambridge: Cambridge University Press.

Polska '93. 1992. Warsaw: Centrum Informacji Polskiej Agencji Informacyjnej.

Prawelska-Skrzypek, G. no date. "Citizen Activism in the Life of Local Communities: Polish Experiences during the Period of Transformations." Unpublished manuscript.

Rocznik Statystyczny (Polish Statistical Yearbook). 1989, 1994. Warsaw: GUS.

Schmitter, P. 1992. "Interest Systems and the Consolidation of Democracies." Pp. 156-181 in *Reexamining Democracy. Essays in Honor of Seymour Martin Lipset*, ed. G. Marks and L. Diamond. Newbury Park: Sage.

Schmitter, P. 1995a. "Some Reflections about the Concept of Civil Society (in general) and Its Role in the Liberalization and Democratization of Europe in the Nineteenth Century." Paper presented at the Conference "Civil Society Before Democracy," Princeton University, October 6-7.

Schmitter, P. 1995b. "Transitology: The Science or Art of Democratization?" Pp. 11-41 in *The Consolidation of Democracy in Latin America,* ed. J. Tulchin. Boulder: Lynne Rienner.

Schmitter, P. and T. L. Karl. 1991. "What Democracy Is ... and Is Not." *Journal of Democracy* 2 (3): 75-88.

Sewerynski, M. 1994. "Dylematy i perspektywy zwiazkow zawodowych w krajach post-komunistycznych." *Przeglad Socjologiczny* 43: 111-131

Shafer, M. 1994. *Winners and Losers. How Sectors Shape the Developmental Prospects of States.* Ithaca, N.Y.: Cornell University Press.

Shin, D. C. 1994. "On the Third Wave of Democratization: A Synthesis and Evaluation of Recent Theory and Research." *World Politics* 47 (October): 135-170.

Siemienska, R. 1991. "Problemy demokracji w Europie Wschodniej," Raport z badan. Warsaw: OBOP.

Stepan, A. 1988. *Rethinking Military Politics.* Princeton: Princeton University Press.

Szawiel, T. 1993. "Partie polityczne w Polsce: stan obecny szanse i zagrozenia." Pp. 39-57 in: *Polska 1989-1992. Fragmenty pejzazu.* Warszawa: IFIS PAN.

Tilly, C. 1978. *From Mobilization to Revolution.* New York: McGraw-Hill.

Valenzuela, J. S. 1992. "Democratic Consolidation in Post-Transitional Setting: Notion, Process, and Facilitating Conditions," Pp. 57-104 in *Issues in Democratic Consolidation,* ed. S. Mainwaring, G. O'Donnell and J. S. Valenzuela. Notre Dame: University of Notre Dame Press.

　　　　　　　　　　　　　　　　　　　　　　　　Grzegorz Ekiert and Jan Kubik

Waller, M. 1994. "Political Actors and Political Roles in East-Central Europe." Pp. 21-36 in *Parties, Trade Unions and Society in East-Central Europe*, ed. M. Waller and M. Myant. Portland: Frank Cass.

Walton, J. 1991. "Debt, Protest and the State in Latin America." Pp. 299-328 in *Power and Popular Protest in Latin American Social Movements*, ed. S. Eckstein. Berkeley: University of California Press.

Walton, J. and C. Ragin. 1990. "Global and National Sources of Political Protest: Third World Responses to the Debt Crisis." *American Sociological Review* 55: 876-890.

Wasilewski, J., ed. 1994. *Konsolidacja elit politycznych w Polsce, 1991-1993*. Warszawa: ISP PAN.

Wasilewski, J. 1995. "The Crystallization of the Post-Communist and Post-Solidarity Political Elite." Pp. 117-133 in *After Communism*, ed. E. Wnuk-Lipinski. Warsaw: ISP PAN.

Wesolowski, W. 1995. "Formowanie sie partii politycznych w postkomunistycznej Polsce." *Studia Polityczne* 4: 7-28.

Zubek, V. 1993. "The Fragmentation of Poland's Political Party System." *Communist and Post-Communist Studies* 26 (1): 47-71.

The Authors

Beissinger, Mark R., Department of Political Science, University of Wisconsin, Madison, Wisconsin, USA.

Crishock, Louis J., Department of Sociology, The Catholic University of America, Washington, D.C., USA.

Ekiert, Grzegorz, Department of Government/Center for European Studies, Harvard University, Cambridge, Massachusetts, USA.

Fillieule, Olivier, Centre National de la Recherche Scientifique, CRESAL, Saint Etienne, France, and Institute of Political Studies (IEP), Paris, France.

Gentile, Pierre, Department of Political Science, University of Geneva, Geneva, Switzerland.

Hocke, Peter, Research Unit "Social Movements and the Public Sphere," Social Science Research Center Berlin (WZB), Berlin, Germany.

Koopmans, Ruud, Research Unit "Social Movements and the Public Sphere," Social Science Research Center Berlin (WZB), Berlin, Germany.

Kubik, Jan, Department of Political Science, Rutgers University, New Brunswick, New Jersey, USA.

McCarthy, John D., Department of Sociology, The Pennsylvania State University, University Park, Pennsylvania, USA.

McPhail, Clark, Department of Sociology, The University of Illinois, Urbana-Champaign, USA.

Neidhardt, Friedhelm, Research Unit "Social Movements and the Public Sphere," Social Science Research Center Berlin (WZB), Berlin, Germany.

Olzak, Susan, Department of Sociology, Stanford University, Stanford, California, USA.

Olivier, Johan L., Human Sciences Research Council, Pretoria, South Africa.

Rucht, Dieter, Research Unit "Social Movements and the Public Sphere," Social Science Research Center Berlin (WZB), Berlin, Germany.

Schweingruber, David, Department of Sociology, The University of Illinois, Urbana-Champaign, USA.

Smith, Jackie, Department of Sociology, State University of New York, Stony Brook, New York, USA.

Tarrow, Sidney, Department of Government, Cornell University, Ithaca, New York, USA.